SHAKESPEARE IN EUROPE

Shakespeare in Europe

EDITED BY

Oswald LeWinter

Meridian Books

THE WORLD PUBLISHING COMPANY

CLEVELAND AND NEW YORK

IN MEMORIAM

Paul Horowitz (1959–1961)

A MERIDIAN BOOK

Published by The World Publishing Company
2231 West 110th Street, Cleveland 2, Ohio
First Meridian printing April 1963

Library of Congress Catalog Card Number: 63-12323
Designed by Larry Kamp
Printed in the United States of America WP463

Contents

CONTENTS

Preface

Like many other anthologies, this one grew out of an essentially personal need, a need to have available in one place the scattered and in many cases untranslated texts of European Shakespeare criticism for study. Nevertheless, had I not felt that such a collection might also be of interest to the general English reader as well as to the special student with little or no competence in some of these foreign languages, I would not have pursued that need to its present point.

There exist already a number of excellent studies of Shakespeare's reception in particular European countries. There have also been issued a number of works of a more comprehensive, supranational nature which deal with continental attitudes to Shakespeare by literary movements or epochs. Among the former group are works by Dr. Joachimi-Dege, Miss Josephine Calina, L. Collison-Morley, and others, while such studies as those of F. E. Halliday and J. G. Robertson fall, with distinction, among the latter. But while these writers have dealt with their materials as literary historians, their methods were those of an earlier generation. They tended to summarize texts and frequently to disrupt them by isolating terms and passages. Rarely have they allowed large portions of texts to speak for themselves. This is one oversight which the present work is intended partially to rectify. Then, too, these writers constructed chronologies for the most part rather than attempting to see European intellectual development in its entirety, an entirety often conspicuously disdainful of political divisions, with the result that even their best works seem to be layer cakes of information and conclusions.

But the present work has several other justifications. The first of these lies in the limited number of works on which previous books were based. Many documents have hitherto been neglected or unknown. Sometimes language difficulties and poor editions have been responsible. More often the fault has been with those commentators who have reconstructed critical traditions in a manner tendentious to the utmost, or ironically, with those at the other extreme who have compiled *museums* of Shakespeare commentary (see Ralli's two-volume *A History of Shakespearean Criticism*), in which masterpieces have been truncated or have suffered the indignities of paraphrase. The present work also includes many selections that are "minor" only in the sense that they are short and little known; they are frequently of "major" importance because of their ideas or because of the contribution they have made to the development of European intellectual consciousness.

The last, and the greatest, justification for this book derives from the definition given by Ralli and others to the term "criticism." Frequently that term has been altered beyond recognizable meaning to include materials devoted to matters of text or to the establishment of the canon, or even to the presentation of translations with accompanying notes concerning variant readings. While all of the foregoing is worthy and extremely important, it is my conviction that criticism is a branch of aesthetics, one which involves the rendering of value judgments, and that at its best it is the practice of that discipline which alone has the power to make the literature of the past contemporary. It is in this spirit that the present volume assembles its documents. But I have not held to any narrow concept of criticism. While there is much of value in the monument of Shakespeare scholarship, I have had to resist the temptation to include even such of its worthies as Gervinus and others of equal caliber. I have included chiefly those men whose response to Shakespeare's work was first and last that of fellow artists; men for whom the English poet represented both the Sphinx before the citadel of art, and the answer to the famous riddle. Only once have I succumbed to the temptation to include materials not specifically of a "critical" nature. That one digression accounts for the presence of the great historian Leopold von Ranke. But I hope that the reader will realize, after concluding the selection which represents this eminent thinker, that the document is not, after all, wholly irrelevant since it embodies two critical tendencies which in our time have had much honor; namely, that of historical criticism and that of sociological criticism, both admittedly in crude form and by implication.

With respect to the choice of selections, it has seemed useful to me to establish three criteria: literary merit, interest, and previous availability. On the ground of the last of these I have omitted the important, illuminating work of A. W. Schlegel, Nietzsche, Schopenhauer, and Pasternak. The first of these has been translated a great many times and appears in various anthologies and source books. Likewise, Pasternak's most extensive essay on Shakespeare ("Translating Shakespeare") is easily available in an excellent translation in the paperbound edition of *I Remember*. The references to Shakespeare in the works of Schopenhauer and Nietzsche, although numerous, are scattered. Only the lack of time to extract and to arrange them, as well as the suspicion that such arrangement would be ultimately paideutic, has prevented their inclusion in the present work. One exclusion pains me deeply, however. I have become aware, only since the completion of this project, of the existence of an important document in Polish Shakespeare criticism, the Polish Romantic poet, Adam Mickiewicz' *O stuce dramatycznij w polsce*. Many other writers, Madame de Staël, Hebbel, Herder, Mendelssohn, Anatole France, Lamartine, Borgese, to mention only a few, I have felt were less interesting than those whom I had the space to include. And as for the criterion of literary merit, to its sharp edge have fallen such writers as Papini and others whom a less capricious taste might have included. One final word about the selections must be devoted to the Danish critic Georg Brandes. His *William Shakespeare* (1895) is in many ways an admirable book, but one which can have no place in serious Shakespeare criticism owing both to Brandes' reconstruction of the poet's life from spurious sources and unsupported suppositions and to the book's method of imposing all manner of psychological theorizing about the influence of "practical" life on the work of art. Such theories, no matter how plausible, have ultimately little to do with an aesthetic judgment of the work.

Given the nature of my own interest, I have found myself unwilling to arrange the selections in any way that would follow any author through his career or any tendency or concept through the centuries covered by the book. Instead, I have neglected national groupings or groupings by movements and have, less haphazardly than it seems, allowed the selections to be arranged according to the birth dates of their authors. I have felt that by this method I would gain what seems to me more valuable than any mechanical or external coherence; to wit, an internal coherence, one which suggests the richness of European intellectual activity in the past three centuries and suggests the simultaneous existence of conflicting tendencies. If, as in the selections from Hugo and Taine, a work of 1864 precedes a work of 1863 (Turgenev's essay of 1860 appears between these two), I have felt that that is all to the good. Intellectual history is not the work of time, but of men. And men may, in old age, remain true to principles of their youth after the wind of taste has begun to blow from another quarter, just as the men of a younger generation may initiate a shift in sensibility before a decaying tendency has ceased to exist.

In the introduction to this book I have tried to describe what appear to me to be the chief tendencies of European Shakespeare criticism and to suggest the place that the figures which I include might have in its vast edifice. My remarks are offered not in the spirit of conclusions. The student of Shakespeare will see without difficulty the many writers he might have included or the many principles by which he might have organized his own work. It is my hope that this will be only the first of many volumes devoted to a fertile, though neglected, area.

As far as the source materials are concerned, I have attempted in all cases to consult the best, often the earliest, editions available. In those instances in which I have used existing translations I have tried to use those that have remained most faithful to the spirit of the original without doing so at the expense of the English language.

The Shakespeare quotations in this book have been conformed to the Globe edition of *Shakespeare's Works,* and act, scene, and line references have been supplied. My own notes to the selections are given in numbered footnotes and are labeled Editor.

So many people have given me invaluable aid and succor in bringing this book to press that I cannot begin to thank all of them. I hope I may be forgiven by all those whom I fail to mention as well as by those whom I shall embarrass by making their altruistic gifts public here. Miss Jane Kronholtz, my agent, has been both whip and salve. Without her dual role this book might have remained a boast. I am deeply grateful to my friends, Mr. Allen Bergson of Columbia University, Mr. Otis T. Bourns, Jr., Professor Leonard Michaels of Paterson State College, and to my teachers, Anthony Ostroff and Mark Linenthal, Jr., in whose company, over a period of years, the notion of this project developed and was refined. Many of my colleagues have been of incalculable aid in their warm discussions with me. To Professors Henry Finch, Department of Philosophy; Gordon Ross Smith, J. Mitchell Morse, Charles T. Davis, of the Department of English; and Thomas F. Magner and Sigmund S. Birkenmayer, both of the Department of Slavic Languages, all of The Pennsylvania State University, my deepest thanks. I also wish to thank the head of my department, Professor Henry W. Sams, for his solicitude and encouragement, and for creating an atmosphere conducive to both satisfying teaching and special research. My thanks to Professor Frederick R. Matson and his staff of the Central Research Fund of The Pennsylvania State University for their material assistance; to Professor William B. Edgerton, Chairman of the Department of Slavic Languages, University of Indiana; to R. T. Tankersley, Librarian of the Paterno Collection of Columbia University; to the anonymous and efficient staffs of the New York Public Library and the Library of Congress; to Misses Margaret K. Spangler, Elsa C. Lisle, and Mildred A.

Ailman, of the Pattee Library of The Pennsylvania State University; to my superb translators, Miss Françoise Rosen and Professor Alfred Triolo, the Department of Romance Languages, Professor Edward C. Thaden, the Department of History, and Professor LaMarr Kopp, the Department of German; to my graduate assistant, Miss Ronalie J. Roper; to my students, Miss Anne Cypher and Mr. Roger Lowenthal; to Miss Leticia Cavalcanti. And last but most important, my thanks, hardly commensurate with their contributions, to Aaron Asher of The World Publishing Company, and to Marcia Dale LeWinter, my wife.

OSWALD LEWINTER

University Park, Pennsylvania
September 1, 1962

SHAKESPEARE IN EUROPE

Introduction

The history of Shakespeare criticism on the Continent is the history of the development of European consciousness since the sixteenth century. In the microcosm of the Continent's reception of the English poet we can observe the struggle that has characterized a large part of European intellectual activity over the past three centuries, between two major and conflicting attitudes to life. We can see the emergence of one of these attitudes and its displacement of the other and older one, the metamorphosis of that newer attitude into several related ones, and the reappearance of the first attitude in new guises. The two attitudes of which I speak have been called *classic* and *romantic*.[1] By using these terms I do not mean to imply that the vast edifice of European culture is easily categorized, or that these theoretical limits are not subject to human energies and human will. We shall see these tendencies, as I prefer to think of them, existing side by side, seesawing, with one and then the other in ascendance. Intellectual history is a process and like any other is marked by vast and mobile forces.

Shakespeare's plays were brought to the Continent in his own lifetime by itinerant actors. Mostly the versions, and they were not much more than that, were garbled. But even that notwithstanding, the plays gave evidence of the presence of an artist of the highest magnitude, and one whose energy appeared, especially to those who knew the England of the time, of one piece with the national energy. While we do not have much mention of Shakespeare by the literati of the period, we do know that his plays found ready audiences even as far away as Warsaw. Shakespeare's bawdiness, dramatic variety,

[1] For the meaning which I am attaching to these terms and for a discussion of their evolution in Shakespeare criticism, see Walter F. Schirmer, *Alte und Neue Wege der Shakespeare-Kritik* (Bonn, Peter Hanstein Verlag, 1953).

involved plots, characters such as Falstaff, and the colorful pomp of his histories as well as the often coarse humor of his comedies must have been popular among the illiterate audiences who had been primed for such fare for some time by the *commedia dell' arte*. But taste, one of the means by which we can observe intellectual development, is not the product of the multitude. On the contrary, it is more often the result of an imposition by a few powerful minds of their thought on the times. Perhaps that is why Shakespeare criticism on the Continent is deserving of special attention. It is one of the few times I know of when the instincts of the illiterate audiences were right long before the *raffiné* minds of the professional critics were willing to take the reins of appreciation from their hands and lead Shakespeare's cart from the barn to the palace. And why Shakespeare should have appealed to these pastoral audiences is obvious. On the most superficial level he appeared to embody many of the elements of folk literature, miraculous elements, superstitions, and the like. But why he was ignored at first and later attacked by the literati of the Continent before his ultimate enthronement in the nineteenth century is more complex in its origins.

The "establishment" of European literature during the seventeenth and most of the eighteenth centuries was dominated by French taste. It was a taste whose basis was a critical theory which had been developed in Italy during the sixteenth century and had been codified into a pseudo-law by the later French critics Boileau, Rapin, and Le Bossu. This theory was based on the narrowest reading of Aristotle's *Poetics* by Italian critics, chiefly Lodovico Castelvetro.[2] In his commentary on the *Poetics*, Castelvetro had assumed that an unimaginative audience, one which desires pleasure, credibility, and marvelous occurrences to excite it, is the audience for whom poems are written. From his theory of the audience's ignorance, an ignorance that wished only pleasure and comfort, Castelvetro derived his precepts of the "unities." Aristotle

[2] See Bernard Weinberg, *A History of Literary Criticism in the Italian Renaissance*, 2 vols. (Chicago, University of Chicago Press, 1961). This is the fullest and best discussion of the manner and architects of the reconstruction of Aristotle of which I have knowledge.

had demanded only that a play have unity of action (a demand which Castelvetro did not consider essential). The former had had little to say about the unity of time (twelve hours in Castelvetro) and nothing to say about the unity of place. But Castelvetro, in his reconstruction of the *Poetics,* insisted on the unities of time and place and made the unity of action actually dependent on these, whose importance he asserted. The result of this neoclassic doctrine was the narrowest latitude in plot, character, choice of materials, and episodes. And when the doctrine found its way to France in the next century, it came with the best of references (since worship of the "ancients" was not confined to Renaissance Italy alone) and found a ground which had been prepared for it from another quarter: the insistence on reason and its virtues by Descartes. It was according to these theories that French classical drama was constructed. And once we realize this, the opinions of Voltaire and others of his position become more comprehensible. But what of such opinions? Were they entirely unfavorable? Not altogether.

While from the first it had been clear, even to his contemporaries at home (e.g. Jonson), that Shakespeare ignored or did not know ancient critical doctrine, and that his dramas seemed constructed according to "rules of their own," it was also clear that an artist whose work transcended all narrow a priori criteria of judgment was at work in such plays as *Othello, The Tempest, Hamlet, Macbeth,* and *A Midsummer Night's Dream.* But doctrines of ancient lineage do not fall like the walls of Jericho. And the power of Shakespeare's work notwithstanding, classical doctrine in the Europe of the eighteenth century had its champion, and that champion was none other than Voltaire. Already by the middle of the century new and more liberal tendencies were beginning to be noticeable. The Abbé Prévost, who had visited England in 1728, discussed Shakespeare in several issues of his journal, *Le Pour et le Contre,* as early as 1738. But Prévost's attitude to Shakespeare, while free to a surprising degree from classical dogma, was radical for its time and made no noticeable impression. In 1745 Pierre Antoine de La Place prefaced his translations of Shakespeare with views of the English poet which, while less profound than Prévost's, were still largely liberal. But the voice of Voltaire dominated Europe and it was his utterances on English drama that were the penultimate word on that subject for France, Italy, and even Germany, until the appearance, in 1769, of a voice quite as powerful and original, and certainly more liberal—that of Lessing.

Whereas Voltaire had praised Shakespeare with reservations about the propriety of his dramas when judged by the only criteria Voltaire was willing to concede existed, Lessing was not bound by dogma in that way. Voltaire's final judgment had been unfavorable: Shakespeare was barbarous, unable to observe the unities, full of flaws, and one could hardly understand how he could still be so moving and impressive. But he was dangerous, and any sensible French dramatist would do well to leave him alone. Castelvetro's insistence on the unities had become the weapon classical writers were to turn against Shakespeare in one form or another for over a century. The battle line had been drawn by these writers and the unities became the focal point. Lessing admitted Shakespeare's irregularities but went on to state that in spite of them (it was too early for any critic to be able to see that it might be because of them) Shakespeare was a poet closer to Aristotle's theory than any French dramatist.

The fight was on. But it would be wrong to think that Lessing had any personal stake in this. His were the highest motives. He saw, as perhaps no other critic of the time, that German literature (and the same might be said of the other continental literatures) would have to free itself from the tyranny of classical doctrine imposed by France if it was to emerge with any character of its own. And, too, his knowledge of Aristotle must have made him aware of how the *Poetics* had been distorted by neoclassical thinkers. Lessing saw the vitality of Germany's folk drama and saw, as well, its resemblance to Shakespearean drama. He realized that Shakespeare had instinctively grasped the nature of tragic dramatization in a way far superior to those writers who began with theories. In his later years, as we can see by his own dramas, Lessing tended to retrogress to a position closer to Voltaire's. But it did not matter. The issues had been clarified and younger writers would appear to take up where he had left off.

By 1773, with the appearance of Herder's pamphlet, *Von Deutscher Art und Kunst,* the new movement had arrived. These critics of the *Sturm und Drang* showed none of the adherence to doctrine of earlier writers. Nature was their law, their chief concept, and the standard by which to judge. It was no longer necessary to compare Shakespeare to classical drama. One had only to appreciate the marvelous in him, the natural, and the transcendent. It was with these critics that Germany began to develop that lead over France in continental Shakespeare criticism which it was not to lose; a lead which was never seriously challenged by France, except for the decade that saw the preface to *Cromwell* and *Racine et Shakespeare* (from 1820 to 1830), or by any other country on the Continent. That lead, and the critical literature it produced, did not have much of an effect in France. There, as late as the last decade of the eighteenth century, classical theory was still flourishing. Marie-Joseph Chénier's drama, *Brutus et Cassius* (1790), was one more of a long line of attempts at dismembering *Julius Caesar* into something acceptable to the law of classicism. It would take at least two more decades, until the end of the Napoleonic period, before French writers would begin the controversies about what should be admired and emulated in Shakespeare.

But the German situation, which was to have its short-lived parallel in France, was more than simply a shift in critical point of view. It was the vanguard of that revolution in sensibility which we associate with the term "Romanticism." Everywhere writers were discovering the vitality of their national folk literatures. They had begun to heed the appeals of Rousseau for subjective analysis and introspection. They had become aware of the manner in which advances in the sciences had outmoded ancient concepts. And, when they cast about for a figure of eminence to support these new views of the nature of man and of life, they found Shakespeare. In him were subjective elements, dark moods, all the paraphernalia which they craved. Now, it is always difficult not to come to the conclusion that much that these writers saw in Shakespeare they put there themselves. But such conclusions tend to give a distorted view of the processes of reasoning which produce them. What had been, for an earlier time, the chief details of drama, the unities, or problems of form and propriety, were yielding to a newer and different view. The subjectivity of the new generation of writers found its critical expression in their preoccupations with the problem of character in drama. Goethe had set the problem in his discussion of Hamlet in *Wilhelm Meister* four years before the turn of the century. And henceforth, it seemed, the duty of the critic was to search for the character in his natural setting. In France, by 1800, the new voice was being heard, albeit weakly, even by critics with predominantly classical leanings. In his *Mélanges littéraires,* Chateaubriand, in the main standing with Voltaire, could still admit:

> I formerly measured Shakespeare with the classic microscope. It is an excellent instrument for observing the ornaments of good or bad taste, the perfect or imperfect details; but it is unfit for the observation of the whole, as the focus of the lens bears only on a single point, and is incapable of embracing the entire surface.

And Madame de Staël, who could not condone much of the barbarity in Shakespeare, had to admit that Shakespeare was the model for Germany and that through his influence German drama had been revitalized. Both *De la littérature* (1800) and *De l'Allemagne* (1810),[3] while constituting a rear guard of classicism, proved enormously influential in most of Europe. In Italy and Russia, the younger writers, already impressed by such plays as Goethe's *Götz von Berlichingen* (1773) and Schiller's *Die Räuber* (1781), were being told by the indefatigable Madame that this exciting new drama was the result of Shakespeare's influence on these admired authors. It was natural that they should turn to the fountainhead. And turn they did, with excellent results, since Madame de Staël had

[3] Napoleon prevented Madame de Staël from publishing *De l'Allemagne* until 1813.

been principally correct. Shakespeare's influence on German literature after Lessing can hardly be overestimated; and it could be asserted that the whole of German literature in the last half of the eighteenth century, and the early decades of the nineteenth, would have been much different, much more within the mainstream of European literature of that period, had it not been for the influence Shakespeare exerted. It was through him, paradoxically, that the German national spirit discovered itself,[4] learned to understand its peculiarities, its depths and heights, and to embody these factors in a truly individual literature. And since these longings for a national literature were awakening at the end of the eighteenth century and were to occupy the chief figures of the early nineteenth century, Madame de Staël's work, inadvertently, offered a *modus vivendi*.

But the French writers of the first decade of the nineteenth century were still unable to shake off the influence of Voltaire. No major literary figure, until Stendhal, found it necessary or wise to disagree. And even Stendhal, whose *Racine et Shakespeare* was a major utterance in the cause of Romanticism, was read less in the 1820s and early thirties than Voltaire. As so often happens, men outlive the time when their vision of life has relevance to the life that is being lived around them. As Professor Eugen Weber has written:

> Voltaire, cold, brittle, brilliant, spurned by the Romantics, is yet carried deep into the heart of their time by reactionary gentlemen, in exile or returned from it, who could not unlearn their youth.[5]

The same, we will see, is true of the aged Victor Hugo, who professes the Romantic creed in 1864, when the tide of taste has turned.

But Stendhal's criticism is more than merely revolutionary. While he still fights on the ground designated by Voltaire, the

[4] Cf. Joachimi-Dege, cited in the Selected Bibliography, for an excellent discussion of Shakespeare's influence on the development of German literature of the period.

[5] Eugen Weber, *Paths to the Present* (New York, Dodd, Mead and Company, 1960), p. 5.

unities, he develops an argument, perhaps unwittingly, which is of great importance. As I have attempted to suggest, the argument of the unities derived from Castelvetro depends, in his scheme, on his theory of an ignorant audience's wishes. Stendhal's refutation of the classical insistence on the unities is the first in continental Shakespeare criticism to invert Castelvetro's argument. He asserts that because of this very audience who can "imagine" more than the classical authors are willing to concede the playwright must give full rein to his imagination. Stendhal also asserts that the insistence on the unities is "a French habit." And while this is hyperbole, its truth lies in the fact that French drama has been only occasionally successful in freeing itself from an adherence to rigorous formal theories. Stendhal paved the way for the unprecedented reception of Victor Hugo's Preface of 1827, and where the younger writer's manifesto is a profession of faith and principles, its predecessor is a model of rational discourse intent on developing the dogma, as it were, to which the new writers could profess their allegiance.[6]

The idealism about art which spread through Europe during the nineteenth century, this deification of nature which has been identified with the complex of ideas known as Romanticism, and which held that no laws could be imposed on the work of art from the outside, produced a great body of criticism. The problem with most of the Romantic critics was, paradoxically, essentially theoretical. A major effort of these critics was to develop a theory of the literary art. But while previous criticism had been engaged in attempting to tailor works to fit its theories, and even when earlier critics had engaged in practical criticism their preoccupation was primarily with the possibility of applying theory to specific works,

[6] In a recent article, "Romanticism and Comparative Literature," *Comparative Literature,* Vol. 14, No. 2 (Spring, 1962), pp. 153–166, Professor D. L. Fanger is of the opinion that Stendhal's "vigorously polemic manifesto lacks any unity beyond what his temperament inevitably gives it." I find it difficult, however, to agree, since it is precisely the unity of "temperament," or organic unity, which Stendhal is implicitly praising in this work. I suspect that a feeling similar to mine may have lurked behind Professor Fanger's evaluation, else why does he feel it necessary to qualify with "inevitably"?

the Romantic critics were continually tailoring their theory to broaden it enough to make room for the specific demands made upon it by any great work of art. Clearly one can see that there is nothing less, at the heart of these two methods, than opposing views of life. And while there have been reactions to the original Romantic position in the later nineteenth century as well as in our own time, it seems to me that many of these reactions have been overestimated. Finally, such labels as Positivism, Humanism, Aestheticism, and the like serve only to distort, not merely their frequent simultaneity in time, but also their real resemblances. Critics like to stress differences in speaking of reactions to things. Often these very reactions are not total, but only partial disavowals of the doctrines of an earlier generation, and even more often they are not that, but only a refinement of terms that masquerades as revolt and novelty. And it is this that we must keep uppermost in mind if we are to find our way through the maze of movement and countermovement that characterizes European literature after the nineteenth century.

As I have said, the Romantic critics shifted the focus in Shakespeare criticism from the unities, which they assumed had been sufficiently discredited, to nature and character. After Tieck, the Schlegels, and others in Germany, it seemed nothing more could be done, nor, indeed, had to be done. Tieck, in his essay on *Hamlet*'s stageworthiness, had refuted the last resurrected form of the "unities" argument, Goethe's assertion that Shakespeare, while a great poet, had not written for the stage. It seemed that the controversy was settled and that later German critics would be free to indulge in an orgy of subjectivity. But in France and Russia, that satellite of French taste, matters were much different. In the latter, after the appearance of Pushkin, it was once again the case of a major writer having, under the influence of Shakespeare, changed the landscape of his native literature for all time to come. In Italy, the same can be said of Manzoni, who had fought the battle of the "unities" in his *Lettre à M. Chauvet* in behalf of the future of Italian literature and of its literary language. But by the middle of the century a new genre had asserted its supremacy; the novel, whose practitioners and critics were interested in a different concept of society, one more realistically related to the society in which they lived. And with this new dominant force in European literature the attitudes to Shakespeare changed accordingly. Taine and Turgenev are both products of a Romanticism which had undergone a metamorphosis whereby it had sloughed off its extravagant idealism and retained its social concerns. These social concerns, their suitability to the novel—that genre's supremacy—and the growing status of the sciences, produce the criticism of the last half of the nineteenth century. It is a criticism which in Taine seems related to classicism, and it surely does derive some of its assertions from it, by a rehearsal of Shakespeare's flaws. And certainly Grillparzer, late in the century, reminds us of Voltaire. But too much water has gone past the old tree. Even the rehearsal of flaws cannot use any of the old "unities" arguments which had been the distinguishing features of the classicists, and Taine does not attempt to use them. Behind Taine's criticism lurks not only the old Romantic impulse of seeing the world in one's own terms, but also the elevation of genius and the assertion of the work of art having laws of its own, both of which underlie the Aestheticism of the same period.

Both here, and in the headnotes, I have tried to suggest several ideas: that Shakespeare criticism on the Continent can be divided into two major tendencies, both of which underwent metamorphosis (though I must admit that it is my own feeling that by the 1870s classicism had died in the sense of being able to exert any lasting influence on the younger writers) and whose transformed, often disguised, descendants exist side by side with one or the other clan in power; that the major contributions to continental Shakespeare criticism have been French and German, perhaps because of the early development of interest in Shakespeare in these two countries, as well as the presence of two powerful critics, Voltaire and Lessing, at the outset (one thing remains to be said about French Shakespeare enthusiasm: unlike England's or Germany's interest, it never became a matter concerning the multitudes, but remained, even at its height, among the literary figures as an intellectual problem); that Shakespeare was from the first enlisted mainly in the cause of freedom from the tyranny of classical doctrine, and as a guide in the development of a national literature by the main figures in the various countries of Europe. For this last idea Germany, Italy, and briefly Russia (during the period of Pushkin) can be offered as evidence. So too, in a negative sense, the case of Spain is of value, since it is my contention that the absence of any *body* of Spanish Shakespeare criticism during the eighteenth and nineteenth centuries is the result of Spain's preoccupation with her own literature; a literature whose great *siglo de oro* figures, Lope de Vega, Tirso de Molina, Gongora, and Cervantes, all in one way or another managed to accomplish for their language and literature what those countries dominated by the narrowest classicism could not have done without the aid of Shakespeare.

Much of the Shakespeare criticism of our own time has been the work of professional critics rather than of great writers. In Europe a few major writers have undertaken the study or the translation of Shakespeare and have, in the process, left us with their responses. But their words have lacked the force and passion of the great Romantic critics. The Romantic critics were certainly not the first critics to see Shakespeare's greatness. But because of the energy with which they lent themselves to Shakespeare, an energy free from the prejudices formed by a priori theories, theirs is, I remain convinced, the best complete body of criticism we possess. It is unfortunate that in our own time we have seen Shakespeare become the property largely of academicians, men such as Schücking, whose imposition of history on Shakespeare criticism has served to interrupt the work begun by critics such as Schlegel and Coleridge, to turn the attention from the plays to matters ultimately outside them, and has, unwittingly, sired a reaction which, while it pretends to follow the Romantics in their preoccupation with character, is flabby and inept. The intellectual force that underlay Romantic criticism in Europe, present even in such of its offspring as Aestheticism and Humanism, is conspicuously absent. Hugo said that "Supreme art is the region of equals." Certainly the great monuments of European Shakespeare criticism would bear him out. I am not suggesting that Europe has had no great writers since the nineteenth century. That would be absurd! Merely that the battles in literature in our time have been between the outgrowths of one generic tendency and that the various European literatures have all arrived beyond that point where Shakespeare's influence in the struggle against narrow rules was necessary.

1. Voltaire

1694–1778

The Shakespearean criticism of Voltaire (François Marie Arouet) is most perplexing. It ranges from early admiration, though with qualifications, to an often foolish antagonism in later life. In order to understand Voltaire's ambivalence it is necessary to realize that he was a product of the French neoclassical tradition whose critical tenets had been codified by Boileau, Rapin, and Le Bossu. Voltaire's was a tradition founded on rules and reason, and it was inevitable that to such a mind the theater of Shakespeare should appear barbarous and bloody, and ignorant of the rules.

Voltaire's first mention of Shakespeare occurs in an essay on poetry (1728) where he states that works of art do not admit of classification. No definition of tragedy could be inclusive enough to contain the Oedipus Tyrannus, *Addison, and* Julius Caesar. *Shakespeare breaks the rules but he is great in spite of his faults. Once again, in 1730, in his preface to the edition of* Oedipe, *he comments on Shakespeare's barbarism, but calls him, along with Lope de Vega, a great genius. Two further discussions of Shakespeare, the* Discours sur la Tragédie *which serves as a preface to* Brutus *(1731), and* Lettres Philosophiques *(1733), complete the first period of Voltaire's Shakespeare criticism. The latter, while still praising the English genius, is no longer as extravagant. It is a recounting of the faults which predominates.*

It is wrong to think, as some critics have, that Voltaire's attitude to Shakespeare has anything of such personal elements as envy in it. Rather, Voltaire saw himself as the champion of all that the Cartesian clarity of the previous century had won, and the opponent of new and dangerous tendencies that were beginning to assert themselves in literature and criticism. His attitude to Shakespeare, beginning with the publication of Appel à toutes les Nations de l'Europe *in 1761, shows an increasing inclination to disparagement. In a preface to his translation of* Julius Caesar *(1764), Voltaire, with the dogmatism characteristic of his last years, all but dismisses Shakespeare while asserting the supremacy of Racine and Corneille.*

The following essay, Discours sur la Tragédie, *addressed to Lord Bolingbroke, is the least equivocal statement on Shakespeare that Voltaire was to make in the early period of his interest in the English dramatist. The essay develops with greater care his earlier, somewhat hurried, claims.*

PREFACE TO Brutus

Discourse on Tragedy

If I dedicate to an Englishman a work performed in Paris, it is not, milord, because there are not also in my country enlightened judges and excellent minds to whom I could have tendered this honor; but you know that the tragedy of Brutus was born in England. You remember that when I had withdrawn to Wandsworth, to the home of Mr. Falkener, that worthy and virtuous citizen, I was busy at his home with writing in English prose the first act of this play, more or less as it is today in French verse. I spoke to you about it sometimes, and we were surprised that no Englishman had dealt with this subject, which, above all others, is perhaps the most suitable to your theater. You used to encourage me to continue this work, which is capable of arousing such great feeling. Permit me, then, to present *Brutus* to you, *docte sermonis utriusque linguae,* although it is written in another language, to you who could give me lessons in French as well as in English, to you, who would teach me at least to endow my language with that force and energy which noble freedom of thought inspires: for

From *Oeuvres complètes de Voltaire,* Tome Second (Paris, Lefèvre-Deterville, 1817), pp. 271–285. Translated by Françoise Rosen.

vigorous feelings of the soul always pass into the language; and whoever thinks forcefully speaks in the same way.

I confess, milord, that on my return from England, where I had spent almost two years in a continual study of your language, I found myself at a loss when I wished to compose a French tragedy. I had almost become accustomed to thinking in English; I felt that the terms of my own language no longer came to my imagination with the same abundance as before: it was like a stream whose source has been diverted; time and effort were required to make it flow in its original bed. I understood then that, to succeed in an art, one must cultivate it all one's life.

What alarmed me most in returning to this career was the severity of our poetry and the slavery to rhyme. I missed that happy freedom which you have of writing your tragedies in unrhymed verse; of lengthening and above all of shortening almost all your words; of running one line on to the next; and of creating, at need, new terms, which are always adopted among you when they are sonorous, intelligible, and necessary. An English poet, I used to say, is a free man who subdues his language to his genius; the Frenchman is a slave to rhyme, obliged sometimes to make four verses to express a thought which an Englishman can render in a single line. The Englishman says everything that he wants to say, the Frenchman says only what he can say; the former runs in a vast arena, and the latter walks fettered on a slippery and narrow path.

In spite of all these reflections and complaints, we shall never be able to shake off the yoke of rhyme; it is essential to French poetry. Our language admits of only a few inversions; our lines do not at all accept enjambment, or at least this license is very rare; our syllables cannot produce an appreciable harmony by their long or short measures; our caesuras and a certain number of feet would not suffice to distinguish prose from poetry: rhyme is thus necessary to French verse. Furthermore, so many great masters have made rhymed verses, such as Corneille, Racine, Despréaux, and have so accustomed our ears to this harmony that we could not endure others, and, I repeat again, whoever would wish to free himself of a burden which the great Corneille has borne would rightly be regarded not as a bold talent who is opening up a new path, but as a very weak man who cannot walk in the ancient lists.

Some have tried to give us tragedies in prose; but I do not believe that this enterprise can in future succeed; who has more could not be satisfied with less. One will always be unwelcome in saying to the public: I am coming to diminish your pleasure. If, in the midst of the paintings of Rubens or of Paul Veronese, someone came and placed his pencil sketches, would he not be wrong to deem himself equal to these painters? One is accustomed at festivals to dances and songs; would it be enough to walk and talk instead, on the pretext that one would walk and talk well, and that that would be more easy and natural?

There is a strong likelihood that poetry will always be necessary in all tragic drama, and, moreover, always rhymed poetry in ours. It is even to this constraint of rhyme and to this extreme severity of our versification that we owe those excellent works that we have in our language. We desire that rhyme never cost anything to the meaning, that it be neither trivial nor too far-fetched. We rigorously require in poetry the same purity, the same exactitude as in prose. We do not permit the least license; we ask that an author wear all these chains without breaking them, and nonetheless that he seem always free; and we recognize as poets only those who have satisfied all these conditions.

That is why it is easier to compose a hundred lines of verse in any other language than four lines in French. The example of our Abbé Regnier-Desmarais,[1] of the French Academy and that of la Crusca, is a very obvious proof of this: he translated Anacreon into Italian successfully, and his French poetry is, with the exception of two or three quatrains, in the most mediocre class. Our Ménage [2] was in the same case. How many of our fine minds have composed some very good Latin poetry, and have not been bearable in their own language!

I know how many disputes I have undergone about our

[1] François Seraphin Regnier-Desmarais (1632–1713), one of the principal editors of the *Dictionary of the French Academy,* and also the author of *Poems in French, Italian, Spanish, and Latin* (1707). Editor.
[2] Gilles Ménage (1613–1692), critic and scholar whose reputation rests chiefly on his *Etymological Dictionary of the French Language.* Editor.

versification in England, and what reproaches the learned Bishop of Rochester often made me about this childish constraint which he claims we impose on ourselves out of sheer wantonness. But be assured, milord, that the more a foreigner knows our language, the more will he reconcile himself to this rhyme that disturbs him at first. Not only is it necessary to our tragedy, but it embellishes even our comedies. A clever remark in verse is the more easily remembered: the portraits of human life will always be more striking in verse than in prose; and whoever says *verse*, in French, necessarily says rhymed verse: in a word, we have prose comedies of the celebrated Molière which had to be cast into verse after his death, and which are no longer played except in this new manner.

Being unable, milord, to hazard in the French theater unrhymed poetry such as is common in Italy and England, I should at least have wished to transfer to our stage certain beauties of your own. It is true, I admit, that English drama is quite defective. I have heard from your own lips that you did not possess one good tragedy; but, in recompense, in those so outrageous plays, you have some admirable scenes. Up till now nearly all the tragic authors of your nation have lacked that purity, that regular deportment, those touches of decorum of action and style, that elegance, and all those refinements of the tragic art which have established the reputation of French drama since the great Corneille; but your most irregular plays have a great merit, namely, action.

In France we have reputable tragedies which are conversations rather than the representation of an event. An Italian author wrote me a letter on drama:

> A critic of (our play) Pastor Fido said that that composition was a quintessence of very beautiful madrigals;[3] I believe, if

[3] *Il Pastor Fido* by Giambattista Guarini (1538–1612), written between 1580 and 1585 and circulated in manuscript form until its publication in 1590, was the occasion for the last of the great cinquecento literary quarrels. Voltaire's unnamed correspondent, in referring to a critic who believes Guarini's tragicomedy to be a series of madrigals, may well have been alluding to Faustino Summo, whose *Discorsi Poetici* (1600), in its last two discourses constituted an attack upon Guarini's work. Summo's arguments are those of Cicero against the mixing of styles and his theory, once again, was that of a narrow classicism. Editor.

> he were living, that he would say concerning French tragedies that they are quintessences of beautiful elegiac poetry and of sumptuous epithalamia.

I am indeed afraid that this Italian was too right. Our excessive delicacy obliges us sometimes to put into narrative what we should wish to expose to sight. We fear to hazard on stage new spectacles before a nation habituated to ridicule everything that is not customary.

The place where one performs drama, and the abuses which have slipped in there, are still a cause of that dryness which one can complain of in some of our plays. The benches which are on the stage, intended for the spectators, shrink the area of the stage and make all action almost impracticable.* This fault is the reason why scenery, so much recommended by the ancients, is rarely suitable to the play. Above all, it prevents the actors from going from one room to another in sight of the spectators, as the Greeks and Romans wisely arranged it, to preserve at the same time unity of place and verisimilitude.

How should we dare on our stage to have appear, for example, Pompey's ghost, or Brutus' spirit, in the midst of so many young people who never look upon the most serious things save as the occasion for making a witticism? How should we bring before them on stage the body of Marcus, in front of his father Cato, who exclaims: "Happy youth who died for your country! O my friends, let me count these glorious wounds! who would not wish to die thus for the fatherland? Why has one only one life to sacrifice for it? . . . My friends, do not weep at all for my loss, do not lament my son; weep for Rome, the mistress of the world is no more. O Liberty! O my country! O virtue!" etc.[4]

That is what the late Mr. Addison did not at all fear to perform in London; that is what was played, translated into Italian, in more than one city in Italy. But if we should venture such a spectacle in Paris, do you not already hear the pit

* Finally these reiterated complaints of Voltaire's have brought about the reform of the stage in France, and these abuses no longer exist.

[4] Voltaire is paraphrasing a speech (IV, iv, 76–95) from Joseph Addison's *Cato* (1713). Editor.

crying out, and do you not see our women turning their heads aside?

You could not imagine to what point this delicacy goes. The author of our tragedy of *Manlius* took his subject from the English play of Mr. Otway, entitled *Venice Preserved.* The subject is drawn from the history of the conspiracy of the Marquis of Bedamar, written by the Abbé de Saint-Réal; [5] and permit me to say in passing that this bit of history, equal perhaps to Sallust, is far above Otway's play and our *Manlius.* Firstly, you will notice the prejudice which has forced the French author to disguise a known adventure under Roman names, which the Englishman has treated naturally under the real names. People did not at all find it ridiculous on the London stage that a Spanish ambassador was named Bedamar, and the conspirators had the names of Jaffeir, Jacques-Pierre, and Elliot; that alone in France would have been able to make the play fail.

But observe that Otway does not at all fear to assemble all the conspirators. Renault takes their oath, assigns his post to each one, prescribes the hour of carnage, and from time to time casts uneasy and suspicious glances at Jaffeir, whom he mistrusts. He delivers before them all this moving speech, translated word for word from the Abbé de Saint-Réal: "Never has such profound tranquillity preceded so great a disturbance. Our good fortune has blinded the most clear-sighted of men, has reassured the most timid, has lulled the most suspicious, has confounded the most subtle: we are still living, my dear friends: we are still living, and our life will be deadly to the tyrants of this place," etc.[6]

What has the French author done? He has feared to venture so many characters on stage; he contents himself with making Renault, under the name of Rutilius, recite a weak portion of this same speech, which he has just delivered, he says, to the conspirators. Do you not feel, from this single account, how

[5] César Vichard, Abbé de Saint-Réal (1639–1692), was primarily a historian, author of *La Conjuration des Espagnoles contre Venise* (1674) and *Vie de Jésus-Christ* (1678). Editor.

[6] Voltaire is paraphrasing Act III, scene ii, 355–364, of Otway's *Venice Preserved* (1682). Editor.

much that English scene is superior to the French, although Otway's play is outlandish?

With what pleasure did I not see in London your tragedy of *Julius Caesar,* which, for one hundred and fifty years, has been the delight of your nation! I surely do not claim to approve the barbaric irregularities with which it is filled; it is only astonishing that there are not more of them in a work composed in a century of ignorance by a man who did not even know Latin, and who had no teacher but his own genius. But in the midst of so many uncouth faults, with what delight I watched Brutus, still holding the dagger stained with Caesar's blood, assemble the Roman mob, and speak to them thus from the height of the speakers' rostrum:

> Romans, countrymen, and lovers! . . . If there be any in this assembly, any dear friend of Caesar's, to him I say, that Brutus' love to Caesar was no less than his. If then that friend demand why Brutus rose against Caesar, this is my answer:— Not that I loved Caesar less, but that I loved Rome more. Had you rather Caesar were living and die all slaves, than that Caesar were dead, to live all free men? As Caesar loved me, I weep for him; as he was fortunate, I rejoice at it; as he was valiant, I honour him; but, as he was ambitious, I slew him. . . . Who is here so base that would be a bondman? If any, speak; for him have I offended. Who is here so rude that would not be a Roman? If any, speak; for him have I offended. . . .
>
> CITIZENS. None, Brutus, none.
>
> BRUTUS. Then none have I offended. . . . Here comes his body, mourned by Mark Antony: who, though he had no hand in his death, shall receive the benefit of his dying, a place in the commonwealth; as which of you shall not? With this I depart,—that, as I slew my best lover for the good of Rome, I have the same dagger for myself, when it shall please my country to need my death.
>
> CITIZENS. Live, Brutus! live, live!
>
> (III, ii, 13–53)

After this scene Antony comes to move by pity those same Romans in whom Brutus had inspired his own harshness and barbarity. Antony, by an artful speech, gradually brings round these haughty spirits and when he sees them softened, then he shows them Caesar's body, and, using the most pathetic expressions, he incites them to tumult and vengeance. Perhaps the French would not permit one to present on their stage a Chorus composed of artisans and plebeian Romans; that Caesar's bloodied body be there exposed to the eyes of the people, and that this people be aroused to vengeance from the height of the speakers' rostrum: it is up to Custom, which is the King of this world, to change the taste of nations, and to turn to pleasure the objects of our aversion.

The Greeks ventured spectacles no less shocking for us. Hippolytus, broken by his fall, comes on stage to count his wounds and utter cries of pain. Philoctetes falls down in his bouts of suffering; black blood drips from his wound. Oedipus, covered with the blood that still flows from the remains of his eyes, which he has just torn out, complains of gods and men. One hears the cries of Clytemnestra, whom her own son slaughters; and Electra cries out on stage, "Strike, do not spare her, she did not spare our father." Prometheus is fixed to a rock by nails which are driven through his stomach and his arms. The furies reply to the bloody ghost of Clytemnestra with inarticulate howls. Many Greek tragedies, in a word, are filled with this terror carried to excess.

I know well that Greek tragedians, who are moreover superior to the English, erred in often taking horror for terror, and the disgusting and unbelievable for the tragic and marvelous. The art was in its infancy, at the time of Aeschylus, as in London, at the time of Shakespeare; but, among the great faults of the Greek poets, and even among your own, one finds a true pathos and singular beauties; and if some Frenchmen who are acquainted with foreign tragedies and manners only through translations and by hearsay condemn them without any restriction, they are, it seems to me, like blind men who would assert that a rose cannot have vivid colors because they would count its thorns by touch. But if you and the Greeks go beyond the bounds of decorum, and if the English especially have put on frightful spectacles, in wishing to mount terrible ones, we French, as fastidious as you have been foolhardy, stop too soon, from fear of being carried away; and sometimes we do not attain the tragic, from fear of passing beyond its limits.

I am very far from suggesting that the stage become a scene of carnage as it is in Shakespeare and his successors, who, not having his genius, imitated only his faults, but I dare to believe that there are situations which still appear merely disgusting to Frenchmen, and which, well handled, presented with art, and above all, softened by the charm of fine poetry, could cause us a sort of pleasure of which we have no notion (now).

> There is no serpent or odious monster
> Which, by imitated art, cannot please the eye.

At least, will someone tell me why it is permitted to our heroes and heroines of the drama to kill themselves, and why they are forbidden to kill anyone else? Is the scene less bloodied by the death of Atalide stabbing herself than it would be by the murder of Caesar? And if the spectacle of Cato's son, who appears dead before his father's eyes, is the occasion of an admirable speech by that old Roman; and if this piece has been applauded in England and in Italy by those who are the greatest partisans of French decorum; if the most delicate women have not been at all shocked by it, why should the French not become accustomed to it? Is not nature the same in all men?

All these laws, of not shedding any blood on stage, of not having more than three interlocutors speak, etc., are laws which, it seems to me, could have some exceptions among us, as they did among the Greeks. These rules of decorum, always a little arbitrary, are not like fundamental rules of drama, which are the three unities: there would be weakness and sterility in extending an action beyond the length of time and suitable place. Ask anyone who may have put too many events in a play the reason for this fault; if he is honest, he will tell you he did not have enough talent to fill his play with a single event; and if he takes two towns and two days for his action, believe that it is because he would not have had the adroitness to compress it within the space of three hours and in the precincts of a palace, as verisimilitude requires. His case is altogether different from that of one who would venture a horrible spectacle on stage: he would not at all offend verisimilitude; and this daring, far from supposing weakness in the author, would require, on the contrary, a great talent to inject true grandeur by his poetry into an action which, without a sublime style, would only be dreadful and disgusting.

This is what our great Corneille attempted once in his *Rodogune*. He presents a mother who, in the presence of the Court and an ambassador, tries to poison her son and daughter-in-law, after having killed her other son with her own hand. She offers them the poisoned goblet, and, upon their refusal and suspicions, drinks it herself, and dies of the poison which she had intended for them. Such terrible blows must not be lavished, and not every one is able to strike them. These novelties demand great circumspection and masterly execution. The English themselves admit that Shakespeare, for example, was the only one among them who knew how to evoke ghosts and make them speak successfully:

> Within that circle none durst move but he.

The more a dramatic action is majestic or frightening, the more insipid it would become if it were often repeated; a little like the details of battles, which, being in themselves most terrible, become lifeless and boring, by dint of reappearing often in histories. The only play in which Monsieur Racine put spectacle was his masterwork, *Athalie*. In it one sees a child on a throne, its nurse and the priests who surround it, a queen commanding her soldiers to massacre it, and Levite armies rushing to its defense. All this action is pathetic; but, if the style were not so as well, it would be merely puerile.

The more one wishes to strike the sight of a brilliant display, the more is one required to say great things; otherwise one would be merely a decorator, and not a tragic poet. Nearly thirty years ago the tragedy of Montezuma was performed in Paris; the scene opened with a new spectacle; it was a palace in magnificent and barbaric style; Montezuma appeared in a remarkable costume; slaves armed with arrows were in the background; around him were eight grandees of his court, prostrate on the ground: Montezuma began the play by saying to them:

> Arise, your king today permits you,
> To see him and to speak with him.

This spectacle pleased; but that is all that was fine in this tragedy.

For myself, I admit that it has not been without some fear that I have introduced on the French stage the Roman senate in red robes, going to deliberate. I remembered that when I formerly introduced in *Oedipus* a Chorus of Thebans who said:

> O Death, we implore thy deadly aid!
> O Death, come save us, come end our days!

the pit, instead of being struck by the pathos which could exist at this point, felt at first only the supposed ludicrousness of having put these words in the mouths of unaccustomed actors, and there was a burst of laughter. That is what has prevented me in *Brutus* from making the Roman senators speak when Titus is accused before them, and from increasing the terror of the situation by expressing the astonishment and grief of these fathers of Rome, who doubtless must have marked their surprise otherwise than by a dumb-show which was not even executed.*

The English give much more to action than we do, they address themselves rather to the eyes: the French give more

* We think it appropriate to recall here the following section which Monsieur de Voltaire curtailed in the editions subsequent to 1738:

"Furthermore, milord, if there are some passable passages in this work, I must confess that I am obliged for them to friends who think as you do. They encouraged me to temper the austerity of Brutus by paternal love, so that one should admire him and pity the effort that he makes in condemning his son. They urged me to give to young Tullia a character of tenderness and innocence, because if I had made of her a haughty princess who would have spoken to Titus only as a subject who must serve his prince, then Titus would have been debased, and the ambassador would have been useless. They wished Titus to be a young man furious in his passions, loving Rome and his father, adoring Tullia, making a duty of loyalty to the senate, even the senate he complained to elegance, to harmony, to the charms of verse. It is certain that it is more difficult to write well than to put on stage assassinations, tortures, sorcerers, and ghosts. Thus, the tragedy of Cato, which does so much honor to Mr. Addison, your successor in the ministry, this tragedy, the only well-written one from one end of your nation to the other, according to what I have heard you yourself say, owes its great reputation only to its fine poetry, that is to say, to bold and true thoughts, expressed in harmonious verse. It is beauties of detail which sustain works of verse, and which preserve them to posterity. It is often the singular manner of saying common things, and it is this art of embellishing by diction what all men think and feel which makes great poets. There are neither far-fetched feelings nor picturesque adventure in the fourth book of Virgil; it is quite natural and that is the effort of the human mind. Monsieur Racine is only so superior to the others who have all said the same things as he, because he has said them better. Corneille is only truly great when he expresses himself as well as he thinks. Let us remember this precept of Despréaux:

> And that all he says, easy to remember,
> Leaves us a long memory of his work.

This is what so many dramatic works do not at all have, which the skill of an actor and the face and voice of an actress have made successful in our theaters. How many badly written plays have had more performances than *Cinna* and *Britannicus!* But no one has ever remembered two lines of these feeble poems, whereas one knows parts of *Britannicus* and

---

of, and carried far from his duty by a passion which he thought he had mastered. In fact, if Titus had been of his mistress' opinion, and had told himself good reasons in favor of kings, Brutus then would have been regarded only as a rebel chief, Titus would no longer have had remorse, and his father would no longer have aroused pity.

"Take care, they said to me, lest the two children of Brutus appear on stage together; you know that interest is lost when it is divided. But above all, let your play be simple; imitate that beauty of the Greeks, believe that the multiplicity of events and of complicated interests is the resource only of sterile talents which do not know how to elicit from a single passion material sufficient to form five acts. Try to work each scene as if it were the only one which you had to write, etc., etc."

Cinna by heart. In vain has Pradon's *Regulus* caused tears to flow by some touching situations; this work and all those which resemble it are scorned, while their authors applaud each other in their prefaces.

Some judicious critics could ask me why I have spoken of love in a tragedy whose title is *Junius Brutus;* why I have mingled this passion with the austere virtue of the Roman senate and the policy of an ambassador.

People reproach our nation with having softened the drama by too much tenderness; and the English have deserved the same reproach for nearly half a century, for you have always, to a small extent, taken our fashions and vices. But do you permit me to express my feeling on this matter?

To desire love in all tragedies seems to me an effeminate taste; to proscribe it always is quite unreasonable bad humor.

Drama, be it tragic, be it comic, is the living portrait of human passions. The ambition of a prince is represented in tragedy; comedy ridicules the vanity of a bourgeois. Here you laugh at the coquetry and intrigues of a middle-class woman; there you weep for the ill-fated passion of Phaedra; in the same way, love entertains you in a novel, and it transports you in Virgil's Dido. Love in a tragedy is no more an essential defect than in the *Aeneid;* it is to be eschewed only if it is inappropriately introduced, or unskillfully treated.

The Greeks rarely ventured this passion on the Athenian stage: first, because, since their tragedies had revolved at first around subjects of terror, the mind of the spectators was bent toward this kind of spectacle; secondly, because, as their women led a much more retired life than ours do, and thus, the language of love was not, as it is today, the subject of all conversations, poets were the less drawn toward treating this passion, which is the most difficult of all to represent, because of the delicate handling it requires. A third reason, which seems rather strong to me, was that they had no actresses; the women's roles were played by masked men: it seems that love would have been ridiculous on their lips.

It is quite different in London or Paris; and one must admit that authors would have scarcely understood their own interests or known their audience, if they had always made

Oldfield, Duclos, and Le Couvreur[7] speak only of ambition and politics.

The trouble is that love is often with our dramatic heroes only gallantry, and that with yours it degenerates sometimes to debauchery. In our *Alcibiades,* a very well-attended play, but poorly written, and thus held in low esteem, people have long admired these bad verses which the Aesopus of the last century (the actor Baron) recited in charming tones:

Ah! when, steeped in a true love
And sighing at the feet of an adorable beloved,
I knew in her timid and heedless eyes
That these cares of my heart were able to trouble her calm:
When, by the secret avowal of mutual ardor,
My own again took on new force:
In these moments so sweet, I a hundred times proved
That a mortal may savor happiness complete.

In your *Venice Preserved,* old Renault tries to violate Jaffeir's wife, and she complains of it in rather indecent terms, so far as to say that he came to her *unbutton'd.*

In order for love to be worthy of tragic drama, it must be the necessary nexus of the play, and not be brought in by force, to fill in the gap in your tragedies and ours, which are all too long; it must be truly tragic passion, regarded as a weakness, and fought against by remorse. Either love must lead to misfortunes and crime, to show how dangerous it is; or virtue must triumph over it, to show that it is not invincible; without that it is no more than the love in an eclogue or in a comedy.

It is up to you, milord, to decide whether I have fulfilled some of these conditions; but may your friends deign above all not to judge of the genius and taste of a whole nation by this essay and by this tragedy I send you. I am perhaps one of those who cultivate literature in France with less success; and if the sentiments which I here submit to your censure are disapproved, it is to me alone that the blame for them belongs.

[7] Anne Oldfield (1683–1730), an actress who excelled in both tragedy and comedy. Marie Anne Duclos (1664–1748), a French actress. Adrienne Le Couvreur (1690–1730), a French actress who was especially popular from 1717 until her death. Editor.

2. Gotthold Ephraim Lessing

1729–1781

Voltaire had been unable to reconcile Shakespearean drama with the classic and humanistic traditions of his time. It remained for the German critic and dramatist Lessing to provide the means of seeing in Shakespeare the continuity of classical tragedy. Lessing felt that under the impact of French neoclassical criticism Aristotle's theory of tragedy had been perverted. Its emphasis had shifted from what was for Lessing of the first importance, the nature of tragedy's impact upon its audience, to a Procrustean catalogue of rules and subject matter. It was not merely to free German drama of the tyranny of French classical criticism, or to assert the natural power of German Volksdrama, *that Lessing chose Shakespeare as the model of tragedy and Voltaire and Corneille as his targets. Lessing's passion was profoundly moral and he had become convinced that Aristotle's terms had been considerably diminished in France.*

Lessing's most famous early statement of this critical attitude is Number 17 of Briefe die neueste Literatur betreffend *(February 16, 1759). The letters, published between 1759 and 1765, and supposedly to a friend in the army, castigated the learned or saccharine imitators of French and English writers with the brilliant irony that became characteristic of Lessing's style. Lessing asserted, as no European critic of the time had been able to do before him, that* Othello, Hamlet, *and* King Lear *were of a power over an audience equal to that of the* Oedipus *of Sophocles.*

But it was not until the period of the Hamburgische Dramaturgie *that Lessing's talent as a critic and polemicist manifested itself most impressively. He accepted an invitation in December 1766 to become a sort of resident critic of the newly formed Hamburg National Theater, a venture which was to last no more than eight months. The total of 104 essays, devoted to the plays that were offered by the company, were published in 1769 by Lessing himself in two volumes and under their present title. In these essays Lessing defined the nature and function of tragedy. He scrutinized French neoclassical drama and the view of tragedy that it presents, contrasting it with what seemed to him far more profoundly moving, and closer to the true spirit of Aristotle, the view of tragedy implicit in Shakespeare and a number of his contemporaries. Lessing, though by no means the first or the only one, was the strongest voice up to that time to insist that Shakespeare's power was attributable to his great natural resources as a poet, and that these resources validated his dramatic "form."*

FROM Hamburg Dramaturgy

Number 5

If Shakespeare was not as great an actor as he was a dramatist, at least he knew as well what was needed for the art of the one as the other. Yes, perhaps he even pondered more about the former because he had the less genius for it. Certainly every word that he puts into Hamlet's mouth when addressing the players should be a golden rule for all actors who care for sensible approbation. "I pray you," he says among other things, "speak the speech as I pronounced it to you, trippingly on the tongue: but if you mouth it, as many of your players do, I had as lief the town-crier spoke my lines. Nor do not saw the air too much with your hand, thus, but use all gently; for in the very torrent, tempest, and, as I may say, the whirlwind of passion, you must acquire and beget a temperance that may give it smoothness" (III, ii, 1–9).

The fire of the actor is often mentioned, discussions are

From *Selected Prose Works of G. E. Lessing*, published in Bohn's Standard Library, c. 1890. Translated by Helen Zimmern.

common as to whether the actor can show too much animation. If those who maintain this cite as an instance that an actor may be passionate or at least more passionate than circumstances require; then those who deny it have a right to say that in such cases the actor has not shown too much animation, but too little intelligence. Altogether it depends greatly what we understand under the word fire. If screams and contortions are fire then it is incontestable that the actor can carry these too far. But if fire consists in the rapidity and vivacity with which all those parts that make the actor bring their properties to bear, to give to his acting the semblance of truth, then we should not desire to see this semblance of truth carried to the extremest illusion, if we deemed it possible that the actor could apply too much fire in this sense. It can therefore not be this fire the moderation of which Shakespeare requires even in the torrent, tempest, and whirlwind of passion. He can only mean that violence of voice and movement; and it is easy to discover why, where the poet has not observed the least moderation, the actor must yet moderate himself in both points. There are few voices that do not become displeasing at their utmost pitch, and movements that are too rapid, too agitated will rarely be dignified. Now our eyes and our ears are not to be offended, and only when everything is avoided in the expression of violent passion that can be unpleasant to these can acting possess that smoothness and polish which Hamlet demands from it even under these circumstances, if it is to make the deepest impression and to rouse the conscience of stiff-necked sinners out of its sleep.

The art of the actor here stands midway between the plastic arts and poetry. As visible painting beauty must be its highest law, but as transitory painting it need not always give to its postures the calm dignity that makes ancient sculpture so imposing. It may, it must at times permit to itself the wildness of a Tempesta, the insolence of a Bernini; and they have in this art all that which is expressive and peculiar without the offensive element that arises in the plastic arts through their permanent posture. Only it must not remain in them too long, it must prepare for them gradually by previous movements, and must resolve them again into the general tone of the conventional. Neither must it ever give to them all the strength which the poet may use in his treatment. For though the art is silent poetry, yet it desires to make itself comprehended immediately to our eyes, and every sense must be gratified if it is to convey unfalsified the proper impressions to the soul.

It might easily come about that the moderation demanded by art, even in the extremes of passion, does not consort well with applause. But what applause? It is true the gallery greatly loves the noisy and boisterous, and it will rarely omit to repay a good lung with loud hand-clappings. The German parterre also shares this taste in part; and there are actors cunning enough to derive advantage from this taste. The most sleepy actor will rouse himself toward the end of the scene, when he is to make his exit, raise his voice and overload the action, without reflecting whether the sense of his speech requires this extra exertion. Not seldom it even contradicts the mood in which he should depart; but what matters that to him? Enough that he has thus reminded the parterre to look at him, and, if it will be so good, to applaud after him. They should hiss after him! But, alas! the spectators are partly not connoisseurs, and in part too good-natured, and they take the desire to please them for the deed.

Number 11

The appearance of a ghost was so bold a novelty on the French stage, and the poet who ventured upon it justified it by such curious reasons, that it really repays the trouble of investigating them a little.

"They cry and write on all sides," says Monsieur de Voltaire, "that we no longer believe in ghosts and that the apparition of a ghost is held childish in the eyes of an enlightened nation. But how," he replies to this, "should all antiquity have believed in such miracles and should we not be permitted to adapt ourselves to antiquity? How? Our own religion has hallowed the belief in such extraordinary dispensations of Providence and it should be held ridiculous to revive them!"

These exclamations appear to me to be more rhetorical than philosophical. Above all things I should wish religion to be left out of the question. In matters of taste and criticism, reasons extorted from religion are all very well to silence an opponent, but not well suited to convince him. Religion as religion has nothing to decide here, and regarded as a form of ancient tradition her testimony has neither more nor less value than all other testimonies of antiquity. Consequently in this instance we have only to deal with antiquity.

Very good then; all antiquity believed in ghosts. Therefore the poets of antiquity were quite right to avail themselves of this belief. If we encounter ghosts among them, it would be unreasonable to object to them according to our better knowledge. But does this accord the same permission to our modern poet who shares our better knowledge? Certainly not. But suppose he transfers his story into these more credulous times? Not even then. For the dramatic poet is no historian, he does not relate to us what was once believed to have happened, but he really produces it again before our eyes, and produces it again not on account of mere historical truth but for a totally different and a nobler aim. Historical accuracy is not his aim, but only the means by which he hopes to attain his aim; he wishes to delude us and touch our hearts through this delusion. If it be true therefore that we no longer believe in ghosts; and if this unbelief must of necessity prevent this delusion, if without this delusion we cannot possibly sympathize, then our modern dramatist injures himself when he nevertheless dresses up such incredible fables, and all the art he has lavished upon them is vain.

Consequently? It is consequently never to be allowed to bring ghosts and apparitions on the stage? Consequently this source of terrible or pathetic emotions is exhausted for us? No, this would be too great a loss to poetry. Besides does she not own examples enough where genius confutes all our philosophy, rendering things that seem ludicrous to our cooler reason most terrible to our imagination? The consequence must therefore be different and the hypotheses when we started false. We no longer believe in ghosts? Who says so? Or rather, what does that mean? Does it mean: we are at last so far advanced in comprehension that we can prove their impossibility; that certain incontestable truths that contradict a belief in ghosts are now so universally known, are so constantly present even to the minds of the most vulgar, that everything that is not in accordance with these truths seems to them ridiculous and absurd! It cannot mean this. We no longer believe in ghosts can therefore only mean this: in this matter concerning which so much may be argued for or against, that is not decided and never can be decided, the prevailing tendency of the age is to incline toward the preponderance of reasons brought to bear against this belief. Some few hold this opinion from conviction, and many others wish to appear to hold it, and it is these who raise the outcry and set the fashion. Meanwhile the mass is silent, and remains indifferent, and thinks now with one side, now with the other, delights in hearing jokes about ghosts recounted in broad daylight and shivers with horror at night when they are talked of.

Now a disbelief in ghosts in this sense cannot and should not hinder the dramatic poet from making use of them. The seeds of possible belief in them are sown in all of us and most frequently in those persons for whom he chiefly writes. It depends solely on the degree of his art whether he can force these seeds to germinate, whether he possesses certain dexterous means to summon up rapidly and forcibly arguments in favor of the existence of such ghosts. If he has them in his power, no matter what we may believe in ordinary life, in the theater we must believe as the poet wills.

Such a poet is Shakespeare and Shakespeare only and alone. His ghost in *Hamlet* makes our hairs stand on end, whether they cover a believing or an unbelieving brain. Monsieur de Voltaire did not do well when he referred to this ghost, he only made himself and his ghost of *Ninus* ridiculous by so doing.

Shakespeare's ghost appears really to come from another world. For it comes at the solemn hour, in the dread stillness of night, accompanied by all the gloomy, mysterious accessories wherewith we have been told by our nurses that ghosts appear. Now Voltaire's ghost is not even fit for a bugbear wherewith to frighten children. It is only a disguised actor, who has nothing, says nothing, does nothing that makes it probable that he is that which he pretends to be. All the circumstances moreover, under which he appears, disturb the illusion and betray the creation of a cold poet who would like to deceive and terrify us without knowing how to set about it. Let us only consider this one thing. Voltaire's ghost steps out of his grave in broad daylight, in the midst of an assembly of the royal parliament, preceded by a thunderclap. Now where did Monsieur de Voltaire learn that ghosts are thus bold? What old woman could not have told him that ghosts avoid sunshine and do not willingly visit large assemblies? No doubt Voltaire knew this also; but he was too timid, too delicate to make use of these vulgar conditions, he wanted to show us a ghost but it should be of a higher type, and just this original type marred everything. A ghost that takes liberties which are contrary to all tradition, to all spectral good manners, does not seem to me a right sort of ghost, and everything that does not in such cases strengthen the illusion seems to weaken it.

If Voltaire had paid some attention to mimetic action he would for other reasons have felt the impropriety of allowing a ghost to appear before a large assembly. All present are forced at once to exhibit signs of fear and horror, and they must all exhibit them in various ways if the spectacle is not to resemble the chilly symmetry of a ballet. Now suppose a troupe of stupid walking gentlemen and ladies have been duly trained to this end, and even assuming that they have been successfully trained, consider how all the various expressions of the same emotion must divide the attention of the spectator and withdraw it from the principal characters. For if these are to make their due impression on us, it is not only needful we should see them but it is well we should see nothing but them. Shakespeare lets only Hamlet see the ghost, and in the scene where his mother is present, she neither sees nor hears it. All our attention is therefore fixed on him, and the more evidences of terror and horror we discover in this fear-stricken soul, the more ready are we to hold the apparition that has awakened such agitation as that for which he holds it. The specter operates on us, but through him rather than by itself. The impression it makes on him passes on to us, and the effect is too vivid and apparent for us to doubt its supernatural cause. How little has Voltaire understood this artistic touch! At his ghost many are frightened, but not much. Semiramis exclaims once: "Heaven! I die," while the rest make no more ado about him than we might make about a friend whom we deemed far away and who suddenly walks into the room.

Number 15

The sixteenth evening *Zaïre* by Voltaire was performed. "To those who care for literary history," says Monsieur de Voltaire, "it will not be displeasing to know how this play originated. Various ladies had reproached the author because his tragedies did not contain enough about love. He replied that in his opinion, tragedy was not the most fitting place for love; still if they would insist on having enamored heroes he also could create them. The play was written in eighteen days and received with applause. In Paris it is named a Christian tragedy and has often been played in the place of *Polyeucte*."[1]

To the ladies therefore we are indebted for this tragedy and it will long remain the favorite play of the ladies. A young ardent monarch, only subjugated by love; a proud conqueror, only conquered by love; a Sultan without polygamy; a seraglio converted into the free and accessible abode of an absolute mistress; a forsaken maiden raised to the highest pinnacle of fortune, thanks solely to her lovely eyes; a heart for which religion and tenderness contest, that is divided between its god and its idol, that would like to be pious if only it need not

[1] A tragedy by Pierre Corneille which appeared in 1643. Editor.

cease loving; a jealous man who recognizes his error and avenges it on himself: if these flattering ideas do not bribe the suffrages of the fair sex, then what indeed could bribe them?

Love itself dictated *Zaïre* to Voltaire! said a polite art critic. He would have been nearer the truth had he said gallantry; I know but one tragedy at which love itself has labored and that is *Romeo and Juliet* by Shakespeare. It is incontestable that Voltaire makes his enamored Zaïre express her feelings with much nicety and decorum. But what is this expression compared with that living picture of all the smallest, most secret artifices whereby love steals into our souls, all the imperceptible advantages it gains thereby, all the subterfuges with which it manages to supersede every other passion until it succeeds in holding the post of sole tyrant of our desires and aversions? Voltaire perfectly understands the—so to speak—official language of love; that is to say the language and the tone love employs when it desires to express itself with caution and dignity, when it would say nothing but what the prudish female sophist and the cold critic can justify. Still even the most efficient government clerk does not always know the most about the secrets of his government; or else if Voltaire had the same deep insight as Shakespeare into the essence of love, he would not exhibit it here, and therefore the poem has remained beneath the capacities of the poet.

Almost the same might be said of jealousy. His jealous Orosman plays a sorry figure beside the jealous Othello of Shakespeare. And yet Othello has unquestionably furnished the prototype of Orosman. Cibber [2] says Voltaire avails himself of the brand that lighted the tragic pile of Shakespeare. I should have said: a brand from out of this flaming pile and moreover one that smoked more than it glowed or warmed. In Orosman we hear a jealous man speak and we see him

[2] Lessing is most likely referring here to Colley Cibber (1671–1757), a comic actor by 1689 who became Poet Laureate in 1730. He produced his first play, *Love's Last Shift, or The Food in Fashion,* in 1695. He is best known for his *Apology for the Life of Colley Cibber,* and for Alexander Pope's satire of him in *The Dunciad.* Editor.

commit a rash deed of jealousy, but of jealousy itself we learn neither more nor less than what we knew before. Othello on the contrary is a complete manual of this deplorable madness; there we can learn all that refers to it and awakens it and how we may avoid it.

But is it always Shakespeare, always and eternally Shakespeare who understood everything better than the French, I hear my readers ask? That annoys us, because we cannot read him. I seize this opportunity to remind the public of what it seems purposely to have forgotten. We have a translation of Shakespeare. It is scarcely finished and yet seems already forgotten. Critics have spoken ill of it. I have a mind to speak very well of it. Not in order to contradict these learned men, nor to defend the faults they have discovered, but because I believe there is no need to make so much ado about these faults. The undertaking was a difficult one, and any other person than Herr Wieland [3] would have made other slips in their haste, or have passed over more passages from ignorance or laziness and what parts he has done well few will do better. Any way his rendering of Shakespeare is a book that cannot be enough commended among us. We have much to learn yet from the beauties he has given to us, before the blemishes wherewith he has marred them offend us so greatly that we require a new translation.

To return to *Zaïre*. It was brought out on the Parisian stage in 1733 by the author; and three years after it was translated into English and played in London at Drury Lane. The translator was Aaron Hill, himself no mean dramatic poet. This greatly flattered Voltaire, and what he said of it in his dedication to the Englishman Falkener deserves to be read, for it is in his peculiar strain of proud humility. Only we must not think everything is as true as he asserts.

Woe to him who does not always read Voltaire's writings in the skeptical spirit wherein he has written a portion of them.

For instance, he says to his English friend: "Your poets had

[3] Christoph Martin Wieland (1733–1813). His eight-volume translation came out between 1762–1766. Editor.

a custom to which even Addison himself submitted; for custom is as mighty as reason or law. This unreasonable custom was that every act must be concluded by verses in a style quite different from that of the rest of the play, and also these verses must of necessity contain a comparison. Phaedra before her exit compares herself poetically to a stag, Cato to a rock, and Cleopatra to children who weep themselves to sleep. The translator of *Zaïre* is the first who has ventured to maintain the laws of nature against such an abnormal taste. He has abolished this custom, for he felt that passion must speak its own language and that the poet must everywhere conceal himself in order that we may recognize the hero."

There are only three untruths in this passage; that is not much for Monsieur de Voltaire. It is true that the English since Shakespeare, or perhaps even before him, had the habit of ending their blank verse acts with a few rhyming lines. But that these rhyming lines consisted only of comparisons, that they necessarily contained such comparisons, is entirely false; and I cannot imagine how Monsieur de Voltaire could say such things to the face of an Englishman who might also be presumed to have read the tragic poets of his nation. Secondly it is not true that Hill departed from this custom in his translation of *Zaïre*. It is indeed almost incredible that Monsieur de Voltaire should not have looked more closely at a translation of his own play than I or someone else. And yet so it must be. For as certainly as it is in blank verse, so certainly does every act close with two or four rhymed lines. Comparisons, it is true, they do not contain, but as I said, among all the rhymed lines with which Shakespeare and Jonson and Dryden and Lee and Otway and Rowe and all the rest conclude their acts, there are certainly a hundred against five that likewise do not contain them. Therefore where is Hill's speciality? But even had he had the speciality that Voltaire confers on him, it is not true, in the third place, that his example has had the influence that Voltaire accords it. Of the tragedies that even now appear in England, half, if not more, have their acts ending with rhymes, rather than without them. Hill himself has never entirely abandoned the old custom even in those plays he has written since the translation of *Zaïre*. And what does it matter whether we hear rhymes at the end or no? If they are there, they may perhaps be useful to the orchestra to warn them to take up their instruments; a sign which in this way would be more prettily given out of the play itself than by means of a whistle or other signal.

Number 73

On the forty-eighth evening Herr Weisse's [4] tragedy of *Richard III* was performed. . . .

This play is unquestionably one of our most important original dramas. It is rich in beauties which sufficiently prove that it would not have been beyond the power of the poet to avoid the faults with which they are intermingled, had he but had sufficient confidence in himself.

Shakespeare had already brought the life and death of the third Richard upon the stage, but Herr Weisse did not recollect this until his own work was already completed. He says: "Although I shall lose much by this comparison, it will at least be found that I have not been guilty of plagiarism. But perhaps it would have been a merit to commit a plagiarism on Shakespeare."

For this end we must suppose such an act to be possible. What has been said of Homer, that it would be easier to deprive Hercules of his club, than him of a verse, can be as truly said of Shakespeare. There is an impress upon the least of his beauties which at once exclaims to all the world: I am Shakespeare's—and woe to the foreign beauty who has the self-confidence to place itself beside it!

Shakespeare must be studied, not plundered. If we have

[4] Christian Felix Weisse (1726–1804), a scholar and poet. His reputation survives mainly because of his translations of children's books. Editor.

genius, Shakespeare must be to us what the *camera obscura* is to the landscape painter. He must look into it diligently to learn how nature reflects herself upon a flat surface, but he must not borrow from it.

Now in Shakespeare's whole play I do not know one single scene, not even a single speech which Herr Weisse could have used as it stands. Even the smallest portions of Shakespeare are cut according to the great measure of his historical plays, and these stand to the tragedies of French taste much as a large fresco stands to a miniature painting intended to adorn a ring. What material can we then take from the former to use in the latter? Perchance a face, a single figure, at most a little group, which must then be worked out into a whole. In the same manner single Shakespearean thoughts must become entire scenes, and entire scenes whole acts. For rightly to use a giant's sleeve for the dress of a dwarf, we must not employ it as a sleeve but make a whole coat out of it.

If this is done, then the author may feel quite at ease on the score of plagiarism. Few persons will be able to recognize the wool from which the threads have been spun. Those few who comprehend the art will not betray the maker, for they know that a grain of gold may be wrought so skillfully that the value of the form far surpasses the value of the material.

I, for my part, sincerely deplore that our poet recollected Shakespeare's Richard too late. He might have known him and yet remained as original as he now is; he might have used him without a single borrowed thought convicting him.

Now if the same thing had occurred to me, I should at least have afterward employed Shakespeare's work as a mirror to wipe from my work all those blemishes which my eye had not been able to perceive immediately. How do I know that Herr Weisse has not done this? And why should he not have done this?

May it not be that what I consider blemishes he holds to be none? And is it not very probable that he is more in the right than I am? I am convinced that in most instances the eye of the artist is more penetrating than that of the most keen-sighted of his observers. Among twenty objections made by the latter, the artist will remember that nineteen of these were made and answered by himself while at work.

Nevertheless he will not be annoyed at hearing them from others also, for he likes his work to be criticized. Whether it be judged profoundly or superficially, justly or unjustly, benevolently or satirically, it is all the same to him. Even the most superficial, the most unjust, the most awkward judgment is of more worth to him than tame admiration. In some form or another he may make use of the former to his advantage; but what is he to do with the latter? He does not like to despise the good honest souls who look up to him as to something extraordinary, and yet he must shrug his shoulders at them. He is not vain, but he is usually proud, and from mere pride he would ten times rather bear an unmerited censure than unmerited praise.

3. Johann Wolfgang von Goethe

1749–1832

Goethe's influence on poetry, criticism, aesthetics, and drama has been uniformly profound. It has been said that the entire Romantic attitude toward Shakespeare grew out of the famous comparison of Hamlet to an oak tree planted in a costly jar, in Wilhelm Meisters Lehrjahre *(1796). It was certainly a new kind of criticism. But it was not without its antecedents.*

The previous generation, Sturm und Drang, *had abandoned Lessing's attempt to relate Shakespeare to Sophocles in favor of a less comparative approach. Its critics had concerned themselves with such matters as Shakespeare's spirit, his "organic" form, and his fidelity to nature. Wilhelm von Gerstenberg,* in Briefe über Merkwürdigkeiten der Literatur, *had stated that Shakespeare's dramas are* "Gemälde der sittlichen Natur."[1] *And the most outstanding literary figure of that generation, J. G. Herder, had seized on these ideas to which he had added his own caution that Shakespeare should not be compared to classical Greek tragedians, nor could he be, since each period had developed under different historical necessities. Herder's statement is perhaps an early variant of what has come to be called historico-realist criticism of Shakespeare. While such attitudes partially underlie Goethe's criticism, his chief tendency is more conventionally related to the type of Romantic attitude to Shakespeare.*

But Goethe's own attitude, like Voltaire's, changed, though not as profoundly as the French writer's, during the course of his lifetime. He began by admiring, a result of his youthful reading of Shakespeare, he tells us in 1771 (Zum Schäkespears Tag). *Twenty-five years later, discussing* Hamlet *in* Wilhelm Meister *(see above), he tempered his youthful ad-*

[1] Reflections of a moral universe.

miration by pointing out certain structural faults in the play. But the attitude was still largely favorable. It was in the years that followed Wilhelm Meister, *the years during which his friendship with Schiller was at its height, that Goethe, in the company of his fellow poet, arrived at a theory of literature, which, although not as strict as the classical French theory had been, was nevertheless hostile to the form and substance of Shakespeare's plays. The best example of Goethe's attitude of these years is, curiously enough, not a critical essay but his translation of* Romeo and Juliet. *Goethe's must be called a version since, under the influence of his classical theory, he considerably and carefully trimmed the play.*

The most complete statement of Goethe's later years is the following essay, Schäkespear und kein Ende! *(1815). A sort of apologia for his version of* Romeo and Juliet, *the essay shows Goethe transcending his prejudices and being able to claim, as Lessing had earlier, that Shakespeare's irregularities, his violations of custom and traditional tragic theory, make his work that much more lifelike. The essay marks the final coronation of Shakespeare in Germany and is of enormous import to the development of later German literature.*

Shakespeare ad Infinitum

There has already been so much said about Shakespeare that it would seem as if there was nothing left to say; and yet it is the characteristic of genius ever to be stimulating other men's genius. In the present case I wish to consider Shakespeare from more than one point of view—first as a poet in general, then in comparison with the classic and modern writers, and finally as a writer of poetic drama. I shall attempt to work out what the imitation of his art has meant to us, and what it can mean in the future. I shall express my agreement with what has been written by reiterating it, and express my dissent briefly and positively, without involving myself in conflict and contradiction. I proceed to the first topic.

I. SHAKESPEARE AS POET IN GENERAL

The highest achievement possible to a man is the full consciousness of his own feelings and thoughts, for this gives him the means of knowing intimately the hearts of others. Now there are men who are born with a natural talent for this and who cultivate it by experience toward practical ends. From this talent springs the ability to profit in a higher sense by the world and its opportunities. Now the poet is born with the same talent, only he cultivates it not for his immediate worldly purposes but for a loftier spiritual and universal purpose. If we call Shakespeare one of the greatest poets, we mean that few have perceived the world as accurately as he, that few who have expressed their inner contemplation of it have given the reader deeper insight into its meaning and consciousness. It becomes for us completely transparent: we find ourselves at once in the most intimate touch with virtue and vice, greatness and meanness, nobility and infamy, and all this through the simplest of means. If we ask what these means are, it seems as if they were directed toward our visual apprehension. But we are mistaken; Shakespeare's works are not for the physical vision. I shall attempt to explain what I mean.

The eye, the most facile of our organs of receptivity, may well be called the clearest of the senses; but the inner sense is still clearer, and to it by means of words belongs the most sensitive and clear receptivity. This is particularly obvious when what we apprehend with the eye seems alien and unimpressive considered in and for itself. But Shakespeare speaks always to our inner sense. Through this, the picture world of imagination becomes animated, and a complete effect results, of which we can give no reckoning. Precisely here lies the ground for the illusion that everything is taking place before our eyes. But if we study the works of Shakespeare enough, we find that they contain much more of spiritual truth than of spectacular action. He makes happen what can easily be conceived by the imagination, indeed what can be better imagined than seen. Hamlet's ghost, Macbeth's witches, many fearful incidents, get their value only through the power of the imagination, and many of the minor scenes get their force from the same source. In reading, all these things pass easily through our minds, and seem quite appropriate, whereas in representation on the stage they would strike us unfavorably and appear not only unpleasant but even disgusting.

Shakespeare gets his effect by means of the living word, and it is for this reason that one should hear him read, for then the attention is not distracted either by a too adequate or a too inadequate stage setting. There is no higher or purer pleasure than to sit with closed eyes and hear a naturally expressive voice recite, not declaim, a play of Shakespeare's. According to the delineation of the characters we can picture to ourselves certain forms, but more particularly are we able by the succession of words and phrases to learn what is passing in their souls; the characters seem to have agreed to leave us in the dark, in doubt, about nothing. To that end conspire heroes and lackeys, gentlemen and slaves, kings and heralds; indeed even the subordinate characters are often more expressive in this way than the leading figures. Everything which in an affair of great importance breathes only secretly through the air, or lies hidden in the hearts of men, is here openly expressed. What the soul anxiously conceals and represses is here brought freely and abundantly to the light. We experience the truth of life—how, we do not know!

Shakespeare associates himself with the World-Spirit; like it, he explores the world; from neither is anything hidden. But whereas it is the business of the World-Spirit to keep its secrets both before and after the event, it is the work of the poet to tell them, and take us into his confidence before the event or in the very action itself. The depraved man of power, the well-intentioned dullard, the passionate lover, the quiet scholar, all carry their heart in their hand, often contrary to verisimilitude. Every one is candid and loquacious. It is enough that the secret must out, and even the stones would publish it. The inanimate insists upon speaking; the elements, the phenomena of sky, earth, and sea, thunder and lightning, wild animals, lift their voice, often apparently and symbolically, but all joining in the revelation.

The whole civilized world too brings its treasures to Shakespeare; Art and Science, Commerce and Industry, all bear him their gifts. Shakespeare's poems are a great animated fair; and it is to his own country that he owes his riches.

For back of him is England, the sea-encircled and mist-covered country, whose enterprise reaches all the parts of the earth. The poet lives at a noble and important epoch, and presents all its glory and its deficiencies with great vivacity; indeed, he would hardly produce such an effect upon us were it not just his own life-epoch that he was representing. No one despised the outer costume of men more than he; but he understood well the inner man, and here all are similar. It is said that he has delineated the Romans with wonderful skill. I cannot see it. They are Englishmen to the bone; but they are human, thoroughly human, and thus the Roman toga presumably fits them. When one takes this into consideration, one finds his anachronisms entirely admirable; indeed, it is just his neglect of the outer form that makes his works so vital.

Enough of these slight words, which cannot begin to sound the praises of Shakespeare. His friends and worshipers will have to add many a word to them. But one more remark: it would be hard to find a poet each of whose works was more thoroughly pervaded by a definite and effective idea than his.

Thus *Coriolanus* is permeated by the idea of anger at the refusal of the lower classes to recognize the superiority of their betters. In *Julius Caesar* everything hinges on the idea that the upper classes are not willing to see the highest place in the State occupied, since they wrongly imagine that they are able to act together. *Antony and Cleopatra* expresses with a thousand tongues the idea that pleasure and action are ever incompatible. And so one will ever find, in searching his works, new cause for astonishment and admiration.

II. SHAKESPEARE COMPARED WITH THE ANCIENTS AND THE MODERNS

The interests which vitalize Shakespeare's great genius are interests which center in this world. For if prophecy and madness, dreams, omens, portents, fairies and gnomes, ghosts, imps, and conjurers introduce a magical element which so beautifully pervades his poems, yet these figures are in no way the basic elements of his works, but rest on a broad basis of the truth and fidelity of life, so that everything that comes from his pen seems to us genuine and sound. It has already been suggested that he belongs not so much to the poets of the modern era, which has been called "romantic," but much more to the "naturalistic" school, since his work is permeated with the reality of the present, and scarcely touches the emotions of unsatisfied desire, except at his highest points.

Disregarding this, however, he is, from a closer point of view, a decidedly modern poet, separated from the ancients by an enormous gulf, not perhaps with regard to his outer form, which is here beside our point, but with regard to his inner and most profound spirit.

Here let me say that it is not my idea to use the following terminology as exhaustive or exclusive; it is an attempt not so much to add another new antithesis to those already recognized, as to indicate that it is already contained in these. These are the antitheses:

Ancient	Modern
Natural	Sentimental
Pagan	Christian
Classic	Romantic
Realistic	Idealistic
Necessity	Freedom
Duty (*sollen*)	Will (*wollen*)*

* "Goethe, in a thoughtful essay, *Schakespear und kein Ende,* written many years later than his famous criticism of *Hamlet* in *Wilhelm Meister,* says that the distinction between the two [ancient and modern drama]

The greatest ills to which men are exposed, as well as the most numerous, arise from a certain inner conflict between duty and will, as well as between duty and its accomplishment, and desire and its accomplishment; and it is these conflicts which bring us so often into trouble in the course of our lives. Little difficulties, springing from a slight error which, though taking us by surprise, can be solved easily, give the clue to situations of comedy. The great difficulties, on the other hand, unresolved and unresolvable, give us tragedy.

Predominating in the old poems is the conflict between duty and performance, in the new between desire and accomplishment. Let us put this decided divergency among the other antitheses and see if it does not prove suggestive. In both epochs, I have said, there predominates now this side, now that; but since duty and desire are not radically separated in men's characters, both will be found together, even if one prevails and the other is subordinate. Duty is imposed upon men; "must" is a bitter pill. The will man imposes upon himself; man's will is his kingdom of heaven. A long-continued obligation is burdensome, the inability to perform it even terrible; but a constant will is pleasurable, and with a firm will men can console themselves for their inability to accomplish their desire.

Let us consider a game of cards as a kind of poem; it consists of both those elements. The form of the game, bound up with chance, plays here the role of necessity, just as the ancients knew it under the form of Fate; the will, bound up with the skill of the player, works in the other direction. In this sense I might call whist "classic." The form of play limits the

---

is the difference between *sollen* and *wollen,* that is, between *must* and *would.* He means that in the Greek drama the catastrophe is foreordained by an inexorable Destiny, while the element of free will, and consequently choice, is the very axis of the modern. The definition is conveniently portable, but it has its limitations. Goethe's attention was too exclusively fixed on the fate tragedies of the Greeks, and upon Shakespeare among the moderns. In the Spanish drama, for example, custom, loyalty, honor, and religion are as imperative and as inevitable as doom. In the *Antigone,* on the other hand, the crisis lies in the character of the protagonist." James Russell Lowell, *Shakespeare Once More.*

operation of chance, and even of the will itself. I have to play, in company with definite partners and opponents, with the cards which come into my hand, make the best of a long series of chance plays, without being able to control or parry them. In omber and similar games the contrary is the case. Here are many openings left for skill and daring. I can disavow the cards that fall to my hand, make them count in different ways, half or completely discard them, get help by luck, and in the play get the best advantage of the worst cards. Thus this kind of game resembles perfectly the modern mode of thought and literature.

Ancient tragedy was based on inescapable necessity, which was only sharpened and accelerated by an opposing will. Here is the seat of all that is fearful in the oracles, the region in which Oedipus lords it over all. Less tragic appears necessity in the guise of duty in the *Antigone;* and in how many forms does it not appear! But all necessity is despotic, whether it belong to the realm of Reason, like custom and civil law, or to Nature, like the laws of Becoming, and Growing and Passing-away, of Life and of Death. Before all these we tremble, without realizing that it is the good of the *whole* that is aimed at. The will, on the contrary, is free, appears free, and is advantageous to the *individual.* Thus the will is a flatterer, and takes possession of men as soon as they learn to recognize it. It is the god of the modern world. Dedicated to it, we are afraid of opposing doctrines, and here lies the crux of that eternal division which separates our art and thought from the ancients. Through the motive of Necessity, tragedy became mighty and strong; through the motive of Will, weak and feeble. Out of the latter arose the so-called Drama, in which dread Necessity is overcome and dissolved through the Will. But just because this comes to the aid of our weakness we feel moved when, after painful tension, we are at last a little encouraged and consoled.

As I turn now, after these preliminaries, to Shakespeare, I must express the hope that the reader himself will make the proper comparisons and applications. It is Shakespeare's unique distinction that he has combined in such remarkable fashion the old and the new. In his plays Will and Necessity struggle to maintain an equilibrium; both contend powerfully, yet always so that Will remains at a disadvantage.

No one has shown perhaps better than he the connection between Necessity and Will in the individual character. The person, considered as a character, is under a certain necessity; he is constrained, appointed to a certain particular line of action; but as a human being he has a will, which is unconfined and universal in its demands. Thus arises an inner conflict, and Shakespeare is superior to all other writers in the significance with which he endows this. But now an outer conflict may arise, and the individual through it may become so aroused that an insufficient will is raised through circumstance to the level of irremissible necessity. These motives I have referred to earlier in the case of Hamlet; but the motive is repeated constantly in Shakespeare—Hamlet through the agency of the ghost; Macbeth through the witches, Hecate, and his wife; Brutus through his friends gets into a dilemma and situation to which they were not equal; even in Coriolanus the same motive is found. This Will, which reaches beyond the power of the individual, is decidedly modern. But since in Shakespeare it does not spring from within, but is developed through external circumstance, it becomes a sort of Necessity, and approaches the classical motive. For all the heroes of ancient poetry willed only what was possible to men, and from this arose that beautiful balance between Necessity, Will, and Accomplishment. Still their Necessity is a little too severe for it really to be able to please us, even though we may wonder at and admire it. A Necessity which more or less, or even completely, excludes human freedom does not chime with our views any longer. It is true that Shakespeare in his own way has approximated this, but in making this Necessity a moral necessity he has, to our pleasure and astonishment, united the spirit of the ancient and the modern worlds. If we are to learn anything from him, here is the point where we must study in his school. Instead of singing the praises of our Romanticism so exclusively, and sticking to it so uncritically—our Romanticism, which need not be chidden or rejected—and thus mistaking and obscuring its strong, solid practical aspect, we should rather attempt to make this great fusion between the old and the new, even though it does seem inconsistent and paradoxical; and all the more should we make the attempt, because a great and unique master, whom we value most highly, and, often without knowing why, give homage to above all others, has already most effectively accomplished this miracle. To be sure, he had the advantage of living in a true time of harvest, and of working in a vigorous Protestant country, where the madness of bigotry was silent for a time, so that freedom was given to a true child of nature, such as Shakespeare was, to develop religiously his own pure inner nature, without reference to any established religion.

The preceding words were written in the summer of 1813; I ask that the reader will not now find fault with me, but simply recall what was said above—that this is merely an individual attempt to show how different poetic geniuses have tried to reconcile and resolve that tremendous antithesis which has appeared in their works in so many forms. To say more would be superfluous, since interest has been centered in this question for the past few years, and excellent explanations have been given us. Above all I wish to mention Blümner's[1] highly valuable treatise, *On the Idea of Fate in the Tragedies of Aeschylus*, and the excellent criticism of it in the supplement of the *Jenaische Literaturzeitung*. Therefore, I come without further comment to my third point, which relates immediately to the German theater and to Schiller's efforts to establish it for the future.

III. SHAKESPEARE AS PLAYWRIGHT

When lovers of art wish to enjoy any work, they contemplate and delight in it as a whole, that is, they try to feel and apprehend the unity which the artist can bring to them.

[1] Hugo Blümner (1844–1919), a German archaeologist whose principal writings are on the fine arts in ancient Greece and Italy. Editor.

Whoever, on the other hand, wishes to judge such works theoretically, to assert some judgment about them, or instruct someone about them, must use his discriminating and analytic faculty. This we attempted to carry out when we discussed Shakespeare, first as poet in general, and then compared him with the ancient and modern poets. Now we intend to close the matter by considering him as a playwright, or poet of the theater.

Shakespeare's fame and excellence belong to the history of poetry; but it is an injustice toward all playwrights of earlier and more recent times to give him his entire merit in the annals of the theater.

A universally recognized talent may make of its capacities some use which is problematical. Not everything which the great do is done in the best fashion. So Shakespeare belongs by necessity in the annals of poetry; in the annals of the theater he appears only by accident. Since we can honor him so unreservedly in the first case, it behooves us in the second to explain the conditions to which he had to accommodate himself, but not therefore to extol those conditions as either admirable or worthy of imitation.

We must distinguish closely related poetic genres, however often they may be confused and merged together in actual treatment—epic, dialogue, drama, play. *Epic* requires the verbal delivery to the crowd through the mouth of an individual; *dialogue,* conversation in a narrow circle, where the crowd may eventually listen; *drama,* conversation bound up with action, even if enacted only before the imagination; *play,* all three together, in so far as they appeal to the sense of vision, and can be embodied under certain conditions of personal presence and stage setting.

Shakespeare's works are in this sense highly dramatic; by his treatment, his revelation of the inner life, he wins the reader; the theatrical demands appear to him unimportant, and so he takes it easy, and we, spiritually speaking, take it easy with him. We pass with him from place to place; our power of imagination provides all the episodes which he omits. We even feel grateful to him for arousing our imagination in so profitable a way. Since he exhibits everything in dramatic form, he renders easy the working of our imaginations; for with the "stage that signifies the world" we are more familiar than with the world itself, and we can read and hear the most fantastic things, and still imagine that they might pass before our eyes on the stage. This accounts for the frequently bungling dramatizations of favorite novels.

Strictly speaking, nothing is theatrical except what is immediately symbolical to the eye: an important action, that is, which signifies a still more important one. That Shakespeare knew how to attain this summit, that moment witnesses where the son and heir in *Henry IV* takes the crown from the side of the slumbering king, who lies sick unto death—takes the crown and marches proudly away with it. But these are only moments, scattered jewels, separated by much that is untheatrical. Shakespeare's whole method finds in the stage itself something unwieldly and hostile. His great talent is that of a universal interpreter, or "epitomizer" (*Epitomator*), and since the poet in essence appears as universal interpreter of Nature, so we must recognize Shakespeare's great genius as lying in this realm; it would be only falsehood—and in no sense is this to his dishonor—were we to say that the stage was a worthy field for his genius. These limitations of the stage, however, have forced upon him certain limitations of his own. But he does not, like other poets, pick out disconnected materials for his separate works, but puts an idea at the center, and to it relates the world and the universe. As he works over and boils down ancient and modern history, he can often make use of the material of old chronicles; indeed, he often adapts them word for word. With romances he does not deal so conscientiously, as *Hamlet* shows us. *Romeo and Juliet* is truer to the original; still he almost destroys the tragic content of it by his two comic characters, Mercutio and the old nurse, played apparently by two favorite actors, the nurse perhaps originally by a male performer. If one examines the construction of the piece carefully, however, one notices that these two figures, and what surrounds them, come in only as farcical interludes, and must be as unbearable to the minds of the lovers on the stage as they are to us.

But Shakespeare appears most remarkable when he revises and pieces together already existing plays. In *King John* and *Lear* we can make this comparison, for the older plays are extant. But in these cases, too, he turns out to be more of a poet than playwright.

In closing, let us proceed to the solution of the riddle. The primitiveness of the English stage has been brought to our attention by scholars. There is no trace in it of that striving after realism, which we have developed with the improvement of machinery and the art of perspective and costuming, and from which we should find it hard to turn back to that child-like beginning of the stage—a scaffolding, where one saw little, where everything was *signified,* where the audience was content to assume a royal chamber behind a green curtain; and the trumpeter, who always blew his trumpet at a certain place, and all the rest of it. Who would be content today to put up with such a stage? But amid such surroundings, Shakespeare's plays were highly interesting stories, only told by several persons, who, in order to make somewhat more of an impression, had put on masks, and, when it was necessary, moved back and forth, entered and left the stage; but left to the spectator nevertheless the task of imagining at his pleasure Paradise and palaces on the empty stage.

How else then did Schroeder [2] acquire the great distinction of bringing Shakespeare's plays to the German stage, except by the fact that he was the "epitomizer" of the "epitomizer"!

Schroeder confined himself exclusively to effect; everything else he discarded, even many necessary things, if they seemed to injure the effect which he wanted to produce on his country and his time. Thus by the omission, for instance, of the first scenes of *King Lear,* he annulled the character of the play. And he was right, for in this scene Lear seems so

[2] Friedrich Ludwig Schroeder (1744–1816), a German actor and dramatist whose translations helped popularize Shakespeare. Editor.

absurd that we are not able, in what follows, to ascribe to his daughters the entire guilt. We are sorry for the old man, but we do not feel real pity for him; and it is pity that Schroeder wishes to arouse, as well as abhorrence for the daughters, who are indeed unnatural, but not wholly blameworthy.

In the old play, which Shakespeare revised, this scene produces in the course of the action the loveliest effect. Lear flees to France; the daughters and the stepson, from romantic caprice, make a pilgrimage over the sea, and meet the old man, who does not recognize them. Here everything is sweet, where Shakespeare's loftier tragic genius has embittered us. A comparison of these plays will give the thoughtful reader ever fresh pleasure.

Many years ago the superstition crept into Germany that Shakespeare must be given literally word for word, even if actors and audience were murdered in the process. The attempts, occasioned by an excellent and exact translation, were nowhere successful, of which fact the painstaking and repeated endeavors of the stage at Weimar are the best witness. If we wish to see a Shakespearean play, we must take up again Schroeder's version; but the notion that in the staging of Shakespeare not an iota may be omitted, senseless as it is, one hears constantly repeated. If the defenders of this opinion maintain the upper hand, in a few years Shakespeare will be quite driven from the stage, which for that matter would be no great misfortune; for then the reader, whether he be solitary or sociable, will be able to get so much the purer pleasure out of him.

They have, however, with the idea of making an attempt along the lines of which we have spoken in detail above, revised *Romeo and Juliet* for the theater at Weimar. The principles according to which this was done we shall develop before long, and it will perhaps become apparent why this version, whose staging is by no means difficult, although it must be handled artistically and carefully, did not take on the German stage. Attempts of a similar kind are going on, and perhaps something is preparing for the future, for frequent endeavors do not always show immediate effects.

4. Johann Friedrich von Schiller

1759–1805

Although Schiller's critical statements concerning Shakespeare are brief it would be folly to underestimate the English dramatist's influence on him. Schiller's early plays like Die Räuber *(1781) and his dissertation for the medical degree (c. 1780) are full of phrases from Shakespeare. There are obvious parallels to Shakespearean characters noticeable even in the later plays. But Schiller did not confine his attention to Shakespeare exclusively to that of an imitator.*

In the beginning Schiller missed in Shakespeare that pathos so remarkable in his own dramas. He resented Shakespeare's frequent release of "sublime" tension by the interspersion of comic effects. The young Schiller, confident in his idealism, rejected all but the ecstatic moments in Shakespeare. But as Schiller became aware of his own sentimentality he began, more and more, to admire the way in which Shakespeare controlled reality by his artistry. On November 28, 1797, in a letter to Goethe, Schiller said of Richard III *that it "was marvelous the way the poet (Shakespeare) could always make the most unpoetic elements yield poetry, and how nimbly he represents the unrepresentable, I mean the art of using symbols where nature cannot be displayed. No piece of Shakespeare's reminded me more strongly of Greek tragedy." It was from Shakespeare, then, that Schiller learned many of those artifices which his contemporaries as well as later writers admired.*

The following selections are both the work of the young Schiller. "The Stage as a Moral Institution" (source of the shorter fragment) was first given as a lecture in Mannheim, June 26, 1784, and later published in the first volume of the "Rhenish Thalia." "On Simple and Sentimental Poetry" was issued over the period 1795–1796. The first paragraphs of "Über die sentimentalischen Dichter" appeared in the twelfth issue of Die Horen *(The Hours) near the end of 1795 and was combined with "Über das Naive," previously published in the same journal. Subsequently Schiller published his "Beschluss der Abhandlung über naive und sentimentalische Dichter." The three fragments were combined under their present title and issued in 1800 in* Kleinen prosaischen Schriften. *Both selections present the poet's youthful candor and moral and aesthetic idealism under the influence, during the early years, of Immanuel Kant.*

FROM On Simple and Sentimental Poetry

When, at a very youthful age, I became first acquainted with Shakespeare, I was displeased with his coldness, with his insensibility, which allows him to jest even in the most pathetic moments, to disturb the impression of the most harrowing scenes in *Hamlet,* in *King Lear,* and in *Macbeth,* etc., by mixing with them the buffooneries of a madman. I was revolted by his insensibility, which allowed him to pause sometimes at places where my sensibility would bid me hasten and bear me along, and which sometimes carried him away with indifference when my heart would be so happy to pause. Though I was accustomed, by the practice of modern poets, to seek at once the poet in his works, to meet *his* heart, to reflect *with him* in his theme—in a word, to see the object in the subject—I could not bear that the poet could in Shakespeare never be seized, that he would never give me an account of himself. For some years Shakespeare had been the object of my study and of all my respect, before I had learned to love his personality. I was not yet able to comprehend nature at first hand. All that my eyes could bear was its image

From Schiller's *Essays Aesthetical and Philosophical* (London, G. Bell & Sons, Ltd., 1884), pp. 281–282, 334. Translator unknown.

only, reflected by the understanding and arranged by rules; and on this score the sentimental poetry of the French, or that of the Germans of 1750 to 1780, was what suited me best. For the rest, I do not blush at this childish judgment; adult critics pronounced in that day in the same way, and carried their simplicity so far as to publish their decisions to the world.

FROM The Stage as a Moral Institution

The sight of Lady Macbeth, while it makes us shudder, will also make us rejoice in a good conscience, when we see her, the sleepwalker, washing her hands and seeking to destroy the awful smell of murder. Sight is always more powerful to man than description; hence the stage acts more powerfully than morality or law.

5. François René de Chateaubriand

1768–1848

In France, following Voltaire's Lettre de M. de Voltaire à l'Académie française *(1776), Shakespeare seemed to have been put firmly in his place. It was not an enviable one. Successive champions of the English dramatist had fallen before the incisive wit of the "sage of Ferney." With the exception of Sebastien Mercier no French critic of any real merit dared to oppose the arbiter of taste. It was not until the appearance, in 1800, twenty-two years after the death of Voltaire, of Madame de Staël's* De la littérature *that a new spirit in French Shakespeare criticism began to appear. It was a spirit of enthusiasm and acceptance that owed much to such German critics as Herder, Gerstenberg, and Goethe, as well as to Mercier. The French Romantic school was in full swing and their critical attitudes found in Shakespeare the perfect example for the elevation of "natural" genius over artifice and rules.*

But Chateaubriand, perhaps the most arresting early figure of the école romantique, *could not completely free himself of the ambivalence of an earlier period. In a real sense, his is a transitional criticism. In his* Mélanges littéraires *(1801) he praises Shakespeare most extravagantly while commenting on his shortcomings. Throughout, Chateaubriand's tone is scholarly and he is clearly the heir of a long cultural tradition. But he cannot contain his enthusiasm and is, in the long run, less certain than his classical predecessors of the value of the rules when a dramatist is attempting to deal with life. Chateaubriand's is the last equivocal statement from a major critic that appears in French criticism.*

FROM Sketches of English Literature
Striking Beauties of Shakespeare

If I were required to say which I consider the finest of the plays of Shakespeare, I should hesitate among *Macbeth, Richard III, Romeo and Juliet, Othello, Julius Caesar,* and *Hamlet*. I do not, however, very highly esteem the much eulogized soliloquy; I always ask myself how the philosophic Prince of Denmark could entertain the doubts which he expresses on the subject of a future state. After his conversation with the "poor ghost" of the King, his father, ought not his doubts to have been at an end?

One of the most powerful dramatic scenes in existence is that of the three queens in *Richard III*. Margaret, after retracing her own misfortunes to harden herself against the miseries of her rival, ends with these words:

> Thou didst usurp my place, and dost thou not
> Usurp the just proportion of my sorrow? . . .
> Farewell, York's wife—and queen of sad mischance.
> (IV, iv, 109–110, 114)

This is tragedy: the sublimest point of tragedy.

I do not believe that any writer ever looked deeper into human nature than Shakespeare. Take for example the following scene from *Macbeth:*

> MACDUFF. See, who comes here?
> MALCOLM. My countryman; but yet I know him not.
> MACDUFF. My ever-gentle cousin, welcome hither.
> MALCOLM. I know him now. Good God, betimes remove
> The means that make us strangers!
> ROSS. Sir, amen.
> MACDUFF. Stands Scotland where it did?
> ROSS. Alas, poor country!

From Chateaubriand's *Sketches of English Literature* (London, Henry Colburn, 1837), pp. 267–278. Translator unknown.

Almost afraid to know itself. It cannot
Be call'd our mother, but our grave; where nothing
But who knows nothing, is once seen to smile;
Where sighs and groans and shrieks that rend the air
Are made, not mark'd; where violent sorrow seems
A modern ecstasy: the dead man's knell
Is there scarce ask'd for who; and good men's lives
Expire before the flowers in their caps,
Dying or ere they sicken.

MACDUFF. O, relation
Too nice, and yet too true!

MALCOLM. What's the newest grief? . . .

ROSS. Your castle is surprised; your wife and babes
Savagely slaughtered. . . .

MACDUFF. My children too?

ROSS. Wife, children, servants, all
That could be found.

MACDUFF. And I must be from thence!
My wife kill'd too?

ROSS. I have said.

MALCOLM. Be comforted:
Let's make us medicines of our great revenge,
To cure this deadly grief.

MACDUFF. He has no children.

(IV, iii, 159–215)

This dialogue resembles that between Flavian and Curiatius in Corneille.[1] Flavian enters to announce to the lover of Camilla that he has been chosen to combat the Horatii.

CURIACE. Albe de trois guerriers a-t-elle fait le choix?
FLAVIAN. Je viens pour vous l'apprendre.
CURIACE. Hé bien! qui sont le trois?
FLAVIAN. Vos deux frères et vous.
CURIACE. Qui?
FLAVIAN. Vous et vos deux frères.

The interrogations of Macduff and Curiatius are beauties of the same order. But Macduff's exclamation: "He has no children!" is unparalleled.

The same hand which drew this picture has traced a charm-

[1] *Les Horaces* (1639). Editor.

ing scene in the farewell of Romeo and Juliet. Romeo has been condemned to banishment, and, on the morning after his secret marriage with Juliet, he is warned by the approaching daylight that it is time to depart.

JULIET. Wilt thou be gone? it is not yet near day:
It was the nightingale, and not the lark,
That pierced the fearful hollow of thine ear;
Nightly she sings on yon pomegranate-tree:
Believe me, love, it was the nightingale.
ROMEO. It was the lark, the herald of the morn,
No nightingale: look, love, what envious streaks
Do lace the severing clouds in yonder east:
Night's candles are burnt out, and jocund day
Stands tiptoe on the misty mountain tops.
I must be gone and live, or stay and die.
JULIET. Yon light is not day-light, I know it, I:
It is some meteor that the sun exhales,
To be to thee this night a torch-bearer,
And light thee on thy way to Mantua:
Therefore stay yet; thou need'st not to be gone.
ROMEO. Let me be ta'en, let me be put to death;
I am content, so thou wilt have it so.
I'll say yon grey is not the morning's eye,
'Tis but the pale reflex of Cynthia's brow;
Nor that is not the lark, whose notes do beat
The vaulty heaven so high above our heads:
I have more care to stay than will to go:
Come, death, and welcome! Juliet wills it so.
How is't my soul? let's talk; it is not day.
JULIET. It is, it is: hie hence, be gone, away!
It is the lark that sings so out of tune,
Straining harsh discords and unpleasing sharps.
Some say the lark makes sweet division;
This doth not so, for she divideth us:
Some say the lark and loathed toad change eyes;
O, now, I would they had changed voices too!
Since arm from arm that voice doth us affray,
Hunting thee hence with hunt's-up to the day,
O, now be gone; more light and light it grows.

(III, v, 1–35)

This contrast of the charms of the dawning of morning and the parting endearments of the lovers, with the catastrophe which is about to follow, is very touching. The sentiment is more natural than that of the Greek tragedies and less pastoral than that of the Italian tragicomedies. I know of only one dramatic scene which bears any resemblance to that which I have just quoted from *Romeo and Juliet*. It occurs in an Indian drama. The resemblance, however, does not consist in the freshness of the imagery in the simplicity of the sorrowful farewell, and certainly not in the interest of the situation. Sacontala,[2] when about to quit her paternal roof, feels herself drawn back by her veil.

> SACONTALA. Who thus seizes the folds of my veil?
> OLD MAN. It is the kid which thou hast so often fed with the grains of the synmaka. He will not quit his benefactress.
> SACONTALA. Why dost thou weep, tender kid? I am forced to forsake our common home. When thou did'st lose thy mother, soon after thy birth, I took thee under my care. Return to thy manger, poor young kid, we must now part.

The farewell scene in *Romeo and Juliet* is very lightly touched by Bandello. It belongs wholly to Shakespeare. Bandello describes the parting of the lovers in the few following words:

> A la fine cominciando l'aurora a voler uscire; si bacciarono; esttretamente abbraciarono gli amanti, e pieni di lagrime e sospiri si dissero addio. *Novelle* (1554)
>
> At length the dawn beginning to appear, the lovers kissed; they closely embraced one another, and full of tears and sighs bade each other adieu.

Shakespeare's Female Characters

Bring together Lady Macbeth, Queen Margaret, Ophelia, Miranda, Cordelia, Jessica, Perdita, Imogen, and the versa-

[2] See my note to Heine's essay on Desdemona, p. 155. Editor.

tility of the poet's genius must excite our wonder. There is a charming ideality in Shakespeare's youthful female characters. The blind King Lear says to his faithful Cordelia:

> When thou dost ask me blessing, I'll kneel down,
> And ask of thee forgiveness: so we'll live,
> And pray, and sing . . .
>
> (V, iii, 10–12)

Ophelia, fantastically decked with flowers, mistaking her brother for Hamlet, whom she loves, and who has killed her father, addresses him thus:

> There's rosemary, that's for remembrance; pray you, love, remember; . . .
>
> (IV, v, 175)
>
> —I would give you some violets; but they withered all, when my father died.
>
> (IV, v, 184)

In *Hamlet;* that tragedy of maniacs, that *Royal Bedlam* in which every character is either crazy or criminal, in which feigned madness is added to real madness, and in which the grave itself furnishes the stage with the skull of a fool; in that Odeon of shadows and specters where we hear nothing but reveries, the challenge of sentinels, the screeching of the night-bird, and the roaring of the sea, Gertrude thus relates the death of Ophelia, who has drowned herself:

> There is a willow grows aslant the brook,
> That shows his hoar leaves in the glassy stream;
> There with fantastic garlands did she come
> Of crow-flowers, nettles, daisies, and long purples
> That liberal shepherds give a grosser name,
> But our cold maids do dead men's fingers call them:
> There, on the pendent boughs her coronet weeds
> Clambering to hang, an envious sliver broke;
> When down her weedy trophies and herself
> Fell in the weeping brook. Her clothes spread wide,
> And, mermaid-like, awhile they bore her up:
> Which time, she chanted snatches of old tunes;
> As one incapable of her own distress,

Or like a creature native and indued
Unto that element: but long it could not be
Till that her garments, heavy with their drink,
Pull'd the poor wretch from her melodious lay
To muddy death.

(IV, vii, 167–184)

The body of Ophelia is carried to the churchyard, and the guilty Queen, bending over the grave, exclaims:

Sweets to the sweet; farewell!
I hoped thou shouldst have been my Hamlet's wife;
I thought thy bride-bed to have deck'd, sweet maid,
And not have strew'd thy grave.

(V, i, 265–268)

The effect of all this is like the spell of enchantment. Othello, in the delirium of his jealousy, thus addresses Desdemona as she sleeps:

O thou weed,
Who art so lovely fair, and smell'st so sweet
That the sense aches at thee—would thou hadst ne'er been born! [3]

(IV, ii, 67–69)

The Moor, when about to smother his wife, kisses her and says:

Oh, balmy breath, that dost almost persuade
Justice to break her sword! . . .
Be thus when thou art dead, and I will kill thee
And love thee after.

(V, ii, 16–19)

In *The Winter's Tale* we find the same poetic grace adapted to feelings of happiness. Perdita thus addresses Florizel:

Now, my fair'st friend,
I would I had some flowers o' the spring that might
Become your time of day; and yours, and yours,
That wear upon your virgin branches yet

[3] Chateaubriand wrongly places this speech in the bedchamber scene (V, ii). It is likely that in his haste to construct a felicitous parallel, Chateaubriand sacrificed exactitude. Editor.

Your maidenhead's growing: O Proserpina,
For the flowers now, that frighted thou let'st fall
From Dis's waggon! daffodils,
That come before the swallow dares, and take
The winds of March with beauty; violets dim,
But sweeter than the lids of Juno's eyes
Or Cytherea's breath; pale primroses,
That die unmarried, ere they can behold
Bright Phoebus in his strength—a malady
Most incident to maids; bold oxlips, and
The crown imperial; lilies of all kinds,
The flower-de-luce being one! O, these I lack,
To make you garlands of, and my sweet friend,
To strew him o'er and o'er.

To this Florizel replies:

When you speak, sweet,
I'ld have you do it ever; when you sing,
I'ld have you buy and sell so, so give alms,
Pray so; and, for the ordering your affairs,
To sing them too: when you do dance, I wish you
A wave o' the sea, that you might ever do
Nothing but that; move still, still so,
And own no other function.

(IV, iv, 112–128, 136–143)

In *Cymbeline,* Imogen being accused of infidelity to Posthumus, exclaims:

False to his bed! What is it to be false?
To lie in watch there and to think on him?
To weep 'twixt clock and clock?

(III, iv, 42–44)

When Arviragus enters the cave, bearing Imogen, as if dead, in his arms, Guiderius says:

O sweetest, fairest lily!
My brother wears thee not the one half so well
As when thou grew'st thyself.

Belarius exclaims:

O melancholy!
Whoever yet could sound thy bottom? find
The ooze, to show what coast thy sluggish crare
Might easiliest harbour in! . . .

(IV, ii, 202–208)

Imogen throws herself on the neck of Posthumus, when he is convinced of his unfounded jealousy, and he exclaims:

Hang there like fruit, my soul
Till the tree die!

Then Cymbeline, addressing his daughter, says:

How now, my flesh, my child!
What, makest thou me a dullard in this act?
Wilt thou not speak to me?

Your blessing, Sir.

(V, v, 263–266)

replies Imogen at his feet.

I have quoted the above passages, merely as examples of beauty of style, without reference to the merits of the plays from which they are taken. I have not attempted to paint the heart-moving madness of Ophelia, the resolute love of Juliet, the nature, the affection, and the terror of Desdemona, when Othello awakens her and declares his intention of killing her, or the piety, tenderness, and generosity which characterize Imogen: in all this the romantic takes place of the tragic, and the picture appeals more forcibly to the senses than to the soul.

6. Georg Wilhelm Friedrich Hegel

1770–1831

To the student of literature Hegel's Shakespeare criticism, if one may apply an epithet so suggestive of systematization to brief and scattered remarks, appears to owe a heavy debt to Herder and to others of the early Romantiker. *To the student of philosophy it is doubtless otherwise. But Hegel's insistence on a basic difference between ancient and more recent tragedy we have heard before. So, too, Hegel's assertions concerning the historical development of tragedy and the place of classical tragedy as a "phase" in that development seems strangely familiar. And we cannot help but relate his remark that Hamlet is a "noble soul (who) is not steeled to this kind of energetic activity," to its ancestry in* Wilhelm Meister.

But these debts, which should only sharpen our perspective, are few and of relatively little importance. The bulk of Hegel's remarks, both on tragedy and on Shakespeare, are unique and remain as perhaps the finest critical doctrines, their brevity on the latter notwithstanding, of the Romantic Movement.

It is Hegel who asserts, with all his finesse of erudition and logic, that Shakespeare's tragic figures embody the deepest essence of tragic knowledge. And it is Hegel who identifies Shakespeare's art as essentially romantic, and who continues to assert that it is romantic art that is "art transcending itself."

The bulk of Hegel's lectures were collected by his students and published posthumously, beginning in 1838.

FROM The Philosophy of Fine Art

Generally speaking, however, in modern tragedy it is not the substantive content of their object in the interest of which men act, and which is maintained as the stimulus of their passion; rather it is the inner experience of their heart and individual emotion, or the particular qualities of their personality, which insist on satisfaction. For even in the examples already referred to we find that to a real extent in those heroes of Spanish honor and love the content of their ultimate ends is so essentially of a personal character that the rights and obligations deducible from the same are able to fuse in direct concurrence with the individual desires of the heart, and to a large extent, too, in the youthful works of Schiller this continual insistence upon Nature, rights of man, and a converted world somewhat savors of the excess of a wholly personal enthusiasm. And if it came about that Schiller in later years endeavored to enforce a more mature type of pathos, this was simply due to the fact that it was his main idea to restore once again in modern dramatic art the principle of ancient tragedy.

In order to emphasize still more distinctly the difference which in this respect obtains between ancient and modern tragedy, I will merely refer the reader to Shakespeare's *Hamlet*. Here we find fundamentally a collision similar to that which is introduced by Aeschylus into his *Choephorae* and by Sophocles into his *Electra*. For Hamlet's father, too, and the King, as in these Greek plays, has been murdered, and his mother has wedded the murderer. That which, however, in the conception of the Greek dramatists possesses a certain ethical justification—I mean the death of Agamemnon—in the contrasted case of Shakespeare's play, can only be viewed as an atrocious crime, of which Hamlet's mother is innocent;

From Hegel's *The Philosophy of Fine Art*, translated by F. P. B. Osmaston. Reprinted by permission of G. Bell & Sons, Ltd. (London).

so that the son is merely concerned in his vengeance to direct his attention to the fratricidal king, and there is nothing in the latter's character that possesses any real claim to his respect. The real collision, therefore, does not turn on the fact that the son, in giving effect to a rightful sense of vengeance, is himself forced to violate morality, but rather on the particular personality, the inner life of Hamlet, whose noble soul is not steeled to this kind of energetic activity, but, while full of contempt for the world and life, what between making up his mind and attempting to carry into effect or preparing to to carry into effect its resolves, is bandied from pillar to post, and finally through his own procrastination and the external course of events meets his own doom.

If we now turn, in close connection with the above conclusions, to our *second* point of fundamental importance in modern tragedy—that is to say, the nature of the characters and their collisions—we may summarily take a point of departure from the following general observations.

The heroes of ancient classic tragedy discover circumstances under which they, so long as they irrefragably adhere to the *one* ethical state of pathos which alone corresponds to their own already formed personality, must infallibly come into conflict with an ethical Power which opposes them and possesses an equal ethical claim to recognition. Romantic characters, on the contrary, are from the first placed within a wide expanse of contingent relations and conditions, within which every sort of action is possible; so that the conflict, to which no doubt the external conditions presupposed supply the occasion, essentially abides within the *character* itself, to which the individuals concerned in their passion give effect, not, however, in the interests of the ethical vindication of the truly substantive claims, but for the simple reason that they are the kind of men they are. Greek heroes also no doubt act in accordance with their particular individuality; but this individuality, as before noted, if we take for our examples the supreme results of ancient tragedy, is itself necessarily identical with an ethical pathos which is substantive. In modern tragedy the peculiar character in its real significance, and to which it as a matter of accident remains constant, whether it happens to grasp after that which on its own account is on moral grounds justifiable, or is carried into wrong and crime, forms its resolves under the dictate of personal wishes and necessities, or among other things purely external considerations. In such a case, therefore, though we may have a coalescence between the moral aspect of the object and the character, yet, for all that, such a concurrence does not constitute, and cannot constitute—owing to the divided character of ends, passions, and the life wholly personal to the individual—the *essential* basis and objective condition of the depth and beauty of the tragic drama.

In view of the great variety of differences which further separates particular characters in this type of poetry, it is impossible to say much in the way of generalization. I will, therefore, restrict myself to a reference to the following fundamental points of view. A primary opposition which at once invites notice is that of an *abstract,* and consequently formal, characterization in its contrast with the actual individuals whom we are accustomed to meet in the concrete living world. As example of this type, we may with exceptional pertinency cite the tragic characters of the French and Italians, which, originating in the imitation of ancient drama, to a greater or less degree merely amount to pure personifications of specific passions, such as love, honor, fame, ambition, tyranny, and so forth, and which, while they present the motives of their actions, as also the gradation and quality of their emotions to the best advantage with a lavish display of declamation, and all the arts of rhetoric, none the less by doing so rather resemble the dramatic failures of Seneca than the dramatic masterpieces of the Greeks. Spanish tragedy also receives the stamp of this abstract style of character-drawing. In this case, however, the pathos of love, in its conflict with honor, friendship, royal prerogative, and the rest is itself of so abstract a subjective character that in the case where the intention is to make this equally subjective substantiality stand out as the genuine object of interest, a more complete particularization of characters is hardly feasible. The characters of Spanish drama, however, often possess a certain kind of solidity, and, if I may use the expression, inflexible personality, however wanting in content it may be, a feature that is absent from French work; and at the same time Spanish writers, here also in contrast to the cold simplicity which the movement of French tragedies exhibits even in their tragic composition, know how to make up with the cleverly invented abundance of interesting situations and developments the deficiency referred to in the matter of characterization.

In contrast to both these schools, and in their mastery of the exposition of fully developed human characters and personality, the English are exceptionally distinguished; and among them, and soaring above the rest at an almost unapproachable height, stands Shakespeare. For even in the cases where a purely formal passion, as for instance ambition in Macbeth, or jealousy in Othello, claims as its field the entire pathos of his tragic hero, such an abstraction impairs by no fraction the full breadth of the personality. Despite this restriction the characters remain throughout entire men. In fact, the more Shakespeare on the infinite embrace of his world-stage proceeds to develop the extreme limits of evil and folly, to that extent, as I have already observed, on these very boundaries—of course, not without real wealth of poetic embellishment—he concentrates these characters in their limitations. While doing so, however, he confers on them intelligence and imagination; and, by means of the image in which they, by virtue of that intelligence, contemplate themselves objectively as a work of art, he makes them free artists of themselves, and is fully able, through the complete virility and truth of his characterization, to awaken our interest in criminals, no less than in the most vulgar and weak-witted lubbers and fools. Of a similar nature is the style of expression he makes his tragic characters adopt. It is at once individual, realistic, emphatically vital, extraordinarily various, and, moreover, where it seems advisable, it can rise to sublimity and is marked by an overwhelming force of utterance. Its ideal intensity and its qualities of invention are displayed in images and similes that flash from each other with lightning rapidity.

Its very rhetoric, here the barren child of no school, but the growth of genuine emotion and penetration into human personality, is such that, if we take into account this extraordinary union of the directness of life itself and ideal greatness of soul, we shall find it hard indeed to point to a single other dramatic poet among the moderns whom we are entitled to rank in his company. No doubt Goethe in his youth made a real effort to achieve some approach to a like natural truth and detailed characterization; but in the ideal force and exaltation of his passion his rivalry collapses. Schiller, again, has shown an increasing tendency toward violence, the tempestuous expatiation of which lacks a true core of reality.

Modern characters also differ in the nature of their *constancy* or their spiritual *vacillation* and distraction. We find, no doubt, the weakness of indecision, the fluctuations of reflection, the weighing of reasons, conformably to which a resolve should be directed, here and there in classic drama, and more particularly in the tragedies of Euripides. But Euripides is a writer whose tendency is already to forsake the wholly plastic completeness of characterization and action and to develop exceptional aspects of personal sensibility. In modern tragedy we meet yet more frequently such vacillating characters, more particularly on the ground that they are essentially under the sway of two opposed passions, which make them fluctuate from one resolve or one kind of deed to another. I have already made some observations on this attitude of vacillation in another context, and will now merely supplement this by stating that, although the tragic action must depend on colliding factors, yet where we find such a division on *one* and the same individual such a concurrence is always attended with precarious consequences. And the reason is that this disruption into interests, which are opposed to each other, is due in part to an obscurity and obtuseness of the intelligence, and in some measure, too, to weakness and immaturity. We come across characters of this type in the creations of Goethe's younger days, notably Weislingen, Fernando in *Stella,* and above all Clavigo. They are, as we may say, double men, who are unable to secure a ready, and so stable, individuality. It is wholly another matter when two opposed spheres of life or moral obligation are equally sacred to a character which, on its own account, is not deficient in stability, and such a person is under the necessity of ranking himself on *one* side to the exclusion of the other. In a case of that kind, the vacillation is merely a moment of passage, and does not itself constitute, as it were, the nervous system of the character. Again, of a somewhat similar kind, is the tragic case where the spiritual life is seduced, despite its nobler purpose, into objects of passion which are contradictory to the same, as in the case of Schiller's *Holy Maid,* and are then forced to seek a recovery from this division of the soul in their own intimate or objective life, or pay the penalty. At the same time, this personal tragedy of inward division, when it is made the pivot on which the tragic action revolves, contains, as a rule, what is merely pitiful and painful, or, from another standpoint, exasperating; and the poet will rather do better to avoid it than go out of his way to find it and develop it. The worst case is that, however, where such a vacillation and veering round of character and the entire personality is—the very dialectic of art being thrown awry for this purpose—made the principle of the entire presentation, as though the truth of all importance was to demonstrate that no character is in itself firmly rooted and self-assured. The one-sided ends of specific passions, it is true, ought not to bring about a realization which is secured without a battle; and also, in everyday life, they cannot fail to experience, through the reactionary power of conditions and individuals which oppose them, their finite character and lack of stability. An issue of this kind, however, before the appearance of which we are unable to get the pertinent conclusion, ought not to be introduced as a dialectical piece of wheel adjustment in the personality itself; if it is, the person concerned, viewed as *this* personal state of the soul, is a wholly empty and undefined form, whose collective living growth is found, no less in respect to its objects than in its character, to be wholly wanting in definition. In much the same way the case, also, is otherwise, where the change in the spiritual condition of the entire man itself appears as a direct consequent of just this, its own kind of self-detachment, so that only that is developed and emphasized which essentially and from the first lay secured in the character. As an example, we find in Shakespeare's *Lear* that the original folly of the old man is intensified to the point of madness much in the same way that Gloucester's spiritual blindness is converted into actual physical blindness, in which for the first time his eyes are opened to the true distinction in the love he entertains for his two sons respectively. It is precisely Shakespeare who, as a contrast to that exposition of vacillating and essentially self-divided characters, supplies us with the finest examples of essentially stable and consequential characters, who go to their doom precisely in virtue of this tenacious hold upon themselves and their ends. Unsupported by the sanction of the moral law, but rather carried onward by the formal necessity of their personality, they suffer themselves to be involved in their acts by the coil of external circumstances, or they plunge blindly therein and maintain themselves there by sheer force of will, even where all that they do is merely done because they are impelled to assert themselves against others, or because they have simply come to the particular point they have reached. The rise of insurgent passion, one essentially consonant with a certain type of character, one which has not as yet fully emerged, but now secures its utmost expansion, this onward movement and process of a great soul, with all the intimate traits of its evolution, this picture of its self-destructive conflict with circumstances, human and objective conditions and results, is the main content of some of Shakespeare's most interesting tragedies.

The last of the subjects which we have still to discuss as proposed is the nature of the *tragic issue* which characters in our present drama have to confront, as also the type of tragic *reconciliation* compatible with such a standpoint. In ancient tragedy it is the eternal justice which, as the absolute might of destiny, delivers and restores the harmony of substantive being in its ethical character by its opposition to the particular forces which, in their strain to assert an independent subsistence, come into collision, and which, in virtue of the rational ideality implied in its operations, satisfied us even where we see the downfall of particular men. Insofar as a justice of the same kind is present in modern tragedy, it is necessarily, in part, more abstract on account of the closer differentiation of ends and characters, and, in part, of a colder nature and one that is more akin to that of a criminal court, in virtue of the fact that the wrong and crime into which individuals are necessarily carried, insofar as they are intent upon executing their designs, are of a profounder significance. Macbeth, for instance, the elder daughters of Lear and their husbands, the president in *Kabale und Liebe,* Richard III, and many similar examples, on account of their atrocious conduct, only deserve the fate they get. This type of dénouement usually is presented under the guise that individuals are crushed by an actual force which they have defied in order to carry out their personal aims. Wallenstein, for example, is shattered on the adamantine wall of the imperial power; but the old Piccolomini, who, in order to maintain the lawful régime, betrays a friend and misuses the rights of friendship, is punished through the death and sacrifice of his son. Götz von Berlichingen, too, attacks a dominant and securely founded political order, and goes to ground, as also Weislingen and Adelheid, who range themselves, no doubt, on the side of this organized power, but, through wrongful deed and disloyalty, prepare the way to disaster. And along with this we have the demand emphasized, in virtue of the personal point of view of such characters, that these should of necessity appear themselves to acknowledge the justice of their fate. Such a state of acceptance may either be of a religious nature, in which case the soul becomes conscious of a more exalted and indestructible condition of blessedness with which to confront the collapse of its mundane personality; or it may be of a more formal, albeit more worldly, type, insofar, that is, as the strength and equanimity of the character persists in its course up to the point of overthrow without breaking asunder; and in this way, despite all circumstances and mischances, preserves with unimpaired energy its personal freedom. Or, as a final alternative, where the substance of such acceptance is of more real value, by the recognition that the lot which the individual receives is the one, however bitter it may be, which his action merits.

From another point of view, however, we may see the tragic issue also merely in the light of the effect of unhappy circumstances and external accidents, which might have brought about, quite as readily, a different result and a happy conclusion. From such a point of view we have merely left us the conception that the modern idea of individuality, with its searching definition of character, circumstances, and developments, is handed over essentially to the contingency of the earthly state, and must carry the fateful issues of such finitude. Pure commiseration of this sort is, however, destitute of meaning; and it is nothing less than a frightful kind of external necessity in the particular case where we see the downfall of essentially noble natures in their conflict thus assumed with the mischance of purely external accidents. Such a course of events can insistently arrest our attention; but in the result it can only be horrible, and the demand is direct and irresistible that the external accidents ought to accord with that which is identical with the spiritual nature of such noble characters. Only as thus regarded can we feel ourselves reconciled with the grievous end of Hamlet and Juliet. From a purely external point of view, the death of Hamlet appears as an accident occasioned by his duel with Laertes and the interchange of the daggers. But in the background of Hamlet's soul, death is already present from the first. The sandbank of finite condition will not content his spirit. As the focus of such mourning and weakness, such melancholy, such a loathing of all the conditions of life, we feel from the first that, hemmed within such an environment of horror, he is a lost man, whom the surfeit of the soul has well-nigh already done to death before death itself approaches him from without. The same thing may be observed in the case of Romeo and Juliet. The ground on which these tender blossoms have been planted is alien to their nature; we have no alternative left us but to lament the pathetic transiency of such a beautiful love, which, as some tender rose in the vale of this world of accident, is broken by rude storms and tempests, and the frangible reckonings of noble and well-meaning devices. This pitiful state of our emotions is, however, simply a feeling of reconciliation that is painful, a kind of *unhappy blessedness* in misfortune.

7. Ludwig Tieck

1773–1853

Few people will doubt that, along with August Wilhelm von Schlegel, Ludwig Tieck is pre-eminent among German Shakespeareans of the Romantic period. While the former has frequently overshadowed his gifted collaborator, it would be wrong to think that the latter made no truly significant contribution. Schlegel's superb essays on Shakespeare began to appear in 1796. They show, systematically, the technical brilliance and coherence of many of Shakespeare's effects. But Schlegel's praise of Shakespeare's "unreal" world owes something to Tieck. Three years earlier, Tieck had written his Shakespeares Behandlung des Wunderbaren. *Although not published until 1796, when it prefaced Tieck's prose rendering of* The Tempest, *the essay was known and discussed favorably among the Jenauer Romantiker (the circle composed of Tieck, Novalis, Schlegel, and other lesser figures). In the essay a new critical attitude, a genuinely romantic one, is noticeable. Tieck praises the dreamlike otherworldliness of Shakespeare's comedies. Ariel, Prospero, and a host of other characters have the same effect on our minds as the figures in a dream. In the presence of such dramas we relinquish the real world and its criteria and abandon ourselves to those of the world in the plays.*

The critics of the Sturm und Drang *had been content to revere Shakespeare with an unbounded awe, and to cite him as the perfect example that to true art all external, pre-existing criteria are irrelevant. But with the Romantic critics, of whom Tieck may be considered the type, admiration without interpretation and comprehension is no longer enough. These critics, unlike any of their predecessors, not only valued the uses of the imagination, but saw, among those uses, the critic's opportunity to bring the literature of an older period down to his subjective present. This, too, was a new view of the social function of the critic. He would no longer lecture the poet. He would, instead, distill, from the poet's work, what was necessary for his own life, and by implication, for those lives that partook of his. This shift in focus which occurs in the period, and which is visible in Shakespeare criticism, has not always been understood.*

It was during this period that the "Germanization" of Shakespeare, begun nearly half a century earlier, reached its zenith. Performances and translations abounded. Between 1797 and 1810 the nine volumes of Schlegel's translations from Shakespeare's plays made their appearance. It is in the Romantic writers that we find the genesis of that "Shakespearomanie" which was to have its bivalent effect on German literature into the early decades of the present century; bivalent because, while it produced, fortunately, the profusion of nineteenth-century German Shakespeare criticism, much of it valuable, it also marred the work of such writers as Grabbe (his Die Hohenstaufen *of 1828 is a poor imitation of the Yorkist cycle) and Immerman.*

Ludwig Tieck's interest in Shakespeare continued throughout his life. In 1811 he issued his Alt Englisches Theater, *translations and prefaces. And in 1826 Tieck followed this with* Über Shakespears Sonette, *and more translations,* Vier Schauspiele von Shakespear, *in 1836. Tieck's critical interest in English renaissance drama had been stimulated by his journey to England (1817). Shortly after settling in Dresden he was invited by Theodor Hell (pseudonym of Theodor Winkler), editor of the Dresden* Abendzeitung, *to become a regular contributor of drama criticism. Tieck accepted and from 1821 until 1824 his criticism appeared in its pages. Tieck, in the manner of Lessing, upheld the highest aesthetic standards and Winkler may have had some cause to regret his invitation. Many of Winkler's coterie, a host of forgettable writers who had gathered under the "poetic" title of "Der Liederkreis," fell before Tieck's ironic invective. It was during this period that the essay* Bemerkungen über einige Charaktere im Hamlet, und über die Art, wie diese auf der Bühne dargestellt werden konnten *was written. The essay appeared in the* Abendzeitung *as a series of articles between February 27 and March 5, 1823. As its title suggests, the essay may have had among its intentions one of disputing the persisting notion that Shakespeare had not been a dramatic poet; a claim that had been advanced as late as 1815 by Goethe in* Schäkespear und kein Ende! *(see above). The articles were gathered under their present title in the volumes of* Dramaturgische Blätter *which Tieck issued in 1825–1826, and which were reissued in 1852 under that title and simultaneously as Vols. III and IV of* Kritische Schriften.

NOTE: *I would like to make public my thanks to Professor Philip A. Shelley, head of the German Department of The Pennsylvania State University, for his assistance and encouragement during the tedious process of dating the following essay when Goedecke (Vol. VI) could offer no specific date.*

FROM Observations Concerning Characters in Hamlet

In *Wilhelm Meister* Goethe, making very careful observations, points out many beautiful aspects of this character [Hamlet]. But if I do not fail to understand Shakespeare altogether, the poet tried to indicate throughout the entire work that the poor girl has experienced such passionate ecstasy and has so thoroughly submitted to the prince that Laertes' warnings and admonitions prove much too late. The way in which this relationship as well as many other details have been woven into the work like a puzzle and yet kept subdued is an accomplishment worthy of the great poet. But at this point Hamlet's behavior becomes bitter and her pain and mental agony are

From *Bemerkungen*, reprinted from *Ludwig Tieck's Ausgewählte Werke*, edited by Georg Witkowski (Leipzig, Max Hesses Verlag, 1903), Vol. IV, pp. 108–130. Translated by LaMarr Kopp.

consistent with her behavior. Yet everything about her, even hell itself, as Laertes says, seems beautiful and lovely, reconciled, making a solution of the problem all the more difficult to present.

When she first appears with Laertes, he compares Hamlet's "trifling of his favors" to a violet; she raises questions naively and smilingly, conscious deep within her of someone quite different. "No more but so?" After her brother has continued his speaking she replies:

> But, good my brother,
> Do not, as some ungracious pastors do,
> Show me the steep and thorny way to heaven;
> Whiles, like a puff'd and reckless libertine,
> Himself the primrose path of dalliance treads,
> And recks not his own rede.
>
> (I, ii, 46–51)

I do not understand how an innocent girl could make such a reply—one which snubs every word of warning. But she is convinced she knows her brother, she senses quite keenly the frightening fact that these admonitions will become meaningful only now, since until this time her relationship with the prince has been either tolerated or ignored. Toward her father she is much more cautious; she does not risk saying too much, a few general remarks suffice. She realizes quite painfully that her father, a stern man, treats the prince with disdain.

Frightened, deeply shaken, quite confused, she announces the prince's visits. Here we already sense how precariously and deceptively her whole existence persists. This scene is invariably played in too cold a manner and with too much matter-of-factness.

In this atmosphere of ill will the poor girl must sound out her mentally deranged lover. To portray the painfulness of this disgraceful task, to show the painfulness of being secretly listened to by her father and the king, especially as she stands facing her lover whom she may never see again and to whom she would otherwise have so much to say—to play this role requires the full artistic power of the actress. She must present herself to him in a strange, forced, unnatural way. She must bear patiently his abuses and the bitterness that sometimes seem little short of brutal. She dare not offer one word in her own defense; finally, quite unobserved by others, the torrent within her breaks. This is certainly a most difficult assignment for any actress. Instead one generally sees the girl go about the whole business quite matter-of-factly; and then, too, when the role of the prince is played sentimentally and with suffering, the greatest possible injustice is done to the poet.

As she tries to return the packet, Hamlet cries: Ha, ha! Are you honest?" which implies something even more disturbing: you are honest? He notes her awkardness and confusion and takes this as still another insult.

During the presentation of the play she is forced to display some impertinence in the presence of Hamlet's assembled court. There he treats her without respect; to him she seems deserving of none. The prince is dismissed, her father has been murdered by him, and her long suppressed anguish, the neglect and disdain, the remembrance of lovely times now passed—all this breaks upon her and threatens her fragile emotions. The pain of her father's death serves as a pretext for her mental distress, concealing its relation to her love affair. Her song of mourning alternates with a gay frolicsome romance in which her own fate is mirrored.

> Then up he rose and donn'd his clothes,
> And dupp'd the chamber-door;
> Let in the maid, that out a maid
> Never departed more.
> (IV, v, 52–55)

To this she adds

> Quoth she, before you tumbled me,
> You promised me to wed.
> So would I ha' done, by yonder sun,
> And thou hadst not come to my bed.
> (IV, v, 63–66)

When Ophelia appears once again in the same scene, her mental condition has grown worse. In Shakespeare, who never deviated from the nature he observed, the mentally disturbed characters always possess a certain consciousness and a kind of reason. For example, Lear expresses some of his most sublime thoughts during his most severe illness. Sometimes, too, such characters tend to fondle or play with certain objects. We see this with Ophelia. She has brought along certain herbs and flowers which in England at that time were associated with an allegorical meaning. (Often on the stage the sick are pictured handling straw to which they give some imaginary name; this would be quite at odds with the purposes of the poet.) She comes up to Laertes and says: "There's rosemary, that's for remembrance; pray, love, remember; and there is pansies, that's for thoughts" (IV, v, 175–176).

In England as in Germany rosemary was a flower strewn at weddings. Even in Germany today, in the rural areas, this is true; sometimes, too, at funerals the flower is used. Perhaps the custom still exists in a few parts of England. It is because of her father, now dead, that she gives Laertes first rosemary and then pansies, the *pensées* of the French. They are meant to preserve the melancholy reminiscences, the "thoughts."

"There's fennel for you and columbines," she continues, extending her hand to the king. Fennel was pregnant with meaning. Proverbially it signifies flattery but it can also allude to sensuality, desire. Columbines, too, mean various things, not infrequently they hint of faithlessness and crass sensuality.

"There's rue for you; and here's some for me: we may call it herb-grace o'Sundays: O, you must wear your rue with a difference.—There's a daisy" (IV, v, 180–183), etc.

In the German language of the Middle Ages the words for repentance, to feel sorry for and regret or lament, were closely allied in meaning; similarly in English the words "rue" and "ruth" have overlapping meanings. Quite frequently in those days the words meant "repentance." Since repentance prepared the heart for improvement and inner devotion, hence making forgiveness possible, the plant rue is here called "herb of grace." It is difficult to realize that even learned persons among the English do not understand that in Shakespeare's day the word "to rue" often meant "to repent." It occurs a number of times in Shakespeare. If my above observations could not be proved in the romances, nevertheless this one passage could serve to justify my assertion. For according to the symbolism of that era, Ophelia—an abandoned lover—could not wear rue but would have to adorn herself with willow (it is with a willow tree that her own suicide is carried out). She offers the queen some rue because of her illicit marriage—we may call this rue an herb of grace o'Sundays—(this may have some reference to Sunday worship service: this passage poses some real problems). You may wear it with a difference (because each of us is guilty of different sins). "There's a daisy—" the flower of lightheartedness, of gaiety as expressed by infatuated girls.

In presenting this scene the poet's intended effect can be achieved only if the action and the speaking move rapidly and flamingly and above all with charm, the way Laertes describes his sister, for example. It is essential to convey that attractiveness, that charming flirtation which Ophelia personifies, even in an intense situation such as this one where the atmosphere is suddenly darkened by insanity as if by a passing black cloud. The transition from joy to sorrow and vice versa must be made suddenly and glaringly but yet be characterized by charm and loveliness. If even a trace of shocking ghostlike horror is tolerated, if the spoken lines are grossly affected, if the accents are altered, making the scene progress hesitatingly, the whole effect by which Shakespeare tried to accomplish so much becomes unpleasant and could grow almost unbearable—something, possibly, that many persons would call a grand and glorious effect.

We have less to say of Laertes. It suffices if the actor refuses to yield to the temptation to interpret him as a thoroughly noble and sensitive son and brother. At the opening he is a gallant young man of the day, admonishing Ophelia in beautiful and flowery speeches that provide him an opportunity of listening to himself—a trait which he shares with the entire cast.

Then we lose sight of him until after the turning point of the play when he suddenly appears once more, this time as a rough, crudely courageous rebel. Although mourning the death of his father as demonstrably as possible (and who would not ascribe such emotions to a man in his position), the agony he displays is but a pretense making the rapidly growing dream of his ambitions more clear. Upon closer consideration, what does his rebellion have to do with his father's death? Meanwhile those nobler qualities within him are aroused by the king's heroic personality. The opportune moment to murder the king has passed and the earlier serious and reflective mood of the stormy young fellow is changed into new theatrical fury by the entrance of his crazed sister. There is no doubt that he loves her, and the sight that confronts him must be disarmingly painful for him—but not in the way he demonstrates in front of the king.

When he is again somewhat more composed we note that in his traitorlike dealings with the king he refuses to relinquish his advantage although he is convinced that the real moment for attaining his goal has already passed. The death of his sister incites him anew. Many a critic has labeled Laertes' language, his expression of pain, unnatural and affected. Actually they are reproaching the poet for something that should call forth praise.

Equally effective is his extravagantly exaggerated speech at the grave which challenges Hamlet to surpass him with even greater exaggerations. I have already discussed the action by which the tragedy is brought about.

Playing the role of the ghost is said to have been one of the most skillful and effective performances Schröder ever accomplished. I can quite believe it although I myself have never seen him play this role. But what has amounted ever since to an imitation of this great artist on the German stage is certainly not to be discredited. I am referring to that dull, slow, monotonous recitation with hardly any gestures, whereby the scene easily begins to drag and hence the illusion is destroyed. It is true that old Hamlet no longer possesses flesh and blood, but none the less he certainly displays all the human passion of anger, revenge, and jealousy. Even when modified, the solemn speech must be understood as such. Therefore let him show anger by his words and energetic gestures. In both theaters of London the ghost was simply a laughable character who, lifeless and without character, wandered back and forth across the stage repeating his lines as in a recitation.

Calling *Hamlet* the most eccentric and capricious of Shakespeare's works does him no injustice if one also understands the drama as the most provocative—a combination resulting in an immensely tragic perception that can be described only with the greatest difficulty. Although the profound elements of tragedy appear intermittently, one senses both the pain and the brightness of an apparent comedy, quite unconscious of a transition. In fact, in no other work has Shakespeare taken his audience more completely into his confidence and actually touched them, so to speak. According to the usual comments of narrow-minded critics it is precisely because of this that illusion and dignity, interest and truth, go by the board. To play specific roles certain actors are engaged. These are not simply chosen at random, generally speaking, but usually come from Globus, particularly those assigned to the role of Hamlet. And to banish all doubts about this, the author alludes to the literary quarrels which the poets and actors of Globus (the Shakespearean troupe) carried on with the children of the royal chapel and its authors. The actor who plays before the Danish prince is none other than Burbadge, the great interpreter of heroic roles in Shakespeare, who played Macbeth, Lear, and Richard III, and who most likely assumed the role of the ghost in this play. This man, the most widely acclaimed of his day and perhaps the greatest tragedian and interpreter of character that had appeared in England (and even in comedies he assumed the most important roles) appeared in this play attired as one was accustomed to see him. The tale of rugged Pyrrhus is the highest form that Shakespeare presents in the entire work. Burbadge changes the tone here, having tears in his eyes. (Incidentally, here we see what Hamlet has to teach the actors concerning wise moderation, primarily as an actual principle; this could have settled long since the old dispute as to the degree to which an actor should be emotionally overpowered.) In the little tragedy this same actor played the role of the king which must be presented with noble precision and majesty, particularly since it is written in ancient verse, quite without any trace of pathos. (At any rate, as mentioned above, it cannot be pushed insignificantly into the background where everything becomes lifeless and unintelligible.) The mimicry must have been a frightful experience for the actual king, for here the similarity to his brother confronted him as if in punishment.

When afterward the ghost passes through his wife's bedroom, it certainly was not dressed in armor but in night clothes.* So a ghost has a wardrobe, chided one critic. Why not? All ghost stories do the same thing; old Hamlet appears during the night watch like a hero in armor, a call to revenge, and in the bedroom he wears a more comfortable costume, in his habit as he lived, to use Hamlet's own words.

In conclusion just one more remark—an observation that is quite contrary to the taste of our theaters. Shakespeare had such abundant troupes of elegant and experienced actors that today we can hardly believe the like was once possible. He, and many of his contemporaries with him, could not have written as they did, massing one difficulty upon another, demanding the bizarre and the unusual, if there had not been many great players. Yet even so it was not uncommon to find a player in more than one role. Then why do we, having much more meager resources at our disposal, reject this solution when we have actors who are particularly versatile? It is nothing but a misunderstood concept of distinction that interprets this as inadmissible; for this we have Shakespeare, Eckhof,[1] and Schröder[2] who set good examples. How advantageous it is for beginning actors, who otherwise are pushed into the background quite frequently, the practice of diversity of various minor roles; how instructive when the experienced artist assists in demonstrating the whole range of his power, the epitome of his training. I hope no one will argue with me about the problem of illusion. A materialistic, crude illusion

* The 1603 edition confirms this: Enter the ghost in his night gowne.

[1] Hans Konrad Dietrich Eckhof (1720–1778). Actor whose influence on the German theater is reckoned equal to Lessing's. Editor.

[2] Antoinette Sophie Schröder (1781–1868), Germany's greatest tragic actress of the nineteenth century. Editor.

that can be destroyed so easily should not and must not be found in the theater. Shoddy work or the ruination of a play that results when a role must be shortened or even omitted due to insufficient players results in a much more serious problem of destroyed illusion.

I have purposely avoided a discussion of the main characters of the work since that would have involved me in much too complicated inquiries, arguments, and interpretations, and because so much has already been said on the subject. Even now it is not my intention to set forth my views concerning Hamlet. I only wish to call the attention of friends of the poet to several verses, specifically, to that famous monologue on suicide. The person who is not well acquainted with the works of the poet still knows Hamlet, no matter how superficially; indeed one may say that even those persons who have never read this monologue have at least heard it recited and have admired it. How often it has been translated, elucidated, imitated. There is not one Frenchman, acquainted with books, nor one educated Spaniard to whom its contents are unfamiliar. It really seems as if one were confronting the quintessence of Shakespeare in these verses, as if here one were experiencing the entire depths of his inexhaustible spirit in the most direct and unmistakable manner, as if one possessed in just a few words the most opportune excerpt for reference to anyone who claimed to question the gloriousness of modern poetry and the depth of our modern art.

I must confess a certain weakness or ungraciousness: long have I struggled to achieve the sensitivity and insight that would enable me to accept enthusiastically the many writers I come across again and again in many books in which this passage was treated with great admiration and which even the opponents of Shakespeare acknowledge with praise.

I referred to this as my weakness because I always find it difficult to isolate this or that individual passage in a successful drama or masterpiece. Already quite early my mind became accustomed to understanding the whole within its essential framework. And with Shakespeare, who for years has been the subject of my undivided study, I found myself so carried along in the flow of his works that I could only pause in astonishment when someone lifted out of context some certain verse which to me, too, seemed indispensable and pointed, but not more so than all the others. I was usually rewarded for my approach by discovering great beauty where others had only negative criticism for the poet and where others wanted to make improvements. By considering only isolated details they had overlooked the meaning, the true sense of the passage in question.

I grant you that even when a poetical work gives us real satisfaction due to its inner compulsion and total harmony, a particular scene may reflect a brighter glow of beauty than another because of its outstanding excellence. This experience I could not deny, and it would be an indication of artistic insensitivity not to be captivated or moved by certain individual passages, especially when the wise poet himself may have made special reference to them. Can one ever forget that scene of rage in *Lear* after he has seen it even once? Or Macbeth's monologue before the murder and his lines afterward? Othello's anger? Clarence's dream in *Richard III*? Or York's death and his final speech, in the third part of *Henry VI*? Talbot's taking leave of his son in the first part? The death of Winchester or Gloucester in the second? Our mind, to be sure, loses many impressions, but these and others like them are never lost or forgotten.

I referred to this too as my ungraciousness because I was totally unable to share the exclusive admiration for this famous passage with any others, no matter how often I read and reread them. The fitting language, the appropriate scenes I understood; but if for centuries the world had not labeled this passage something special, I would have read over it, just as over many others, and would not have been especially struck if a certain ambiguity, yes, a certain inappropriateness had not arrested me against my will.

It seemed to me, if I may say so, as if the great poet might have afforded the brooding, melancholy Hamlet, just on the verge of voluntarily giving up his life, somewhat different lines. For actually, up to this point, he had never demonstrated that kind of character. In his epic poem Lucretia forms a resolution under different circumstances and with a different determination; Brutus and Cassius think and die like Romans; Othello, the excesses of his grief making life unbearable for him, hastily and unpremeditatingly commits suicide. Likewise Juliet, and similarly Romeo. Nowhere else in this poet do we find an attempt to portray this state of mind which tolerates and toys with a suicide drive. Hamlet is the only one who, already in his first monologue, when the whole of life disgusts him, says, "O, that this too too solid flesh would melt, thaw, and resolve itself into a dew! Or that the Everlasting had not fix'd his canon 'gainst self-slaughter" (I, ii, 129–132). But afterward he does not actually commit suicide, and hence his later speech cannot contain that forcefulness, that dreadful depth such as we see in *Werther*. Yet some of the gripping effect of that German, Werther, may have been passed on to this Dane, Hamlet, some fragments of that gripping truth which Goethe's *Werther*, by its power and conviction, portrays so uniquely. It is understandable that Hamlet, at the beginning of the play, filled with grief over the loss of his dear father and over the displeasure of a mother whom he once loved, and denied his rightful claims, forced from the throne—it is understandable, I say, that he, conscious of a certain moral weakness, wishes it were pardonable to arrange his own escape from this repulsive world. But after he has discovered quite strangely and strikingly that his father has not died a natural death but rather has been shamefully murdered, and after he has had to promise the ghost both revenge and reparation, that is, after he has committed himself to a role which rather than bringing him closer to his goal exposes him to even greater problems, he rebukes himself in a passionate speech for his rashness and his indecision. At this point, being in a completely different situation than the one in which we first saw him, can he forget that divine canon which he fears and decide rather to abandon this life in order to relieve himself from that commissioned task? It was here that I found contradiction and a lack of clarity; Hamlet's mood, however confused, was utterly incomprehensible to me.

But is it absolutely essential that we ascribe to this monologue a reference to suicide? Did Shakespeare really have that in mind? As a reply to this question my remarks, otherwise superfluous, are intended to stimulate the reader to reflect on this question. I already anticipate what ordinary judgments and opinions will oppose my ideas. I know, too, how difficult it was for me to dismiss everything I had read by the authorities on this subject. Nevertheless, for years now, I have become more and more convinced that both interpreters and admirers of Shakespeare have been in error and that this monologue cannot possibly mean what they read into it.

In Shakespeare's day this monologue was not understood this way either, although there is no concrete evidence for this assertion. Every time *Hamlet* was performed before his contemporaries the critics ridiculed this character and even this monologue. At any rate I know of no passage in which the modern interpretation was given. I cannot say whether Betterton interpreted these verses as referring to suicide or not; that Garrick [3] and many others before him did so exclusively is an established fact. I do not have Rowe's [4] edition of Shakespeare available to check whether he supplies any clues to this famous monologue or whether he refers to an earlier interpretation or tradition.

At first it may seem that the passage allows for no other interpretation. Those who know this passage only in translation will be all the more of this opinion since any translator necessarily conveys his own interpretations and hence unconsciously propagates the notion even if only to a very slight degree. Of importance is an attempt to explain the passage first in light of the whole of the work and then in light of the individual words, placing it in the proper perspective so that it convinces every one of the poet's admirers.

Right from the beginning Hamlet appears in a very bad mood, and the audience scene only tends to increase his

[3] Thomas Betterton (1635–1710), David Garrick (1717–79). Actors. Editor.

[4] Cf. *The Works of William Shakespeare,* ed. Nicholas Rowe, 7 vols. (London, 1709–1710); 9 vols. (1714). Editor.

vexation. His bitterness toward his mother is demonstrated nearly without restraint and in a badly behaved manner; hence, from the king, who always impresses him, he has to suffer a considerable reprimand—all this after the more important concerns of the hereditary prince, feeling a compulsion to become king, have been ignored in favor of Laertes' less significant petition. And now comes his monologue, revealing his disgust with life, expressing the desire for pardon in ending his life at will, and showing his bitterness against his mother and the king. The news of the ghost's appearance occupies all his attention. During the night his whole being collapses at the ghost's appearance and the story it relates. Being at a loss to pull himself together, he devises a plan of acting insane—a plan about which it is difficult to ascertain whether he is able to avoid insanity at all or whether he is already in the clutches of mental illness (when he devises the scheme). He terrifies Ophelia with this resolution. He uses his feigned illness to give Polonius a sharp rebuke, and then afterward forgets himself almost entirely when he is in the company of the friends of his youth and the players. But no matter how cheerful, and at certain moments even exuberant, he becomes, his melancholy often returns suddenly and he proclaims his disgust with the world and with people in beautiful orations. Yet it would be wrong to take these too literally, for when he tells Rosencrantz that he has abandoned all his normal activities, his conceit, shortly before the duel with Laertes, contradicts this when he assures Horatio that ever since Laertes' departure he has been a diligent fencer. In a moment of loneliness, when the players have left him, his own lack of courage and determination strikes him bitterly, he blasphemes the usurper, and himself even more; he is repulsive to himself, realizing that neither the murder of his father nor the ghost's call for revenge have sufficed to drive him to action. "Am I a coward?" he asks himself; "would I tolerate abuse and misdeed against myself and not seek instant revenge?—Yes," he cries, reproaching himself: "I would tolerate all, because I lack gall, lack power of animosity to punish offense." [5]

[5] Tieck is paraphrasing Hamlet's soliloquy (II, ii, 598–606). Editor.

Reaching no resolution he suddenly stops, like a person thoroughly beside himself; finding some excuse for himself he is momentarily calmed. It may have been some evil apparition whose words were only lies intended to ensnare his melancholy mood. Once before it occurred to him to test his uncle by means of a drama in which the murder is enacted just the way the ghost revealed. If the uncle should not withstand the test, he would then take the necessary measures.

He was quieted but for a few moments; he cannot dismiss so easily his thoughts, his reflections about himself. Once more, in a calm mood, he tries to discover why it is so difficult for him to follow through the decision, to carry out the deed demanded of him by the ghost. Re-examining this deep-rooted question within himself he makes another appearance. It is true, Shakespeare often makes great demands upon us, but here even more so than usual; but of course (in his day) he could trust the actor's interpretation. If we permit the curtain to fall between that powerful monologue and this more composed one, the train of thought which the poet asks us to follow is broken somewhat too abruptly. I remind you that only on occasion did Shakespeare assume a division into acts; most of his works were planned in uninterrupted sequence. If there must be a break, then here, at least, is definitely not the place for it. The first act should close after the scene of Hamlet in the presence of the ghost and then with his friends; the second should conclude only after the famous monologue and the king's speech about the prince. The third act should extend up to the time of Hamlet's departure; and the fifth should begin with the gravediggers.

So Hamlet exits after the actors have gone and after his powerful monologue. Directly the king enters with Polonius and Ophelia. The latter is given instructions by her father; the king, together with his councilor, hides in order to eavesdrop on the prince, who is still disturbed by the thoughts just uttered: Am I a coward? Would I tolerate abuse against myself? What restrains me from being avenger?

> To be, or not to be: that is the question.
>
> (III, i, 1)

It all depends, he says to himself—and here the audience must remember all that has preceded and must follow the apparent transition of thought—it all depends whether the individual lives or does not live, that is to say, I do not dare more than life itself and then lose; therefore it is all a matter of life, whether I want to go to it! This remark is quite correct, this thought has often been expressed, for he who does not fear death has nothing left to fear.

> Whether 'tis nobler in the mind to suffer
> The slings and arrows of outrageous fortune,

It can be an indication of great magnanimity, he continues after a pause, when one bears the extremes of life calmly and quietly, exercising that patience which in praise is called Christian, and which demands just as much strength and magnitude of soul as resistance.

> Or to take arms against a sea of troubles,
> And by opposing, end them?

By "them" he means his troubles: but how? by suicide? Would that be "opposing"—actually opposing? Would it be proper and fitting, then, to "take arms," if these arms were to be directed only against those who "take" them? No. Hence I myself destroy these troubles, I make utter ruin my opponent. But I must make a success of it, in case my patience fail to endure when I possess the power to refrain from evaluating my life too highly; for surely that can be dangerous: but I must shun this danger all the less since death is but repose from all earthly cares.

> To die: to sleep;
> No more; and by a sleep to say we end
> The heart-ache and the thousand natural shocks
> That flesh is heir to, 'tis a consummation
> Devoutly to be wish'd. To die, to sleep.

But this, to be sure, is not the moment of death, and the pain which pursues him is not that associated with quitting that life which so often activates our fears—no, it is not that which prevents us from a determination that renders our enemy helpless in harming us or—something that would lame our arm—that punishes him.

> To sleep: perchance to dream: ay, there's the rub;

That, literally, is the impulse; in bowling, that corresponds to the thrust which either keeps the ball on a straight course or sends it off in a different direction.

> For in that sleep of death what dreams may come
> When we have shuffled off this mortal coil,
> Must give us pause: There's the respect
> That makes calamity of so long life.

It is this secret fear, this fear of the unknown that causes misery, misfortune, vexation, and sorrow to mortals for so many years.

> For who would bear the whips and scorns of time,

This could be meant in a general sense, or more specifically, might be an example of the lampoons and poisonous precipitation of the age that many writers enjoyed and from which even Shakespeare had to suffer more than once. Frequently, as we see it now, Shakespeare is alluding to his immediate surroundings and to himself; this is especially true in *Hamlet*.

> The oppressor's wrong, the proud man's contumely.

The phrase "the oppressor's wrong" implies more than the German translation would indicate, for here it refers not merely to pressure exerted but rather to an injustice, to an offense which the oppressor commits. For the words "proud man's," the Folio—the text followed precisely by the editors elsewhere in this scene—substitutes the words "poor man's." This also conveys the meaning well. For there are cases where those higher beings despair because of the scorn, offenses, and slander of a lesser one and would like to destroy him for it, if he were certain he could.

> The pangs of despised love, the law's delay.

The tortured soul who practices his revenge on his loved one or on a rival who invokes his disdain. A better word for "despised" is used in the Folio, at least in my opinion: disregarded love—a relationship such as that between Othello and Desdemona, when Othello kills her and even tries to do away with Cassio, or a relationship as that between Posthumus and Imogen. To be sure, there were "pangs"—agony or anguish, as we might call it in German—as she experienced them. Not every misjudged emotion will demand such bloody revenge at once.

> The insolence of office, and the spurns
> That patient merit of the unworthy takes,
> *who could bear all this,*
> When he himself might his quietus make
> With a bare bodkin?

Here is the passage where the translation says something not contained in the original and which refers explicitly to the idea of suicide. Schröder reads even more into this by translating this way: "For who would bear . . . when he himself might with a bare knife do that he were with the death-bell tolled." "Quietus" can mean "state of rest" only in a metaphysical sense, not a literal. At court the word refers to the conclusion of procedures, when all is finished; in auditor's terminology it is the completely eradicated receipt; i.e., a legal term, an expression from the affairs of everyday life. In *The Player* by Shirley (Dodsley IX), the player's guardian, to whom he wants to give the girl in marriage, says:

> A brace of thousands, Will, she has to her portion:
> I hop'd to put her off with half the sum;
> That's truth: some younger brother would ha' thanked me
> And given my quietus.

"Bodkin" is an old word that occurs already in Chaucer and always means a small dagger, but may also mean awl (bradawl), an instrument with which ribbon is drawn through trimming, or an object to curl the hair. As far as I know the word is never used for needle or pinneedle. It has the same connotation as *stelo, stilo, stiletto* in Italian, which in German would be *Stilett*—a word we have borrowed from the Italian: a dagger which is not carried like a sword or worn on the belt, but is generally concealed. Perhaps "bodkin," like "stiletto" is a diminutive. In Italy, primarily in rural areas, young girls and older women wear such large and strong pins in their hair that they could conveniently be used as daggers.

A "bare bodkin" can also be a bare, exposed dagger. Had the poet wished to convey the idea of a trifle, as did the translator, he would have had to add the word "but"; the word "bare" means this pointed piece of metal—without a sheath making it easier to conceal—is adequate. The meaning of the passage is therefore the following: Who would bear all those previously related afflictions if he could achieve, with the aid of a mere small dagger, his quietus, that is, his complete balance sheet, or further, if he could force the opponent to silence or drive the sea of suffering from his shores by a single thrust of the dagger; it does not mean that the suffering one take his own life; a small, concealed dagger is adequate where the sword could not be used; even the mighty enemy could be subdued with it. Anyone contemplating suicide has at his command water, like Ophelia, or starvation or even poison. Meanwhile it is unnecessary to continue the exposition "too nicely."

who would fardels bear
To grunt and sweat under a weary life,
But that the dread of something after death,
The undiscover'd country from whose bourn
No traveller returns, puzzles the will
And makes us rather bear those ills we have
Than fly to others we know not of?
Thus conscience does make cowards of us all.

This therefore is the thing that lames the courage not only of mine but of all men's. At this point the speaker closes his musings with that moving monologue of wrath. It is expressed with particular beauty in the original as well as in the translation.

And thus the native hue of resolution
Is sicklied o'er with the pale cast of thought,
And enterprises of great pitch and moment,
With this regard their currents turn awry,
And lose the name of action.

The Folio expresses "turn awry" as "turn away," which is somewhat better. For anyone who has been able to hold to the previous interpretation right down to this last verse, no matter how hard that would be, this conclusion must be quite difficult if not altogether impossible. Is, then, every suicide an act or undertaking of resolve and determination? And could Hamlet deceive himself so completely that he would speak so elegantly about that common cowardice of committing suicide under these circumstances just to escape a task repulsive to him? He is no hero at all; as he acknowledges to Ophelia, he displays all kinds of weaknesses; nearly all the good and all the evil of mankind is expressed in him; but it would mean sinking too deeply if he were now to reflect on whether he should not rather take his own life, and then, merely out of fear, abandon the idea. My only surprise is that his friends and admirers have been willing to let him sink to such a level without turning from him in indignation. A certain longing for suicide, a kind of disdain for life that dominated the whole atmosphere for a while is perhaps the reason that this monologue has been so misunderstood and so admired in both a biased as well as exaggerated way. But if we now, after reading this conclusion, go back and read the passage again with my exposition in mind, everything seems natural, significant, and fitting. Acts that are deliberate and determined—for example, snatching the kingdom from a usurper, revenging a murdered father, assuming the position as king, to which both birth and law lend support, winning soldiers, the masses, and leaders over to his side for the great revolution—yes, all this is action and venture, and all this, just as similar extensive plans, is changed and dies while still a resolution, all because the initiator of such plans hesitates and because he is not indifferent to the possibility of his own annihilation in the struggle. We must note, too, that Hamlet demonstrates only the kind of suffering that is caused and can be punished by others—not suffering that could pardon suicide. Examples: incurable diseases, deep melancholy, an incorrigible aversion to life, grief over a friend or a loved one, or grief over irreplaceable qualities that so easily rob life of all its appeal, or the misery of an involuntary murder, or the like. Nothing is affected by these.

According to my exposition I understand everything in Hamlet's character that preceded as well as all that follows, such as his admonishing the players, his forgetting himself during the play in the king's presence, yet missing the opportunity when the king's conscience has betrayed him. When he finds the king in prayer he again hesitates to perform the decisive deed, imagining rather a more than inhuman vengefulness—an explanation by which he explains away any reason and excuses himself. The opposite extreme is presented by Laertes, who, in spite of the insolence he demonstrates upon entering, likewise vacillates when facing the king, doubting, letting the unique moment of opportunity pass, imagining he will have a second one and an even better opportunity some time in the future. In his mother's presence the prince gives free rein to his anger; the ghost admonishes him again, but he, having worked out no definite scheme, takes leave of the king and sails for England. As if by accident Polonius has been murdered. There is so little real tragedy associated with his death that there seems to be a slight trace of the comic about it. During his journey Hamlet is rescued in a miraculous manner. Upon his return he spends his precious time philosophizing somberly, as if to celebrate his animosity toward life. His conceit and his mood together cause him to forget himself with Laertes. He dallies, he is moved by fearful imaginings when challenged to a duel; and again he ponders the dread of hazarding life and reflects on how cheaply life must be valued. And thus he proceeds toward not only the destruction of the king but of himself as well.

This disdain for life, coupled with an unusually determined dependence upon it, characterizes Hamlet throughout most of the scenes. This is also an indication of all those emotions which have abandoned not only the freshness of human existence because of wounded pride and hurt feelings but have also lost that quiet secure confidence by excessive brooding. In Hamlet's melancholy soul are lodged many dark passions; revenge, anger, jealousy, pride, and awe are frightfully in evidence, but so mitigated and transformed by mood, wit, taste, knowledge, and nobility of personality that this miracle-like phenomenon charms and enchains, that even its repulsive qualities are not without splendor even when stripped of all greatness. This bizarre, impenetrable combination of foolishness and wisdom, magnanimity and pettiness, love and hate, conceit and genuine pride; this lover who shows passion and yet to whom no love can be entrusted, who speaks and feels like a noble friend, who by assuming charm at will is an idol of the people, who in a certain sense closes his eyes to his whole environment and yet is actually betrayed by one person; this mixture of heterogenous ingredients which we generally find in real life only in a much smaller measure and which in more recent times we have come to call "interesting"; these beautiful contradictions from which nearly every gifted individual suffers to a greater or lesser degree—in short, what is here combined and summed up is certainly the reason why this character and this tragedy have had such universal success. Everyone claims, and not without a certain justification, to understand the poet in this work; nearly everyone believes that he himself has experienced those same emotions or at least very similar ones. Hence this most wonderful creation in the history of poetry was epoch-making. How many English poets have tried ever since to imitate or even continue *Hamlet*? And among the German poets, in how many works does one discover this Danish prince, or at least a memory of him? This work afforded its own age as well as ours new insights, as if through a third eye or a new sense. Before its creation the human soul had never been probed so penetratingly and so thoroughly. The secrets of the heart had never before been divulged with such boldness, with a gaiety near despair and a sense of the tragic veiled in the simple voice of a child. The horror of the world of spirits and ghosts, the sham politics of the palace, the absurdity of ordinary perception, of melancholy, of merriment, had never been sensed in such close proximity. Like Buonarotti's "Last Judgment," for a while this work caused great excitement in England, just as among us it stimulates in many a weak spirit serious fears or a tantalizing temptation to imitate or surpass it. In its hazarded greatness it stands so daringly on the most extreme limits of the possible, like *Macbeth* and *Lear*, that even the slightest excess must necessarily thrust it into the absurd.

Even though the world was captivated and overpowered by this inexhaustible creation, none the less many became so engrossed that they were unable to sense the directing spirit, the *spiritus rector,* behind the work. Most persons committed the human error of considering the hero all too charming, of overlooking his weaknesses, of finding him noble, tender, and mild, a personification of wonderful melancholy. At that time Schröder was perhaps justified in yielding to this requirement as much as possible; hence his *Hamlet* continued to live. Otherwise the fascination of the tragedy would likely have not appealed to our people. It is precarious even today to allow the work to speak wholly for itself. We have still been elaborating and reworking it. Squenz [6] and his cohorts are not far wrong when they repeatedly warn: "And the women just can't stand that!" But many of the men neither. Actually the world has changed very little.

[6] Herr Peter Squenz, a stock German comic figure, derives from Peter Quince (*A Midsummer Night's Dream*). Shakespeare's play, probably brought to Germany by itinerant actors, was robbed of its carpenter-dramatist by Daniel Schwenter (1585–1636), from whose lampoon Andreas Gryphius created his own *Absurda Comica oder Herr Peter Squenz* (around 1650). Editor.

8. Stendhal

1783–1842

*Chateaubriand had exhibited, though to a lesser degree, Voltaire's ambivalence toward Shakespeare. But other predecessors of the French Romantic school, Madame de Staël and Charles Nodier, had been closer in their responses to the earliest German enthusiasts. These writers had found a special appeal in Shakespeare's darker and more cosmic aspects. But the specter of classicism continued to hang on. English companies were unable to present any of the tragedies in Paris. Frequently audiences became abusive. Hacks such as Lemercier plagiarized from Shakespeare in their dramas and deplored his bizarre elements in their criticism (*Cours Analytique de Littérature Générale, *1817). But the borrowings were unscrupulously thrust into classical formats. It was not until the arrival of a major literary figure that the struggle for the future of French literature began to go against the conservative elements.*

Despite the contemporaneity of Stendhal (Marie Henri Beyle) with the chief French Romantics, it is difficult to consider him as one of them. Stendhal himself felt that he was ahead of his time, a feeling with which subsequent literary taste seems to have agreed. Certainly Stendhal's manner of analyzing character is to one side of the main concerns of the école romantique. *Nevertheless, Stendhal saw, with great clarity, that classicism was a static art, and that Romanticism was not merely dynamic but ultimately brought even vanished historical periods into the present.*

In 1823 Stendhal published Racine et Shakespeare *and, by asserting that there is more art in the latter than in the former, deprived such critics as Ducis and other post-classical holdovers of the core of their argument. There is no ambivalence in*

Stendhal. Neither is there any lack of evidence for his assertions. Like Lessing, he links Shakespeare to Euripides and Sophocles. But Stendhal's unique contribution to all of later criticism, not merely of Shakespeare, is his denial that the unities are necessary to produce deep emotional and dramatic effects. It is the emotion which carries the spectator from one moment of dramatic tension to the next. And it is the passions that underly these dramatic moments which are the true concern of the audience.

With these bold assertions Stendhal paved the way for the enormous, if brief, influence of Shakespeare on French literature of the nineteenth century; an influence which seemed, for a time, as though it might permanently tear loose French literature from its anchorage to the critical traditions of many centuries.

FROM Racine and Shakespeare

EXCERPT FROM CHAPTER 1—On the Construction of Interesting Tragedies

The whole dispute between Racine and Shakespeare amounts to knowing whether, in observing the two unities of *place* and *time*, one can create plays which would deeply interest spectators of the nineteenth century, plays which would make them weep and tremble, or, in other terms, which would afford them *dramatic* pleasures instead of the *epic* pleasures which make us run to the fiftieth performance of the *Pariah* or of *Regulus*.

I say that the observation of the two unities of *place* and *time* is a French habit, a deeply rooted habit, a habit of which we can rid ourselves with difficulty, because Paris is the salon of Europe and gives it its tone; but I say that these unities

From Stendhal's *Racine et Shakespeare* (Paris, Calmann-Levy, 1854), pp. 7–20, 31. Translated by Françoise Rosen.

are in no way necessary to produce profound emotion and true dramatic effect.

Why, I shall say to the partisans of *classicism*, do you demand that the action represented in a tragedy shall last no longer than twenty-four or thirty-six hours, and that (the place of) the scene shall not change, or, as Voltaire said, that the changes of place shall not extend beyond the various suites of a palace?

The Academician. Because it is not plausible that an action performed in two hours' time should include the duration of a week or a month, nor that, in the space of a few moments, the actors should go from Venice to Cyprus, as in Shakespeare's *Othello*, or from Scotland to the court of England, as in *Macbeth*.

The Romantic. Not only is that implausible and impossible; but it is equally impossible that the action should include twenty-four or thirty-six hours.[1]

The Academician. Heaven forbid that we should be so absurd as to claim that the fictional duration of the action must correspond exactly to the *material* time employed for the performance. It is then that the rules would be real impediments to genius. In the arts of imitation one must be severe, but not rigorous. The spectator can very well imagine that, in the interval of the intermissions, several hours are passing, all the better as he is distracted by the concerts which the orchestra plays.

The Romantic. Take care what you say, sir, you are giving me an immense advantage; you concede, then, that the spectator can *imagine* a more considerable period of time is passing than that during which he is sitting in the theater. But, tell me, will he be able to imagine that the passing time is a period

[1] Stendhal is here echoing Ermes Visconti, whose series of six articles published in six consecutive issues of *Il Conciliatore,* Milan, between November 19 and December 6, 1818, constitutes the most systematic definition of literary romanticism by any of the *conciliatoristi.* Visconti was a close friend of Manzoni's. For a fuller discussion of his influence and thought see Grazia Avitabile, *The Controversy on Romanticism in Italy:* First Phase 1816–1823 (New York, 1959), particularly Chapter 7. Editor.

double the real time, triple, quadruple, or one hundred times more considerable? Where shall we stop?

The Academician. You are singular, you modern philosophers; you find fault with poetic rules, because, you say, they restrain genius; and now, you would like the rule of *unity of time,* in order to be plausible, to be applied by us with all the rigor and all the exactitude of mathematics. Does it not suffice you then, that it is evidently contrary to all plausibility that the spectator could imagine that a year, a month, or even a week has passed, since he took his ticket and entered the theater?

The Romantic. And who has told you that the spectator cannot imagine that?

The Academician. It is reason which tells me.

The Romantic. I beg your pardon; reason would not be able to teach you that. How would you manage to know that the spectator can imagine that twenty-four hours have passed, while in fact he has been seated only two hours in his loge, if experience did not teach you? How could you know that the hours which seem so long to a man who is bored seem to fly for one who is entertained, if experience did not teach you? In a word, it is experience alone which must decide between you and me.

The Academician. Without doubt, experience.

The Romantic. Well, then! experience has already spoken against you. In England, for two centuries; in Germany, for fifty years, tragedies have been presented whose action lasts for whole months, and the spectators' imagination lends itself to this perfectly.

The Academician. There you are citing foreigners—and, moreover, even Germans!

The Romantic. Another day, we shall talk of that incontestable superiority which the Frenchman in general, and in particular the inhabitant of Paris, has over all the peoples of the world. I give you your due, this feeling of superiority among you is quite sincere; you are despots spoiled by two centuries of flattery. Chance has determined that it should be you, Parisians, who should be entrusted with making literary reputations in Europe; and a woman of wit, known for her *enthusiasm* for the beauties of nature, exclaimed, in order to please the Parisians, "The most beautiful stream in the world is (the one that flows in) the gutter of the rue du Bac!" All the writers in good society, not only of France but of all Europe, have flattered you to obtain from you in exchange a little literary renown; and what you call *inner feeling, moral evidence,* is nothing other than the moral evidence of a spoiled child, in other words, the habit of flattery.

But let us return to the subject. Can you deny that the dweller in London or in Edinburgh, that the compatriots of Fox and of Sheridan, who are perhaps not complete fools, see performed without being in any way shocked, tragedies such as *Macbeth,* for example? Now, this play, which each year is applauded an infinite number of times in England and America, begins with the assassination of the King and the flight of his sons, and ends with the return of these same princes at the head of an army which they have mustered in England, in order to dethrone the bloodthirsty Macbeth. This series of actions necessarily requires several months.

The Academician. Ah! You will never persuade me that the English and the Germans, foreigners though they are, really imagine that whole months are passing while they are at the theater.

The Romantic. Just as you will never persuade me that French spectators believe that twenty-four hours are passing while they are seated at a performance of *Iphigenia at Aulis.*

The Academician (losing patience). What a difference!

The Romantic. Let us not take offense, and kindly observe what is going on in your mind. Try to set aside for a moment the veil cast by habit over the acts which take place so quickly that you have almost lost the power of following them with your eye and of seeing them happen. Let us be clear on this word *illusion.* When one says that the spectator's imagination fancies that the time is passing which is necessary for the events portrayed on the stage, one does not understand by that that the spectator's illusion goes to the point of believing that all this time has really elapsed. The fact is that the spectator, swept along by the action, is shocked by nothing; he does not think at all of the time that has passed. Your Parisian spectator sees Agamemnon awaken Arcas at seven o'clock precisely; he is witness to the arrival of Iphigenia; he sees her conducted to the altar, where the Jesuitical Calchas awaits her; he could certainly reply, if one asked him, that it took several hours for all these events. However, if, during the dispute of Achilles with Agamemnon, he pulls out his watch, it will tell him a quarter past eight. What spectator would be surprised at this? And yet the play which he is applauding has already lasted for several hours.

The fact is that even your Parisian spectator is accustomed to seeing time walk with a different pace on stage and in the hall. There is a fact which you cannot deny.

It is clear that, even at Paris, even in the French theater in the rue de Richelieu, the spectator's imagination lends itself easily to the poet's suppositions. The spectator naturally pays no attention to the intervals of time which the poet needs, no more than in sculpture does he take it into his head to reproach Dupaty or Bosio because their figures lack movement. That is one of the infirmities of the art. The spectator, when he is not a pedant, is concerned solely with the events and the developments of passions which are put before his eyes. Precisely the same thing is happening in the mind of the Parisian who applauds *Iphigenia at Aulis,* and in that of the Scot who admires the history of his ancient kings, Macbeth and Duncan. The only difference is that the Parisian, offspring of a good family, has taken the habit of mocking the other.

The Academician. That is to say, according to you, that the dramatic illusion would be the same for both of them?

The Romantic. To have illusions, to be *in illusion,* means to be mistaken, according to the dictionary of the Academy. An illusion, says M. Guizot,[2] is the effect of a thing or an idea which deceives us by its misleading appearance. Illusion means, then, the action of a man who believes the thing which is not, as in dreams, for example. Dramatic illusion will be the

[2] François Pierre Guillaume Guizot (1787–1874), a French historian and statesman who edited translations of Shakespeare and Hallam. Editor.

action of a man who believes to be truly existing the things which are happening on the stage.

Last year (August 1822), the soldier who was on guard duty inside the Baltimore theater, seeing Othello, who, in the fifth act of the tragedy of this name, was about to kill Desdemona, shouted: "It will never be said that in my presence a confounded Negro has killed a white woman!" At the same moment the soldier fires his gun and breaks an arm of the actor who was playing Othello. A year does not go by without the newspapers' reporting similar stories. Well! that soldier had *illusion,* believed to be true the action which was taking place on the stage. But an ordinary spectator, in the sharpest instant of his pleasure, at the moment when he is enthusiastically applauding Talma-Manlius, saying to his friend, "Do you know this work?" by the mere fact that he applauds does not have *complete illusion,* for he is applauding Talma,[3] and not the Roman Manlius; Manlius is doing nothing worthy of applause, his action is very simple and quite in his own interest.

The Academician. Excuse me, my friend; but what you are saying there is a platitude.

The Romantic. Excuse me, my friend; but what you are saying to me there is the evasion of a man whom a long habit of indulging in elegant phrases has rendered incapable of reasoning in a concise manner.

It is impossible for you not to acknowledge that the illusion which one goes to seek at the theater is not a perfect illusion. The *perfect illusion* was that of the soldier on guard duty in the Baltimore theater. It is impossible for you not to admit that the spectators know perfectly well that they are at the theater and that they are present at the performance of a work of art, and not at a real event.

The Academician. Who dreams of denying that?

The Romantic. You concede to me that *imperfect illusion.* Take care! Do you believe that from time to time, for example, two or three times in an act, and at each time lasting for a second or two, the illusion is complete?

[3] François Joseph Talma (1763–1826) was a French tragedian who specialized in accuracy of costume. Editor.

The Academician. This is not at all clear. In order to reply to you, I should have to return several times to the theater, and observe myself react.

The Romantic. Ah! There is a charming reply and one full of good faith! One sees that you belong to the Academy, and that you no longer need the votes of your colleagues in order to enter it. A man who still had his reputation to make as a learned *littérateur* would take pains to avoid being so clear, and reasoning in so precise a manner. Watch out for yourself; if you continue to be so candid, we are going to agree.

It seems to me that these moments of *perfect illusion* are more frequent than one generally believes and, above all, than one admits as true in literary discussions. But these moments last an infinitely small time, for example, a half second or a quarter second. One very quickly forgets Manlius to see only Talma; these moments have greater duration for young women and it is for this reason that they shed so many tears at a tragedy.

But let us inquire in what moments of tragedy the spectator may hope to encounter these delightful instants of *perfect illusion.*

These charming instants are met neither at the moment of a change of scene, nor at the precise moment when the poet makes the spectator span a gap of twelve or fifteen days at once, nor at the moment when the poet is obliged to put a long narrative in the mouth of one of his characters, simply in order to inform the spectator of a previous event, the knowledge of which is necessary to him, nor at the moment when three or four lines occur that are admirable, and remarkable *as verse.*

These delightful and so rare instants of *perfect illusion* can only be met in the heat of a spirited scene, when the actors' replies press on, for example, as when Hermione says to Orestes, who has just assassinated Pyrrhus at her command:

> Who told you so? [4]

Never will one find these moments of *perfect illusion,* neither

[4] Racine, *Andromaque* (1667). Act V, iii, 1543. Editor.

at the instant when a murder is committed on stage, nor when guards come to arrest a character to take him to prison. All these things we cannot believe to be true, and they never produce illusion. These passages are done only to lead into the scenes in which the spectators may encounter these demi-seconds that are so delightful; moreover, I say that these brief moments of *perfect illusion are found more often in the tragedies of Shakespeare than in the tragedies of Racine.*

All the pleasure that one finds in the tragic spectacle depends on the frequency of these little moments of illusion, and *on the state of emotion in which, during the intervals between them, they leave the spectator's soul.*

One of the things which most opposes the birth of these moments of illusion is admiration, however justified it may be in other respects, for the beautiful lines of a tragedy.

It is much worse, if one begins to wish to pass judgment on the lines of a tragedy. Moreover, this is exactly the situation of the soul for the Parisian spectator, when he goes to see for the first time the celebrated tragedy of the *Pariah.*

There is the question of *romanticism* reduced to its final terms. If you are insincere, or if you are insensitive, or if you are petrified by Laharpe,[5] you will deny me my little moments of perfect illusion.

And I admit that I can reply nothing to you. Your feelings are not something material that I can extract from your own heart, and put before your eyes in order to confound you.

I say to you: You ought to have such a feeling at this moment; all well-constituted men generally experience such a feeling at this moment; you will reply to me: Forgive (me) the expression, *that is not true.*

For my part, I have nothing to add. I have come to the last boundaries of what logic can grasp in poetry.

The Academician. There is abominably obscure metaphysics; and do you believe, with that, to cause Racine to be hissed?

The Romantic. Furthermore, it is only charlatans who claim

[5] Jean François de Laharpe (1739–1803), a French poet and critic whose best-known works are his lectures, *Lycée, ou Cours de littérature.* Editor.

to teach algebra without effort, or to pull teeth without pain. The question which we are debating is one of the most difficult with which the human mind can concern itself.

As for Racine, I am indeed glad you have named that great man. People have made of his name a term of abuse for us; but his glory is imperishable. He will always be one of the greatest geniuses to have been offered to the amazement and admiration of men. Is Caesar any the less a great general because, since the time of his campaigns against our ancestors the Gauls, gunpowder has been invented? All that we claim is that, if Caesar should return to this world, his first care would be to have some cannon in his army. Are we to say that Catinat or Luxembourg are greater captains than Caesar, because they had an artillery park and took in three days strongholds that would have stopped the Roman legions for a month? That would have been a fine argument to make to Francis the First at Marignan, to say to him: "Take care not to use your artillery, Caesar had no cannons; would you believe yourself more adroit than Caesar?"

If people of undeniable talent, such as Messieurs Chénier, Lemercier, Delavigne, had dared to infringe the rules whose absurdity has been recognized since Racine, they would have given us better than *Tiberious, Agamemnon,* or the *Sicilian Vespers.* Is not *Pinto* a thousand times superior to *Clovis, Orovius, Cyrus,* or some such other very correct tragedy by M. Lemercier?

Racine did not believe that one could make tragedy in any other way. If he were living in our time, and if he dared follow the new rules, he would do a hundred times better than *Iphigenia.* Instead of inspiring admiration, a somewhat chilly sentiment, he would have made torrents of tears flow. Who is the man, a little enlightened, who does not have greater pleasure in seeing (aux Français) *Marie Stuart* by Monsieur Lebrun than *Bajazet* by Racine? And yet M. Lebrun's verse is quite weak; the immense difference in the quantity of pleasure comes from the fact that M. Lebrun has dared to be halfway romantic.

The Academician. You have spoken at length; perhaps you have spoken well, but you have not convinced me at all.

The Romantic. I expected that. But here is a somewhat long intermission coming to an end, the curtain is being raised. I wished to dispel boredom in making you a little angry. Admit that I have succeeded.

Here ends the dialogue of the two adversaries, a dialogue of which I was really a witness in the pit (of the theater) in the rue Chantereine, and of which it only rests with me to name the interlocutors. The Romantic was polite; he did not wish to push the amiable Academician, much older than himself; otherwise he would have added: In order to be able still to read in one's own heart; in order to tear the veil of habit; in order to be able to plunge into experience for the moments of *perfect illusion* we are talking about, one must still have a soul susceptible to vivid impression, one must not be forty years old.

We have habits; offend these habits, and we will be sensitive for a long time only to the opposition you show us. Let us suppose that Talma appears on stage, and plays Manlius with powdered hair arranged in pigeon-wing fashion; we would do nothing but laugh during the whole time of the spectacle. Will he be any the less sublime in reality? No; but we will not see this sublimity. Thus, Lekain [6] would have produced *exactly the same effect* in 1760 if he had presented himself without powdered hair for this same role of Manlius. The spectators for the whole duration of the spectacle would have been sensitive only to their *contradicted habit.* There precisely is where we stand in France with regard to Shakespeare. He contradicts a great number of those ridiculous habits which the assiduous reading of Laharpe and other little perfumed rhetoricians of the eighteenth century has caused us to develop. What is worse is the fact that we expend vanity in supporting the argument that these bad habits are founded on nature.

Young people can still come back from this error of "self-esteem." Their soul being susceptible to vivid impressions, pleasure can make them forget vanity; moreover, that is what it is impossible to ask of a man over forty. The people of this

[6] Henri Louis Lekain (1728–1778), the most successful and popular actor of his day. He was championed by Voltaire. Editor.

age in Paris have made up their minds on all things, and even on things of an importance quite different from that of knowing whether, to make interesting tragedies in 1823, one must follow Racine's system or Shakespeare's.

EXCERPT FROM CHAPTER 2—On Laughter

Shakespeare was romantic because he presented to the Englishmen of 1590, first, the bloody catastrophes brought on by the civil wars, and, to provide a respite from these sad spectacles, a crowd of fine paintings of the movements of the heart, and of the nuances of the most delicate passions. One hundred years of civil wars and almost continual disturbances, numerous treacheries, torments, generous zeal, had prepared the subjects of Elizabeth for this sort of tragedy, which produces almost none of the artificiality of the life of the courts and the civilization of tranquil peoples. The Englishmen of 1590, happily quite ignorant, liked to contemplate at the theater the image of the misfortunes which the firm character of their Queen had just removed from real life. These same naive details, which our Alexandrian verse would reject with disdain, and on which one sets such a high value in *Ivanhoe* and *Rob Roy*, would have appeared to lack dignity in the eyes of the haughty marquises of Louis XIV.

These details would have mortally frightened the sentimental and perfumed dolls who, under Louis XV, could not see a spider without fainting. (There, I feel it indeed, is a scarcely dignified sentence.)

9. Alessandro Manzoni

1785–1873

Until the end of the eighteenth century the Italian attitude to Shakespeare was content to be a reflection of the French. If Voltaire's was the commanding critical voice in much of Europe, this was especially true of Italy. It was not until the last decade of that century that one could detect a growing and individualized interest in the English poet.

In 1796 Ugo Foscolo, a major poet of the Napoleonic period, and one more romantic than he would have cared to admit (although the hero of his novel Le Ultime Lettere di Jacopo Ortis *remarks that Shakespeare, among other masters of the superhuman genius "possessed" his imagination and "fired my heart"), ranks Shakespeare with Alfieri, Sophocles, and Voltaire as a great tragedian who deserves to be studied. But although Foscolo's was a strong voice, it was not enough to offset the Voltairean, ambivalent attitude toward Shakespeare.*

It was not until the Romantic period reached Italy that interest in Shakespeare grew to proportions equal to those of Germany and France. In 1814 Madame de Staël's De l'Allemagne *was published in translation and might be said to have taken Italian critics by storm. Such younger writers as Michele Leoni and the great poet, Giacomo Leopardi, became her disciples. Translations and critical prefaces in abundance followed. Once again it is possible to detect that the English poet is being used to overthrow classical critical doctrine, particularly that which deals with the unities.*

If Voltaire was the major influence on Italian Shakespeare appreciation in the eighteenth century, Manzoni became the central figure of Italian Shakespeare criticism in the following one.

Manzoni ranked Shakespeare with Virgil. And Manzoni's

own plays are full of the influence of the former. Even in I Promessi Sposi *(1827), one of the major novels of Romantic literature, and one enormously influential in Italy, the ghost of Shakespeare is audible. But Manzoni, like so many other writers who have studied Shakespeare for the sake of their own works, did not confine his interest to borrowing alone. His* Lettre à M. Chauvet sur l'Unité de Temps et de Lieu dans la Tragédie *remains one of the most important, if little read, pieces of Romantic Shakespeare criticism. In it Manzoni contrasts* Othello *with* Zaïre *as an argument against the unity of time, stating that the former is more believable because Shakespeare has allowed Othello's jealousy to develop while Voltaire must depend on chance since twenty-four hours is hardly enough time to make human events believable. Manzoni also examines* Richard II, *a play he, like Coleridge, much admired, and points out how a classical construction would have ruined that play.*

FROM Letter to M. Chauvet on the Unity of Time and Place in Tragedy

Let us consider, for example, Shakespeare's *Richard II,* which is not, moreover, the most beautiful of his plays drawn from the history of England.

The action of this tragedy is the overthrow of Richard from the throne of England and the elevation of Bolingbroke in his place. The play begins at the moment when the designs of these two characters appear in open opposition; when the king, having conceived a genuine uneasiness concerning the ambitious projects of his cousin, in order to thwart these ambitions, throws himself into measures which end by bringing on their execution. He banishes Bolingbroke: the Duke of Lancaster, the latter's father, being dead, the king seizes his prop-

From Manzoni's *Lettere,* reprinted from *Opere Complète* (Paris, 1843), pp. 257–260. Translated by Françoise Rosen.

erties and leaves for Ireland, Bolingbroke infringes the order of exile and returns to England on the pretext of claiming the inheritance which has been taken away from him by an illegal act. His partisans flock to him in crowds: as their number increases, he changes his language, passes by degrees from claims to threats; and soon the subject who has come to demand justice is a potent rebel who lays down laws. The uncle and lieutenant of the king, the Duke of York, who goes to meet Bolingbroke in order to oppose him, ends by treating with him. The character of this figure unfolds with the action in which he is engaged: the duke speaks successively, first to the rebellious subject, then to the chief of a numerous faction, finally to the new king; and this progress is so natural, so exactly parallel to events that the spectator is not surprised to find at the end of the play a good servant of Henry IV in the same character who had learned with the greatest indignation of Bolingbroke's landing. As the first successes of the latter become known, it is naturally toward Richard that interest and curiosity turn. One is eager to know the effect of so great a blow on the soul of this irascible and haughty king. Thus, Richard is summoned to the scene by the expectation of the audience at the same time as by the course of the action.

He has been warned of the disobedience of Bolingbroke and of his attempt: he hurriedly leaves Ireland and lands in England at the moment when his adversary is seizing the county of Gloucester; but certainly, the king ought not to march straight against the bold aggressor without having prepared to resist him. Here plausibility denied, as expressly as history itself, the unity of place, and Shakespeare has not followed the latter more rigorously than the former. He shows us Richard in the land of Wales: he could without difficulty have arranged his subject so as to produce the two rivals successively on the same terrain; but what would he not have had to sacrifice for that? and what would his tragedy have gained thereby? Unity of action? By no means; for where would one find a tragedy in which the action is more strictly unified than in this one? Richard deliberates, with his remaining friends, as to what he ought to do; and it is here that the character of this king begins to assume a development so natural and so unexpected. The spectator had already made the acquaintance of this astounding personality and flattered himself that he had fathomed it; but there was in it something secret and profound which had not appeared at all in prosperity and which adversity alone could elicit. The foundation of the character is still the same; it is still pride, it is still the highest ideal of its own dignity: but this same pride which, when it was accompanied by power, showed itself by levity, by impatience with every obstacle, by a thoughtlessness which did not permit it even to suspect that all human power has its judges and its limits: this pride, once deprived of force, has become grave and serious, solemn and measured. What supports Richard is an unalterable consciousness of his own greatness, it is the certainty that no human event has been able to destroy, since nothing can cancel his birth and his kingship. The enjoyments of power have escaped him; but the idea of his calling to the highest rank remains: in what he is, he persists in honoring what he was; and this obstinate respect for a title which no one any longer acknowledges to be his removes from the sense of his misfortune everything which could humiliate or dishearten him. The ideas, the emotions through which this revolution in Richard's character is manifested have great originality, are expressed in the most exalted poetry, and are even very touching.

But this historical tableau of Richard's soul and of the events which modify it necessarily embraces more than twenty hours, and the same is true for the progress of the other deeds, passions, and characters developed in the rest of the action. The clash of the two factions, the ardor and increasing activity of the king's enemies, the tergiversations of those who are waiting for victory in order to know positively to which cause respectable people ought to be attached, the courageous loyalty of one single man, loyalty which the poet has described just as history has sanctioned it, with all the ideas true and false that determined this man to render homage to adversity in spite of force: all these are admirably depicted in this tragedy. A few improprieties, which one could remove without altering its order, could not impose upon the grandeur and beauty of the whole.

I am almost ashamed to give so fleshless a sketch of so majestic a tableau. But I flatter myself that I have said enough about it to show at least that what is characteristic in this subject requires more latitude than the rule of the two unities accords. Let us now suppose that Shakespeare, having composed his *Richard II,* had shown it to a critic convinced of the necessity of this rule. The latter would probably have said to him: "There are in your play some very fine situations, and above all some admirable sentiments; but plausibility is deplorably offended. You transport your public from London to Coventry, from the county of Gloucester to the land of Wales, from parliament to Flint Castle; it is impossible for the spectator to create for himself the illusion necessary to follow you. There is a contradiction between the various situations in which you wish to place the spectator and the real situation he is in. He is too certain of not having changed position to be able to imagine that he has made all these journeys which you demand of him."

I don't know, but it seems to me that Shakespeare would have been quite astonished by such objections. "Oh Good Heavens!" he might have replied, "how you talk of displacements and journeys. There is no question of that here; I never dreamed of it, nor did my spectators, either. I place before their eyes an action which is unfolded by degrees, which is composed of events that arise successively from one another and that occur in different places; it is the mind of the spectator which follows them—he has no traveling to do except to imagine to himself that he is traveling. Do you think that he has come to the theater to see real events? and has it ever entered my mind to create for him such an illusion? to make him believe that what he knows has already happened several hundred years ago is happening now once more? that these actors are men really engrossed in the passions and concerns which they are speaking of, and speaking of in verse?"

But I have too much forgotten, sir, that it is not on the objection drawn from plausibility that you base the maintenance of the rules, but rather on the impossibility of preserving without them unity of action and stability of character. Let us see, then, whether this objection can be applied to the tragedy of *Richard II*. Well! How would one set about proving, I ask you with some curiosity, that the action is not unified, that the characters are not constant, and this, because the poet has remained in the places and times given by history, instead of shutting himself up in the space and length of time which the critics have measured out on their own authority for all tragedies? What more would Shakespeare have replied to a critic who had come to oppose to him the law of twenty-four hours! "Twenty-four hours!" he would have said, "but why? Reading the chronicles of Holinshed supplied my mind with the idea of an action simple and great, unified and varied, full of interest and of lessons; and this action—I should have had to distort, to mutilate from pure caprice! The impression which a chronicler has produced on me—I should not have sought to render, after my fashion, to spectators who asked nothing better! I should have been less a poet than he (Holinshed)! I see an event of which each incident relates to all the others and serves to motivate them; I see fixed characters develop in a certain time and in certain places; and in order to give the idea of this event, in order to depict these characters, it will be absolutely necessary for me to mutilate both the one and the others to the point where the duration of twenty-four hours and the precincts of a palace might suffice for their development!"

There would be in your system, sir, I admit, another reply to make to Shakespeare: one could tell him that these pains he has taken to reproduce the facts in their natural order with their most authenticated principal circumstances makes him like a historian rather than like a poet. One could add that it is the rule of the two unities which would have rendered him a poet, in forcing him to create one action, a nexus, of the peripaties; for "it is thus," you say, "that the limits of art give impetus to the artist's imagination and force him to become a creator." That is precisely, I agree, the true consequence of this rule; and the slightest acquaintance with the drama which has accepted it proves, moreover, that it has not failed in its effect. That is a great advantage, according to you: I dare not to be of this opinion and on the contrary to regard the effect which is involved as the gravest disadvantage of this rule from which it results; yes, this necessity to create, imposed arbitrarily on art, separates it from truth and mars it, both in its results and in its means.

I don't know whether I am going to say something contrary to received ideas: but I believe that I am merely stating a very simple truth, in advancing the idea that the essence of poetry does not consist in inventing facts: that invention is what is most easy and most vulgar in the work of the mind, what requires the least reflection and even the least imagination. Thus there is nothing more prevalent than creations of this kind; whereas all the great monuments of poetry have as their basis events given by history, or, what comes down to the same thing, by what has once been regarded as history.

As for dramatic poets in particular, the greatest ones in each country have avoided, with all the more care as they have had more genius, putting into drama facts of their own creation; and on each occasion that has occurred of telling them that they have substituted, on essential points, invention for history—far from accepting this judgment as praise, they have rejected it as blame. If I did not know how much temerity there is in too general historical assertions, I should dare to assert that there is not, in all that remains to us of the tragic drama of the Greeks, nor even in all their poetry, a single example of this sort of creation, which consists in substituting for the principal known causes of a great action, causes wantonly invented. The Greek poets took their subjects, with all their important circumstances, from the national traditions. They did not invent the facts; they received them just as their contemporaries had transmitted them: they accepted, they respected history just as individuals, peoples, and time had made it.

10. Franz Grillparzer

1791–1872

By the middle of the nineteenth century the German Romantic Movement had lost its vigor and a new kind of criticism made its appearance. Hegel's aesthetics were being tendentiously reconstructed by such critics as Ulrici and Gervinus into something predominantly anti-Romantic and metaphysical with an increasing focus on such issues as tragic guilt and moral purpose. But while the critical situation moved more and more toward a confusion of aesthetics with morality, the theatrical situation held on for a time with many régisseurs *staging Shakespeare along the lines which had been urged by Tieck.*

Among the most successful companies was Heinrich Laube's; under Laube's direction the Vienna Court Theater, fortunate in having actors like Lewinski, Charlotte Wolter, and the immortal Sonnenthal, continued to present Shakespeare in a hitherto unrivaled manner. It was this theater of Laube's which attracted to its performances Austria's major literary figure of the nineteenth century, Franz Grillparzer.

If seen against the background of the Romantic Movement, Grillparzer becomes something of an anachronism. From the first he admired Lope de Vega and Shakespeare and his admiration of the latter surely influenced the form and subject of his historical drama König Ottokars Glück und Ende *(1825). Yet in spite of this admiration Grillparzer's own works show little of the Romantic subjectivity and extravagance, and his attitude to Shakespeare is more judicious, more reminiscent of the early Voltaire than of either the German or French Romantics.*

But if Grillparzer saw errors in Shakespeare neither could he abide the new critical tendencies of such as Gervinus, whose work he calls "absurd." In his Studien zur Englischen Literatur, *a collection of remarks dating back to 1821, Grillparzer attempted to place Shakespeare in a rational perspective—a perspective somewhere between Voltaire's and Byron's.*

FROM Studies in English Literature

1821

What was Shakespeare trying to accomplish in making Iago more than twenty-eight years of age? I have looked upon the world for four times seven, he says. His hypocrisy, his knowledge of the world and of people would indicate a somewhat older person, probably about forty. Wasn't Shakespeare himself hardly more than thirty when he wrote *Othello*? Is not his villainy, however refined and always well calculated, nevertheless quite rash in relation to the consequences, at least to the far-distant consequences, just as is typical of a young, heedless planner?

Measure for Measure

1849

In his absurd commentary on Shakespeare, Gervinus is inclined to put this work on the same plane as *Othello.* Foolishly asserting that the chief virtue of a dramatic work lies in its emphasis upon the didactic, he feels obligated to suggest certain improvements for each of Shakespeare's masterpieces. Now admittedly *Measure for Measure* has certain masterful and unexcelled qualities, yet it belongs to the more mediocre works of Shakespeare. From the beginning the work suffers

From Grillparzer's *Studien,* reprinted from *Gesammelte Werke* (Vienna, 1887), Vol. XIV, pp. 89–93. Translated by LaMarr Kopp.

from the absurd assumption which underlies it. A law imparting punishment by death to everyone who has had physical contact with a woman is plausible only under some fairy-tale caliph in *Thousand and One Nights.* Hence the entire work seems somewhat arbitrary. This does disappear in the more gripping scenes but somehow always hovers in the background, making everything seem more like a play and transferring it from real life to the theatrical stage. Shakespeare himself sensed this quite correctly, for in none of his serious works does he allow the comic element to assume such proportions. This fairy-tale quality extends even to the action. One can give his consent to this sublimation of Mariana for the sake of Isabella as well as to some other things without detracting from his enjoyment. But no one will be convinced he is observing a scene from life—and that is, after all, the task of drama. The work's major merit lies in the characters, particularly Isabella, who certainly belongs to Shakespeare's most admirable creations of this kind. Still she demonstrates a unique relatedness to Shakespeare's characters. All are drawn with equal effectiveness and remain consistent as long as the action permits. This is true of all the main characters in his best works. In the works of second rank, he modifies the characters according to the events that take place. He has no conscience against satisfying his own wishes by moving them to the side whenever some gaiety or even some absurdity of action stands in the way of their development. This has even happened in one of his undisputed masterpieces with the character of Lady Macbeth. As soon as she has fulfilled her purpose of inciting her husband to murder, the poet moves her aside since he has no need for her any further. Until her last unexcelled scene she remains subordinate and sometimes almost anxious—a fact which confounded Tieck, who, acknowledging no error in Shakespeare, preferred to abandon everything rather than relinquish a part. Tieck finally interpreted her as a tender wife and loving mother. The same is true of Isabella. From the start she is one of the most wonderful characters the genius of a poet has ever created. The fact that here she demonstrates some grossness as well as impropriety without any indication of antipathy we are prepared to excuse as a part of those times which found fewer things disgusting than our own. As soon as Mariana appears, however, the action becomes more legendary and colorful, she forgets her former stringency to such an extent that she succumbs willingly to the reckless confusion of her own role with that of Mariana's, and yields to the sinfulness of carnal desires; only at the end does she find a return to the nobility of her own nature once more. Indeed at the very end beyond that strength of character, which formerly determined her life in a cloister, is the marriage to the duke arranged without questionings. Even Angelo's character with its undeniably good qualities, demonstrated anew at his reprieve at the end and contrasting to his shamelessness and dishonesty, seems to belong to the land of fable and the realm of the impossible. The fact that of all those who are guilty only the one least guilty—chattering Lucio—is punished makes the title, *Measure for Measure,* a vivid satire. Even in construction the work reveals weaknesses, especially in the fourth act which is quite without content and exists merely to carry the action into Act V. The number five at that time was a canonical requirement similar to the many murders in a tragedy.

What I have said above is not a reproof against Shakespeare, for even in this work he has achieved so much that for any other poet it would suffice to make him revered forever. The reproof is directed to those insensitive critics who, lacking discrimination and truly competent judgment for praise, do an injustice to the real masterpieces of Shakespeare by placing this work on the same level.

Othello
1849

Germans consider Shakespeare the perfect copy of nature. When they correctly hold him above all other poets of the new age, they are calling attention especially to the truth of his creative work. It is noteworthy, however, that this quality of natural truth has not been sensed universally and at all times. Voltaire, a man so gifted the world has seen his kind but once and also a poet who in some of his dramas is not to be scorned, spoke rather disparagingly of Shakespeare. It might be justified to consider him prejudiced. But then England's second greatest poet, Lord Byron, who in no way lacked a sense of natural truth, was nothing less than permeated with the excellence of his fellow countryman. How does one account for this difference of opinion on a matter such as nature and truth which should be and always are the same? Othello, psychologically the truest picture of human passion, offers a welcome contribution to the solution of the problem. Iago's slander, his fragmentary speech, Othello's struggle between love and suspicion—nothing can be closer to truth than these: here we see how passion is aroused, how it grows, and finally how it becomes something frightful—but not at such a rapid pace. Shakespeare frequently presents a compendium, a précis, an *abrégé* of nature rather than nature itself. What could hardly be accomplished in five acts is here compressed into the limits of a single act (the fourth). Othello discharged his lieutenant more for the sake of official procedure than because he was displeased with him. He discovers him not secretly but beyond all suspicion in the presence of hs wife pleading for her intercession. She intercedes. What could be more simple, natural, or guiltless? And yet it is possible for Othello to grow so suspicious within the dimensions of a single act that the remainder of the play scarcely adds a thing other than the murder. I am omitting the incident of the handkerchief which in itself actually presents no real test. The fact that Desdemona uses such a valuable and significant love token as an ordinary handkerchief can hardly be considered natural. Shakespeare always follows the path of nature but frequently he allows himself a few shortcuts. This points up both the truth and the violation of truth in his poetry.

The same is true of his characters. Desdemona is an angel of purity and likely the most angelic character ever created by any poet. How is it, then, that this tender, obedient, and childishly dependent girl fled from her father's home? Explanations exist in abundance. If being true to character were really important to Shakespeare, then he should have offered some clarification, especially relating to this incongruity, by indicating something concerning the course of events. It is quite generally conceded that Iago's character is impossible. For the sake of human nature, I am quite prepared to believe it!

So, then, there are quite a few errors! However, how is it that during the presentation or while reading these errors we are not in the least disturbed? Why, rather, do they strike us as signs of genius? Shakespeare's truth is a truth of impression and not of analysis. The precision of the presentation, the force of all that it embodies, is so overpowering that we never ponder the actual possibilities, since it is reality that confronts us.

The art of presentation to this degree can make any imaginable claim upon nature, even if we fail to understand that claim.

He was probably forced into taking these shortcuts of nature by his audience, desiring colorful events rather than psychological complexity; but also the content of his subject matter which he found ready and waiting, which he accepted as reality, and from which he deviated only on rare occasion was responsible.

But we who strive to do something similar with infinitely less ability should recognize these weaknesses and find in Shakespeare an example but not a model. The feeling of necessity follows only the footsteps of genius; the rest of us keep normal probability and succession of events clearly in view; we will be convincing only when we can justify.

11. Leopold von Ranke

1795–1886

Ranke is generally considered the first modern historian. During the fifty years of his association with the University of Berlin he was of enormous influence as both teacher and scholar. One cannot say that he exhibited, to any great degree, an "interest" in Shakespeare, and certainly he avoided any discussion of the English poet's art and its characteristics in his numerous works. But what he has had to say is of interest, nevertheless, because of his scrupulous avoidance of any of the many theories, such as Hegelianism, Romanticism, and others, which marred the work of other historians.

Of interest, too, in his remarks on Shakespeare in the History of England, Principally in the 17th Century *(published originally as* Englische Geschichte, vornehmlich im 16 und 17 Jahrhundert *between 1859 and 1868) is Ranke's placing of Shakespeare within the social context of his period, and his attempt to see Shakespeare as a product of those social forces.*

FROM History of England

EXCERPT FROM VOLUME IV, CHAPTER 6

While the town theaters and their productions were thus struggling to rise in mutual rivalry, the genius of William Shakespeare developed itself: at that time he was lost among the crowd of rivals, but his fame has increased from age to age among posterity.

From Ranke's *History of England* (Oxford, The Clarendon Press, 1875), Vol. IV, pp. 460–463. Translator unknown.

It especially concerns us to notice that he brought on the stage a number of events taken from English history itself. In the praise which has been lavishly bestowed on him, of having rendered them with historical truth, we cannot entirely agree. For who could affirm that his King John and Henry VIII, his Gloucester and Winchester, or even his Maid of Orleans, resemble the originals whose names they bear? The author forms his own conception of the great questions at issue. While he follows the chronicle as closely as possible, and adopts its characteristic traits, he yet assigns to each of the personages a part corresponding to the peculiar view he adopts: he gives life to the action by introducing motives which the historian cannot find or accept: characters which stand close together in tradition, as they probably did in fact, are set apart in his pages, each of them in a separately developed homogeneous existence of its own: natural human motives, which elsewhere appear only in private life, break the continuity of the political action, and thus obtain a twofold dramatic influence. But if deviations from fact are found in individual points, yet the choice of events to be brought upon the stage shows a deep sense of what is historically great. These are almost always situations and entanglements of the most important character: the interference of the spiritual power in an intestine political quarrel in *King John;* the sudden fall of a firmly seated monarchy as soon as it departs from the strict path of right in *Richard III;* the opposition which a usurping prince, Henry IV, meets with at the hands of the great vassals who have placed him on the throne, and which brings him by incessant anxiety and labor to a premature grave; the happy issue of a successful foreign enterprise, the course of which we follow from the determination to prepare for it, to the risk of battle, and to final victory; and then again in *Henry V* and *Henry VI,* the unhappy position into which a prince not formed by nature to be a ruler falls between violent contending parties, until he envies the homely swain who tends his flocks and lets the years run by in peace; lastly the path of horrible crime which a king's son not destined for the throne has to tread in order to ascend it: all these are great elements in the history of states, and are not only important for England, but are symbolic for all people and their sovereigns. The poet touches on parliamentary or religious questions extremely seldom; and it may be observed that in *King John* the great movements which led to Magna Charta are as good as left out of sight; on the contrary he lives and moves among the personal contrasts offered by the feudal system, and its mutual rights and duties. Bolingbroke's feeling that though his cousin is King of England yet he is Duke of Lancaster reveals the conception of these rights in the Middle Ages. The speech which Shakespeare puts into the mouth of the Bishop of Carlisle is applicable to all times. The crown that secures the highest independence appears to the poet the most desirable of all possessions, but the honored gold consumes him who wears it by the restless care which it brings with it.

Shakespeare depicts the popular storms which are wont to accompany a free constitution in the plots of some of his Roman dramas; of these Plutarch instead of Holinshed furnishes the basis. He is right in taking them from a foreign country: for events nearer to his audience would have roused an interest of a different kind, and yet would not have had so universal a meaning. What could be more dramatic, for example, and at the same time more widely applicable than the contrast between the two speeches, by the first of which Caesar's murder is justified, while by the second the memory of his services is revived? The conception of freedom which the first brings to life is set in opposition to the thought of the virtues and services of the possessor of absolute power, and thrust by them into the background; but these same feelings are the deepest and most active in all ages and among all nations.

But the attested traditions of ancient and modern times do not satisfy the poet in his wish to lay bare the depths of human existence. He takes us into the cloudy regions of British and Northern antiquity known only to fable, in which other contrasts between persons and in public affairs make their appearance. A king comes on the stage, who in the plenitude of enjoyment and power is brought by overhasty confidence in his nearest kin to the extremest wretchedness into which men can fall. We see the heir to a throne who, dispossessed of his rights by his own mother and his father's murderer, is directed by mysterious influences to take revenge. We have before us a great nobleman, who by atrocious murders has gained possession of the throne, and is slain in fighting for it. The poet brings us into immediate proximity with the crime, its execution, and its recoil; it seems like an inspiration of hell and of its deceitful prophecies. We wander on the confines of the visible world and of that other world which lies on the other side, but extends over into this, where it forms the borderland between conscious sense and unconscious madness: the abysses of the human breast are opened to view, in which men are chained down and brought to destruction by powers of nature that dwell there unknown to them: all questions about existence and nonexistence, about heaven, hell, and earth, about freedom and necessity, are raised in these struggles for the crown. Even the tenderest feelings that rivet human souls to one another he loves to display upon a background of political life. Then we follow him from the cloudy North into sunny Italy. Shakespeare is one of the intellectual powers of nature; he takes away the veil by which the inward springs of action are hidden from the vulgar eye. The extension of the range of human vision over the mysterious being of things which his works offer constitutes them a great historical fact.

We do not here enter upon a discussion of Shakespeare's art and characteristics, of their merits and defects: they were no doubt of a piece with the needs, habits, and mode of thought of his audience; for in what case could there be a stronger reciprocal action between an author and his public than in that of a young stage depending upon voluntary support? The very absence of conventional rule made it easier to put on the stage a drama by which all that is grandest and mightiest is brought before the eyes as if actually present in that medley of great and small things which is characteristic of human life. Genius is an independent gift of God: whether it is allowed to expand or not depends on the receptivity and taste of its contemporaries.

12. Heinrich Heine

1797–1856

If Heine presents us with little that is original in his critique of Shakespeare, still he is worthy of being read. His Shakespeare's Maidens and Women *(1839) is full of the sharp irony, the felicitous turn of speech, the outrageously refreshing assertions so characteristic of the style of the master satirist. In the introduction to the book he reviews, with more passion than discernment, the German Shakespeare criticism up to and including his own time. In his treatment of the female characters, Heine follows the main line, a somewhat sentimental one, of the Romantic critics, except when speaking of love. Here Heine brings to bear the perceptions of a psychologist and his comments are frequently astute.*

Heine must be seen as a transitional figure. He stands at the back door of Romanticism, so to speak, headed out toward the realism which flourished in the later nineteenth century. Like Carlyle, he makes obeisance to genius. Like the later Swinburne, he is at the mercy of his grand feelings. But at their best his perceptions reach below logic to an intuitive level of truth.

FROM Shakespeare's Maidens and Women

EXCERPT FROM Introduction

The Germans have comprehended Shakespeare better than the English. And here I must again recall that great name

From *Shakespeare's Maidens and Women* in Vol. II of *The Prose and Poetical Works of Heinrich Heine*, 20 vols. (New York, Groscup and Sterling, 1901). Translated by C. G. Leland.

which is ever to be found where there is question of a great beginning. Gotthold Ephraim Lessing was the first man who raised his voice in Germany for Shakespeare. He it was who bore the first and greatest stone for a temple to the greatest of all poets, and, what was more praiseworthy, he took the pains to clear the ground on which this temple was to be raised of all its ancient rubbish. Without pity he tore down the light French stage show which spread wide over the place, so inspired was he with a genial love of building. Gottsched shook the locks of his peruke so despairingly that all Leipzig trembled, and the cheeks of his spouse grew white with fear—or from pearl powder. One may say that the whole dramaturgy of Lessing was written in the interest of Shakespeare.

Next to Lessing we have Wieland.[1] By his translation of the great poet he increased more practically the recognition of his merits in Germany. Strange that the poet of Agathon and of Musarion, the trifling, toying *cavalière servante* of the Graces, the hanger-on and imitator of the French, was the man who all at once grasped the British *earnestness* so powerfully that he himself raised on his shield the hero who was to put an end to his own supremacy.

The third great voice which rang for Shakespeare in Germany was that of our dearly loved Herder, who declared himself with unconditional enthusiasm for the British bard. Goethe also paid him honor with a grand flourish on his trumpet; in short, it was an array of kings, who, one after the other, threw their votes into the urn, and elected William Shakespeare the Emperor of Literature.

This Emperor was already firmly seated on his throne when the knight August Wilhelm von Schlegel and his squire, Court Councilor Ludwig Tieck, succeeded in kissing his hand, and assured all the world that now his realm and reign were really sure—the thousand-year-long rule of the great William.

But it would be unjust should I deny to A. W. von Schlegel

[1] *Vide* my note to Number 15 of Lessing's *Hamburgische Dramaturgie*, p. 51. Editor.

the merit which he won by his translation of Shakespeare's dramas, and his lectures on them. Honorably confessed that the latter lack the philosophic basis, they sweep along too superficially in a frivolous dilettantism, and certain ugly reserved reflections or back thoughts came too visibly forward for me to pronounce unreserved praise over them. Herr A. W. von Schlegel's inspiration is always artificial, a deliberately intended shamming oneself into an intoxication without drunkenness; and with him, as with all the rest of the Romantic school, the apotheosis of Shakespeare is indirectly meant for a degradation of Schiller. Schlegel's translation is certainly the best as yet, and fulfills every requisition which can be made for a metrical version. The feminine nature of his talents is here an admirable aid to the writer, and in his artistic ready skill without character, he can adapt himself admirably and accurately to the foreign spirit.

And yet I confess that, despite these merits, I often prefer to read the old translation of Eschenburg [2] (which is all in prose) to that of Schlegel, and for these reasons:

The language of Shakespeare is not peculiarly his own, but was derived from his predecessors and contemporaries; it is the traditional theatrical language which the dramatic poet of those days must use, whether he found it fitted to his genius or not. One has only to look superficially over Dodsley's *Collection of Old Plays,* and observe that in all the tragedies and comedies of the time there prevails the same manner of speech, the same euphuism, the same exaggeration of refinement, the same forced meaning of words, and the same "conceits," jests, witty flourishes, and elaborate fancies which we find in Shakespeare, and which are blindly admired by men of small or narrow minds, but which are excused by the intelligent reader—when he does not blame them—as extraneous, or belonging to the conditions of an age which exacted them. Only in the passages where his highest revelations are shown, and where the whole genius of Shakespeare appears, does

[2] Johann Joachim Eschenburg (1743–1820) translated Shakespeare into German prose (13 vols., Zurich, 1775–1782) and also wrote a *Manual of Classical Literature.* Editor.

he voluntarily strip away that traditional language of the stage, and show himself in a grandly beautiful nakedness, in a simplicity which vies with unadorned Nature and fills us with delighted awe.

Yes, in such passages Shakespeare manifests, even in language, a decided originality, but one which the metrical translator who comes limping along behind on the feet of the measure fitted to the thought cannot faithfully reflect. With such a translator these unusual passages are lost in the ordinary wheel ruts of theatrical language, and even Schlegel cannot avoid this fate. But why then take the trouble to translate metrically, when the best work of the poet is thereby lost and only the faulty reproduced? A prose translation which more easily reproduces the unadorned, plain, natural purity of certain passages therefore deserves preference to the metrical.

While directly following Schlegel, Ludwig Tieck deserves credit as an elucidator of Shakespeare. This was set forth in his "Dramaturgic Pages," which appeared fourteen years ago [1823] in the *Abendzeitung,* and which awoke the utmost interest in "the theatergoing public," as well as among actors. Unfortunately there prevails in these pages a wide-ranging or straying, wearisome, pedantic tone, which the delightful good-for-nothing, as Gutzkow [3] called him, assumed with a certain lurking spirit of roguery. What he lacked in a knowledge of classic tongues, or even in philosophy, he made up in decorum and gravity, and we are reminded of Sir John in the chair, when he delivers his harangue to the Prince. But in spite of the puffed-out doctrinal gravity under which little Ludwig sought to conceal his philologic and philosophic deficiencies or *ignorantia,* there are to be found here and there in these leaves the shrewdest comments on the character of the Shakespearean heroes, and ever and anon we find that poetic power of perception which we ever admired in his earlier writings, and recognized with joy.

[3] Cf. my headnote to the Ludwig Tieck selection, p. 95. Karl Ferdinand Gutzkow (1811–1878) was a popular German novelist, playwright, and director. Editor.

Ah, this Tieck, who was once a poet, and reckoned, if not among the highest, at least with those who had the highest aims, how low has he fallen since then! How miserably mournful is the negligently reeled-off task, which he gives us annually, compared to the free outpourings of his muse from the early moonlit time of Fairy Tale! As dear as he once was, even so repulsive is he now—the powerless Neidhart, who calumniates the inspired sorrows of German youth in his gossiping novels. Unto him are truly applicable those words of Shakespeare:

> For sweetest things turn sourest by their deeds:
> Lilies that fester smell far worse than weeds.

Among the German commentators on the great poet, the late Franz Horn [4] should not be omitted. His elucidations of Shakespeare are certainly the fullest, and are in five volumes. There is, indeed, in them the spirit of wit and intelligence, but it is a spirit so diluted and thinned down that it is even less refreshing than the most spiritless narrow-mindedness. Strange that this man, who out of love for Shakespeare devoted a whole life to his study of him, and was one of his most zealous worshipers, was a pitifully petty pietist. But it may be that a sense of his own wretched weakness of soul awoke in him an endless amazement at Shakespeare's power, and so, whenever and anon the British Titan, in his most passionate scenes, piles Pelion on Ossa and storms the heights of heaven, then the poor elucidator in awe lets fall his pen and pauses, mildly sighing and grimacing. As a pietist he must naturally, according to his canting-pious nature, hate the poet whose soul, inspired with the springlike air of the gods, breathes in every word the most joyous heathenism—yes, he should hate that believer in life, to whom the faith of death is in secret detestable, and who, reveling in the most enchanting delirium of antique heroic power, shuns the pitiful pleasures of humility, self-denial, and abasement! And yet he

[4] Franz Christoph Horn (1781–1837), a German poet and critic who, besides translating Shakespeare, wrote a *Critical History of German Poetry and Eloquence* (1822–1829). Editor.

loves him all the same, and in his unwearied love would fain convert Shakespeare to the true Church; he comments a Christian sense into him—be it pious fraud or self-delusion; he finds this Christian feeling everywhere in Shakespeare's dramas, and the holy water of his commentary is also a bath of baptism in five volumes, which he pours on the head of the great heathen.

And yet, I repeat, these comments are not quite without wit and sense. Many a time Franz Horn brings forth a happy thought, then he makes wearisome, sweet-sourish grimaces, and groans and twists and twines himself round on the stool of childbirth; and when finally the clever idea has come to light, he looks at it with emotion and wearied smiles, like a midwife who has got through with her job. It is really both vexatious and amusing that just this weak and pious Franz commented on Shakespeare. In a comedy by Grabbe the affair is delightfully reversed, and Shakespeare is represented in hell as writing explanations of Horn's works.

But all the glosses and explanations and laborious laudation of commentators was of less practical use as regarded making Shakespeare known to the public than the inspired love with which talented actors produced his dramas, and thereby made them a subject for popular judgment. Lichtenberg,[5] in his letters from England, gives us important intelligence as to the skill and method by which Shakespeare's characters were given on the London stage in the middle of the last century. I say characters—not the works in their fullness, since to this day British actors have only felt or known what is characteristic, not the poetry, and still less the art. Such one-sidedness of apprehension is found, but in far more limited degree, among the commentators, who were never able to see through the dusty spectacles of erudition that which was the simplest and nearest, or the nature which was in Shakespeare's dramas. Garrick saw more clearly into the Shakes-

[5] Georg Christoph Lichtenberg (1742–1799) was one of the literati of his day. His writing, full of humor and satire, is chiefly responsible for the success of his book *Ample Commentary on the Engravings of Hogarth,* which was incomplete at the time of his death. Editor.

pearean thoughts than Dr. Johnson, the John Bull of Learning, on whose nose Queen Mab doubtless cut the drollest capers while he wrote on the *Midsummer Night's Dream;* truly he never knew why he, when at work on Shakespeare, felt more tickling o' the nose and wish to sneeze than over any other poet whom he criticized.

While Dr. Johnson dissected the Shakespearean characters like dead corpses, dealing out thereby his dullest dogmatisms in Ciceronian English, balancing himself with heavy self-conceit on the antitheses of his Latin periods, Garrick on the stage thrilled all the people of England, as he called with thrilling invocation the dead to life, that they might set forth to all their fearful, bloody or gay, and festive work. But Garrick loved the great poet, and as reward for that love he lies buried in Westminster near the pedestal of Shakespeare's statue, like a faithful dog at the feet of his master.

We are indebted to the celebrated Schröder for a transference of Garrick's acting to Germany. He also adapted several of Shakespeare's best dramas to the German stage. Like Garrick, Schröder understood neither the poetry nor art which is revealed in those dramas—he only cast an intelligent glance at the nature which expresses itself in them; nor did he so much attempt to reproduce the charming harmony and inner perfection of a piece, as to give the single characters with the most one-sided truth to nature. I am guided in this opinion by the traditions of his plays as they are preserved till today in the Hamburg theater, and also his "make up" of the dramas for the stage, in which all poetry and art are wiped out, and in which only a certain generally attainable naturalness and sharp outline of character appear to be developed by a combination of the most striking traits.

The method of the great Devrient [6] was developed out of this system of naturalness. I saw him once at Berlin at the same time with the great Wolf, who, however, in his play manifested a deeper feeling for art. But though they took opposite directions—one from nature, the other from art—both

[6] Heine is probably referring to Ludwig Devrient (1784–1832), a popular actor of the day and member of a famous theatrical family. Editor.

were one in poetry, and they thrilled or enraptured the souls of their audience by the most dissimilar methods.

The muses of music and of painting have done less than might have been expected to exalt Shakespeare. Were they envious of their sisters Melpomene and Thalia, who won their most immortal wreaths by means of the great Briton? With the exception of *Romeo and Juliet* and *Othello,* no play by Shakespeare has inspired any composer of any note to any great creation. The value of those sweetly sounding flowers which sprung from the exulting nightingale heart of Zingarelli [7] I need not praise, any more than those sweetest sounds with which the swan of Pesaro sung the bleeding tenderness of Desdemona, and the black flames of her lover! Painting, and especially the arts of design, have still more scantily sustained the fame of our poet. The so-called Shakespeare gallery in Pall Mall shows a good will, but at the same time the chilly weakness of British painters. There we see sober portrayals, quite in the spirit of the old French school, but without the taste which the latter never quite lost. There is something in which the English are as ridiculous bunglers as in music. That is, painting. Only in portraits have they shown the world anything remarkable, and when they execute them with the graver—not with colors—they surpass the artists of the rest of Europe. What can the cause be that the English, to whom sense of color is so scantily allotted, are still the most remarkable draftsmen and produce masterpieces of copper and steel engraving? That this last remark is true is shown by the portraits of Women and Maidens from the dramas of Shakespeare which are given with this work. Their superior excellence requires no comment, but the question or subject here is not of comment at all. These pages are only intended as a fleeting introduction or greeting to the delightful work, as use and custom go. I am the porter who opens this gallery to you, and what you have so far heard is only the rattling of my keys. And while I lead you round I shall often intrude a brief word of gossip on your reflections, and often imitate the

[7] Niccolo Zingarelli (1752–1837), an Italian composer who attained a brief popularity in his day. Editor.

cicerone who never allows a man to become too deeply inspired amid his own reflections while looking at a picture, and is ever ready with a trivial word to wake you from your contemplative dream.

In any case, I trust with this publication to cause some pleasure to my friends at home. May the sight of these beautiful women's faces drive from their brows the shadows, which at present have only too much cause to be there! Ah that I could offer you more substantial consolation than is afforded by these shadowy forms of beauty!—alas that I cannot give you the rosy reality! Once I would fain have broken the halberds with which the Gardens of Delight are guarded; but my hand was too weak, and the halberdiers laughed and thrust their points against my breast, and the too forward, great-souled heart was silent for shame, if it was not from fear. Ye sigh!

Desdemona (OTHELLO)

I have incidentally remarked in the foregoing paper that the character of Romeo has in it something of Hamlet. In fact, a Northern serious earnestness casts its side shadows on this glowing mind. And if we compare Juliet with Desdemona, the same Northern element appears in all the power of her passion; she is always self-conscious, and in clearest self-consciousness mistress of her deeds. Juliet loves and thinks and acts—Desdemona loves, feels, and obeys not her own will, but the stronger impulse. Her admirable excellence lies in this, that the bad can in no respect act on her noble nature like the good. She would certainly have remained in the palazzo of her father, a modest child fulfilling household duties; but the voice of the Moor was heard, and though she looked down she saw his countenance in his words, in his stories of his life, or, as she says, in his soul, and this suffering, magnanimous, beautiful white face of the soul wrought on her heart with irresistibly attracting magic. Yes, her father, the dignified and wise Brabantio, was quite in the right; she was so bound in chains of magic that the timid, tender child felt herself drawn to the Moor, and had no fear of the hideous black mask which the multitude regarded as the face of Othello.

Juliet's love is active, that of Desdemona passive. She is the sunflower, herself unconscious that her head is ever turned toward the high star of day. She is a true daughter of the South—tender, sensitive, patient, like those slender, great-eyed lights of women who beam so lovingly, so softly and dreamily, from the Sanskrit poems or plays. She ever reminds me of the *Sakuntala* of Kalidasa,[8] the Indian Shakespeare.

The English engraver to whom we are indebted for the present picture of Desdemona has given to her great eyes a somewhat too strong expression of passion. But I believe that I have already remarked that the contrast between face and character always has its peculiar charm. In any case this face is very fair, and it must specially please the writer of these pages that it recalls that noble and beautiful woman who, thank God!—never found any deep defect in his own face, and who as yet has only seen it in his soul.

OTHELLO. Her father loved me; oft invited me;
Still question'd me the story of my life,
From year to year, the battles, sieges, fortunes,
That I have pass'd.
I ran it through, even from my boyish days,
To the very moment that he bade me tell it;
Wherein I spake of most disastrous chances,
Of moving accidents by flood and field,
Of hair-breadth scapes i' the imminent deadly breach,
Of being taken by the insolent foe
And sold to slavery, of my redemption thence
And portance in my travels' history:
Wherein of antres vast and deserts idle,
Rough quarries, rocks and hills whose heads touch heaven,

[8] Kalidasa, about whom little is known, flourished supposedly 450 A.D. His extant dramas are *Sakuntala, Vikrama and Urvasi,* and *Agnimitra and Malavika,* a comedy. Editor.

It was my hint to speak,—such was the process;
And of the Cannibals that each other eat,
The Anthropophagi and men whose heads
Do grow beneath their shoulders. This to hear
Would Desdemona seriously incline:
But still the house-affairs would draw her thence:
Which ever as she could with haste dispatch,
She'ld come again, and with a greedy ear
Devour up my discourse: which I observing,
Took once a pliant hour, and found good means
To draw from her a prayer of earnest heart
That I would all my pilgrimage dilate,
Whereof by parcels she had something heard,
But not intentively: I did consent,
And often did beguile her of her tears,
When I did speak of some distressful stroke
That my youth suffer'd. My story being done,
She gave me for my pains a world of sighs:
She swore, in faith, 'twas strange, 'twas passing strange,
'Twas pitiful, 'twas wondrous pitiful:
She wish'd she had not heard it, yet she wish'd
That heaven had made her such a man: she thank'd me,
And bade me, if I had a friend that loved her,
I should but teach him how to tell my story,
And that would woo her. Upon this hint I spake:
She loved me for the dangers I had pass'd,
And I loved her that she did pity them.
This only is the witchcraft I have used:
Here comes the lady; let her witness it.

(I, iii, 128–170)

This tragedy is believed to be the last work of Shakespeare, as *Titus Andronicus* was the first. In both the love of a fair lady for an ugly Negro is treated with predilection. The man matured, returned to the problem which had busied his youth. Has he here found the solution of it? Is this solution as true as it is beautiful? A gloomy grieving seizes me when I give place to the thought that the honorable Iago, with his evil comments on the love of Desdemona for the Moor, is not all in the wrong. Most repulsive of all to me are Othello's remarks on the damp hand of his wife.

There is just such a marvelous and significant example of love for a Negro, such as we see in *Titus Andronicus* and *Othello,* in the Arabian Nights' Entertainments, where a beautiful princess, who is also a sorceress, keeps her husband bound in a statuelike immovability, and beats him daily with rods because he slew her Negro lover. Heart-rending are the wails of the princess over the bier of the black corpse, which she by her magic art keeps in a kind of apparent life and covers with the kisses of despair, and which she would fain, by the greater magic of love, wake from its twilight-dimmering half death to the full truth of life. Even as a boy I was struck in reading the Arabian tale with this picture of passionate and incomprehensible love.

Virgilia (CORIOLANUS)

She, the wife of Coriolanus, is a shy dove who dares not so much as coo in the presence of her overhaughty husband. When he returns victorious from the field, and all is exultation and loud rejoicing over him, she in humility looks down, and the smiling hero calls her "My gracious Silence!" In this silence lies her whole character; she is silent as the blushing rose, as the chaste pearl, as the yearning evening star, as the enraptured human heart—a perfect, precious, glowing silence, which tells more than eloquence, more than all rhetorical bombast. She is an ever mild and modest dame; and in her tender loveliness forms the clearest contrast to her mother-in-law, the Roman she-wolf Volumnia, who once suckled with her iron milk the wolf Caius Marcius. Yes, the latter is the real matron, and from her aristocratic nipples the young brood sucked nothing but wild self-will, unbridled defiance, and scorn of the people.

How a hero may win the laurel crown of fame from the early imbibing of such virtues and vices, but on the other hand lose the civic oaken wreath, and finally descending to the most atrocious crime, or treason to his native land, disgracefully perish, is shown by Shakespeare in his drama entitled *Coriolanus.*

After *Troilus and Cressida,* in which our poet took his material from the old Greek heroic time, I take up *Coriolanus,* because we here see how he understood treating Roman affairs. In this drama he sketches the partisan strife of the patricians and plebeians in ancient Rome.

I will not directly assert that this portrayal agrees exactly in every detail with the annals of Roman history; but our poet has understood and depicted the real life and nature of that strife with deepest truthfulness. We can judge of this the more accurately because our own times afford so many subjects which recall those of the troubled discord which once raged in old Rome between the privileged patricians and the degraded plebeians. We might often deem that Shakespeare was a poet of the present day, who lived in the London of our own life, sketching the Tories and Radicals of our own time disguised as Romans. What might confirm us in such a fancy is the great resemblance which really exists between the ancient Romans and modern Englishmen, and the statesmen of both races. In fact, a certain prosaic hardness, greed, love of blood, unwearying perseverance and firmness of character, is as peculiar to the English of today as to the old Romans, only that the latter were more land rats than water rats; but in the *unamiableness,* in which both attained the utmost height, they are perfectly equal and alike. The most striking elective affinity is to be observed between the nobility of both races. The English nobleman, like the same character of yore in Rome, is patriotic; love for his native land keeps him, in spite of all political-legal differences, intimately allied to the plebeian, and this sympathetic bond so brings it about that the English aristocrats and democrats, like the Romans before them, form one and a united race. In other countries where nobility is bound, less to the land than to the person of him who is their prince, or are devoted to the peculiar interests of their class, this is not the case. Then again we find among the English, as once among the Roman nobles, a striving toward established authority as the highest, most glorious, and also indirectly the most profitable—I say *indirectly* the most profitable, because, as once in Rome, so now in England, the management of the highest offices under government is made profitable only by misuse of influence and traditional exactions, that is to say, indirectly. Those offices are the aim of youthful education in the great families of England, just as they were among the Romans, and with the one as with the other, skill in war and oratory avail as the means to future position. So among the English, as it was among the Romans, the tradition of reigning and of administration is the hereditary endowment of noble families, and through this it may be that the English Tories will long be indispensable—yes, and so long in power as were the senatorial families of old Rome.

But nothing under present circumstances in England is so resemblant as the "soliciting suffrages," as we see it depicted in *Coriolanus.* With what bitter and restrained sourness, with what scornful irony, does the Roman Tory beg for the votes of the good citizens whom he so deeply despises in his soul, and whose approbation is to him so absolutely necessary that he may become consul. There being, however, this difference—that most English lords have got their wounds, not in battle but in fox-hunting, and being better trained by their mothers in the art of dissimulation, do not when electioneering manifest their ill-temper and scorn as did the stubborn Coriolanus.

As in all things, Shakespeare has exercised in this drama the strictest impartiality. The aristocrat is here quite in the right when he despises his plebeian masters of votes, for he feels that he was braver in war—such bravery being among the Romans the greatest virtue. Yet the poor electors, the people, are withal quite right in opposing him, despite this virtue, for he distinctly declared that as consul he would oppose giving bread to the people, although bread is the people's first right.

13. Aleksandr Sergeyevich Pushkin

1799–1837

Russian literary taste in the eighteenth and nineteenth centuries, like that of Italy, may be said to have been, by and large, pseudo-classical (e.g., such major figures as Derzhavin) and little more than a reflex of the Francophilia that dominated Russian intellectual life. And as the wind shifted in France so, too, one could notice a change in the Russian critical atmosphere. Under the influence of Madame de Staël, that indefatigable literary provocateur, *and of Victor Hugo (see below), younger writers like Zhukovski and Karamzin flocked to the banners of Romanticism. Theirs was not an easy allegiance to bestow. In 1817, the year that Pushkin left the Lyceum, one of the bitterest battles was being fought over the future literary language of Russia. One group, led by an admiral, favored Church Slavic over both the demotic language and the gallicisms of Karamzin. Pushkin aligned himself with the Karamzinists but soon went beyond them to favor the demotic.*

Throughout his brief life Pushkin acknowledged his debt to Byron and Shakespeare. At school he had read Boileau, Racine, Molière, and the other French classical writers. The English poets were the discovery of his young manhood and maturer years and with all the fervor one devotes to things self-discovered, Pushkin devoted himself to their study. The Byronic period was brief. After his return from his southern exile, a much deeper and more lasting influence, Shakespeare's, became noticeable. With an early fragment, O drame, *Pushkin had entered the Church Slavic vs. demotic controversy by stating his preference for the rough eloquence of Shakespeare's characters over the correct speech of Racine's. If such assertions were difficult for the followers of French taste to countenance, Pushkin's much bolder attack on Molière in the 1833 fragment* Shailok, Andzhelo i Falstaf Shekspira *was even harder to swallow. That fragment, perhaps conceived in the period during which Pushkin was at work on his* Boris Godunov *(1825), a drama full of Shakespearean effects, is remarkable for the insight it gives the reader to Pushkin's preoccupations at the time. The detailed attention to the delineation of the hypocritical characters in Shakespeare and Molière might almost be notes to guide Pushkin toward his conception of the master hypocrite, Shuiski, in* Boris. *Whether or not the following fragment was conceived during the* Boris *period and kept among notes until its inclusion in the* Table-talk *under the date of 1833 is unimportant. It remains as one of the few direct statements about Shakespeare's dramatic sense by the one poet important and excellent enough to have used him to free Russian drama from its staleness and French tyranny.*

FROM Shylock, Angelo, and Falstaff

Shakespeare's characters are not, like Molière's, the personification of one certain passion or vice. They are living beings imbued with many passions, many vices; their variegated and multiple characters evolve before the spectator by the force of circumstance. Molière's miser is miserly—and no more; Shakespeare's Shylock is miserly, shrewd, vengeful, child-loving, and witty. Molière's hypocrite courts his benefactor's wife—hypocritically; assumes guardianship over the estate—hypocritically; asks for a glass of water—hypocritically. Shakespeare's hypocrite pronounces sentences with vain severity, but in accordance with justice; he justifies his cruelty by the grave considerations of a statesman; he tempts innocence

From *Shailok, Andzhelo i Falstaf Shekspira,* reprinted from Pushkin's *Polnoe Sobranie Sochineni v Shesti Tomakh* (Works in Six Volumes), 2nd edition (Moscow, Gosudarstvennoe Izdatelstvo Khudozhestvennoi Literatury, 1934), Vol. VI, pp. 340–342. Translated by the editor.

with powerful and luring sophistry, not with a funny mixture of piety and flirtation. Angelo is a hypocrite because his overt actions contradict his secret passions. What depth there is in his character!

Yet nowhere, perhaps, is Shakespeare's versatile genius so richly fulfilled as in the character of Falstaff, whose vices, when considered in totality, constitute a funny, horrid chain, resembling an ancient bacchanal. An analysis of Falstaff's character shows us that its foundation is sensuousness. Probably since his youth, coarse, cheap wooing has been his chief preference. But now, in his fifties, he is obese and frail; gluttony and wine have discharged him from the service of Venus. Furthermore, he is a coward: but spending his life with young rakes, the constant target of their jests and bidding, he conceals his cowardice under crafty and derisive audacity: he is boastful from habit and plan. But Falstaff is never stupid; he even displays a few of the manners of a person who occasionally has been present in the best society. He is a stranger to principles. He is weak, like an old woman. His chief necessities are strong Spanish wine (the sack), a prodigious lunch, and money for his mistresses: and he will do anything at all to come by them, so long as no bodily harm is involved in it.

14. Victor Marie Hugo

1802–1885

Stendhal's Racine et Shakespeare *(see above) had ushered in a new period in French Shakespeare appreciation. Four years later, in 1827, a group led by Edmund Kean began to offer Shakespeare in English to Parisians. The result was electrifying. French literati crowded the theater. If any nostalgia for classicism had still been lurking in the corners of French taste it was about to receive its* coup de grâce *from Victor Hugo.*

Young and flamboyant, attached to the Romantic creed by the natural dispositions of his personality, Hugo issued his preface to Cromwell *in 1827, a preface which became the manifesto of the new movement. This movement, in whose ranks were de Vigny, Dumas, de Musset, and more of the best writers of the period as well as such artists as Delacroix and Berlioz, seemed as though it were about to divert centuries of critical theory and literary taste from their common course. It seemed, too, for a time, as though the "Shakespearomanie" had come to France. Translations followed translations. No director could make his reputation without having done Shakespeare. The mark of an actor's ability became his creation of a Shakespearean role. Even the newspapers of the day reflect the new attitude. It was, however, primarily an emotional one and it was this which distinguished it from the* anglomanie *of the previous century. It was at this time that it became abundantly clear that no serious French critic would ever again question the supremacy of Shakespeare among modern writers.*

But if this period of enthusiasm was passionate it was also brief. By the end of the fourth decade of the century Romantic theory was moving in a new direction. The Shakespeare fever had passed. He was no longer the subject of controversy, and critics such as Guizot and Mézières, while still admiring, could devote themselves to the serious study of his work and times without having to defend their desire to do so.

Some older writers like Hugo remained true to the enthusiasms of their youth and in 1864 the poet published his William Shakespeare. *The book has all the fervor of the earlier preface. Hugo expands his youthful remarks and reasserts his opinions. Published originally as an accompaniment to the Shakespeare translations of the poet's son, François Victor Hugo, the book is one of the last extended professions of the Romantic faith by a French writer of the nineteenth century. One need only look at the work of Taine (see below) to realize that a reaction to Romanticism had begun.*

FROM William Shakespeare

EXCERPT FROM PART II, BOOK II, CHAPTER 5

Shakespeare's Work

One of the probable causes of the feigned madness of Hamlet has not been, up to the present time, indicated by critics. It has been said, "Hamlet acts the madman to hide his thought, like Brutus." In fact, it is easy for apparent imbecility to hatch a great project; the supposed idiot can take aim deliberately. But the case of Brutus is not that of Hamlet. Hamlet acts the madman for his safety. Brutus screens his project, Hamlet his person. Given the manners of those tragic courts, from the moment that, through the revelation of the ghost, Hamlet is acquainted with the crime of Claudius, he is in danger. The superior historian within the poet is manifested, and one feels the deep insight of Shakespeare into the darkness of the ancient royalty. In the Middle Ages and in the Eastern Empire,

From Hugo's *William Shakespeare* (Chicago, A. C. McClurg and Company, 1906), pp. 234–240, 274–277. Translated by Melville B. Anderson.

and even at earlier periods, woe unto him who found out a murder or a poisoning committed by a king! Ovid, according to Voltaire's conjecture, was exiled from Rome for having seen something shameful in the house of Augustus. To know that the king was an assassin was a state crime. When it pleased the prince not to have had a witness, it was a matter of life and death to know nothing; it was bad policy to have good eyes. A man suspected of suspicion was lost. He had but one refuge, madness, to pass for "an innocent"; he was despised, and that was all. You remember the advice that, in Aeschylus, the Ocean gives to Prometheus: "To seem mad is the secret of the sage." When the Chamberlain Hugolin found the iron spit with which Edric of Mercia had impaled Edmund II,[1] "he hastened to put on madness," says the Saxon chronicle of 1016, and saved himself in that way. Heraclides of Nisbis, having discovered by chance that Rhinometer was a fratricide, had himself declared insane by the doctors, and succeeded in getting himself shut up for life in a cloister. He thus lived peaceably, growing old, and waiting for death with a vacant stare. Hamlet runs the same risk, and has recourse to the same means. He gets himself declared insane like Heraclides, and puts on madness like Hugolin. This does not prevent the uneasy Claudius from twice making an effort to get rid of him—in the middle of the drama by the ax or the dagger, and toward the end by poison.

The same indication is again found in *King Lear:* the Earl of Gloucester's son takes refuge also in apparent lunacy. Herein is a key to open and understand Shakespeare's thought. To the eyes of the philosophy of Art, the feigned madness of Edgar throws light upon the feigned madness of Hamlet.

The Hamblet of Belleforest is a magician; the Hamlet of Shakespeare is a philosopher. We just now spoke of the singular reality which characterizes poetical creations. There is no more striking example than this type, Hamlet. Hamlet is not

[1] E. A. Freeman states: "The chronicles are silent as to the manner of Eadmund's death."—*History of the Norman Conquest* (London, 1867–1879), Vol. I, p. 470. Freeman makes no mention of the story of Hugolin, hence I would doubt the tradition on which Hugo is relying. Editor.

in the least an abstraction. He has been at the university; he has the Danish savageness softened by the Italian politeness; he fences well, but is soon out of breath; he is short, plump, somewhat lymphatic. He does not care to drink too soon during the fencing bout with Laertes—probably for fear of sweating. After having thus supplied his personage with real life, the poet can launch him into the full ideal; there is ballast enough.

Other works of the human mind equal *Hamlet;* none surpasses it. There is in *Hamlet* all the majesty of the mournful. A drama issuing from an open sepulcher—this is colossal. *Hamlet* is to our mind Shakespeare's capital work.

No figure among those that poets have created is more poignant and more disquieting. Doubt counseled by a ghost—such is Hamlet. Hamlet has seen his dead father and has spoken to him. Is he convinced? No; he shakes his head. What shall he do? He does not know. His hands clench, then fall by his side. Within him are conjectures, systems, monstrous apparitions, bloody recollections, veneration for the ghost, hate, tenderness, anxiety to act and not to act, his father, his mother, conflicting duties—a profound storm. His mind is occupied with ghastly hesitation. Shakespeare, wonderful plastic poet, makes the grandiose pallor of this soul almost visible. Like the great specter of Albrecht Dürer, Hamlet might be named "Melancholia." Above his head, too, there flits the disemboweled bat; at his feet are science, the sphere, the compass, the hourglass, love; and behind him, at the horizon, a great and terrible sun, which seems to make the sky but darker.

Nevertheless, at least one-half of Hamlet is anger, transport, outrage, hurricane, sarcasm to Ophelia, malediction on his mother, insult to himself. He talks with the gravediggers, almost laughs, then clutches Laertes by the hair in the very grave of Ophelia, and tramples furiously upon that coffin. Sword-thrusts at Polonius, sword-thrusts at Laertes, sword-thrusts at Claudius. At times his inaction gapes open, and from the rent, thunderbolts flash out.

He is tormented by that possible life, interwoven of reality and dream, concerning which we are all anxious. Somnambulism is diffused through all his actions. One might almost consider his brain as a formation: there is a layer of suffering, a layer of thought, then a layer of dream. It is through this layer of dream that he feels, comprehends, learns, perceives, drinks, eats, frets, mocks, weeps, and reasons. There is between life and him a transparency—the wall of dreams; one sees beyond it, but one cannot step over it. A kind of cloudy obstacle everywhere surrounds Hamlet. Have you never, while sleeping, had the nightmare of pursuit or flight, and tried to hasten on, and felt the ankylosis of your knees, the heaviness of your arms, the horrible paralysis of your benumbed hands? This nightmare Hamlet suffers while awake. Hamlet is not upon the spot where his life is. He has ever the air of a man who talks to you from the other side of a stream. He calls to you at the same time that he questions you. He is at a distance from the catastrophe in which he moves, from the passer-by he questions, from the thought he bears, from the action he performs. He seems not to touch even what he crushes. This is isolation carried to its highest power. It is the loneliness of a mind, even more than the unapproachableness of a prince. Indecision is, in fact, a solitude; you have not even your will to keep you company. It is as if your own self had departed and had left you there. The burden of Hamlet is less rigid than that of Orestes; it fits patter to his form: Orestes bears fatality, Hamlet destiny.[2]

And thus, apart from men, Hamlet still has within him an undefined something which represents them all. *Agnosco fratrem.* If at certain hours we felt our own pulse, we should be conscious of his fever. His strange reality is our own reality, after all. He is the mournful man that we all are in certain situations. Unhealthy as he is, Hamlet expresses a permanent condition of man. He represents the discomfort of the soul in a life unsuited to it. He represents the shoe that pinches

[2] The remarkable thing about this passage is that Hugo is dealing with the two characters as archetypes, an approach which anticipates Gilbert Murray. Cf. "Hamlet and Orestes" (the annual Shakespeare Lecture, 1914) in revised form in Murray, *The Classical Tradition in Poetry* (Cambridge, Mass., 1927; New York, 1957), especially pp. 180, 206. Editor.

and stops our walking: this shoe is the body. Shakespeare delivers him from it, and rightly. Hamlet—prince if you like, but king never—is incapable of governing a people, so wholly apart from all does he exist. On the other hand, he does better than to reign; he *is*. Take from him his family, his country, his ghost, the whole adventure at Elsinore, and even in the form of an inactive type he remains strangely terrible. This results from the amount of humanity and the amount of mystery in him. Hamlet is formidable—which does not prevent his being ironical. He has the two profiles of destiny.

Let us retract a word said above. The capital work of Shakespeare is not *Hamlet:* the capital work of Shakespeare is all Shakespeare. This is, moreover, true of all minds of this order. They are mass, block, majesty, Bible; and their unity is what renders them impressive.

Have you ever gazed upon a beclouded headland running out beyond eyeshot into the deep sea? Each of its hills contributes to its make-up. No one of its undulations is lost upon it. Its bold outline is sharply marked upon the sky, and juts far out amid the waves; and there is not a useless rock. Thanks to this cape, you can go amidst the boundless waters, walk among the winds, see closely the eagles soar and the monsters swim, let your humanity wander in the eternal uproar, penetrate the impenetrable. The poet renders this service to your mind. A genius is a headland into the infinite.

EXCERPT FROM PART II, BOOK IV, CHAPTER 1

Criticism

All Shakespeare's plays, with the exception of *Macbeth* and *Romeo and Juliet*—thirty-four plays out of thirty-six—offer to the observer one peculiarity which seems to have escaped, up to this day, the most eminent commentators and critics; one which is unnoticed by the Schlegels, and even by M. Villemain[3] himself, in his remarkable labors, and of which it is

[3] Abel François Villemain (1790–1870) had a high reputation for being a perspicuous literary critic, with a highly polished style. Editor.

impossible not to speak. It is the double action which traverses the drama and reflects it on a small scale. Beside the tempest in the Atlantic is the tempest in the teacup. Thus, Hamlet makes beneath himself a Hamlet; he kills Polonius, father of Laertes—and there stands Laertes over against him exactly as he stands over against Claudius. There are two fathers to avenge. There might be two ghosts. So, in *King Lear*, side by side and simultaneously, Lear, driven to despair by his daughters Goneril and Regan, and consoled by his Cordelia, is repeated in Gloucester, betrayed by his son Edmund and loved by his son Edgar. The idea bifurcated, the idea echoing itself, a lesser drama copying and elbowing the principal drama, the action attended by its moon—a smaller action like it—unity cut in two; surely the fact is a strange one. These double actions have been strongly condemned by the few commentators who have pointed them out. In this condemnation we do not sympathize. Do we then approve and accept as good these double actions? By no means. We recognize them, and that is all. The drama of Shakespeare—as we said with all our force as far back as 1827 [4] in order to discourage all imitation—the drama of Shakespeare is peculiar to Shakespeare; it is a drama inherent in this poet; it is his own essence; it is himself. Thence his originalities, which are absolutely personal; thence his idiosyncrasies, which exist without establishing a law.

These double actions are purely Shakespearean. Neither Aeschylus nor Molière would admit them; and we should certainly agree with Aeschylus and Molière.

These double actions are, moreover, the sign of the sixteenth century. Each epoch has its own mysterious stamp. The centuries have a signature which they affix to masterpieces, and which it is necessary to know how to decipher and recognize. The signature of the sixteenth century is not that of the eighteenth. The Renaissance was a subtle time, a time of reflection. The spirit of the sixteenth century was reflected in a mirror. Every idea of the Renaissance has a double compartment. Look at the rood lofts in the churches. The Renaissance,

[4] Hugo is referring to his famous preface to *Cromwell*. Editor.

with an exquisite and fantastical art, always makes the Old Testament an adumbration of the New. The double action is there in everything. The symbol explains the personage by repeating his gesture. If, in a bas-relief, Jehovah sacrifices his son, he has for a neighbor, in the next bas-relief, Abraham sacrificing his son. Jonah passes three days in the whale, and Jesus passes three days in the sepulcher; and the jaws of the monster swallowing Jonah answer to the mouth of hell engulfing Jesus.

The carver of the rood loft of Fécamp, so stupidly demolished, goes so far as to give for a counterpart to St. Joseph—whom?—Amphitryon.

These singular parallels constitute one of the habits of the profound and far-sought art of the sixteenth century. Nothing can be more curious in that manner than the use which was made of St. Christopher. In the Middle Ages and in the sixteenth century, in paintings and sculptures, St. Christopher—the good giant martyred by Decius in 250, recorded by the Bollandists, and accepted imperturbably by Baillet [5] is always triple, an opportunity for the triptych. To begin with, there is a first Christ-bearer, a first Christophorus; this is Christopher with the infant Jesus on his shoulders. Next, the Virgin with child is a Christopher, since she carries Christ. Lastly, the cross is a Christopher; it also carries Christ. This treble illustration of the idea is immortalized by Rubens in the cathedral of Antwerp. The twin idea, the triple idea—such is the stamp of the sixteenth century.

Shakespeare, faithful to the spirit of his time, must needs add Laertes avenging his father to Hamlet avenging his father, and cause Hamlet to be pursued by Laertes at the same time that Claudius is pursued by Hamlet; he must needs make the filial piety of Edgar a comment on the filial piety of Cordelia, and bring out in contrast, weighed down by the ingratitude of unnatural children, two wretched fathers, each bereaved of one of the two kinds of light—Lear mad, and Gloucester blind.

[5] Adrien Baillet (1649–1706) was a French writer, scholar, and minor historian. Editor.

15. Ivan Sergeyevich Turgenev

1818–1883

In Russia, by the end of the 1840s, the satirical naturalism of Gogol combined with an older sentimental realism revived by the influential George Sand to produce what has come to be known as the Russian "realistic" novel. Among its chief practitioners was Ivan Turgenev.

Turgenev's Western education, sympathies, and long residence have frequently caused critics to overlook the thoroughly Russian nature of his work. It is the Russia of the thirties and forties that finds its expression in A Sportsman's Sketches *(1852),* Rudin *(1856),* A House of Gentlefolk *(1859),* On the Eve *(1860), and his finest novel,* Fathers and Sons *(1862).*

The realistic writers were no longer interested in Shakespeare's imaginative genius or in the problem of unities. These questions had been foremost for the Romantic critics, but "realism" was predominantly the art of the novel and the novel was concerning itself with a new concept of society. The Romantic idealism had, in Russia, deteriorated by Turgenev's time to social paralysis covered by Utopian rhetoric. Rudin, the hero of Turgenev's first full novel, typifies the self-conscious, introspective idealist who is ultimately ineffective. He was a hero who dissatisfied his author. In On the Eve *Turgenev turned from the type and created the Bulgarian, Insanov. The new hero, although ultimately lifeless, was strong-willed, single-minded, courageous, and willing to act even in the face of ridicule. Insanov is clearly the predecessor of Bazarov in* Fathers and Sons.

In the same year that he had written On the Eve *Turgenev gave his famous lecture* Hamlet and Don Quixote—The Two Eternal Human Types. *Although little read in English, the essay is in Europe considered a classic of nineteenth-century criticism. It is rarely reproduced in English and is not included in either of the standard editions of Turgenev in that language. The address is here given in full, except that some of the prefatory and concluding remarks, intended for hearers rather than readers, have been omitted.*

Turgenev saw that the Russia of his day was faced with the dilemma that thought and the will to action had become separated from one another in the best minds. He believed that a synthesis of the two was needed before social change would be possible. Turgenev's essay is concerned less with Shakespeare and Cervantes than with the implications for society of their characters.

Hamlet and Don Quixote—The Two Eternal Human Types

The first edition of Shakespeare's tragedy *Hamlet* and the first part of Cervantes' *Don Quixote* appeared in the same year at the very beginning of the seventeenth century.

This coincidence seems to me significant. . . . It seems to me that in these two types are embodied two opposite fundamental peculiarities of man's nature—the two ends of the axis about which it turns. I think that all people belong, more or less, to one of these two types; that nearly every one of us resembles either Don Quixote or Hamlet. In our day, it is true, the Hamlets have become far more numerous than the Don Quixotes, but the Don Quixotes have not become extinct.

Let me explain.

All people live—consciously or unconsciously—on the strength of their principles, their ideals; that is, by virtue of what they regard as truth, beauty, and goodness. Many get their ideals all ready-made, in definite, historically developed forms. They live trying to square their lives with this ideal, deviating from

From *Current Literature*, Number 42, January 1907 (London), pp. 290–293, 349–352. Translated by David A. Modell.

it at times, under the influence of passions or incidents, but neither reasoning about it nor questioning it. Others, on the contrary, subject it to the analysis of their own reason. Be this as it may, I think I shall not err too much in saying that for all people this ideal—this basis and aim of their existence—is to be found either outside of them or within them; in other words, for every one of us it is either his own "I" that forms the primary consideration or something else which he considers superior. I may be told that reality does not permit of such sharp demarcations; that in the very same living being both considerations may alternate, even becoming fused to a certain extent. But I do not mean to affirm the impossibility of change and contradiction in human nature; I wish merely to point out two different attitudes of man to his ideal. And now I will endeavor to show in what way, to my mind, these two different relations are embodied in the two types I have selected.

Let us begin with Don Quixote.

What does Don Quixote represent? We shall not look at him with the cursory glance that stops at superficialities and trifles. We shall not see in Don Quixote merely "the Knight of the sorrowful figure"—a figure created for the purpose of ridiculing the old-time romances of knighthood. It is known that the meaning of this character had expanded under its immortal creator's own hand, and that the Don Quixote of the second part of the romance is an amiable companion to dukes and duchesses, a wise preceptor to the squire-governor—no longer the Don Quixote he appears in the first part, especially at the beginning of the work; not the odd and comical crank, who is constantly belabored by a rain of blows. I will endeavor, therefore, to go to the very heart of the matter. I repeat: What does Don Quixote represent?

Faith, in the first place; faith in something eternal, immutable; faith in the truth, in short, existing *outside* of the individual, which cannot easily be attained by him, but which is attainable only by constant devotion and the power of self-abnegation. Don Quixote is entirely consumed with devotion to his ideal, for the sake of which he is ready to suffer every possible privation and to sacrifice his life; his life itself he values only insofar as it can become a means for the incarnation of the ideal, for the establishment of truth and justice on earth. I may be told that this ideal is borrowed by his disordered imagination from the fanciful world of knightly romance. Granted—and this makes up the comical side of Don Quixote; but the ideal itself remains in all its immaculate purity. To live for oneself, to care for oneself, Don Quixote would consider shameful. He lives—if I may so express myself—outside of himself, entirely for others, for his brethren, in order to abolish evil, to counteract the forces hostile to mankind—wizards, giants, in a word, the oppressors. There is no trace of egotism in him; he is not concerned with himself, he is wholly a self-sacrifice—appreciate this word; he believes, believes firmly, and without circumspection. Therefore is he fearless, patient, content with the humblest fare, with the poorest clothes—what cares he for such things! Timid of heart, he is in spirit great and brave; his touching piety does not restrict his freedom; a stranger to variety, he doubts not himself, his vocation, or even his physical prowess; his will is indomitable. The constant aiming after the same end imparts a certain monotonousness to his thoughts and one-sidedness to his mind. He knows little, but need not know much; he knows what he is about, why he exists on earth—and this is the chief sort of knowledge. Don Quixote may seem to be either a perfect madman, since the most indubitable materialism vanishes before his eyes, melts like tallow before the fire of his enthusiasm (he really does see living Moors in the wooden puppets, and knights in the sheep); or shallow-minded, because he is unable lightly to sympathize or lightly to enjoy; but, like an ancient tree, he sends his roots deep into the soil, and can neither change his convictions nor pass from one subject to another. The stronghold of his moral constitution (note that this demented, wandering knight is everywhere and on all occasions the moral being) lends especial weight and dignity to all his judgments and speeches, to his whole figure, despite the ludicrous and humiliating situations into which he endlessly falls. Don Quixote is an enthusiast, a servant of an idea, and therefore is illuminated by its radiance.

Now what does Hamlet represent?

Analysis, first of all, and egotism, and therefore incredulity. He lives entirely for himself; he is an egotist. But even an egotist cannot believe in himself. We can only believe in that which is outside of and above ourselves. But this I, in which he does not believe, is dear to Hamlet. This is the point of departure, to which he constantly returns, because he finds nothing in the whole universe to which he can cling with all his heart. He is a skeptic, and always pothers about himself; he is ever busy, not with his duty, but with his condition. Doubting everything, Hamlet, of course, spares not himself; his mind is too much developed to be satisfied with what he finds within himself. He is conscious of his weakness; but even this self-consciousness is power; from it comes his irony, in contrast with the enthusiasm of Don Quixote. Hamlet delights in excessive self-depreciation. Constantly concerned with himself, always a creature of introspection, he knows minutely all his faults, scorns himself, and at the same time lives, so to speak, nourished by this scorn. He has no faith in himself, yet is vainglorious; he knows not what he wants nor why he lives, yet is attached to life. He exclaims:

> Or that the Everlasting had not fix'd
> His canon 'gainst self-slaughter! O God! God!
> Most weary, stale, flat and unprofitable,
> Seem to me all the uses of this world!
>
> (I, ii, 131–134)

But he will not sacrifice this flat and unprofitable life. He contemplates suicide even before he sees his father's ghost, and receives the awful commission which breaks down completely his already weakened will—but he does not take his life. The love of life is expressed in the very thought of terminating it. Every youth of eighteen is familiar with such feelings as this: "When the blood boils, how prodigal the soul!"

I will not be too severe with Hamlet. He suffers, and his sufferings are more painful and galling than those of Don Quixote. The latter is pummeled by rough shepherds and convicts whom he has liberated; Hamlet inflicts his own wounds—teases himself. In his hands, too, is a lance—the two-edged lance of self-analysis.

Don Quixote, I must confess, is positively funny. His figure is perhaps the most comical that ever poet has drawn. His name has become a mocking nickname even on the lips of Russian peasants. Of this our own ears could convince us. The mere memory of him raises in our imagination a figure gaunt, angular, rugged-nosed, clad in caricature armor, and mounted on the withered skeleton of the pitiable Rosinante, a poor, starved and beaten nag, to whom we cannot deny a semi-amusing and semi-pathetic co-operation. Don Quixote makes us laugh, but there is a conciliatory and redeeming power in this laughter; and if the adage be true, "You may come to worship what you now deride," then I may add: Whom you have ridiculed, you have already forgiven—are even ready to love.

Hamlet's appearance, on the contrary, is attractive. His melancholia; his pale though not lean aspect (his mother remarks that he is stout, saying, "Our son is fat"); his black velvet clothes, the feather crowning his hat; his elegant manners, the unmistakable poetry of his speeches; his steady feeling of complete superiority over others, alongside of the biting humor of his self-denunciation—everything about him pleases, everything captivates. Everybody flatters himself on passing for a Hamlet. None would like to acquire the appellation of "Don Quixote." "Hamlet Baratynski," [1] wrote Pushkin to his friend. No one ever thought of laughing at Hamlet, and herein lies his condemnation. To love him is almost impossible; only people like Horatio become attached to Hamlet. Of these I will speak later. Everyone sympathizes with Hamlet, and the reason is obvious: nearly everyone finds in Hamlet his own traits; but to love him is, I repeat, impossible, because he himself does not love anyone.

Let us continue our comparison.

[1] Jewgenij Abramovich Baratynski (1800–1844), a Russian lyric poet, was a contemporary and successful follower of Pushkin. Such poems as "Eda" and "The Gypsy" exhibited the melancholy which occasioned Pushkin's comment. Editor.

Hamlet is the son of a king, murdered by his own brother, the usurper of the throne; his father comes forth from the grave—from "the jaws of Hades"—to charge Hamlet to avenge him; but the latter hesitates, keeps on quibbling with himself, finds consolation in self-depreciation, and finally kills his stepfather by chance.

A deep psychological feature, for which many wise but short-sighted persons have ventured to censure Shakespeare! And Don Quixote, a poor man, almost destitute, without means or connections, old and lonely, undertakes the task of destroying evil and protecting the oppressed (total strangers to him) all over the world. It matters not that his first attempt to free innocence from the oppressor brings redoubled suffering upon the head of innocence. (I have in mind that scene in which Don Quixote saves an apprentice from a drubbing by his master, who, as soon as the deliverer is gone, punishes the poor boy with tenfold severity.) It matters not that, in his crusades against harmful giants, Don Quixote attacks useful windmills. The comical setting of these pictures should not distract our eyes from their hidden meaning. The man who sets out to sacrifice himself with careful forethought and consideration of all the consequences—balancing all the probabilities of his acts proving beneficial—is hardly capable of self-sacrifice. Nothing of the kind can happen to Hamlet; it is not for him, with his penetrative, keen, and skeptical mind, to fall into so gross an error. No, he will not wage war on windmills; he does not believe in giants, and would not attack them if they did exist. We cannot imagine Hamlet exhibiting to each and all a barber's bowl, and maintaining, as Don Quixote does, that it is the real magic helmet of Mambrin. I suppose that, were truth itself to appear incarnate before his eyes, Hamlet would still have misgivings as to whether it really was the truth. For who knows but that truth, too, is perhaps non-existent, like giants? We laugh at Don Quixote, but, my dear sirs, which of us, after having conscientiously interrogated himself, and taken into account his past and present convictions, will make bold to say that he always, under all circumstances, can distinguish a barber's pewter bowl from a magic golden helmet? It seems to me, therefore, that the principal thing in life is the sincerity and strength of our convictions—the result lies in the hands of fate. This alone can show us whether we have been contending with phantoms or real foes, and with what armor we covered our heads. Our business is to arm ourselves and fight.

Remarkable are the attitudes of the mob, the so-called mass of the people, toward Hamlet and Don Quixote. In *Hamlet* Polonius, in *Don Quixote* Sancho Panza, symbolize the populace.

Polonius is an old man—active, practical, sensible, but at the same time narrow-minded and garrulous. He is an excellent chamberlain and an exemplary father. (Recollect his instructions to his son, Laertes, when going abroad—instructions which vie in wisdom with certain orders issued by Governor Sancho Panza on the Island of Barataria.) To Polonius Hamlet is not so much a madman as a child. Were he not a king's son, Polonius would despise him because of his utter uselessness and the impossibility of making a positive and practical application of his ideas. The famous cloud scene, the scene where Hamlet imagines he is mocking the old man, has an obvious significance, confirming this theory. I take the liberty of recalling it to you:

POLONIUS: My lord, the queen would speak with you, and presently.
HAMLET: Do you see yonder cloud that's almost in shape of a camel?
POLONIUS: By the mass, and 'tis like a camel, indeed
HAMLET: Methinks it is like a weasel.
POLONIUS: It is backed like a weasel.
HAMLET: Or like a whale?
POLONIUS: Very like a whale.
HAMLET: Then will I come to my mother by and by.
(III, ii, 391–402)

Is it not evident that in this scene Polonius is at the same time a courtier who humors the prince and an adult who would not cross a sickly, capricious boy? Polonius does not in the least believe Hamlet, and he is right. With all his natural, narrow presumptiveness, he ascribes Hamlet's capriciousness to his love for Ophelia, in which he is, of course, mistaken, but he makes no mistake in understanding Hamlet's character. The Hamlets are really useless to the people; they give it nothing, they cannot lead it anywhere, since they themselves are bound for nowhere. And, besides, how can one lead when he doubts the very ground he treads upon? Moreover, the Hamlets detest the masses. How can a man who does not respect himself respect any one or anything else? Besides, is it really worth while to bother about the masses? They are so rude and filthy! And much more than birth alone goes to make Hamlet an aristocrat.

An entirely different spectacle is presented by Sancho Panza. He laughs at Don Quixote, knows full well that he is demented; yet thrice forsakes the land of his birth, his home, wife, and daughter, that he may follow this crazy man; follows him everywhere, undergoes all sorts of hardships, is devoted to him to his very death, believes him and is proud of him, then weeps, kneeling at the humble pallet where his master breathes his last. Hope of gain or ultimate advantage cannot account for this devotion. Sancho Panza has too much good sense. He knows very well that the page of a wandering knight has nothing save beatings to expect. The cause of his devotion must be sought deeper. It finds its root (if I may so put it) in what is perhaps the cardinal value of the people—in its capability of a blissful and honest blindness (alas! it is familiar with other forms of blindness), the capability of disinterested enthusiasm, the disregard of direct personal advantages, which to a poor man is almost equivalent to scorn for his daily bread. A great, universally historic virtue!

The masses of the people invariably end by following, in blind confidence, the very persons they themselves have mocked, or even cursed and persecuted. They give allegiance to those who fear neither curses nor persecution—nor even ridicule—but who go straight ahead, their spiritual gaze directed toward the goal which they alone see—who seek, fall, and rise, and ultimately find. And rightly so; only he who is led by the heart reaches the ultimate goal. "*Les grandes pensées viennent du coeur,*" said Vovenarg. And the Hamlets find nothing, invent nothing, and leave no trace behind them, save that of their own personality—no achievements whatsoever. They neither love nor believe, and what can they find? Even in chemistry—not to speak of organic nature—in order that a third substance may be obtained, there must be a combination of two others; but the Hamlets are concerned with themselves alone—they are lonely, and therefore barren.

"But," you will interpose, "how about Ophelia—does not Hamlet love her?"

I shall speak of her, and, incidentally, of Dulcinea.

In their relations to woman, too, our two types present much that is noteworthy.

Don Quixote loves Dulcinea, a woman who exists only in his own imagination, and is ready to die for her. (Recall his words when, vanquished and bruised, he says to the conqueror, who stands over him with a spear: "Stab me, Sir Knight . . . Dulcinea del Toboso is the most beautiful woman in the world, and I the most unfortunate knight on earth. It is not fit that my weakness should lessen the glory of Dulcinea.") He loves purely, ideally; so ideally that he does not even suspect that the object of his passion does not exist at all; so purely that, when Dulcinea appears before him in the guise of a rough and dirty peasant woman, he trusts not the testimony of his eyes, and regards her as transformed by some evil wizard.

I myself have seen in my life, on my wanderings, people who laid down their lives for equally nonexistent Dulcineas or for a vulgar and oftentimes filthy something or other, in which they saw the realization of their ideal, and whose transformation they likewise attributed to evil—I almost said bewitching—events and persons. I have seen them, and when their like shall cease to exist, then let the book of history be closed forever: there will be nothing in it to read about. Of sensuality there is not even a trace in Don Quixote. All his thoughts are chaste and innocent, and in the secret depths of his heart he hardly hopes for an ultimate union with Dulcinea—indeed, he almost dreads such a union.

And does Hamlet really love? Has his ironic creator, a most profound judge of the human heart, really determined to give this egotist, this skeptic, saturated with every decomposing poison of self-analysis, a loving and devout heart? Shakespeare did not fall into the contradiction; and it does not cost the attentive reader much pains to convince himself that Hamlet is a sensual man, and even secretly voluptuous. (It is not for nothing that the courtier Rosencrantz smiles slyly when Hamlet says in his hearing that he is tired of women.) Hamlet does not love, I say, but only pretends—and mawkishly—that he loves. On this we have the testimony of Shakespeare himself. In the first scene of the third act Hamlet says to Ophelia: "I did love you once." Then ensues the colloquy:

OPHELIA: Indeed, my lord, you made me believe so.
HAMLET: You should not have believed me . . . I loved you not.
(III, i, 115–120)

And having uttered this last word, Hamlet is much nearer the truth than he supposed. His feelings for Ophelia—an innocent creature, pure as a saintess—are either cynical (recollect his words, his equivocal allusions, when, in the scene representing the theater, he asks her permission to lie . . . in her lap), or else hollow (direct your attention to the scene between him and Laertes, when Hamlet jumps into Ophelia's grave and says, in language worthy of Bramarbas [2] or of Captain Pistol: "Forty thousand brothers could not, with all their quantity of love, make up my sum. . . . Let them throw millions of acres on us," etc. V, i, 292–303).

All his relations with Ophelia are for Hamlet only the occasions for preoccupation with his own self, and in his exclamation, "Nymph! in thy orisons be all my sins remember'd!" (III, i, 88–89) we see but the deep consciousness of his own sickly inanition, a lack of strength to love, on the part of the almost superstitious worshiper before "the Saintess of Chastity."

But enough has been said of the dark sides of the Hamlet type, of those phases which irritate us most because they are nearer and more familiar to us. I will endeavor to appreciate

[2] An expression denoting a braggart that derives from Ludwig von Holberg's (1684–1754) play *Jakob von Thyboe* (1723), whose chief character, named Bramarbas, is a boastful officer. Editor.

whatever may be legitimate in him, and therefore enduring. Hamlet embodies the doctrine of negation, that same doctrine which another great poet has divested of everything human and presented in the form of Mephistopheles. Hamlet is the self-same Mephistopheles, but a Mephistopheles embraced by the living circle of human nature: hence his negation is not an evil, but is itself directed against evil. Hamlet casts doubt upon goodness, but does not question the existence of evil; in fact, he wages relentless war upon it. He entertains suspicions concerning the genuineness and sincerity of good; yet his attacks are made not upon goodness, but upon a counterfeit goodness, beneath whose mask are secreted evil and falsehood, its immemorial enemies. He does not laugh the diabolic, impersonal laughter of Mephistopheles; in his bitterest smile there is pathos, which tells of his sufferings and therefore reconciles us to him. Hamlet's skepticism, moreover, is not indifferentism, and in this consists his significance and merit. In his make-up good and evil, truth and falsehood, beauty and ugliness, are not blurred into an accidental, dumb, and vague something or other. The skepticism of Hamlet, which leads him to distrust things contemporaneous—the realization of truth, so to speak—is irreconcilably at war with falsehood, and through this very quality he becomes one of the foremost champions of a truth in which he himself cannot fully believe. But in negation, as in fire, there is a destructive force, and how can we keep it within bounds or show exactly where it is to stop, when that which it must destroy and that which it should spare are frequently blended and bound up together inseparably? This is where the oft-observed tragedy of human life comes into evidence: doing presupposes thinking, but thought and the will have separated, and are separating daily more and more. "And thus the native hue of resolution is sicklied o'er with the pale cast of thought," Shakespeare tells us in the words of Hamlet.

And so, on the one side stand the Hamlets—reflective, conscientious, often all-comprehensive, but as often also useless and doomed to immobility; and on the other the half-crazy Don Quixotes, who help and influence mankind only to the extent that they see but a single point—often nonexistent in the form they see it. Unwillingly the questions arise: Must one really be a lunatic to believe in the truth? And, must the mind that has obtained control of itself lose, therefore, all its power?

We should be led very far indeed even by a superficial consideration of these questions.

I shall confine myself to the remark that in this separation, in this dualism which I have mentioned, we should recognize a fundamental law of all human life. This life is nothing else than an eternal struggle and everlasting reconcilement of two ceaselessly diverging and continually uniting elements. If I did not fear startling your ears with philosophical terms, I would venture to say that the Hamlets are an expression of the fundamental centripetal force of nature, in accordance with which every living thing considers itself the center of creation and looks down upon everything else as existing for its sake. Thus the mosquito that settled on the forehead of Alexander the Great, in calm confidence of its right, fed on his blood as food which belonged to it; just so Hamlet, though he scorns himself—a thing the mosquito does not do, not having risen to this level—always takes everything on his own account. Without this centripetal force—the force of egotism—nature could no more exist than without the other, the centrifugal force, according to whose law everything exists only for something else. This force, the principle of devotion and self-sacrifice, illuminated, as I have already stated, by a comic light, is represented by the Don Quixotes. These two forces of inertia and motion, of conservatism and progress, are the fundamental forces of all existing things. They explain to us the growth of a little flower; they give us a key to the understanding of the development of the most powerful peoples.

I hasten to pass from these perhaps irrelevant speculations to other considerations more familiar to us.

I know that, of all Shakespeare's works, *Hamlet* is perhaps the most popular. This tragedy belongs to the list of plays that never fail to crowd the theater. In view of the modern attitude of our public and its aspiration toward self-consciousness and reflection, its scruples about itself and its buoyancy of spirit, this phenomenon is clear. But, to say nothing of the beauties in which this most excellent expression of the modern spirit abounds, one cannot help marveling at the master genius who, though himself in many respects akin to his Hamlet, cleft him from himself by a free sweep of creative force, and set up his model for the lasting study of posterity. The spirit which created this model is that of a Northern man, a spirit of meditation and analysis, a spirit heavy and gloomy, devoid of harmony and bright color, not rounded into exquisite, oftentimes shallow, forms; but deep, strong, varied, independent, and guiding. Out of his very bosom he has plucked the type of Hamlet; and in so doing has shown that, in the realm of poetry, as in other spheres of human life, he stands above his child, because he fully understands it.

The spirit of a Southerner went into the creation of Don Quixote, a spirit light and merry, naive and impressionable, —one that does not enter into the mysteries of life, that reflects phenomena rather than comprehends them.

At this point I cannot resist the desire, not to draw a parallel between Shakespeare and Cervantes, but simply to indicate a few points of likeness and of difference. Shakespeare and Cervantes—how can there be any comparison? some will ask. Shakespeare, that giant, that demigod! . . . Yes, but Cervantes is not a pygmy beside the giant who created *King Lear*. He is a man—a man to the full; and a man has the right to stand on his feet even before a demigod. Undoubtedly Shakespeare presses hard upon Cervantes—and not him alone—by the wealth and power of his imagination, by the brilliancy of his greatest poetry, by the depth and breadth of a colossal mind. But then you will not find in Cervantes' romance any strained witticisms or unnatural comparisons or feigned concepts; nor will you meet in his pages with decapitations, picked eyes, and those streams of blood, that dull and iron cruelty, which are the terrible heirloom of the Middle Ages, and are disappearing less rapidly in obstinate Northern natures. And yet Cervantes, like Shakespeare, lived in the epoch that witnessed St. Bartholomew's Night; [3] and long after that time heretics were burned and blood continued to flow—shall it ever cease to flow? *Don Quixote* reflects the Middle Ages, if only in the provincial

[3] Tradition generally refers to St. Bartholomew's Day. See also p. 367. Editor.

poetry and narrative grace of those romances which Cervantes so good-humoredly derided, and to which he himself paid the last tribute in *Persiles and Sigismunda.* Shakespeare takes his models from everywhere—from heaven and earth—he knows no limitations; nothing can escape his all-pervading glance. He seizes his subjects with irresistible power, like an eagle pouncing upon its prey. Cervantes presents his not over-numerous characters to his readers gently, as a father his children. He takes only what is close to him, but with that how familiar he is! Everything human seems subservient to the mighty English poet; Cervantes draws his wealth from his own heart only—a heart sunny, kind, and rich in life's experience, but not hardened by it. It was not in vain that during seven years of hard bondage Cervantes was learning, as he himself said, the science of patience. The circle of his experience is narrower than Shakespeare's, but in that, as in every separate living person, is reflected all that is human. Cervantes does not dazzle you with thundering words; he does not shock you with the titanic force of triumphant inspiration; his poetry—sometimes turbid, and by no means Shakespearean—is like a deep river, rolling calmly between variegated banks; and the reader, gradually allured, then hemmed in on every side by its transparent waves, cheerfully resigns himself to the truly epic calm and fluidity of its course.

The imagination gladly evokes the figures of these two contemporary poets, who died on the very same day, the twenty-sixth of April, 1616.[4] Cervantes probably knew nothing of Shakespeare, but the great tragedian in the quietude of his Stratford home, whither he had retired for the three years preceding his death, could have read through the famous novel, which had already been translated into English. A picture worthy of the brush of a contemplative artist—Shakespeare reading *Don Quixote!* Fortunate are the countries where such men arise, teachers of their generation and of posterity. The unfading wreath with which a great man is crowned rests also upon the brow of his people.

A certain English Lord—a good judge in the matter—once

[4] It is generally agreed now that Cervantes was in captivity five years, died April 23, and was entombed April 24. Editor.

spoke in my hearing of Don Quixote as a model of a real gentleman. Surely, if simplicity and a quiet demeanor are the distinguishing marks of what we call a thorough gentleman, Don Quixote has a good claim to his title. He is a veritable hidalgo—a hidalgo even when the jeering servants of the prince are lathering his whole face. The simplicity of his manners proceeds from the absence of what I would venture to call his self-love, and not his self-conceit. Don Quixote is not busied with himself, and, respecting himself and others, does not think of showing off. But Hamlet, with all his exquisite setting, is, it seems to me—excuse the French expression—*ayant des airs de parvenu;* he is troublesome—at times even rude—and he poses and scoffs. To make up for this, he was given the power of original and apt expression, a power inherent in every being in whom is implanted the habit of reflection and self-development—and therefore utterly unattainable so far as Don Quixote is concerned. The depth and keenness of analysis in Hamlet, his many-sided education (we must not forget that he studied at the Wittenberg University), have developed in him a taste almost unerring. He is an excellent critic; his advice to the actors is strikingly true and judicious. The sense of the beautiful is as strong in him as the sense of duty in Don Quixote.

Don Quixote deeply respects all existing orders—religions, monarchs, and dukes—and is at the same time free himself and recognizes the freedom of others. Hamlet rebukes kings and courtiers, but is in reality oppressive and intolerant.

Don Quixote is hardly literate; Hamlet probably kept a diary. Don Quixote, with all his ignorance, has a definite way of thinking about matters of government and administration; Hamlet has neither time nor need to think of such matters.

Many have objected to the endless blows with which Cervantes burdens Don Quixote. I have already remarked that in the second part of the romance the poor knight is almost unmolested. But I will add that, without these beatings, he would be less pleasing to children, who read his adventures with such avidity; and to us grownups he would not appear in his true light, but rather in a cold and haughty aspect, which would be incompatible with his character. Another interesting point is involved here. At the very end of the romance, after Don Quixote's complete discomfiture by the Knight of the White Moon, the disguised college bachelor, and following his renunciation of knight-errantry, shortly before his death, a herd of swine trample him underfoot. I once happened to hear Cervantes criticized for writing this, on the ground that he was repeating the old tricks already abandoned; but herein Cervantes was guided by the instinct of genius, and this very ugly incident has a deep meaning. The trampling under pigs' feet is always encountered in the lives of Don Quixotes, and just before their close. This is the last tribute they must pay to rough chance, to indifference and cruel misunderstanding; it is the slap in the face from the Pharisees. Then they can die. They have passed through all the fire of the furnace, have won immortality for themselves, and it opens before them.

Hamlet is occasionally double-faced and heartless. Think of how he planned the deaths of the two courtiers sent to England by the king. Recall his speech on Polonius, whom he murdered. In this, however, we see, as already observed, a reflection of the medieval spirit recently outgrown. On the other hand, we must note in the honest, veracious Don Quixote the disposition to a half-conscious, half-innocent deception, to self-delusion—a disposition almost always present in the fancy of an enthusiast. His account of what he saw in the cave of Montesinos was obviously invented by him, and did not deceive the smart commoner, Sancho Panza.

Hamlet, on the slightest ill success, loses heart and complains; but Don Quixote, pummeled senseless by galley slaves, has not the least doubt as to the success of his undertaking. In the same spirit Fourier is said to have gone to his office every day, for many years, to meet an Englishman he had invited, through the newspapers, to furnish him with a million francs to carry out his plans; but, of course, the benefactor of his dreams never appeared. This was certainly a very ridiculous proceeding, and it calls to mind this thought: The ancients considered their gods jealous, and, in case of need, deemed it useful to appease them by voluntary offerings (recollect the ring cast into the sea by Polycrates); why, then, should we not believe that some share of the ludicrous must inevitably be mingled with the acts, with the very character of people moved unto great and novel deeds—as a bribe, as a soothing offering, to the jealous gods? Without these comical crank-pioneers, mankind would not progress, and there would not be anything for the Hamlets to reflect upon.

The Don Quixotes discover; the Hamlets develop. But how, I shall be asked, can the Hamlets evolve anything when they doubt all things and believe in nothing? My rejoinder is that, by a wise dispensation of Nature, there are neither thorough Hamlets nor complete Don Quixotes; these are but extreme manifestations of two tendencies—guideposts set up by the poets on two different roads. Life tends toward them, but never reaches the goal. We must not forget that, just as the principle of analysis is carried in Hamlet to tragedy, so the element of enthusiasm runs in Don Quixote to comedy; but in life, the purely comic and the purely tragic are seldom encountered.

Hamlet gains much in our estimation from Horatio's attachment for him. This character is excellent, and is frequently met with in our day, to the credit of the times. In Horatio I recognize the type of the disciple, the pupil, in the best sense of the word. With a stoical and direct nature, a warm heart, and a somewhat limited understanding, he is aware of his shortcomings, and is modest—something rare in people of limited intellect. He thirsts for learning, for instruction, and therefore venerates the wise Hamlet, and is devoted to him with all the might of his honest heart, not demanding even reciprocation. He defers to Hamlet, not as to a prince but as to a chief. One of the most important services of the Hamlets consists in forming and developing persons like Horatio; persons who, having received from them the seeds of thought, fertilize them in their hearts, and then scatter them broadcast through the world. The words in which Hamlet acknowledges Horatio's worth, honor himself. In them is expressed his own conception of the great worth of Man, his noble aspirations, which no skepticism is strong enough to weaken.

Give me that man
That is not passion's slave, and I will wear him
In my heart's core, ay, in my heart of hearts,
As I do thee.
(III, ii, 76–79)

The honest skeptic always respects a stoic. When the ancient world had crumbled away—and in every epoch like unto that—the best people took refuge in stoicism as the only creed in which it was still possible to preserve man's dignity. The skeptics, if they lacked the strength to die—to betake themselves to the "undiscovered country from whose bourn no traveler returns"—turned epicureans; a plain, sad phenomenon, with which we are but too familiar.

Both Hamlet and Don Quixote die a touching death; and yet how different are their ends! Hamlet's last words are sublime. He resigns himself, grows calm, bids Horatio live, and raises his dying voice in behalf of young Fortinbras, the unstained representative of the right of succession. Hamlet's eyes are not turned forward. "The rest is silence," says the dying skeptic, as he actually becomes silent forever. The death of Don Quixote sends an inexpressible emotion through one's heart. In that instant the full significance of this personality is accessible to all. When his former page, trying to comfort Don Quixote, tells him that they shall soon again start out on an expedition of knight-errantry, the expiring knight replies: "No, all is now over forever, and I ask everyone's forgiveness; I am no longer Don Quixote, I am again Alonzo the good, as I was once called —Alonso el Bueno."

The word is remarkable. The mention of this nickname for the first and last time makes the reader tremble. Yes, only this single word still has a meaning, in the face of death. All things shall pass away, everything shall vanish—the highest station, power, the all-inclusive genius—all to dust shall crumble. "All earthly greatness vanishes like smoke." But noble deeds are more enduring than resplendent beauty. "Everything shall pass," the apostle said, "love alone shall endure."

16. Hippolyte Taine

1828–1893

The mid-nineteenth century saw a reaction to Romanticism in much of Europe. Among the French leaders of this reaction toward a more rational, scientific approach was Hippolyte Taine. He and his followers asserted that the lessons learned from the recent advances in the biological sciences could be applied to art, literature, history, or any of man's activities which, like the aforementioned, are ruled by fixed laws and are thereby subject to scientific methods of analysis.

Although the theories he proselytized have largely fallen into disrepute, Taine's own work is still noteworthy, particularly his remarks on Shakespeare, which, despite his insistence on a rational approach, are much more subjective and impressionistic than he himself knew. In fact, many of the underlying assumptions of such critics as Carlyle appear in one or another disguise. But on the whole Taine's attitude is negative. He judges Shakespeare's world to be immoral and denies that his noblest characters act consciously. But it is no longer possible to take Voltaire's position and Taine cannot deny Shakespeare's great art.

Taine's chief interest for the student of Shakespeare lies in the fact that he ultimately typifies French Shakespeare criticism. His tangential admiration is characteristic of a distance, true even at the height of French enthusiasm for the English poet, that has existed between English and French taste.

FROM A History of English Literature

EXCERPT FROM BOOK II, CHAPTER 4, PART 2

Let us then look for the man, and in his style. The style explains the work; whilst showing the principal features of the genius, it infers the rest. When we have once grasped the dominant faculty, we see the whole artist developed like a flower.

Shakespeare imagines with copiousness and excess; he spreads metaphors profusely over all he writes; every instant abstract ideas are changed into images; it is a series of paintings which is unfolded in his mind. He does not seek them, they come of themselves; they crowd within him, covering his arguments; they dim with their brightness the pure light of logic. He does not labor to explain or prove; picture on picture, image on image, he is forever copying the strange and splendid visions which are engendered one within another, and are heaped up within him. Compare to our dull writers this passage, which I take at hazard from a tranquil dialogue:

> The single and peculiar life is bound,
> With all the strength and armour of the mind,
> To keep itself from noyance; but much more
> That spirit upon whose weal depend and rest
> The lives of many. The cease of majesty
> Dies not alone; but, like a gulf, doth draw
> What's near it with it: it is a massy wheel,
> Fix'd on the summit of the highest mount,
> To whose huge spokes ten thousand lesser things
> Are mortised and adjoin'd; which, when it falls,
> Each small annexment, petty consequence,
> Attends the boisterous ruin. Never alone
> Did the king sigh, but with a general groan.
>
> (*Hamlet*, III, iii, 11–23)

From Taine's *A History of English Literature*, Vol. I, Book II (New York, Henry Holt and Company, 1871), pp. 307–311, 316–323, 328–340. Translated by H. Van Laun. Reprinted by permission of Holt, Rinehart and Winston, Inc.

Here we have three successive images to express the same thought. It is a whole blossoming; a bough grows from the trunk, from that another, which is multiplied into numerous fresh branches. Instead of a smooth road, traced by a regular line of dry and well-fixed stakes, you enter a wood, crowded with interwoven trees and luxuriant bushes, which conceal you and close your path, which delight and dazzle your eyes by the magnificence of their verdure and the wealth of their bloom. You are astonished at first, modern mind that you are, businessman, used to the clear dissertations of classical poetry; you become cross; you think the author is joking, and that through self-esteem and bad taste he is misleading you and himself in his garden thickets. By no means; if he speaks thus, it is not from choice, but necessity; metaphor is not his whim, but the form of his thought. In the height of passion, he imagines still. When Hamlet, in despair, remembers his father's noble form, he sees the mythological pictures with which the taste of the age filled the very streets:

> A station like the herald Mercury
> New-lighted on a heaven-kissing hill.
> (III, iv, 59–60)

This charming vision, in the midst of a bloody invective, proves that there lurks a painter underneath the poet. Involuntarily and out of season, he tears off the tragic mask which covered his face; and the reader discovers, behind the contracted features of this terrible mask, a graceful and inspired smile of which he had not dreamed.

Such an imagination must needs be vehement. Every metaphor is a convulsion. Whosoever involuntarily and naturally transforms a dry idea into an image, has his brain on fire: true metaphors are flaming apparitions, which are like a picture in a flash of lightning. Never, I think, in any nation of Europe, or in any age of history, has so deep a passion been seen. Shakespeare's style is a compound of furious expressions. No man has submitted words to such a contortion. Mingled contrasts, raving exaggerations, apostrophes, exclamations, the whole fury of the ode, inversion of ideas, accumulation of images, the horrible and the divine, jumbled into the same line; it seems to my fancy as though he never writes a word without shouting it. "What have I done?" the queen asks Hamlet. He answers:

Such an act
That blurs the grace and blush of modesty,
Calls virtue hypocrite, takes off the rose
From the fair forehead of an innocent love,
And sets a blister there, makes marriage-vows
As false as dicers' oaths: O, such a deed
As from the body of contraction plucks
The very soul, and sweet religion makes
A rhapsody of words: heaven's face doth glow;
Yea, this solidity and compound mass,
With tristful visage, as against the doom,
Is thought-sick at the act.
(III, iii, 40–51)

It is the style of frenzy. Yet I have not given all. The metaphors are all exaggerated, the ideas all verge on the absurd. All is transformed and disfigured by the whirlwind of passion. The contagion of the crime, which he denounces, has marred his whole nature. He no longer sees anything in the world but corruption and lying. To vilify the virtuous were little; he vilifies virtue herself. Inanimate things are sucked into the whirl of grief. The sky's red tint at sunset, the pallid shade spread by night over the landscape, become the blush and the pallor of shame, and the wretched man who speaks and weeps sees the whole world totter with him in the dimness of despair.

Hamlet, it will be said, is half mad; this explains his vehemence of expression. The truth is that Hamlet, here, is Shakespeare. Be the situation terrible or peaceful, whether he is engaged on an invective or a conversation, the style is excessive throughout. Shakespeare never sees things tranquilly. All the powers of his mind are concentrated in the present image or idea. He is buried and absorbed in it. With such a genius, we are on the brink of an abyss; the eddying water dashes in headlong, devouring whatever objects it meets, bringing them to light again, if at all, transformed and mutilated. We pause stupefied before these convulsive metaphors, which might have been written by a fevered hand in a night's delirium, which gather a pageful of ideas and pictures in half a sentence, which scorch the eyes they would enlighten. Words lose their sense; constructions are put out of joint; paradoxes of style, apparently false expressions, which a man might occasionally venture upon with diffidence in the transport of his rapture, become the ordinary language; he dazzles, he repels, he terrifies, he disgusts, he oppresses; his verses are a piercing and sublime song, pitched in too high a key, above the reach of our organs, which offends our ears, of which our mind alone can divine the justice and beauty.

Yet this is little; for that singular force of concentration is redoubled by the suddenness of the dash which it displays. In Shakespeare there is no preparation, no adaptation, no development, no care to make himself understood. Like a too fiery and powerful horse, he bounds, but cannot run. He bridges in a couple of words an enormous interval; is at the two poles in a single instant. The reader vainly looks for the intermediate track; confounded by these prodigious leaps, he wonders by what miracle the poet has entered upon a new idea the very moment when he quitted the last, seeing perhaps between the two images a long scale of transitions, which we pace painfully step by step, but which he has spanned in a stride. Shakespeare flies, we creep. Hence comes a style made up of conceits, bold images shattered in an instant by others still bolder, barely indicated ideas completed by others far removed, no visible connection, but a visible incoherence; at every step we halt, the track failing; and there, far above us, lo, stands the poet, and we find that we have ventured in his footsteps, through a craggy land, full of precipices, which he threads, as if it were a straightforward road, but on which our greatest efforts barely carry us along.

What will you think, further, if we observe that these vehement expressions, so unexpected, instead of following one after the other, slowly and with effort, are hurled out by hundreds, with an impetuous ease and abundance, like the bubbling waves from a welling spring, which are heaped together, rise one above another, and find no place wide enough to spread themselves and fall? You may find in *Romeo and Juliet* a score of examples of this inexhaustible inspiration. The two lovers pile up an infinite mass of metaphors, impassioned exaggerations, clenches, contorted phrases, amorous extravagances. Their language is like the trill of nightingales. Shakespeare's wits, Mercutio, Beatrice, Rosalind, his clowns, buffoons, sparkle with far-fetched jokes, which rattle out like a musketry fire. There is none of them but provides enough play of words to stock a whole theater. Lear's curses, or Queen Margaret's, would suffice for all the madmen in an asylum, or all the oppressed of the earth. The sonnets are a delirium of ideas and images, turned out with an energy enough to make a man giddy. His first poem, "Venus and Adonis," is the sensual ecstasy of a Correggio, insatiable and excited. This exuberant fecundity intensifies qualities already in excess, and multiplies a hundredfold the luxuriance of metaphor, the incoherence of style, and the unbridled vehemence of expression.

All that I have said may be compressed into a few words. Objects were taken into his mind organized and complete; they pass into ours disjointed, decomposed, fragmentarily. He thought in the lump, we think piecemeal; hence his style and our style—two languages not to be reconciled. We, for our part, writers and reasoners, can note precisely by a word each isolated fraction of an idea, and represent the due order of its parts by the due order of our expressions. We advance gradually; we affiliate, go down to the roots, try and treat our words as numbers, our sentences as equations; we employ but general terms, which every mind can understand, and regular constructions, into which any mind can enter; we attain justness and clearness, not life. Shakespeare lets justness and clearness look out for themselves, and attains life. From amidst his complex conception and his colored semi-vision he grasps a fragment, a quivering fiber, and shows it; it is for you, from this fragment, to divine the rest. He, behind the word, has a whole picture, an attitude, a long argument abridged, a mass of swarming ideas; you know them, these abbreviative, condensive words: these are they which we launch out from the furnace of invention, in a fit of passion—words of slang or of fashion, which appeal to local memory or individual experience; little concocted and incorrect phrases, which, by their irregularity, express the suddenness and the breaks of the inner sensation; trivial words, exaggerated figures. There is a gesture beneath each, a quick contraction of the brows, a curl of laughing lips, a clown's trick, an unhinging of the whole machine. None of them mark ideas; each is the extremity and issue of a complete mimic action; none is the expression and definition of a partial and limited idea. This is why Shakespeare is strange and powerful, obscure and original, beyond all the poets of his or any other age; the most immoderate of all violators of language, the most marvelous of all creators of souls, the farthest removed from regular logic and classical reason, the one most capable of exciting in us a world of forms, and of placing living beings before us.

EXCERPT FROM BOOK II, CHAPTER 4, PART 4

On this common background stands out a population of distinct living figures, illuminated by an intense light, in striking relief. This creative power is Shakespeare's great gift, and it communicates an extraordinary significance to his words. Every word pronounced by one of his characters enables us to see, besides the idea which it contains and the emotion which prompted it, the aggregate of the qualities and the entire character which produced it—the mood, physical attitude, bearing, look of the man, all instantaneously, with a clearness and force approached by no one. The words which strike our ears are not the thousandth part of those we hear within; they are like sparks thrown off at intervals; the eyes catch rare flashes of flame; the mind alone perceives the vast conflagration of which they are the signs and the effect. He gives us two dramas in one: the first strange, convulsive, curtailed, visible; the other consistent, immense, invisible: the one covers the other so well that as a rule we do not realize that we are perusing words: we hear the roll of those terrible voices, we see contracted features, glowing eyes, pallid faces; we see the rages, the furious resolutions which mount to the brain with the feverish blood, and descend to the sharp-strung nerves. This property possessed by every phrase to exhibit a world of sentiments and forms, comes from the fact that the phrase is actually caused by a world of emotions and images. Shakespeare, when he wrote, felt all that we feel, and much besides. He had the prodigious faculty of seeing in a twinkling of the eye a complete character, body, mind, past and present, in every detail and every depth of his being, with the exact attitude and the expression of face, which the situation demanded. A word here and there of Hamlet or Othello would need for its explanation three pages of commentaries; each of the half-understood thoughts, which the commentator may have discovered, has left its trace in the turn of the phrase, in the nature of the metaphor, in the order of the words; nowadays, in pursuing these traces, we divine the thoughts. These innumerable traces have been impressed in a second, within the compass of a line. In the next line there are as many, impressed just as quickly, and in the same compass. You can gauge the concentration and the velocity of the imagination which creates thus.

These characters are all of the same family. Good or bad, gross or delicate, refined or awkward, Shakespeare gives them all the same kind of spirit which is his own. He has made of them imaginative people, void of will and reason, impassioned machines, vehemently hurled one upon another, who were the representation of whatever is most natural and most abandoned in human nature. Let us act the play to ourselves, and see in all its stages this clanship of figures, this prominence of portraits.

Lowest of all are the stupid folk, babbling or brutish. Imagination already exists there, where reason is not yet born; it exists also here, where reason is dead. The idiot and the brute blindly follow the phantoms which exist in their benumbed or mechanical brains. No poet has understood this mechanism like Shakespeare. His Caliban, for instance, a deformed savage, fed on roots, growls like a beast under the hand of Prospero, who has subdued him. He howls continually against his master, though he knows that every curse will be paid back with "cramps and aches." He is a chained wolf, trembling and fierce, who tries to bite when approached, and who crouches when he sees the lash raised above him. He has a foul sensuality, a loud base laugh, the gluttony of degraded humanity. He wished to violate Miranda in her sleep. He cries for his food, and gorges himself when he gets it. A sailor who had landed in the island, Stephano, gives him wine; he kisses his feet, and takes him for a god; he asks if he has not dropped from heaven, and adores him. We find in him rebellious and baffled passions, which are eager to be avenged and satiated. Stephano had beaten his comrade. Caliban cries, "Beat him enough: after a little time I'll beat him too." He prays Stephano to come with him and murder Prospero in his sleep; he thirsts to lead him there, and sees his master already with his throat cut, and his brains scattered on the earth:

> Prithee, my king, be quiet. See'st thou here,
> This is the mouth o' the cell: no noise, and enter.
> Do that good mischief which may make this island
> Thine own for ever, and I, thy Caliban,
> For aye thy foot-licker.
>
> (*Tempest*, IV, i, 216–220)

Others, like Ajax and Cloten, are more like men, and yet it is pure mood that Shakespeare depicts in them, as in Caliban. The clogging corporeal machine, the mass of muscles, the thick blood coursing in the veins of these fighting brutes, oppress the intelligence, and leave no life but for animal passions. Ajax uses his fists, and devours meat; that is his existence; if he is jealous of Achilles, it is pretty much as a bull is jealous of his fellow. He permits himself to be restrained and led by Ulysses, without looking before him: the grossest flattery decoys him. The Greeks have urged him to accept Hector's challenge. Behold him puffed up with pride, scorning to answer anyone, not knowing what he says or does. Thersites cries,

"Goodmorrow, Ajax"; and he replies, "Thanks, Agamemnon." He has no further thought than to contemplate his enormous frame, and roll majestically his great stupid eyes. When the day comes, he strikes at Hector as on an anvil. After a good while they are separated. "I am not warm yet," says Ajax, "let us fight again." Cloten is less massive than this phlegmatic ox; but he is just as idiotic, just as vainglorious, just as coarse. The beautiful Imogen, urged by his insults and his scullion manners, tells him that his whole body is not worth as much as Posthumus' garment. He is stung to the quick, repeats the word ten times; he cannot shake off the idea, and runs at it again and again with his head down, like an angry ram:

> CLOTEN. "His garment?" Now, the devil–
> IMOGEN. To Dorothy my woman hie thee presently–
> CLOTEN. "His garment?" . . . You have abused me: "His meanest garment!" . . . I'll be revenged: "His meanest garment!" Well.
>
> (*Cymbeline*, II, iii, 142–160)

He gets some of Posthumus' garments, and goes to Milford Haven, expecting to meet Imogen there. On his way he mutters thus:

> With that suit upon my back, will I ravish her: first kill him, and in her eyes; there shall she see my valour, which will then be a torment to her contempt. He on the ground, my speech of insultment ended on his dead body, and when my lust has dined,—which, as I say, to vex her I will execute in the clothes that she so praised,—to the court I'll knock her back, foot her home again.
>
> (III, v, 141–150)

Others, again, are but babblers: for example, Polonius, the grave brainless counselor; a great baby, not yet out of his "swathing clouts"; a solemn booby, who rains on men a shower of counsels, compliments, and maxims; a sort of court speaking trumpet, useful in grand ceremonies, with the air of a thinker, but fit only to spout words. But the most complete of all these characters is that of the nurse in *Romeo and Juliet*, a gossip, loose in her talk, a regular kitchen oracle, smelling of the stew pan and old boots, foolish, impudent, immoral, but otherwise a good creature, and affectionate to her child. Mark this disjointed and never-ending gossip's babble:

> NURSE. Faith I can tell her age unto an hour.
> LADY CAPULET. She's not fourteen. . . .
> NURSE. On Lammas-eve at night shall she be fourteen;
> Susan and she—God rest all Christian souls!—
> Were of an age: well, Susan is with God;
> She was too good for me: but, as I said,
> On Lammas-eve at night shall she be fourteen;
> That shall she, marry; I remember it well.
> 'Tis since the earthquake now eleven years;
> And she was wean'd,—I never shall forget it,—
> Of all the days of the year, upon that day:
> For I had then laid wormwood to my dug,
> Sitting in the sun under the dove-house wall;
> My lord and you were then at Mantua:—
> Nay, I do bear a brain:—but, as I said,
> When it did taste the wormwood on the nipple
> Of my dug and felt it bitter, pretty fool,
> To see it tetchy and fall out with the dug!
> 'Shake,' quoth the dove-house: 'twas no need, I trow,
> To bid me trudge:
> And since that time it is eleven years;
> For then she could stand alone; nay, by the rood,
> She could have run and waddled all about;
> For even the day before, she broke her brow.
> (I, iii, 12–38)

Then she tells an indecent anecdote, which she begins over again four times. She is silenced: what then? She has her anecdote in her head, and cannot cease repeating it and laughing to herself. Endless repetitions are the mind's first step. The vulgar do not pursue the straight line of reasoning and of the story; they repeat their steps, as it were merely marking time: struck with an image, they keep it for an hour before their eyes, and are never tired of it. If they do advance, they turn aside to a hundred chance ideas before they get at the phrase required. They let themselves be diverted by all the thoughts which come across them. This is what the nurse does; and when she brings Juliet news of her lover, she torments and wearies her, less from a wish to tease than from a habit of wandering from the point:

> NURSE. Jesu, what haste? can you not stay awhile?
> Do you not see that I am out of breath?
> JULIET. How art thou out of breath, when thou hast breath
> To say to me that thou art out of breath? . . .
> Is thy news good, or bad? answer to that;
> Say either, and I'll stay the circumstance:
> Let me be satisfied: is't good or bad?
> NURSE. Well, you have made a simple choice; you know not how to choose a man. Romeo! no, not he; though his face be better than any man's, yet his leg excels all men's; and for a hand, and a foot, and a body, though they be not to be talked on, yet they are past compare: he is not the flower of courtesy, but, I'll warrant him, as gentle as a lamb. Go thy ways, wench; serve God. What, have you dined at home?
> JULIET. No, no: but all this did I know before.
> What says he of our marriage? what of that?
> NURSE. Lord, how my head aches! what a head have I!
> It beats as it would fall in twenty pieces.
> My back o' t' other side,—O, my back, my back!
> Beshrew your heart for sending me about,
> To catch my death with jaunting up and down!
> JULIET. I'faith, I am sorry that thou are not well.
> Sweet, sweet, sweet nurse, tell me, what says my love?
> NURSE. Your love says, like an honest gentleman, and a courteous, and a kind, and a handsome, and, I warrant, a virtuous,—Where is your mother?
>
> (II, v, 29–59)

It is never-ending. Her gabble is worse when she comes to announce to Juliet the death of her cousin and the banishment of Romeo. It is the shrill cry and chatter of an overgrown asthmatic magpie. She laments, confuses the names, spins roundabout sentences, ends by asking for aqua vitae. She curses Romeo, then brings him to Juliet's chamber. Next day Juliet is ordered to marry Earl Paris; Juliet throws herself into her nurse's arms, praying for comfort, advice, assistance. The other finds the true remedy: Marry Paris.

O, he's a lovely gentleman!
Romeo's a dishclout to him: an eagle, madam,
Hath not so green, so quick, so fair an eye
As Paris hath. Beshrew my very heart,
I think you are happy in this second match,
For it excels your first.
(III, v, 220–225)

This cool immorality, these weather-cock arguments, this fashion of estimating love like a fishwoman, completes the portrait.

EXCERPT FROM BOOK II, CHAPTER 4, PART 5

The mechanical imagination produces Shakespeare's fool characters: a quick venturesome dazzling, unquiet imagination produces his men of wit. Of wit there are many kinds. One, altogether French, which is but reason, a foe to paradox, scorner of folly, a sort of incisive common sense, having no occupation but to render truth amusing and evident, the most effective weapon with an intelligent and vain people: such was the wit of Voltaire and the drawing rooms. The other, that of improvisators and artists, is a mere inventive transport, paradoxical, unshackled, exuberant, a sort of self-entertainment, a phantasmagoria of images, quibbles, strange ideas, dazing and intoxicating, like the movement and illumination of a ball. Such is the wit of Mercutio, of the clowns, of Beatrice, Rosalind, and Benedick. They laugh, not from a sense of the ridiculous, but from the desire to laugh. You must look elsewhere for the campaigns which aggressive reason makes against human folly. Here folly is in full bloom. Our folk think of amusement, and nothing more. They are good-humored; they let their wit ride gaily over the possible and the impossible. They play upon words, contort their sense, draw absurd and laughable inferences, exchange them alternately, like shuttlecocks, one after another, and vie with each other in singularity and invention. They dress all their ideas in strange or sparkling metaphors. The taste of the time was for masquerades; their conversation is a masquerade of ideas. They say nothing in a simple style; they only seek to heap together subtle things, far-fetched, difficult to invent and to understand; all their expressions are overrefined, unexpected, extraordinary; they strain their thought and change it into a caricature. "Alas, poor Romeo!" says Mercutio, "he is already dead; stabbed with a white wench's black eye; shot through the ear with a love-song, the very pin of his heart cleft with the blind bow-boy's butt-shaft." (II, iv, 13–15). Benedick relates a conversation he has just held with his mistress: "O, she misused me past the endurance of a block! an oak, but with one green leaf on it would have answered her; my very visor began to assume life, and scold with her" (*Much Ado,* II, i, 246–249). These gay and perpetual extravagances show the bearing of the interlocutors. They do not remain quietly seated in their chairs, like the Marquis in the *Misanthrope;* they wheel about, leap, paint their faces, gesticulate boldly their ideas; their wit-rockets end with a song. Young folk, soldiers and artists, they let off their fireworks of phrases, and gambol round about. "There was a star danced, and under that was I born" (*Much Ado,* II, i, 349). This expression of Beatrice's aptly describes the kind of poetical, sparkling, unreasoning, charming wit, more akin to music than to literature, a sort of outspoken and wide-awake dream, not unlike that described by Mercutio:

> O, then, I see Queen Mab hath been with you.
> She is the fairies' midwife, and she comes
> In shape no bigger than an agate-stone
> On the fore-finger of an alderman,
> Drawn with a team of little atomies
> Athwart men's noses as they lie asleep;
> Her waggon-spokes made of long spinners' legs,
> The cover of the wings of grasshoppers,
> The traces of the smallest spider's web,
> The collars of the moonshine's watery beams,
> Her whip of cricket's bone, the lash of film,
> Her waggoner a small grey-coated gnat,

Not half so big as a round little worm
Prick'd from the lazy finger of a maid;
Her chariot is an empty hazel-nut,
Made by the joiner squirrel or old grub,
Time out o' mind the fairies' coachmakers.
And in this state she gallops night by night
Through lovers' brains, and then they dream of love;
O'er courtiers' knees, that dream on court'sies straight,
O'er lawyers' fingers, who straight dream on fees,
O'er ladies' lips, who straight on kisses dream, . . .
Sometime she gallops o'er a courtier's nose,
And then dreams he of smelling out a suit;
And sometime comes she with a tithe-pig's tail
Tickling a parson's nose as a' lies asleep,
Then dreams he of another benefice:
Sometime she driveth o'er a soldier's neck,
And then dreams he of cutting foreign throats,
Of breaches, ambuscadoes, Spanish blades,
Of healths five-fathom deep; and then anon
Drums in his ear, at which he starts and wakes,
And being thus frighted swears a prayer or two
And sleeps again. This is that very Mab
That plats the manes of horses in the night,
And bakes the elf-locks in foul sluttish hairs,
Which once untangled much misfortune bodes: . . .
This is she . . .

(I, iv, 54–95)

Romeo interrupts him, or he would never end. Let the reader compare with the dialogue of the French theater this little poem,

Child of an idle brain,
Begot of nothing but vain fantasy

introduced without incongruity into a conversation of the sixteenth century, and he will comprehend the difference between the wit which devotes itself to reasoning, or to record a subject for laughter, and that imagination which is self-amused with its own act.

Falstaff has the passions of an animal, and the imagination of a man of wit. There is no character which better exemplifies the dash and immorality of Shakespeare. Falstaff is a great supporter of disreputable places, swearer, gamester, brawler, wine-bag, as low as he well can be. He has a big belly, bloodshot eyes, bloated face, shaking leg; he spends his life huddled up among the tavern jugs, or asleep on the ground behind the arras; he only wakes to curse, lie, brag, and steal. He is as big a swindler as Panurge, who had sixty-three ways of making money, "of which the honestest was by sly theft." And what is worse, he is an old man, a knight, a courtier, and well-bred. Must he not be odious and repulsive? By no means; you cannot help liking him. At bottom, like his brother Panurge, he is "the best fellow in the world." He has no malice in his composition; no other wish than to laugh and be amused. When insulted, he bawls out louder than his attackers, and pays them back with interest in coarse words and insults; but he owes them no grudge for it. The next minute he is sitting down with them in a tavern, drinking their health like a brother and comrade. If he has vices, he exposes them so frankly that we are obliged to forgive him them. He seems to say to us: "Well, so I am, what then? I like drinking: isn't the wine good? I take to my heels when hard hitting begins: isn't fighting a nuisance? I get into debt, and do fools out of their money: isn't it nice to have money in your pocket? I brag: isn't it natural to want to be well thought of?"—"Dost thou hear, Hal? thou knowest, in the state of innocency, Adam fell; and what should poor Jack Falstaff do in the days of villany? Thou seest I have more flesh than another man, and therefore more frailty." Falstaff is so frankly immoral, that he ceases to be so. Conscience ends at a certain point; nature assumes its place, and the man rushes upon what he desires, without more thought of being just or unjust than an animal in the neighboring wood. Falstaff, engaged in recruiting, has sold exemptions to all the rich people, and only enrolled starved and half-naked wretches. There's but a shirt and a half in all his company: that does not trouble him. Bah! "they'll find linen enough on every hedge." The prince, who has seen them pass muster, says, "I did never see such pitiful rascals." "Tut, tut," answers Falstaff, "good enough to toss; food for powder; they'll fill a pit as well as better; tush, man, mortal men, mortal men." His second excuse is his unfailing spirit. If ever there was a man who could talk, it is he. Insults and oaths, curses, jobations, protests flow from him as from an open barrel. He is never at a loss; he devises a shift for every difficulty. Lies sprout out of him, fructify, increase, beget one another, like mushrooms on a rich and rotten bed of earth. He lies still more from his imagination and nature than from interest and necessity. It is evident from the manner in which he strains his fictions. He says he fought alone against two men. The next moment it is four. Presently we have seven, then eleven, then fourteen. He is stopped in time, or he would soon be talking of a whole army. When unmasked, he does not lose his temper, and is the first to laugh at his boastings. "Gallants, lads, boys, hearts of gold. . . . What, shall we be merry? shall we have a play extempore?" He does the scolding part of *King Henry* with so much truth that one might take him for a king, or an actor. This big pot-bellied fellow, a coward, a jester, a brawler, a drunkard, a lewd rascal, a pothouse poet, is one of Shakespeare's favorites. The reason is that his manners are those of pure nature, and Shakespeare's mind is congenial with his own.

EXCERPT FROM BOOK II, CHAPTER 4, PART 8

How much more visible is this impassioned and unfettered genius of Shakespeare in the great characters which sustain the whole weight of the drama! The startling imagination, the furious velocity of the manifold and exuberant ideas, the unruly passion, rushing upon death and crime, hallucinations, madness, all the ravages of delirium bursting through will and reason: such are the forces and ravings which engender them. Shall I speak of the dazzling Cleopatra, who holds Antony in the whirlwind of her devices and caprices, who fascinates and kills, who scatters to the winds the lives of men as a handful of desert dust, the fatal Eastern sorceress who sports with life and death, headstrong, irresistible, child of air and fire, whose life is but a tempest, whose thought, ever repointed and broken, is like the crackling of a lightning flash? Of Othello, who, beset by the concise picture of physical adultery, cries at every word of Iago like a man on the rack; who, his nerves hardened by twenty years of war and shipwreck, grows mad and swoons for grief, and whose soul, poisoned by jealousy, is distracted and disorganized in convulsions and in stupor? Or of old King Lear, violent and weak, whose half-unseated reason is gradually toppled over under the shocks of incredible treacheries, who presents the frightful spectacle of madness, first increasing, then complete, of curses, howlings, superhuman sorrows, into which the transport of the first access of fury carries him, and then of peaceful incoherence, chattering imbecility, into which the shattered man subsides: a marvelous creation, the supreme effort of pure imagination, a disease of reason which reason could never have conceived? Amid so many portraitures let us choose two or three to indicate the depth and nature of them all. The critic is lost in Shakespeare, as in an immense town; he will describe a couple of monuments, and entreat the reader to imagine the city.

Plutarch's Coriolanus is an austere, coldly haughty patrician, a general of the army. In Shakespeare's hands he becomes a coarse soldier, a man of the people as to his language and manners, an athlete of war, with a voice like a trumpet; whose eyes by contradiction are filled with a rush of blood and anger, proud and terrible in mood, a lion's soul in the body of a steer. The philosopher Plutarch told of him a lofty philosophic action, saying that he had been at pains to save his landlord in the sack of Corioli. Shakespeare's Coriolanus has indeed the same disposition, for he is really a good fellow; but when Lartius asks him the name of this poor Volscian, in order to secure his liberty, he yawns out:

> By Jupiter! forgot.
> I am weary; yea, my memory is tired.
> Have we no wine here?
>
> (*Coriolanus*, I, ix, 90–92)

He is hot, he has been fighting, he must drink; he leaves his Volscian in chains, and thinks no more of him. He fights like a porter, with shouts and insults, and the cries from that deep chest are heard above the din of the battle like the sounds from a brazen trumpet. He has scaled the walls of Corioli, he has butchered till he is gorged with slaughter. Instantly he turns to the other army, and arrives red with blood, "as he were flay'd." "Come I too late?" Cominius begins to compliment him. "Come I too late?" he repeats. The battle is not yet finished: he embraces Cominius:

O, let me clip ye
In arms as sound as when I woo'd, in heart
As merry as when our nuptial day was done.
(I, vi, 29–31)

For the battle is a real holiday to him. Such senses, such a frame, need the outcry, the din of battle, the excitement of death and wounds. This haughty and indomitable heart needs the joy of victory and destruction. Mark the display of his patrician arrogance and his soldier's bearing, when he is offered the tenth of the spoils:

I thank you, general;
But cannot make my heart consent to take
A bribe to pay my sword.
(I, ix, 36–38)

The soldiers cry, "Marcius! Marcius!" and the trumpets sound. He gets into a passion; rates the brawlers:

No more, I say! For that I have not wash'd
My nose that bled, or foil'd some debile wretch,— . . .
You shout me forth
In acclamations hyperbolical;
As if I loved my little should be dieted
In praises sauced with lies.
(I, ix, 47–53)

They are reduced to loading him with honors: Cominius gives him a war horse; decrees him the cognomen of Coriolanus: the people shout Caius Marcius Coriolanus! He replies:

I will go wash;
And when my face is fair, you shall perceive
Whether I blush or no: howbeit, I thank you.
I mean to stride your steed.
(I, ix, 68–71)

This loud voice, loud laughter, blunt acknowledgment of a man who can act and shout better than speak, foretell the mode in which he will treat the plebeians. He loads them with insults; he cannot find abuse enough for the cobblers, tailors, greedy cowards, down on their knees for a copper. "To beg of Hob and Dick!" "Bid them wash their faces and keep their teeth clean." But he must do this, if he would be consul; his friends constrain him. It is then that the passionate soul, incapable of self-restraint, such as Shakespeare knew how to paint, breaks forth without let. He is there in his candidate's gown, gnashing his teeth, and getting up his lesson in this style:

What must I say?
"I pray, sir"—Plague upon't! I cannot bring
My tongue to such a pace:—"Look, sir, my wounds!
I got them in my country's service, when
Some certain of your brethren roar'd and ran
From the noise of our own drums."
(II, iii, 55–60)

The tribunes have no difficulty in stopping the election of a candidate who begs in this fashion. They taunt him in full senate, reproach him with his speech about the corn. He repeats it, with aggravations. Once roused, neither danger nor prayer restrains him:

His heart's his mouth: . . .
And, being angry, does forget that ever
He heard the name of death.
(III, i, 257–260)

He rails against the people, the tribunes, street magistrates, flatterers of the plebs. "Come, enough," says his friend Menenius. "Enough, with over-measure," says Brutus the tribune. He retorts:

No, take more:
What may be sworn by, both divine and human,
Seal what I end withal! . . . At once pluck out
The multitudinous tongue: let them not lick
The sweet which is their poison.

(III, i, 140–157)

The tribune cries, "Treason!" and bids seize him. He cries:

Hence, old goat! . . .
Hence, rotten thing! or I shall shake thy bones
Out of thy garments!

(III, i, 176–179)

He strikes him, drives the mob off: he fancies himself amongst Volscians. "On fair ground I could beat forty of them!" And when his friends hurry him off, he threatens still, and

Speak(s) o' the people,
As if you (he) were a god to punish, not a man
Of their infirmity.[1]

(III, i, 80–81)

Yet he bends before his mother, for he has recognized in her a soul as lofty and a courage as intractable as his own. He has submitted from his infancy to the ascendancy of this pride which he admires. Volumnia reminds him: "My praises made thee first a soldier." Without power over himself, continually tossed on the fire of his too hot blood, he has always been the arm, she the thought. He obeys from involuntary respect, like a soldier before his general, but with what effort!

CORIOLANUS. The smiles of knaves
Tent in my cheeks, and schoolboys' tears take up
The glasses of my sight! a beggar's tongue
Make motion through my lips, and my arm'd knees,
Who bow'd but in my stirrup, bend like his
That hath received an alms! I will not do't, . . .

VOLUMNIA. Do as thou list.
Thy valiantness was mine, thou suck'dst it from me,
But owe thy pride thyself.

[1] Taine may be relying on his memory or on a corrupt text since this speech does not follow Coriolanus' boast but occurs much earlier in the scene, is spoken by Brutus, and does not precede a departure. Editor.

CORIOLANUS. Pray, be content:
Mother, I am going to the market-place;
Chide me no more. I'll mountebank their loves,
Cog their hearts from them, and come home beloved
Of all the trades in Rome.
(III, ii, 115–134)

He goes, and his friends speak for him. Except for a few bitter asides, he appears to be submissive. Then the tribunes pronounce the accusation, and summon him to answer as a traitor:

CORIOLANUS. How! traitor!
MENENIUS. Nay, temperately: your promise.
CORIOLANUS. The fires i' the lowest hell fold-in the people!
Call me their traitor! Thou injurious tribune!
Within thine eyes sat twenty thousand deaths,
In thy hands clutch'd as many millions, in
Thy lying tongue both numbers, I would say,
"Thou liest," unto thee with a voice as free
As I do pray the gods.
(III, iii, 66–73)

His friends surround him, entreat him: he will not listen; he foams, he is like a wounded lion:

Let them pronounce the steep Tarpeian death,
Vagabond exile, flaying, pent to linger
But with a grain a day, I would not buy
Their mercy at the price of one fair word.
(III, iii, 88–91)

The people vote exile, supporting by their shouts the sentence of the tribune:

CORIOLANUS. You common cry of curs! whose breath I hate
As reek o' the rotten fens, whose love I prize
As the dead carcasses of unburied men
That do corrupt my air, I banish you. . . . Despising,
For you, the city, thus I turn my back:
There is a world elsewhere.
(III, iii, 120–135)

Judge of his hatred by these raging words. It goes on increasing by the expectation of vengeance. We find him next with the Volscian army before Rome. His friends kneel before him, he lets them kneel. Old Menenius, who had loved him as a son, comes now only to be driven away. "Wife, mother, child, I know not." It is himself he knows not. For this power of hating in a noble heart is equal with the power of loving. He has transports of tenderness as of hating, and can contain himself no more in joy than in grief. He runs, in spite of his resolution, to his wife's arms; he bends his knee before his mother. He had summoned the Volscian chiefs to make them witnesses of his refusals; and before them, he grants all, and weeps. On his return to Corioli, an insulting word from Aufidius maddens him, and drives him upon the daggers of the Volscians. Vices and virtues, glory and misery, greatness and feebleness, the unbridled passion which composes his nature endowed him with all.

If the life of Coriolanus is the history of a mood, that of Macbeth is the history of a monomania. The witches' prophecy was buried in his heart, instantaneously, like a fixed idea. Gradually this idea corrupts the rest, and transforms the man. He is haunted; he forgets the thanes who surround him and "who stay upon his leisure"; he already sees in the future an indistinct chaos of images of blood:

> Why do I yield to that suggestion
> Whose horrid image doth unfix my hair
> And make my seated heart knock at my ribs, . . .
> My thought, whose murder yet is but fantastical,
> Shakes so my single state of man that function
> Is smother'd in surmise, and nothing is
> But what is not.
>
> (*Macbeth*, I, iii, 134–142)

This is the language of hallucination. Macbeth's hallucination becomes complete when his wife has resolved on the assassination of the king. He sees in the air a blood-stained dagger, "in form as palpable as this which now I draw" (II, i, 40–41). His whole brain is filled with grand and terrible phantoms, which the mind of a common murderer would never have conceived; the poetry of which indicates a generous heart, enslaved to an idea of fate, and capable of remorse:

Now o'er the one half-world
Nature seems dead, and wicked dreams abuse
The curtain'd sleep; witchcraft celebrates
Pale Hecate's offerings, and wither'd murder,
Alarum'd by his sentinel, the wolf,
Whose howl's his watch, thus with his stealthy pace,
With Tarquin's ravishing strides, towards his design
Moves like a ghost. . . . (*A bell rings.*)
I go, and it is done; the bell invites me.
Hear it not, Duncan; for it is a knell
That summons thee to heaven or to hell.
(II, i, 49–64)

He has done the deed, and returns tottering, haggard, like a drunken man. He is horrified at his bloody hands, "these hangman's hands." Nothing now can cleanse them. The whole ocean might sweep over them, but they keep the hue of murder. "What hands are here? ha, they pluck out mine eyes!" He is disturbed by a word which the sleeping chamberlains uttered:

One cried, "God bless us!" and "Amen," the other;
As they had seen me with these hangman's hands.
Listening their fear, I could not say "Amen,"
When they did say "God bless us!" . . .
But wherefore could not I pronounce "Amen"?
I had most need of blessing, and "Amen"
Stuck in my throat.
(II, ii, 26–33)

Then comes a strange dream; a frightful vision of punishment descends upon him.

Above the beating of his heart, the tingling of the blood which boils in his brain, he had heard them cry:

"Sleep no more!
Macbeth does murder sleep," the innocent sleep,
Sleep that knits up the ravell'd sleave of care,
The death of each day's life, sore labour's bath,
Balm of hurt minds, great nature's second course,
Chief nourisher in life's feast.

And the voice, like an angel's trumpet, calls him by his titles:

> "Glamis hath murder'd sleep, and therefore Cawdor
> Shall sleep no more; Macbeth shall sleep no more!"

This mad idea, incessantly repeated, beats in his brain, with monotonous and hard-pressing strokes, like the tongue of a bell. Insanity begins; all the force of his mind is occupied by keeping before him, in spite of himself, the image of the man whom he has murdered in his sleep:

> To know my deed, 'twere best not know myself. (*Knock.*)
> Wake Duncan with thy knocking! I would thou couldst!

Thenceforth, in the rare intervals in which the fever of his mind is assuaged, he is like a man worn out by a long malady. It is the sad prostration of maniacs worn out by their fits of rage:

> Had I but died an hour before this chance,
> I had lived a blessed time; for from this instant
> There's nothing serious in mortality:
> All is but toys: renown and grace is dead;
> The wine of life is drawn, and the mere lees
> Is left this vault to brag of.
>
> (II, iii, 96–101)

When rest has restored some force to the human machine, the fixed idea shakes him again, and drives him onward, like a pitiless horseman, who has left his panting horse only for a moment, to leap again into the saddle, and spur him over precipices. The more he has done, the more he must do:

> I am in blood
> Stepp'd in so far that, should I wade no more,
> Returning were as tedious as go o'er.
>
> (III, iv, 136–138)

He kills in order to preserve the fruit of his murders. The fatal circlet of gold attracts him like a magic jewel; and he beats down, from a sort of blind instinct, the heads which he sees between the crown and him:

But let the frame of things disjoint, both the worlds suffer,
Ere we will eat our meal in fear and sleep
In the affliction of these terrible dreams
That shake us nightly: better be with the dead,
Whom we, to gain our peace, have sent to peace,
Than on the torture of the mind to lie
In restless ecstasy. Duncan is in his grave;
After life's fitful fever he sleeps well;
Treason has done his worst: nor steel, nor poison,
Malice domestic, foreign levy, nothing,
Can touch him further.

(III, ii, 16–26)

Macbeth has Banquo murdered, and in the midst of a great feast he is informed of the success of his plan. He smiles, and proposes Banquo's health. Suddenly, conscience-smitten, he sees the ghost of the murdered man; for this phantom, which Shakespeare summons, is not a mere stage trick: we feel that here the supernatural is unnecessary, and that Macbeth would create it, even if hell would not send it. With stiffened muscles, dilated eyes, his mouth half open with deadly terror, he sees it shake its bloody head, and cries with that hoarse voice which is only to be heard in maniacs' cells:

Prithee, see there! behold! look! lo! how say you?
Why, what care I? If thou canst nod, speak too.
If charnel-houses and our graves must send
Those that we bury back, our monuments
Shall be the maws of kites. . . .
Blood hath been shed ere now, i' the olden time, . . .
Ay, and since too, murders have been perform'd
Too terrible for the ear: the time has been
That, when the brains were out, the man would die,
And there an end; but now they rise again,
With twenty mortal murders on their crowns,
And push us from our stools: . . .
Avaunt! and quit my sight! let the earth hide thee!
Thy bones are marrowless, thy blood is cold;
Thou hast no speculation in those eyes
Which thou dost glare with!

(III, iv, 69–96)

His body trembling like that of an epileptic, his teeth clenched, foaming at the mouth, he sinks on the ground, his limbs beat against the floor, shaken with convulsive quiverings, whilst a dull sob swells his panting breast, and dies in his swollen throat. What joy can remain for a man besieged by such visions? The wide dark country, which he surveys from his towering castle, is but a field of death, haunted by deadly apparitions; Scotland, which he is depopulating, a cemetery,

> Where . . . the dead man's knell
> Is there scarce ask'd for who; and good men's lives
> Expire before the flowers in their caps,
> Dying or ere they sicken.
>
> (IV, iii, 168–171)

His soul is "full of scorpions." He has "supp'd full with horrors," and the faint odor of blood has disgusted him with all else. He goes stumbling over the corpses which he has heaped up, with the mechanical and desperate smile of a maniac-murderer. Thenceforth death, life, all is one to him; the habit of murder has placed him beyond humanity. They tell him that his wife is dead:

> She should have died hereafter;
> There would have been a time for such a word.
> To-morrow, and to-morrow, and to-morrow,
> Creeps in this petty pace from day to day
> To the last syllable of recorded time,
> And all our yesterdays have lighted fools
> The way to dusty death. Out, out, brief candle!
> Life's but a walking shadow, a poor player
> That struts and frets his hour upon the stage,
> And then is heard no more: it is a tale
> Told by an idiot, full of sound and fury,
> Signifying nothing.
>
> (V, v, 17–28)

There remains for him the hardening of the heart in crime, the fixed belief in destiny. Hunted down by his enemies, "bear-like, tied to a stake," he fights, troubled only by the prediction of the witches, sure of being invulnerable so long as the man whom they have pointed at, does not appear. His thoughts inhabit a supernatural world, and to the last he walks with his eyes fixed on the dream, which has possessed him, from the first.

The history of Hamlet, like that of Macbeth, is the story of a moral poisoning. Hamlet's is a delicate soul, an impassioned imagination, like that of Shakespeare. He has lived hitherto, occupied in noble studies, apt in bodily and mental exercises, with a taste for art, loved by the noblest father, enamored of the purest and most charming girl, confiding, generous, not yet having perceived, from the height of the throne to which he was born, aught but the beauty, happiness, grandeur of nature and humanity. On this soul, which character and training make more sensitive than others, misfortune suddenly falls, extreme, overwhelming, of the very kind to destroy all faith and every spring of action: with one look he has seen all the vileness of humanity: and this insight is given him in his mother. His mind is yet intact; but judge from the violence of his style, the crudity of his exact details, the terrible tension of the whole nervous machine, whether he has not already one foot on the verge of madness:

> O, that this too, too solid flesh would melt,
> Thaw and resolve itself into a dew!
> Or that the Everlasting had not fix'd
> His canon 'gainst self-slaughter! O God! God!
> How weary, stale, flat and unprofitable,
> Seem to me all the uses of this world!
> Fie on't! ah fie! 'tis an unweeded garden,
> That grows to seed; things rank and gross in nature
> Possess it merely. That it should come to this!
> But two months dead: nay, not so much, not two:
> So excellent a king; . . . so loving to my mother,
> That he might not beteem the winds of heaven
> Visit her face too roughly. Heaven and earth! . . .
> and yet, within a month—
> Let me not think on't—Frailty, thy name is woman!—
> A little month, or ere those shoes were old
> With which she follow'd my poor father's body, . . .
> Ere yet the salt of most unrighteous tears

Had left the flushing in her galled eyes,
She married. O, most wicked speed, to post
With such dexterity to incestuous sheets!
It is not nor it cannot come to good:
But break, my heart; for I must hold my tongue!
(*Hamlet*, I, ii, 129–158)

Here already are contortions of thought, earnests of hallucination, the symptoms of what is to come after. In the middle of the conversation the image of his father rises before his mind. He thinks he sees him. How then will it be when the "canonized bones have burst their cerements," "the sepulchre hath oped his ponderous and marble jaws," and when the ghost comes in the night, upon a high "platform" of land, to hint to him of the tortures of his prison of fire, and to tell him of the fratricide, who has driven him thither? Hamlet grows faint, but grief strengthens him, and he has a cause for living:

Hold, hold, my heart;
And you, my sinews, grow not instant old,
But bear me stiffly up! Remember thee!
Ay, thou poor ghost, while memory holds a seat
In this distracted globe. Remember thee!
Yea, from the table of my memory
I'll wipe away all trivial fond records,
All saws of books, all forms, all pressures past, . . .
And thy commandment all alone shall live . . .
O villain, villain, smiling, damned villain!
My tables,—meet it is I set it down,
That one may smile, and smile, and be a villain;
At least I'm sure it may be so in Denmark:
So, uncle, there you are.
(I, v, 93–110)

This convulsive outburst, this fevered writing hand, this frenzy of intentness prelude the approach of a monomania. When his friends come up, he treats them with the speeches of a child or an idiot. He is no longer master of his words; hollow phrases whirl in his brain, and fall from his mouth as in a dream. They call him; he answers by imitating the cry of a sportsman whistling to his falcon: "Hillo, ho, ho, boy! come, bird, come." Whilst he is in the act of swearing them to secrecy, the ghost below repeats "Swear." Hamlet cries, with a nervous excitement and a fitful gaiety:

> Ah ha, boy! say'st thou so? art thou there, truepenny?
> Come on—you hear this fellow in the cellarage—
> Consent to swear. . . .
> GHOST (*Beneath*). Swear.
> HAMLET. *Hic et ubique?* then we'll shift our ground.
> Come hither, gentlemen. . . .
> Swear by my sword.
> GHOST (*Beneath*). Swear.
> HAMLET. Well said, old mole! canst work i' the earth so fast?
> A worthy pioner!
>
> (I, v, 149–163)

Understand that as he says this his teeth chatter, "pale as his shirt, his knees knocking each other." Intense anguish ends with a burst of laughter, which is nothing else than a spasm. Thenceforth Hamlet speaks as though he had a continuous nervous attack. His madness is feigned, I admit; but his mind, as a door whose hinges are twisted, swings and bangs to every wind with a mad precipitance and with a discordant noise. He has no need to search for the strange ideas, apparent incoherencies, exaggerations, the deluge of sarcasms which he accumulates. He finds them within him; he does himself no violence, he simply gives himself up to them. When he has the piece played which is to unmask his uncle, he raises himself, lounges on the floor, would lay his head in Ophelia's lap; he addresses the actors, and comments on the piece to the spectators; his nerves are strung, his excited thought is like a waving and crackling flame, and cannot find fuel enough in the multitude of objects surrounding it, upon all of which it seizes. When the king rises unmasked and troubled, Hamlet sings, and says, "Would not this, sir, and a forest of feathers—if the rest of my fortunes turn Turk with me—with two Provincial roses on my razed shoes, get me a fellowship in a cry of players, sir?" And he laughs terribly, for he is resolved on murder. It is clear that this state is a disease, and that the man will not survive it.

In a soul so ardent of thought, and so mighty of feeling, what is left but disgust and despair? We tinge all nature with the color of our thoughts; we shape the world according to our own ideas; when our soul is sick, we see nothing but sickness in the universe:

> . . . this goodly frame, the earth, seems to me a sterile promontory, this most excellent canopy, the air, look you, this brave o'erhanging firmament, this majestical roof fretted with golden fire, why, it appears no other thing to me than a foul and pestilent congregation of vapours. What a piece of work is a man! how noble in reason! how infinite in faculty! in form and moving how express and admirable! in action how like an angel! in apprehension how like a god! the beauty of the world! the paragon of animals! And yet, to me, what is this quintessence of dust! man delights not me: no, nor woman neither.
>
> (II, ii, 309–321)

Henceforth his thought tarnishes whatever it touches. He rails bitterly before Ophelia against marriage and love. Beauty! Innocence! Beauty is but a means of prostituting innocence:

> Get thee to a nunnery: why wouldst thou be a breeder of sinners? . . . What should such fellows as I do crawling between earth and heaven? We are arrant knaves, all; believe none of us.
>
> (III, i, 122–131)

When he has killed Polonius by accident, he hardly repents it; it is one fool less. He jeers lugubriously:

> KING. Now, Hamlet, where's Polonius?
> HAMLET. At supper.
> KING. At supper! where?
> HAMLET. Not where he eats, but where he is eaten: a certain convocation of politic worms are e'en at him.
>
> (IV, iii, 17–22)

And he repeats in five or six fashions these gravedigger jests. His thoughts already inhabit a churchyard: to this hopeless philosophy your true man is a corpse. Duties, honors, passions, pleasures, projects, science, all this is but a borrowed mask, which death removes, that we may see ourselves what we are, an evil-smelling and grinning skull. It is this sight he goes to see by Ophelia's grave. He counts the skulls which the grave-digger turns out: this was a lawyer's, that a courtier's. What salutations, intrigues, pretensions, arrogance! And here now is a clown knocking it about with his spade, and playing "at loggats with 'em." Caesar and Alexander have turned to clay, and make the earth fat; the masters of the world have served to "patch a wall." "Now get you to my lady's chamber, and tell her, let her paint an inch thick, to this favour she must come; make her laugh at that" (V, i, 211–214). When one has come to this, there is nothing left but to die.

This heated imagination, which explains Hamlet's nervous disease and his moral poisoning, explains also his conduct. If he hesitates to kill his uncle, it is not from horror of blood or from our modern scruples. He belongs to the sixteenth century. On board ship he wrote the order to behead Rosencrantz and Guildenstern, and to do so without giving them "shriving-time." He killed Polonius, he caused Ophelia's death, and has no great remorse for it. If for once he spared his uncle, it was because he found him praying, and was afraid of sending him to heaven. He thought he was killing him, when he killed Polonius. What his imagination robs him of is the coolness and strength to go quietly and with premeditation to plunge a sword into a breast. He can only do the thing on a sudden suggestion; he must have a moment of enthusiasm; he must think the king is behind the arras, or else, seeing that he himself is poisoned, he must find his victim under his foil's point. He is not master of his acts; occasion dictates them; he cannot plan a murder, but must improvise it. A too lively imagination exhausts energy, by the accumulation of images and by the fury of intentness which absorbs it. You recognize in him a poet's soul, made not to act, but to dream, which sees the imaginary world too clearly to play a part in the real world; an artist whom evil chance has made a prince, whom worse chance has made an avenger of crime, and who, destined by nature for genius, is condemned by fortune to madness and unhappiness. Hamlet is Shakespeare, and, at the close of this gallery of portraits which have all some features of his own, Shakespeare has painted himself in the most striking of all.

If Racine or Corneille had framed a psychology, they would have said, with Descartes: Man is an incorporeal soul, served by organs, endowed with reason and will, living in palaces or porticos, made for conversation and society, whose harmonious and ideal action is developed by discourse and replies, in a world constructed by logic beyond the realms of time and space.

If Shakespeare had framed a psychology, he would have said, with Esquirol: [2] Man is a nervous machine, governed by a mood, disposed to hallucinations, transported by unbridled passions, essentially unreasoning, a mixture of animal and poet, having no rapture but mind, no sensibility but virtue, imagination for prompter and guide, and led at random, by the most determinate and complex circumstances, to pain, crime, madness, and death.

[2] Jean Étienne Dominique Esquirol (1772–1840) was a French physician who founded a model institution for the insane. Editor.

17. Leo Nikolayevich Tolstoy

1828–1910

Tolstoy's Shakespeare and the Drama *(1906) is easily the most vexing document in the long history of European Shakespeare criticism. Admittedly, it is unjust, wrongheaded, and wholly negative. But it cannot be ignored, as it has been by some critics, or dismissed lightly, as it has been by others. That such a document could be written by the man whom many critics would rank beside the object of his attack, and that it could be written in the twentieth century, are themselves of great interest. But of greater interest are the possible causes of Tolstoy's attitude.*

After 1880 Tolstoy became more and more dissatisfied with the growing alienation of art from the "masses." And with the zeal of a reformer and the natural messianic strain of the Slav, Tolstoy launched on a program of polemical works culminating in What Is Art? *(1898) and the present essay. The flaws of these works are only too obvious. The reformer's passion has intimidated the critic's judgment. But the impulse is honest. Its motivation lies in Tolstoy's rationalist Christianity, his* visio pacis*—the eventual establishment of a classless Christian society based on brotherhood. In* What Is Art? *Tolstoy had promulgated his doctrine of "infection," a doctrine which supposes that anything which does not "infect" one with sympathy is not art. Tolstoy's elevation of folk art to the highest level, and his equation of simplicity with artistic virtue are all of a piece with the doctrine.*

We must remember that Tolstoy's humanism was one of religious orientation. He was dismayed by the decay of traditional values, the growing religion of "art" with its concomitant —the refusal to judge literary works from an ethical basis, and the rise of science with its growing moral relativism. Against such a background Tolstoy's attack on Shakespeare, whom the Romantics he blamed for the above-mentioned tendencies had all but canonized, becomes intelligible. And given Tolstoy's maximalist personality, a passionate strain he never quite subdued, even the vituperativeness of the essay can be understood. Thus, injudicious as the essay is it must be seen as one of the great attempts at stemming the tide of aestheticism and decadence, directed less against Shakespeare than against that tradition which had used him as the exemplum of its own predilections. Had Tolstoy made this more explicit than he was able to do, the essay, today, would have more currency.

Shakespeare and the Drama

Mr. Crosby's article on Shakespeare's attitude toward the working classes [1] has suggested to me the idea of expressing my own long-established opinion about the works of Shakespeare, in direct opposition as it is to that established in the whole European world. Calling to mind all the struggles of doubt and self-deceit, all the efforts to attune myself to Shakespeare—which I went through owing to my complete disagreement with this universal adulation, and presuming that many have experienced and are experiencing the same, I think that it may not be unprofitable to express definitely and frankly this view of mine opposed to that of the majority, the more so as the conclusions to which I came when examining the causes of my disagreement with the universally established opinion, are, it seems to me, not without interest and significance.

My disagreement with the established opinion about Shakespeare is not the result of an accidental frame of mind nor of

From *Tolstoy on Shakespeare* (London, The Free Age Press, Everett and Company, 1907), pp. 7–81. Translated by V. Tchertkoff.

[1] Tolstoy intended this essay as a preface to an article by Ernest Crosby, with which it appeared. Crosby's article, while of little value to Shakespeare criticism, has had a greater vogue than it deserves, for example, among critics such as Smirnov. Editor.

a light-minded attitude toward the matter, but is the outcome of many years' repeated and insistent endeavors to harmonize my own views of Shakespeare with those established amongst all civilized men of the Christian world.

I remember the astonishment I felt when I first read Shakespeare. I expected to receive a powerful aesthetic pleasure, but having read, one after the other, works regarded as his best: *King Lear, Romeo and Juliet, Hamlet,* and *Macbeth,* not only did I feel no delight, but I felt an irresistible repulsion and tedium, and doubted as to whether I was senseless in feeling works regarded as the summit of perfection by the whole of the civilized world to be trivial and positively bad, or whether the significance which this civilized world attributes to the works of Shakespeare was itself senseless. My consternation was increased by the fact that I always keenly felt the beauties of poetry in every form; then why should artistic works recognized by the whole world as those of a genius—the works of Shakespeare—not only fail to please me, but be disagreeable to me? For a long time I could not believe in myself, and during fifty years, in order to test myself, I several times recommenced reading Shakespeare in every possible form, in Russian and in English and in German and in Schlegel's translation, as I was advised. Several times I read the dramas and the comedies and historical plays, and I invariably underwent the same feelings: repulsion, weariness, and bewilderment. At the present time, before writing this preface, being desirous once more to test myself, I have as an old man of seventy-five, again read the whole of Shakespeare, including the historical plays: the *Henry's, Troilus and Cressida, The Tempest, Cymbeline,* etc., and I have felt with even greater force the same feelings—this time, however, not of bewilderment, but of firm, indubitable conviction that the unquestionable glory of a great genius which Shakespeare enjoys, and which compels writers of our time to imitate him and readers and spectators to discover in him nonexistent merits—thereby distorting their aesthetic and ethical understanding—is a great evil, as is every untruth.

Although I know that the majority of people believe so firmly in the greatness of Shakespeare that in reading this judgment of mine they will not admit even the possibility of its justice, and will not give it the slightest attention, nevertheless I will endeavor as well as I can to show why I believe that Shakespeare cannot be recognized either as a great genius, or even as an average author.

For illustration of my purpose I will begin by taking one of Shakespeare's most extolled dramas, *King Lear,* in the enthusiastic praise of which the majority of critics agree.

"The tragedy of Lear is deservedly celebrated among the dramas of Shakespeare," says Dr. Johnson. "There is perhaps no play which so much agitates our passions and interests our curiosity."

"We wish that we could pass this play over and say nothing about it," says Hazlitt. "All that we can say must fall far short of the subject, or even of what we ourselves conceive of it. To attempt to give a description of the play itself or of its effects upon the mind is mere impertinence; yet we must say something. It is then the best of Shakespeare's plays, for it is the one in which he was the most in earnest."

"If the originality of invention did not so much stamp almost every play of Shakespeare," says Hallam, "that to name one as the most original seems a disparagement to others, we might say that this great prerogative of genius was exercised above all in *Lear*. It diverges more from the model of regular tragedy than *Macbeth* or *Othello* or even more than *Hamlet,* but the fable is better constructed than in the last of these, and it displays full as much of the almost superhuman inspiration of the poet as the other two."

"King Lear may be recognized as the perfect model of the dramatic art of the whole world," says Shelley.

"I am not minded to say much of Shakespeare's Arthur," says Swinburne. "There are one or two figures in the world of his work of which there are no words that would be fit or good to say. Another of these is Cordelia. The place they have in our lives and thoughts is not one for talk. The niche set apart for them to inhabit in our secret hearts is not penetrable by the lights and noises of common day. There are chapels in the cathedral of man's highest art, as in that of his inmost life, not made to be set open to the eyes and feet of the world. Love and Death and Memory keep charge for us in silence of some beloved names. It is the crowning glory of genius, the final miracle and transcendent gift of poetry that it can add to the number of these, and engrave on the very heart of our remembrance fresh names and memories of its own creation."

"Lear is the occasion for Cordelia," says Victor Hugo. "Maternity of the daughter toward the father; profound subject; maternity venerable among all other maternities, so admirably rendered by the legend of that Roman girl, who in the depths of a prison nurses her old father. The young breast near the white beard. There is not a spectacle more holy. This filial breast is Cordelia. Once this figure dreamed of and found, Shakespeare created his drama. . . . Shakespeare carrying Cordelia in his thoughts, created that tragedy, like a God who, having an aurora to put forward, makes a world expressly for it."

"In *King Lear,* Shakespeare's vision sounded the abyss of horror to its very depths, and his spirit showed neither fear, nor giddiness, nor faintness at the sight," says Brandes. "On the threshold of this work, a feeling of awe comes over one, as on the threshold of the Sistine Chapel, with its ceiling frescoes by Michelangelo, only that the suffering here is far more intense, the wail wilder, and the harmonies of beauty more definitely shattered by the discords of despair."

Such are the judgments of the critics about this drama, and therefore I believe I am not wrong in selecting it as a type of Shakespeare's best.

As impartially as possible I will endeavor to describe the contents of the drama, and then to show why it is not that acme of perfection it is represented to be by critics, but is something quite different.

II

The drama of *Lear* begins with a scene giving the conversation between two courtiers, Kent and Gloucester. Kent, pointing to a young man present, asks Gloucester whether that is not his son. Gloucester says that he has often blushed to acknowledge the young man as his son, but has now ceased doing so. Kent says he "cannot conceive him." Then Gloucester, in the presence of this son of his, says: "The fellow's mother could, and grew round-wombed, and had a son for her cradle ere she had a husband for her bed." "I have another, a legitimate son," continues Gloucester, "but although this one came into the world before he was sent for, his mother was fair and there was good sport at his making, and therefore I acknowledge this one also."

Such is the introduction. Not to mention the language of King Lear, the same in which all Shakespeare's kings speak, the reader or spectator cannot conceive that a king, however old and stupid he may be, could believe the words of the vicious daughters with whom he had passed his whole life, and not believe his favorite daughter, but curse and banish her; and therefore the spectator or reader cannot share the feelings of the persons participating in this unnatural scene.

The second scene opens with Edmund, Gloucester's illegitimate son, soliloquizing on the injustice of men, who concede rights and respect to the legitimate son, but deprive the illegitimate son of them, and he determines to ruin Edgar, and usurp his place. For this purpose, he forges a letter to himself as from Edgar, in which the latter expresses a desire to murder his father. Awaiting his father's approach, Edmund, as if against his will, shows him this letter, and the father immediately believes that his son Edgar, whom he tenderly loves, desires to kill him. The father goes away, Edgar enters, and Edmund persuades him that his father for some reason desires to kill him. Edgar immediately believes this and flees from his parent.

The relations between Gloucester and his two sons, and the feelings of these characters, are as unnatural as Lear's relation to his daughters, or even more so, and therefore it is still more difficult for the spectator to transport himself into the mental condition of Gloucester and his sons and sympathize with them, than it is to do so into that of Lear and his daughters.

In the fourth scene, the banished Kent, so disguised that Lear does not recognize him, presents himself to Lear who is already staying with Goneril. Lear asks who he is, to which Kent answers, one doesn't know why, in a tone quite inappropriate to his position: "A very honest hearted fellow and as poor as the King." "If thou be as poor for a subject as he is for a King, thou art poor enough. . . . How old art thou?" asks the King. "Not so young, Sir, to love a woman, *etc.*, nor so old to dote on her." To this the King says, "If I like thee no worse after dinner, I will not part from thee yet."

These speeches follow neither from Lear's position, nor his relation to Kent, but are put into the mouths of Lear and Kent, evidently because the author regards them as witty and amusing.

Goneril's steward appears, and behaves rudely to Lear, for which Kent knocks him down. The King, still not recognizing Kent, gives him money for this and takes him into his service. After this appears the fool, and thereupon begins a prolonged conversation between the fool and the King, utterly unsuited to the position and serving no purpose. Thus, for instance, the fool says, "Give me an egg and I'll give thee two crowns." The King asks, "What crowns shall they be?" "Why," says the fool, "after I have cut the egg i' the middle and eat up the meat, the two crowns of the egg. When thou clovest thy crown i' the middle, and gavest away both parts, thou borest thine ass on thy back o'er the dirt: thou hadst little wit in thy bald crown when thou gavest thy golden one away. If I speak like myself in this, let him be whipp'd that first finds it so" (I, iv, 173–180).

In this manner lengthy conversations go on, calling forth in the spectator or reader that wearisome uneasiness which one experiences when listening to jokes which are not witty.

This conversation is interrupted by the approach of Goneril. She demands of her father that he should diminish his retinue: that he should be satisfied with fifty courtiers instead of one hundred. At this suggestion, Lear gets into a strange and unnatural rage, and asks:

> Doth any here know me? This is not Lear:
> Doth Lear walk thus? speak thus? Where are his eyes?
> Either his notion weakens, his discernings
> Are lethargied—Ha! waking? 'tis not so,
> Who is it that can tell me who I am?
>
> (I, iv, 246–250)

And so forth.

While this goes on the fool does not cease to interpolate his humorless jokes. Goneril's husband then enters and wishes to appease Lear, but Lear curses Goneril, invoking for her either sterility or the birth of such an infant monster as would return laughter and contempt for her motherly cares, and would thus show her all the horror and pain caused by a child's ingratitude.

These words, which express a genuine feeling, might have been touching had they stood alone. But they are lost amongst long and high-flown speeches which Lear keeps incessantly uttering quite inappropriately. He either invokes "blasts and fogs" upon the head of his daughter, or desires his curse to "pierce every sense about her," or else appealing to his own eyes says that should they weep he will pluck them out and "cast them with the waters that they lost to temper clay." And so on.

After this, Lear sends Kent, whom he still fails to recognize, to his other daughter, and notwithstanding the despair he has just manifested, he talks with the fool, and elicits his jokes. The jokes continue to be mirthless and besides creating an unpleasant feeling, similar to shame, the usual effect of unsuccessful witticisms, they are also so drawn out as to be positively dull. Thus the fool asks the King whether he can tell why one's nose stands in the middle of one's face? Lear says he cannot. "Why, to keep one's eyes of either side 's nose; that what a man cannot smell out, he may spy into."

> FOOL. Canst tell how an oyster makes his shell?
> LEAR. No.
> FOOL. Nor I either; but I can tell why a snail has a house.
> LEAR. Why?

FOOL. Why, to put his head in; not to give it away to his daughters, and leave his horns without a case. . . .

LEAR. Be my horses ready?

FOOL. Thy asses are gone about 'em. The reason why the seven stars are no more than seven is a pretty reason.

LEAR. Because they are not eight?

FOOL. Yes, indeed: thou would'st make a good fool.

(I, v, 28–41)

And so on.

After this lengthy scene, a gentleman enters and announces that the horses are ready. The fool says:

> She that's a maid now, and laughs at my departure,
> Shall not be a maid long, unless things be cut shorter
>
> (I, v, 55–56)

and departs.

The second part of the first scene of the second act begins by the villain Edmund persuading his brother, when their father enters, to pretend that they are fighting with their swords. Edgar consents, although it is utterly incomprehensible why he should do so. The father finds them fighting. Edgar flies and Edmund scratches his arm to draw blood and persuades his father that Edgar was working charms for the purpose of killing his father and had desired Edmund to help him, but that he, Edmund, had refused and that then Edgar flew at him and wounded his arm. Gloucester believes everything, curses Edgar, and transfers all the rights of the elder and legitimate son to the illegitimate Edmund. The Duke, hearing of this, also rewards Edmund.

In the second scene, in front of Gloucester's palace, Lear's new servant, Kent, still unrecognized by Lear, without any reason, begins to abuse Oswald, Goneril's steward, calling him "A knave, a rascal, an eater of broken meats; a base, proud, shallow, beggarly, three-suited, hundred pound, filthy worsted-stockinged knave . . . the son and heir of a mongrel bitch" (II, ii, 14–22). And so on. Then drawing his sword, he demands that Oswald should fight with him, saying that he will make a "sop o' the moonshine" of him—words which no commentators can explain. When he is stopped, he continues to give vent to the strangest abuse, saying that a tailor made Oswald, as "a stone cutter or a painter could not have made him so ill, though they had been but two hours o' the trade!" He further says that, if only leave be given him, he will "tread this unbolted villain into mortar and daub the wall of a jakes with him."

Thus Kent, whom nobody recognizes, although both the King and the Duke of Cornwall, as well as Gloucester who is present, ought to know him well, continues to brawl, in the character of Lear's new servant, until he is taken and put in the stocks.

The third scene takes place on a heath. Edgar, flying from the persecutions of his father, hides in a wood and tells the public what kinds of lunatics exist there—beggars who go about naked, thrust wooden pricks and pins into their flesh, scream with wild voices and enforce charity, and says that he wishes to simulate such a lunatic in order to save himself from persecution. Having communicated this to the public he retires.

The fourth scene is again before Gloucester's castle. Enter Lear and the fool. Lear sees Kent in the stocks, and, still not recognizing him, is inflamed with rage against those who dared so to insult his messenger, and calls for the Duke and Regan. The fool goes on with his jokes.

Lear with difficulty restrains his ire. Enter the Duke and Regan. Lear complains of Goneril, but Regan justifies her sister. Lear curses Goneril, and when Regan tells him he had better return to her sister, he is indignant and says: "Ask for forgiveness?" and falls down on his knees demonstrating how indecent it would be if he were abjectly to beg food and clothing as charity from his own daughter, and he curses Goneril with the strangest curses and asks who put his servant in the stocks. Before Regan can answer, Goneril arrives. Lear becomes yet more exasperated and again curses Goneril, but when he is told that it was the Duke himself who ordered the stocks, he does not say anything, because, at this moment, Regan tells him that she cannot receive him now, and that he had best return to Goneril, with, however, not a hundred but fifty servants, and that in a month's time she herself will receive him. Lear again curses Goneril and does not want to go to her, continuing to hope that Regan will accept him with the whole hundred servants. But Regan says she will receive him only with twenty-five and then Lear makes up his mind to go back to Goneril, who admits fifty. But when Goneril says that even twenty-five are too many, Lear pours forth a long argument about the superfluous and the needful being relative, and says that if a man is not allowed more than he needs he is not to be distinguished from a beast. Lear, or rather the actor who plays Lear's part, adds that there is no need for a lady's finery, which does not keep her warm. After this he flies into a mad fury and says that to take vengeance on his daughters he will do something dreadful, but that he will not weep, and so he departs. A storm begins.

Such is the second act, full of unnatural events, and yet more unnatural speeches, not flowing from the position of the characters, and finishing with a scene between Lear and his daughters which might have been powerful if it had not been permeated with the most absurdly foolish, unnatural speeches —which, moreover, have no relation to the subject—put into the mouth of Lear. Lear's vacillations between pride, anger, and the hope of his daughters giving in would be exceedingly touching if they were not spoiled by the verbose absurdities to which he gives vent, about being ready to divorce himself from Regan's dead mother, should Regan not be glad to receive him—or about "fen-suck'd fogs," which he invokes upon the head of his daughter, or about the heavens being obliged to patronize old people because they themselves are old.

The third act begins with thunder, lightning—a storm of some special kind such as, according to the words of the characters in the piece, had never before taken place. On the heath, a gentleman tells Kent that Lear, banished by his daughters from their homes, is running about the heath alone, tearing his hair and throwing it to the wind, and that none but the fool is with him. In return Kent tells the gentleman that the Dukes have quarreled, and that the French army has landed at Dover, and having communicated this intelligence, he dispatches the gentleman to Dover to meet Cordelia.

The second scene of the third act also takes place on the heath, but in another part of it. Lear walks about the heath and says words which are meant to express his despair: he desires that the winds should blow so hard that they (the winds) should crack their cheeks and that the rain should flood everything, that lightning should singe his white head, and the thunder flatten the world and destroy all germs "that make ungrateful man!" The fool keeps uttering still more senseless words. Enter Kent; Lear says that for some reason during this storm all criminals shall be found out and convicted. Kent, still unrecognized by Lear, endeavors to persuade him to take refuge in a hovel. At this point the fool pronounces a prophecy in no wise related to the situation and they all depart.

The third scene is again transferred to Gloucester's castle. Gloucester tells Edmund that the French King has already landed with his troops, and intends to help Lear. Learning this, Edmund decides to accuse his father of treason in order that he may get his heritage.

The fourth scene is again on the heath in front of the hovel. Kent invites Lear into the hovel, but Lear answers that he has no reason to shelter himself from the tempest, that he does not feel it, having in his mind a tempest, called forth by the ingratitude of his daughters, which extinguishes all else. This true feeling, expressed in simple words, might elicit sympathy, but amidst the incessant pompous raving, it escapes one and loses its significance.

The hovel into which Lear is led turns out to be the same which Edgar has entered, disguised as a madman, i.e., naked. Edgar comes out of the hovel, and, although all have known him, no one recognizes him—as no one recognizes Kent—and Edgar, Lear, and the fool begin to say senseless things which continue with interruptions for many pages. In the middle of this scene, enters Gloucester (who also does not recognize either Kent or his son Edgar), and tells them how his son Edgar wanted to kill him.

This scene is again cut short by another in Gloucester's castle, during which Edmund betrays his father and the Duke of Cornwall promises to avenge himself on Gloucester. Then the scene shifts back to Lear. Kent, Edgar, Gloucester, Lear, and the fool are at a farm and talking. Edgar says: "Frateretto calls me: and tells me Nero is an angler in the lake of darkness. . . ." The fool says: "Tell me whether a madman be a gentleman or a yeoman?" Lear, having lost his mind, says that the madman is a king. The fool says no, the madman is the yeoman who has allowed his son to become a gentleman. Lear screams: "To have a thousand with red burning spits come hissing in upon 'em"—while Edgar shrieks that the foul fiend bites his back. At this the fool remarks that one cannot believe "in the tameness of a wolf, a horse's health, a boy's love, or a whore's oath." Then Lear imagines he is judging his daughters. "Sit thou here, most learned justicer," says he, addressing the naked Edgar; "Thou, sapient sir, sit here. Now, you she foxes." To this Edgar says: "Look where he stands and glares! Wantest thou eyes at trial, madam? Come o'er the bourn, Bessy, to me."

The fool sings:

> Her boat hath a leak,
> And she must not speak,
> Why she dares not come over to thee.

Edgar goes on in his own strain. Kent suggests that Lear should lie down, but Lear continues his imaginary trial: "Bring in the evidence," he cries. "Thou robed man of justice, take thy place," he says to Edgar, "and thou" (to the fool) "his yoke-fellow of equity, bench by his side. You are o' the commission, sit you too," addressing Kent.

"Purr, the cat is grey," shouts Edgar.

"Arraign her first, 'tis Goneril," cries Lear. "I here take my oath before this honourable assembly, she kicked the poor king her father."

"Come hither, mistress. Is your name Goneril?" says the fool, addressing the seat.

"And here's another whose warped looks proclaim what store her heart is made of," cries Lear. "Stop her there! arms, arms, sword, fire! Corruption in the place! False justicer, why hast thou let her 'scape?"

This raving terminates by Lear falling asleep, and Gloucester persuading Kent, still without recognizing him, to carry Lear to Dover, and Kent and the fool carry off the King.

The scene is transferred to Gloucester's castle. Gloucester himself is about to be accused of treason. He is brought forward and bound. The Duke of Cornwall plucks out one of Gloucester's eyes and sets his foot on it. Regan says, "One side will mock another; the other too." The Duke wishes to pluck the other out also, but a servant, for some reason, suddenly takes Gloucester's part and wounds the Duke. Regan kills the servant, who, dying, says to Gloucester that he has "one eye left to see some mischief on him." The Duke says, "Lest it see more, prevent it," and he tears out Gloucester's other eye and throws it on the ground. Here Regan says that it was Edmund who betrayed his father, and then Gloucester immediately understands that he has been deceived and that Edgar did not wish to kill him.

Thus ends the third act.

The fourth act is again on the heath. Edgar, still attired as a lunatic, i.e., naked, soliloquizes in stilted terms about the instability of fortune and the advantages of a humble lot. Then there comes to him, somehow into the very place on the heath where he is, his father, the blinded Gloucester, led by an old man. In that characteristic Shakespearean language—the chief peculiarity of which is that the thoughts are bred either by the consonance or the contrasts of words—Gloucester also speaks about the instability of fortune. He tells the old man who leads him to leave him, but the old man points out to him that he cannot *see* his way. Gloucester says he has no way and therefore does not require *eyes*. And he argues about his having stumbled when he *saw*, and about defects often proving commodities. "Ah! dear son Edgar," he adds, "might I but live to *see* thee in my touch, I'd say I had *eyes* again."

Edgar, naked and in the character of a lunatic, hearing this, still does not disclose himself to his father, who does not recognize his voice but regards him as a wandering madman. Gloucester avails himself of the opportunity to deliver himself of a witticism: "'Tis the times' plague when madmen lead the blind," and he insists on dismissing the old man, obviously not from motives which might be natural to Gloucester at that moment, but merely in order, when left alone with Edgar, to enact the later scene of the imaginary leaping from the cliff.

Notwithstanding Edgar has just seen his blinded father and has learned that his father repents of having banished him, he puts in utterly unnecessary interjections which Shakespeare might know, having read them in Harouet's book,[2] but which Edgar had no means of becoming acquainted with, and above all, which it was quite unnatural for him to repeat in his present position. He says, "Five fiends have been in poor Tom at once: of lust, as Obidicut; Hobbididence, prince of dumbness; Mahu of stealing; Modo, of murder; Flibbertigibbet, of mopping and mowing; who since possesses chambermaids and waiting women." Hearing these words, Gloucester makes a present of his purse to Edgar, saying:

That I am so wretched
Makes thee the happier: heavens, deal so still!
Let the superfluous and lust-dieted man,
That slaves your ordinance, that will not see
Because he doth not feel, feel your power quickly;
So distribution should undo excess,
And each man have enough.

(IV, i, 68–74)

Having pronounced these strange words, the blind Gloucester requests Edgar to lead him to a certain cliff overhanging the sea, and they depart.

The second scene of the fourth act takes place before the

[2] Tolstoy must be referring to Harsnet's *Declaration of Egregious Popish Impostures,* which was entered in the Stationers' Register March 16, 1603. Professor W. W. Greg, in "The Date of King Lear and Shakespeare's Use of Earlier Versions," *The Library,* Vol. XX, No. 4, London (March 1940), pp. 377–400, calls attention to the fact that this work is the source of Edgar's devils. Editor.

Duke of Albany's palace. Goneril is not only cruel, but also depraved. She despises her husband and discloses her love for the villain Edmund, who has inherited the title of his father Gloucester. Edmund leaves, and a conversation takes place between Goneril and her husband. The Duke of Albany, the only figure with human feelings, who had been already dissatisfied with his wife's treatment of her father, now resolutely takes Lear's side, but expresses his emotion in such words as to shake one's confidence in his feelings. He says that a bear would lick Lear's reverence, that if the heavens do not send their visible spirits to tame these vile offenses, humanity must prey on itself like monsters, etc.

Goneril does not listen to him, and then he begins to abuse her:

> See thyself, devil,
> Proper deformity seems not in the fiend
> So horrid as in woman.

"O vain fool," says Goneril. "Thou changed and self-cover'd thing, for shame," continues the Duke:

> Be-monster not thy feature. Were't my fitness
> To let these hands obey my blood,
> They are apt enough to dislocate and tear
> Thy flesh and bones; howe'er thou art a fiend,
> A woman's shape doth shield thee.
>
> (IV, iii, 63–68)

After this a messenger enters and announces that the Duke of Cornwall, wounded by his servant while plucking out Gloucester's eyes, had died. Goneril is glad, but already anticipates with fear that Regan, now a widow, will deprive her of Edmund. Here the second scene ends.

The third scene of the fourth act represents the French camp. From a conversation between Kent and a gentleman, the reader or spectator learns that the King of France is not in the camp, and that Cordelia has received a letter from Kent and is greatly grieved by what she has learned about her father. The gentleman says that her face reminded one of sunshine and rain.

. . . her smiles and tears
Were like a better way; those happy smilets,
That play'd on her ripe lip, seem'd not to know
What guests were in her eyes; which parted thence,
As pearls from diamonds dropp'd.

(IV, iii, 20–24)

The gentleman says that Cordelia desires to see her father, but Kent says that Lear is ashamed of seeing this daughter whom he has treated so unkindly.

In the fourth scene, Cordelia, talking with a physician, tells him that Lear has been seen, that he is quite mad, wearing on his head a wreath of various weeds, that he is roaming about and that she has sent soldiers in search of him, adding that she desires all secret remedies to spring with her tears, and the like.

She is informed that the armies of the Dukes are approaching; but she is concerned only about her father and departs.

The fifth scene of the fourth act lies in Gloucester's castle. Regan is talking with Oswald, Goneril's steward, who is carrying a letter from Goneril to Edmund, and she announces to him that she also loves Edmund, and that, being a widow, it is better for her to marry him than for Goneril to do so, and she begs him to persuade her sister of this. Further, she tells him that it was very unreasonable to blind Gloucester and yet leave him alive, and therefore advises Oswald, should he meet Gloucester, to kill him, promising him a great reward if he does this.

In the sixth scene, Gloucester again appears with his still unrecognized son Edgar, who (now in the guise of a peasant) pretends to lead his father to the cliff. Gloucester is walking along on level land, but Edgar persuades him that they are with difficulty ascending a steep hill. Gloucester believes this. Edgar tells his father that the noise of the sea is heard; Gloucester believes this also. Edgar stops on a level place and persuades his father that he has ascended the cliff and that in front of him lies a dreadful abyss, and then leaves him alone. Gloucester, addressing the Gods, says that he shakes off his affliction, as he can bear it no longer, and that he does not condemn them—the Gods. Having said this, he leaps on the level ground and falls, imagining that he has jumped off the cliff. On this occasion Edgar, soliloquizing, gives vent to a yet more entangled utterance:

> . . . I know not how conceit may rob
> The treasury of life when life itself
> Yields to the theft; had he been where he thought,
> By this, had thought been past.
>
> (IV, vi, 43–46)

He approaches Gloucester, in the character of yet a different person, and expresses astonishment at the latter not being hurt by his fall from such a dreadful height. Gloucester believes that he has fallen and prepares to die, but he feels that he is alive and begins to doubt that he has fallen from such a height. Then Edgar persuades him that he has indeed jumped from the dreadful height and tells him that the individual who had been with him at the top was the devil, as he had eyes like two full moons and a thousand noses and wavy horns. Gloucester believes this, and is persuaded that his despair was the work of the devil, and therefore decides that he will henceforth despair no more, but will quietly await death. Hereupon enters Lear, for some reason covered with wild flowers. He has lost his senses and says things wilder than before. He speaks about coining, about the moon, calls for a clothier's yard—then he cries that he sees a mouse, which he wishes to entice by a piece of cheese. Then he suddenly demands the password from Edgar, and Edgar immediately answers him with the words, "Sweet marjoram." Lear says "Pass," and the blind Gloucester, who has not recognized either his son or Kent, recognizes the King's voice.

Then the King, after his disconnected utterances, suddenly begins to speak ironically about flatterers who agreed to all he said: "Ay and no too was no good divinity," but when he had got into a storm without shelter, he had seen all this was not true; and then he goes on to say that as all creation addicts itself to adultery, and Gloucester's bastard son had treated his father more kindly than his daughters had treated him (although Lear, according to the development of the drama could not know how Edmund had treated Gloucester); therefore, let dissoluteness prosper, the more so as being a King, he needs soldiers. He here addresses an imaginary hypocritically virtuous lady who acts the prude, whereas

> The fitchew, nor the soiled horse goes to 't
> With a more riotous appetite.
> Down from the waist they are Centaurs,
> Though women all above:
> But to the girdle do the gods inherit,
> Beneath is all the fiends'.
>
> (IV, vi, 124–129)

and saying this Lear screams and spits from horror. This monologue is evidently meant to be addressed by the actor to the audience, and probably produces an effect on the stage, but it is utterly uncalled for in the mouth of Lear—as well as his words: "It smells of mortality," uttered while wiping his hand as Gloucester expresses a desire to kiss it. Then Gloucester's blindness is referred to, which gives occasion for a play of words on *eyes,* about blind Cupid, at which Lear says to Gloucester, "No *eyes* in your head, nor no money in your *purse*? Your eyes are in a *heavy* case, your *purse* in a *light.*" Then Lear declaims a monologue on the unfairness of legal judgment, which is quite out of place in the mouth of the insane Lear. After this enters a gentleman with attendants, sent by Cordelia to fetch her father. Lear continues to act as a madman and runs away. The gentleman sent to fetch Lear does not run after him, but lengthily describes to Edgar the position of the French and British armies. Oswald enters, and seeing Gloucester, and desiring to receive the reward promised by Regan, attacks him; but Edgar with his club kills Oswald, who, in dying, transmits to his murderer Edgar, Goneril's letter to Edmund, the delivery of which would insure reward. In this letter, Goneril promises to kill her husband and marry Edmund. Edgar drags out Oswald's body by the legs, and then returns and leads his father away.

The seventh scene of the fourth act takes place in a tent in the French camp. Lear is asleep on a bed. Enter Cordelia and Kent, still in disguise. Lear is awakened by the music, and seeing Cordelia, does not believe she is a living being, thinks she is an apparition, does not believe that he himself is alive. Cordelia assures him that she is his daughter, and begs him to bless her. He falls on his knees before her, begs her pardon, acknowledges that he is old and foolish, says he is ready to take poison, which he thinks she has probably prepared for him, as he is persuaded she must hate him. "For your sisters," he says, "have done me wrong: you have some cause, they have not." Then he gradually comes to his senses and ceases to rave. His daughter suggests that he should take a walk. He consents and says: "You must bear with me. Pray you now forget and forgive: I am old and foolish." They depart. The gentlemen and Kent, remaining on the scene, hold a conversation which explains to the spectator that Edmund is at the head of the troops and that a battle must soon begin between Lear's defenders and his enemies. So the fourth act closes.

In this fourth act, the scene between Lear and his daughter might have been touching, if it had not been preceded in the course of the earlier acts by the tediously drawn-out monotonous ravings of Lear, and if, moreover, this expression of his feelings constituted the last scene. But the scene is not the last.

In the fifth act, the former cold, pompous, artificial ravings of Lear go on again, destroying the impression which the previous scene might have produced.

The first scene of the fifth act begins by representing Edmund and Regan; the latter is jealous of her sister, and offers herself. Then comes Goneril, her husband, and some soldiers. The Duke of Albany, although pitying Lear, regards it as his duty to fight against the French who have invaded his country, and so he prepares for battle.

Then Edgar enters, still disguised, and hands to the Duke of Albany the letter he had received from Goneril's dying steward, and tells him if he gains the victory to sound the trumpet, saying that he can produce a champion who will confirm the contents of the letter.

In the second scene, Edgar enters leading his father, Gloucester, seats him by a tree, and goes away himself. The noise of battle is heard, Edgar runs back and says that the battle is lost, and Lear and Cordelia are prisoners. Gloucester again falls into despair. Edgar, still without disclosing himself to his father, counsels endurance, and Gloucester immediately agrees with him.

The third scene opens with a triumphal progress of the victor Edmund. Lear and Cordelia are prisoners. Lear, although no longer insane, continues to utter the same senseless inappropriate words, as, for example, that in prison he will sing with Cordelia, she will ask his blessing, and he will kneel down (this process of kneeling down is repeated three times) and will ask her forgiveness. And he further says that while they are living in prison they will wear out "packs and sects of great ones"; that he and Cordelia are sacrifices upon which the gods will throw incense, and that he that parts them "shall bring a brand from heaven and fire us hence like foxes; wipe thine eyes; the good-years shall devour them, flesh and fell, ere they shall make us weep."

Edmund orders Lear and his daughter to be led away to prison, and having called the officer to do this—says he requires another duty and asks him whether he'll do it. The captain says he cannot draw a cart nor eat dried oats, but if it be a man's work, he can do it. Enter the Duke of Albany, Goneril, and Regan. The Duke of Albany wishes to champion Lear, but Edmund does not allow it. The daughters take part in the dialogue and begin to abuse each other, being jealous of Edmund. Here everything becomes so confused that it is difficult to follow the action. The Duke of Albany wishes to arrest Edmund, and tells Regan that Edmund has long ago entered into guilty relations with his wife, and that therefore Regan must give up her claims on Edmund, and if she wishes to marry, should marry him, the Duke of Albany.

Having said this, the Duke of Albany calls Edmund, orders the trumpet to be sounded, saying that if no one appears, he will fight him himself.

Here Regan, whom Goneril has evidently poisoned, falls

deadly sick. Trumpets are sounded, and Edgar enters with a visor concealing his face, and without giving his name, challenges Edmund. Edgar abuses Edmund; Edmund throws all the abuses back on Edgar's head. They fight and Edmund falls. Goneril is in despair. The Duke of Albany shows Goneril her letter. Goneril departs.

The dying Edmund discovers that his opponent was his brother. Edgar raises his visor and pronounces a moral lesson to the effect that the father having begotten his illegitimate son Edmund, has paid for it with his eyesight. After this Edgar tells the Duke of Albany his adventures and how he has only just now, before entering the recent combat, disclosed everything to his father, and the father could not bear it and died from emotion. Edmund is not yet dead, and wants to know all that has taken place.

Then Edgar relates that while he was sitting over his father's body a man came and closely embraced him, and shouting as loudly as if he wished to burst heaven, threw himself on the body of Edgar's father, and told the most piteous tale about Lear and himself, and that while relating this, the strings of life began to crack, but at this moment the trumpet sounded twice and Edgar left him "tranced." And this was Kent.

Edgar has hardly finished this narrative when a gentleman rushes in with a bloody knife, shouting "Help!" In answer to the question, "Who is killed?" the gentleman says that Goneril is killed, having poisoned her sister: she has confessed it.

Enter Kent, and at this moment the corpses of Goneril and Regan are brought in. Edmund here says that the sisters evidently loved him, as one has poisoned the other for his sake and then slain herself. At the same time, he confesses that he had given orders to kill Lear and to hang Cordelia in prison, and to pretend that she had taken her own life; but now he wishes to prevent these deeds, and having said this, he dies, and is carried away.

After this enters Lear with the dead Cordelia in his arms, although he is more than eighty years old and ill. Again begin

Lear's awful ravings, at which one feels ashamed, as at unsuccessful jokes. Lear demands that all should howl, and alternately believes that Cordelia is dead, and that she is alive.

> Had I your tongues and eyes [he says], I'ld use them so
> That heaven's vault should crack.
>
> (V, iii, 258–259)

Then he says that he killed the slave who hanged Cordelia. Next he says that his eyes see badly; but at the same time he recognizes Kent, whom all along he had not recognized.

The Duke of Albany says that he will resign during the life of Lear, and that he will reward Edgar and Kent and all who have been faithful to him. At this moment, the news is brought that Edmund is dead, and Lear, continuing his ravings, begs that they will undo one of his buttons—the same request which he had made when roaming about the heath. He expresses his thanks for this, tells everyone to look at something, and thereupon dies.

In conclusion, the Duke of Albany, having survived the others, says:

> The weight of this sad time we must obey;
> Speak what we feel, not what we ought to say.
> The oldest hath borne most: we that are young
> Shall never see so much, nor live so long.
>
> (V, iii, 322–325)

All depart to the music of a dead march. Thus ends the fifth act and the drama.

III

Such is this celebrated drama. However absurd it may appear in my rendering (which I have endeavored to make as impartial as possible), I may confidently say that in the original it is yet more absurd. For any man of our time—if he were not under the hypnotic suggestion that this drama is the height of perfection—it would be enough to read it to its end (had he sufficient patience for this) to be convinced that far from its being the height of perfection, it is a very bad, carelessly composed production, which, if it could have been of interest to a certain public at a certain time, cannot evoke amongst us anything but aversion and weariness. Every reader of our time who is free from the influence of suggestion will also receive exactly the same impression from all the other extolled dramas of Shakespeare, not to mention the senseless dramatized tales, *Pericles, Twelfth Night, The Tempest, Cymbeline, Troilus and Cressida.*

But such free-minded individuals, not inoculated with Shakespeare worship, are no longer to be found in our Christian society. On every man of our society and time, from the first period of his conscious life, it has been inculcated that Shakespeare is a genius as poet and dramatist, and that all his writings are the height of perfection. Yet however hopeless it may seem, I will endeavor to demonstrate in the selected drama—*King Lear*—all those faults, equally characteristic of all the other tragedies and comedies of Shakespeare, on account of which he is not only no model of dramatic art, but does not satisfy the most elementary demands of art recognized by all.

Dramatic art, according to the laws established by those very critics who extol Shakespeare, demands that the persons represented in the play should be, in consequence of actions proper to their characters, and owing to a natural course of events, placed in positions requiring them to struggle with the surrounding world to which they find themselves in opposition—and in this struggle should display their inherent qualities.

In *King Lear,* the persons represented are indeed placed externally in opposition to the outward world, and they struggle with it. But their strife does not flow from the natural course of events nor from their own characters, but is quite arbitrarily established by the author, and therefore cannot produce on the reader that illusion which represents the essential condition of art.

Lear has no necessity or motive for his abdication, also having lived all his life with his daughters, he has no reason to believe the words of the two elder and not the truthful statement of the youngest; yet upon this is built the whole tragedy of his position.

Similarly unnatural is the subordinate action: the relation of Gloucester to his sons. The positions of Gloucester and Edgar flow from the circumstance that Gloucester, just like Lear, immediately believes the coarsest untruth, and does not even endeavor to inquire of his injured son whether the accusation against him be true, but at once curses and banishes him. The fact that Lear's relations with his daughters are the same as those of Gloucester with his sons makes one feel yet more strongly that in both cases the relations are quite arbitrary and do not flow from the characters nor the natural course of events. Equally unnatural and obviously invented is the fact that, all through the tragedy, Lear does not recognize his old courtier Kent, and therefore the relations between Lear and Kent fail to excite the sympathy of the reader or spectator. In a yet greater degree the same holds true of the position of Edgar, who, unrecognized by anyone, leads his blind father and persuades him that he has leaped off a cliff when in reality Gloucester jumps on level ground.

These positions into which the characters are placed quite arbitrarily are so unnatural that the reader or spectator is unable, not only to sympathize with their sufferings, but even to be interested in what he reads or sees. This in the first place.

Secondly, in this, as in the other dramas of Shakespeare, all the characters live, think, speak, and act quite unconformably with the given time and place. The action of *King Lear* takes place 800 years B.C. and yet the characters are placed in conditions possible only in the Middle Ages: participating in the drama are kings, dukes, armies, and illegitimate children, and gentlemen, courtiers, doctors, farmers, officers, soldiers, and knights with visors, etc. It may be that such anachronisms (with which Shakespeare's dramas abound) did not injure the possibility of illusion in the sixteenth century and the beginning of the seventeenth; but in our time it is no longer possible to follow with interest the development of events which one knows could not take place in the conditions which the author describes in detail. The artificiality of the positions, not flowing from the nature of the characters, and their want of conformity with time and space, is further increased by those coarse embellishments which are continually added by Shakespeare in the places intended to appear particularly touching. The extraordinary storm, during which King Lear roams about the heath, or the grass which for some reason he puts on his head—like Ophelia in *Hamlet*—or Edgar's attire, or the fool's speeches, or the appearance of the helmeted horseman, Edgar—all these effects not only fail to enhance the impression but produce an opposite effect. "*Man sieht die Absicht und man wird verstimmt,*" [3] as Goethe says. It often happens that even during these obviously intentional efforts after effect—as for instance the dragging out by the legs of half a dozen corpses with which all Shakespeare's tragedies terminate—instead of feeling fear and pity, one is tempted rather to laugh.

But it is not enough that Shakespeare's characters are placed in tragic positions which are impossible, do not flow from the course of events, are inappropriate to time and space—besides this, these personages act in a way which is out of keeping with their definite character, and is quite arbitrary. It is generally asserted that in Shakespeare's dramas the characters are especially well expressed, that notwithstanding their vividness, they are many-sided like those of living people; that while exhibiting the characteristics of a given individual they at the same time wear the features of man in general; it is usual to say that the delineation of character in Shakespeare is the height of perfection.

This is asserted with much confidence and repeated by all as indisputable truth; but however much I endeavored to find confirmation of this in Shakespeare's dramas, I always found the opposite. In reading any of Shakespeare's dramas whatever, I was from the very first instantly convinced that he was lacking in the most important, if not the only means of portraying characters: individuality of language, i.e., the style of speech of every person being natural to his character. This

[3] After realizing the intention one turns against it. Editor.

is absent from Shakespeare. All his characters speak, not their own, but always one and the same Shakespearean pretentious and unnatural language, in which not only they could not speak, but in which no living man ever has spoken or does speak.

No living man could or can say as Lear says—that he would divorce his wife in the grave should Regan not receive him, or that the heavens would crack with shouting, or that the winds would burst, or that the wind wishes to blow the land into the sea, or that the curled waters wish to flood the shore, as the gentleman describes the storm, or that it is easier to bear one's grief, and the soul leaps over many sufferings when grief finds fellowship; or that Lear has become childless while I am fatherless, as Edgar says, or use similar unnatural expressions with which the speeches of all the characters in all Shakespeare's dramas overflow.

Again, it is not enough that all the characters speak in a way in which no living men ever did or could speak—they all suffer from a common intemperance of language. Those who are in love, who are preparing for death, who are fighting, who are dying, all alike speak much and unexpectedly about subjects utterly inappropriate to the occasion, being evidently guided rather by consonances and play of words than by thoughts. They all speak alike. Lear raves exactly as does Edgar when feigning madness. Both Kent and the fool speak alike. The words of one of the personages might be placed in the mouth of another, and by the character of the speech it would be impossible to distinguish who speaks. If there is a difference in the speech of Shakespeare's various characters, it lies merely in the different dialogues which are pronounced for these characters—again by Shakespeare and not by themselves. Thus Shakespeare always speaks for kings in one and the same inflated empty language. Also in one and the same Shakespearean, artificially sentimental language speak all the women who are intended to be poetic: Juliet, Desdemona, Cordelia, Imogen, Marina. In the same way also, it is Shakespeare alone who speaks for his villains—Richard, Edmund, Iago, Macbeth—expressing for them those vicious feelings which villains never express. Yet more similar are the speeches of the madmen with their horrible words and those of fools with their mirthless puns. So that in Shakespeare there is no language of living individuals—that language which in the drama is the chief means of setting forth characters. (If gesticulation be also a means of expressing character, as in ballets, this is only a secondary means.) Moreover if the characters speak at random and in a random way, and all in one and the same diction, as is the case in Shakespeare's work, then even the action of gesticulation is wasted. Therefore, whatever the blind panegyrists of Shakespeare may say, in Shakespeare there is no expression of character. Those personages who in his dramas stand out as characters, are characters borrowed by him from former works which have served as the foundation of his dramas, and they are mostly depicted, not by the dramatic method which consists in making each person speak with his own diction, but in the epic method of one person describing the features of another.

IV

The perfection with which Shakespeare expresses character is asserted chiefly on the ground of the characters of Lear, Cordelia, Othello, Desdemona, Falstaff, Hamlet. But all these characters, as well as all the others, instead of belonging to Shakespeare are taken by him from dramas, chronicles, and romances anterior to him. All these characters not only are not rendered more powerful by him, but in most cases, they are weakened and spoiled. This is very striking in this drama of *King Lear,* which we are examining, taken by him from the drama *King Leir* by an unknown author. The characters of this drama, that of King Lear, and especially of Cordelia, not only were not created by Shakespeare, but have been strikingly weakened and deprived of expression by him, as compared with their appearance in the older drama.

In the older drama, Leir abdicates because, having become a widower, he thinks only of saving his soul. He asks his daughters as to their love for him—that by means of a certain device he has invented he may retain his favorite daughter on his island. The elder daughters are betrothed, while the youngest does not wish to contract a loveless union with any of the neighboring suitors whom Leir proposes to her, and he is afraid that she may marry some distant potentate.

The device which he has invented, as he informs his courtier Perillus (Shakespeare's Kent), is this: that when Cordelia tells him that she loves him more than anyone or as much as her elder sisters do, he will tell her that she must in proof of her love marry the prince he will indicate on his island. All these motives for Lear's conduct are absent in Shakespeare's play. Then, when according to the old drama, Leir asks his daughters about their love for him, Cordelia does not say, as Shakespeare has it, that she will not give her father all her love, but will love her husband too, should she marry—to say which is quite unnatural—but simply says that she cannot express her love in words and hopes that her actions will prove it. Goneril and Regan remark that Cordelia's answer is not an answer, and that the father cannot meekly accept such indifference, so that what is wanting in Shakespeare—i.e., the explanation of Lear's anger which caused him to disinherit his youngest daughter—exists in the old drama. Leir is annoyed by the failure of his scheme, and the poisonous words of his elder daughters irritate him still more. After the division of the kingdom between the elder daughters there follows in the older drama a scene between Cordelia and the King of Gaul, setting forth, instead of the colorless Cordelia of Shakespeare, a very definite and attractive character of the truthful, tender, and self-sacrificing youngest daughter. While Cordelia, without grieving that she has been deprived of a portion of the heritage, sits sorrowing at having lost her father's love, and looking forward to earn her bread by her labor, there comes the King of Gaul, who, in the disguise of a pilgrim, desires to choose a bride from amongst Leir's daughters. He asks Cordelia why she is sad. She tells him the cause of her grief. The King of Gaul, still in the guise of a pilgrim, falls in love with her, and offers to arrange a marriage for her with the King of Gaul, but she says she will marry only a man whom she loves. Then the pilgrim, still disguised, offers her his hand and heart and Cordelia confesses that she loves the pilgrim and consents to marry him, notwithstanding the poverty that awaits her. Thereupon the pilgrim discloses to her that it is he who is the King of Gaul, and Cordelia marries him. Instead of this scene, Lear, according to Shakespeare, proposes to Cordelia's two suitors to take her without dowry, and one cynically refuses, while the other, one does not know why, accepts her. After this, in the old drama, as in Shakespeare's, Leir undergoes the insults of Goneril, into whose house he has removed, but he bears these insults in a very different way from that represented by Shakespeare: he feels that by his conduct toward Cordelia he has deserved this, and humbly submits. As in Shakespeare's drama, so also in the older drama, the courtier—Kent—who had interceded for Cordelia and was therefore banished—comes to Leir and assures him of his love, but under no disguise, simply as a faithful old servant who does not abandon his king in a moment of need. Leir tells him—what, according to Shakespeare, he tells Cordelia in the last scene—that if the daughters whom he has benefited hate him, a retainer to whom he has done no good cannot love him. But Perillus—Kent—assures the King of his love toward him, and Leir, pacified, goes on to Regan. In the older drama there are no tempests nor tearing out of gray hairs, but there is the weakened and humbled old man, Leir, overpowered with grief, and banished by his other daughter also, who even wishes to kill him. Turned out by his elder daughters, Leir, according to the older drama, as a last resource, goes with Perillus to Cordelia. Instead of the unnatural banishment of Lear during the tempest, and his roaming about the heath, Leir, with Perillus, in the older drama, during their journey to France, very naturally reach the last degree of destitution, sell their clothes in order to pay for their crossing over the sea, and, in the attire of fishermen, exhausted by cold and hunger, approach Cordelia's house. Here again, instead of the unnatural combined ravings of the fool, Lear and Edgar, as represented by Shakespeare, there follows in the older drama a natural scene of reunion between the daughter and the father. Cordelia—who, notwithstanding her happiness, has all the time been grieving about her father and praying God to forgive her sisters who had done him so much wrong—meets her father in his extreme want, and wishes immediately to disclose herself to him, but her husband advises her not to do this, in order not to agitate the weak old man. She accepts the counsel and takes Leir into her house without disclosing herself to him and nurses him. Leir gradually revives, and then the daughter asks him who he is and how he lived formerly.

> If from the first [says Leir] I should relate the cause,
> I would make a heart of adamant to weep.
> And thou, poor soul, kind hearted as thou art,
> Dost weep already, ere I do begin.

Cordelia replies:

> For God's love tell it, and when you have done
> I'll tell the reason why I weep so soon.

And Leir relates all he has suffered from his elder daughters, and says that now he wishes to find shelter with the child who would be in the right even were she to condemn him to death. "If, however," he says, "she will receive me with love, it will be God's and her work, and not my merit." To this Cordelia says, "Oh, I know for certain that thy daughter will lovingly receive thee." "How canst thou know this without knowing her?" says Leir. "I know," says Cordelia, "because not far from here, I had a father who acted towards me as badly as thou hast acted towards her, yet if I were only to see his white head, I would creep to meet him on my knees." "No, this cannot be," says Leir, "for there are no children in the world so cruel as mine." "Do not condemn all for the sins of some," says Cordelia, and falls on her knees. "Look here, dear father," she says, "look at me: I am thy loving daughter." The father recognizes her and says: "It is not for thee, but for me to beg thy pardon on my knees for all my sins towards thee."

Is there anything approaching this exquisite scene in Shakespeare's drama?

However strange this opinion may seem to worshipers of Shakespeare, yet the whole of this old drama is incomparably and in every respect superior to Shakespeare's adaptation. It is so, firstly, because it has not got the utterly superfluous characters of the villain Edmund and the unlifelike Gloucester and Edgar, who only distract one's attention; secondly, because it has not got the completely false "effects" of Lear running about the heath, his conversations with the fool, and all these impossible disguises, failures to recognize, and accumulated deaths; and above all, because in this drama there is the simple natural and deeply touching character of Leir and the yet more touching and clearly defined character of Cordelia, both absent in Shakespeare. Therefore there is in the older drama, instead of Shakespeare's long drawn-out scene of Lear's interview with Cordelia and of Cordelia's unnecessary murder—the exquisite scene of the interview between Leir and Cordelia, unequaled by any in all Shakespeare's dramas.

The old drama also terminates more naturally and more in accordance with the moral demands of the spectator than does Shakespeare's: namely, by the King of the Gauls conquering the husbands of the elder sisters, and by Cordelia, instead of being killed, restoring Leir to his former position.

Thus it is in the drama we are examining which Shakespeare has borrowed from the drama *King Leir*. So is it also with Othello, taken from an Italian romance, and, again, with the famous Hamlet. The same may be said of Antony, Brutus, Cleopatra, Shylock, Richard, and all Shakespeare's characters, all taken from antecedent work. Shakespeare, while profiting by character already given in preceding dramas or romances or chronicles or *Plutarch's Lives*, not only fails to render them more truthful and vivid, as his eulogists affirm, but on the contrary, always weakens them and often completely destroys them, as with Lear, compelling his characters to commit actions unnatural to them and above all to utter speeches natural neither to them nor to anyone whatever. Thus in *Othello*, although that is perhaps, I will not say the best, but the least bad, and the least encumbered by pompous volubility, the characters of Othello, Iago, Cassio, Emilia, according to Shakespeare, are much less natural and lifelike than in the Italian romance. Shakespeare's Othello suffers from epilepsy of which he has an attack on the stage; moreover, in Shakespeare's version, Desdemona's murder is preceded by the strange vow of the kneeling Othello. Othello, according to Shakespeare, is a Negro and not a Moor. All this is erratic, inflated, unnatural, and violates the unity of the character. All this is absent in the romance. In that romance, the reasons for Othello's jealousy are represented more naturally than in Shakespeare. In the romance, Cassio, knowing whose the handkerchief is, goes to Desdemona to return it, but approaching the back door of Desdemona's house sees Othello and flies from him. Othello perceives the escaping Cassio, and this it is that chiefly confirms his suspicions. Shakespeare has not got this, and yet this casual incident explains Othello's jealousy more than anything else. With Shakespeare, this jealousy is founded entirely on Iago's persistent machinations and treacherous words which Othello blindly believes. Othello's monologue over the sleeping Desdemona, about his desiring her when killed to look as she is alive, about his going to love her even dead, and now wishing to smell her "balmy breath," etc., is utterly impossible. A man who is preparing for the murder of a beloved being does not utter such phrases; still less after committing a murder would he speak about the necessity of an eclipse of sun and moon, and of the globe yawning, nor can he, Negro though he be, address devils, inviting them to burn him in hot sulfur and so forth. Lastly, however effective may be his suicide, absent in the romance, it completely destroys the conception of his clearly defined character. If he indeed suffered from grief and remorse, he would not, intending to kill himself, pronounce phrases about his own services, about the pearl and about his eyes dropping tears *"as fast as the Arabian trees medicinal gum";* and yet less about the Turks beating an Italian, and how he, Othello, smote him—*thus!* So that notwithstanding the powerful expression of emotions in Othello when, under the influence of Iago's hints, jealousy rises in him, and then in his scenes with Desdemona, one's conception of Othello's character is constantly infringed by his false pathos and the unnatural speeches he pronounces.

So it is with the chief character, Othello, but notwithstanding its alteration and the disadvantageous features which it is made thereby to present in comparison with the character in the romance from which it was taken, this character still remains a character, but all the other personages are completely spoiled by Shakespeare.

Iago, according to Shakespeare, is an unmitigated villain, deceiver, and thief, a robber who robs Roderigo and always succeeds even in his most impossible designs and therefore is a person quite apart from real life. In Shakespeare, the motive of his villainy is, firstly, that Othello did not give him the post he desired, secondly, that he suspects Othello of an intrigue with his wife, and thirdly, that as he says, he feels a strange kind of love for Desdemona. There are many motives, but they are all vague. Whereas in the romance there is but one simple and clear motive: Iago's passionate love for Desdemona, transmuted into hatred toward her and Othello after she had preferred the Moor to him and had resolutely repulsed him. Yet more unnatural is the utterly unnecessary Roderigo whom Iago deceives and robs, promising him Desdemona's love, and whom he forces to fulfill all he commands: to intoxicate, provoke, and then kill Cassio. Emilia, who says anything it may occur to the author to put into her mouth, has not even the slightest semblance of a live character.

"But Falstaff, the wonderful Falstaff," Shakespeare's eulogists will say, "of him, at all events, one cannot say that he is not a living character, or that having been taken from the comedy of an unknown author, it has been weakened."

Falstaff, like all Shakespeare's characters, was taken from a drama or comedy by an unknown author, written on a really living person, Sir John Oldcastle, who had been the friend of some Duke. This Oldcastle had once been convicted of heresy, but had been saved by his friend the Duke. But afterward he was condemned and burned at the stake for his religious beliefs which did not conform with Catholicism. It was on this same Oldcastle that an anonymous author, in order to please the Catholic public, wrote a comedy or drama, ridiculing this martyr for conscience's sake and representing him as a good-for-nothing man, the boon companion of the Duke, and it is from this comedy that Shakespeare borrowed, not only the character of Falstaff, but also his own ironical attitude toward it. In Shakespeare's first works, when this character appeared, it was frankly called Oldcastle, but later, in Elizabeth's time, when Protestantism again triumphed, it was awkward to bring out with mockery a martyr in the strife with Catholicism, and besides, Oldcastle's relatives had protested, and Shakespeare accordingly altered the name of Oldcastle to that of Falstaff, also a historical figure, known for having fled from the field of battle at Agincourt.

Falstaff is indeed quite a natural and typical character; but then it is perhaps the only natural and typical character depicted by Shakespeare. And this character is natural and typical because of all Shakespeare's characters, it alone speaks a language proper to itself. And it speaks thus because it speaks in the same Shakespearean language full of mirthless jokes and unamusing puns which, being unnatural to all Shakespeare's other characters, is quite in harmony with the boastful, distorted, and depraved character of the drunken Falstaff. For this reason alone does this figure truly represent a definite character. Unfortunately, the artistic effect of this character is spoiled by the fact that it is so repulsive by its gluttony, drunkenness, debauchery, rascality, deceit, and cowardice, that it is difficult to share the feeling of gay humor with which the author treats it. Thus it is with Falstaff.

But in none of Shakespeare's figures is his—I will not say incapacity to give, but utter indifference to giving—his personages a typical character, so strikingly manifest as in *Hamlet.* In connection with none of Shakespeare's works do we see so strikingly displayed that blind worship of Shakespeare, that unreasoning state of hypnotism owing to which even the mere thought is not admitted that any of Shakespeare's productions can be wanting in genius or that any of the principal personages in his dramas can fail to be the expression of a new and deeply conceived character.

Shakespeare takes an old story, not bad in its way, relating:

"Avec quelle ruse Amlette, qui depuis fut Roy de Dannemarch vengea la mort de son père Horwendille, Occis par Fengon son frère, et autre occurrence de son histoire," [4] or a drama which was written on this theme fifteen years before him. On this subject he writes his own drama, introducing quite inappropriately (as indeed he always does) into the mouth of the principal person all such thoughts of his own as appeared to him worthy of attention. Putting into the mouth of his hero these thoughts: about life (the gravedigger), about death ("To be or not to be")—the same which are expressed in his Sixty-sixth Sonnet—about the theater, about women, he is utterly unconcerned as to the circumstances under which these words are said, and it naturally turns out that the person expressing all these thoughts is a mere phonograph of Shakespeare, without character, whose actions and words do not agree.

In the old legend, Hamlet's personality is quite comprehensible: he is indignant at his uncle's and his mother's deeds, and wishes to revenge himself upon them, but is afraid his uncle may kill him as he had killed his father. Therefore he simulates insanity, desiring to bide his time and observe all that goes on in the palace. Meanwhile his uncle and mother, being afraid of him, wish to test whether he is feigning or is really mad, and send to him a girl whom he loves. He persists, then sees his mother in private, kills a courtier who is eavesdropping, and convicts his mother of her sin. Afterward he is

[4] "With what cunning Hamlet, who has since become King of Denmark, avenged the death of his father, Horwendille, killed by his own brother Fengon, and other incidents of his life." Tolstoy is quoting here only the synopsis of the plot as it appears before *Histoire Troisiesme* in *Le Cinquiesme Tome des Histoires Tragiques* par F. de Belleforest, Paris, 1582. The *Histoires,* a collection of tragic tales translated from the Italian of Matteo Bandello (1480?–1561), appeared in successive volumes, Number 1 privileged in 1565. In Vol. 5, dated 1576, but privileged in 1570, there is the story of Hamlet, absent from Bandello, and clearly derived from Saxo Grammaticus, whose history Belleforest knew and had used for his *Harengues Militaires* privileged February 4, 1570. Tolstoy had probably seen the Belleforest in *Shakespeares Hamlet Quellen* (1881) where Gericke had given Moltke's text of the *Histoires* based on the 1581 Lyons edition together with all of the variants from the 1582 Paris edition which Gericke felt was a superior edition. Editor.

sent to England, but intercepts letters, and returning from England, takes revenge on his enemies, burning them all.

All this is comprehensible and flows from Hamlet's character and position. But Shakespeare, putting into Hamlet's mouth speeches which he himself wishes to express, and making him commit actions which are necessary to the author in order to produce scenic effects, destroys all that constitutes the character of Hamlet and of the legend. During the whole of the drama, Hamlet is doing not what he would really desire, but what is necessary for the author's plan. One moment he is awestruck at his father's ghost, another moment he begins to chaff it, calling it "old mole"; one moment he loves Ophelia, another moment he teases her, and so forth. There is no possibility of finding any explanation whatever of Hamlet's actions or words, and therefore no possibility of attributing any character to him.

But as it is recognized that Shakespeare, the genius, cannot write anything bad, therefore learned people use all the powers of their minds to find extraordinary beauties in what is an obvious and crying failure, demonstrated with especial vividness in *Hamlet,* where the principal figure has no character whatever. And lo! profound critics declare that in this drama, in the person of Hamlet, is expressed a singularly powerful, perfectly novel and deep personality, consisting in this person having no character; and that precisely in this absence of character consists the genius of creating a deeply conceived character. Having decided this, learned critics write volumes upon volumes, so that the praise and explanation of the greatness and importance of the representation of the character of a man who has no character, constitute whole libraries. It is true that some of the critics timidly express the idea that there is something strange in this figure, that Hamlet is an unsolved riddle, but no one has the courage to say (as in Hans Andersen's story) that the King is naked, i.e., that it is as clear as day that Shakespeare did not succeed and did not even wish to give any character to Hamlet, did not even understand that this was necessary. And learned critics continue to investigate and extol this puzzling production, which reminds one of the famous stone with an inscription which Pickwick found near a cottage doorstep, and which divided the scientific world into two hostile camps.

So that neither do the characters of Lear nor Othello, nor Falstaff nor yet Hamlet, in any way confirm the existing opinion that Shakespeare's power consists in the delineation of character.

If in Shakespeare's dramas one does meet figures having certain characteristic features—for the most part secondary figures, such as Polonius in *Hamlet* and Portia in *The Merchant of Venice*—these few lifelike characters amongst five hundred or more other secondary figures, with the complete absence of character in the principal figures, do not at all prove that the merit of Shakespeare's dramas consists in the expression of character.

That a great talent for depicting character is attributed to Shakespeare arises from his actually possessing a peculiarity which, for superficial observers and in the play of good actors, may appear to be the capacity of depicting character. This peculiarity consists in the capacity of representing scenes expressing the play of emotion. However unnatural the positions may be in which he places his characters, however improper to them the language which he makes them speak, however featureless they are, the very play of emotion, its increase and alteration and the combination of many contrary feelings are expressed correctly and powerfully in some of Shakespeare's scenes, and, in the play of good actors, evokes, even if only for a time, sympathy with the persons represented. Shakespeare, himself an actor, and an intelligent man, knew how to express by the means not only of speech, but of exclamation, gesture, and the repetition of words, states of mind and developments or changes of feeling taking place in the persons represented. So that, in many instances, Shakespeare's characters, instead of speaking, merely make an exclamation, or weep, or in the middle of a monologue, by means of gestures, demonstrate the pain of their position (just as Lear asks someone to unbutton him) or in moments of great agitation, repeat a question several times, or several times demand the repetition of a word which has particularly struck them, as do Othello, Macduff, Cleopatra, and others. Such clever methods of expressing the development of feeling, giving good actors the possibility of demonstrating their powers, were and are often mistaken by many critics for the expression of character. But however strongly the play of feeling may be expressed in one scene, a single scene cannot give the character of a figure when this figure, after a correct exclamation or gesture, begins in a language not its own, at the author's arbitrary will, volubly to utter words which are neither necessary nor in harmony with its character.

V

"Well, but what of the profound utterances and sayings expressed by Shakespeare's characters," Shakespeare's panegyrists will retort. "See Lear's monologue on punishment, Kent's speech about vengeance, or Edgar's about his former life, Gloucester's reflections on the instability of fortune, and in other dramas, the famous monologues of Hamlet, Antony, and others."

Thoughts and sayings may be appreciated, I will answer, in a prose work, in an essay, a collection of aphorisms, but not in an artistic dramatic production, the object of which is to elicit sympathy with what is represented. Therefore the monologues and sayings of Shakespeare, even did they contain very many deep and new thoughts, which is not the case, do not constitute the merits of an artistic poetic production. On the contrary, these speeches, expressed in unnatural conditions, can only spoil artistic works.

An artistic, poetic work, particularly a drama, must first of all excite in the reader or spectator the illusion that whatever the person represented is living through, or experiencing, is lived through or experienced by himself. For this purpose it is as important for the dramatist to know precisely what he should make his characters both do and say as what he should not make them say and do so as not to destroy the illusion of the reader or spectator. However eloquent and profound they may be, speeches, when put into the mouths of dramatic characters, if they be superfluous or unnatural to the position and character, destroy the chief condition of dramatic art—the illusion owing to which the reader or spectator lives in the feelings of the persons represented. Without putting an end to the illusion, one may leave much unsaid—the reader or spectator will himself fill this up and sometimes, owing to this, his illusion is even increased, but to say what is superflous is the same as to overthrow a statue composed of separate pieces and thereby scatter them, or to take away the lamp from a magic lantern: the attention of the reader or spectator is distracted, the reader sees the author, the spectator sees the actor, the illusion disappears and to restore it is sometimes impossible—therefore without the feeling of measure, there cannot be an artist, and especially a dramatist.

Shakespeare is devoid of this feeling. His characters continually do and say what is not only unnatural to them, but utterly unnecessary. I do not cite examples of this, because I believe that he who does not himself see this striking deficiency in all Shakespeare's dramas will not be persuaded by any examples and proofs. It is sufficient to read *King Lear* alone, with its insanity, murders, plucking out of eyes, Gloucester's jump, its poisonings, and wranglings—not to mention *Pericles, Cymbeline, The Winter's Tale, The Tempest*—to be convinced of this. Only a man devoid of the sense of measure and of taste could produce such types as Titus Andronicus or Troilus and Cressida, or so mercilessly mutilate the old drama *King Leir*.

Gervinus [5] endeavors to prove that Shakespeare possessed the feeling of beauty, "*Schönheit's sinn,*" but all Gervinus' proofs prove only that he himself, Gervinus, is completely destitute of it. In Shakespeare everything is exaggerated: the actions are exaggerated, so are their consequences, the speeches of the characters are exaggerated, and therefore at every step the possibility of artistic impression is interfered with. Whatever people may say, however they may be enraptured by

[5] Georg Gottfried Gervinus (1805–1871), one of the greatest of the nineteenth-century German Shakespeare scholars. Editor.

Shakespeare's works, whatever merits they may attribute to them, it is perfectly certain that he was not an artist and that his works are not artistic productions. Without the sense of measure, there never was nor can be an artist, as without the feeling of rhythm, there cannot be a musician. Shakespeare might have been whatever you like, but he was not an artist.

"But one should not forget the time at which Shakespeare wrote," say his admirers. "It was a time of cruel and coarse habits, a time of the then fashionable euphuism, i.e., artificial way of expressing oneself—a time of forms of life strange to us, and therefore, to judge about Shakespeare, one should have in view the time when he wrote. In Homer as in Shakespeare, there is much that is strange to us, but this does not prevent us from appreciating the beauties of Homer," say these admirers. But in comparing Shakespeare with Homer, as does Gervinus, that infinite distance which separates true poetry from its semblance manifests itself with especial force. However distant Homer is from us, we can, without the slightest effort, transport ourselves into the life he describes, and we can thus transport ourselves because, however alien to us may be the events Homer describes, he believes in what he says and speaks seriously, and therefore he never exaggerates, and the sense of measure never abandons him. This is the reason why, not to speak of the wonderfully distinct, lifelike, and beautiful characters of Achilles, Hector, Priam, Odysseus, and the eternally touching scenes of Hector's leave-taking, of Priam's embassy, of Odysseus' return, and others—the whole of the *Iliad*, and still more the *Odyssey*, are so humanly near to us that we feel as if we ourselves had lived and are living amongst its gods and heroes. Not so with Shakespeare. From his first words, exaggeration is seen: the exaggeration of events, the exaggeration of emotion, and the exaggeration of effects. One sees at once that he does not believe in what he says, that it is of no necessity to him, that he invents the events he describes and is indifferent to his characters—that he has conceived them only for the stage and therefore makes them do and say only what may strike his public, and so we do not believe either in the events or in the actions or in the sufferings of the characters. Nothing demonstrates so clearly the complete absence of aesthetic feeling in Shakespeare as comparison between him and Homer. The works which we call the works of Homer are artistic, poetic, original works, lived through by the author or authors; whereas the works of Shakespeare—borrowed as they are and externally, like mosaics, artificially fitted together piecemeal from bits invented for the occasion—have nothing whatever in common with art and poetry.

VI

But perhaps the height of Shakespeare's conception of life is such that though he does not satisfy the aesthetic demands he discloses to us a view of life so new and important for men that, in consideration of its importance, all his failures as an artist become imperceptible. So indeed say Shakespeare's admirers. Gervinus says distinctly that besides Shakespeare's significance in the sphere of dramatic poetry in which, according to his opinion, Shakespeare equals "Homer in the sphere of Epos, Shakespeare being the very greatest judge of the human soul, is a teacher of most indisputable ethical authority and the most select leader in the world and in life."

In what then consists this indisputable authority of the most select leader in the world and in life? Gervinus devotes the concluding chapter of his second volume—about fifty pages—to an explanation of this.

The ethical authority of this supreme teacher of life consists in the following: the starting point of Shakespeare's conception of life, says Gervinus, is that man is gifted with powers of activity and therefore first of all, also according to Gervinus, Shakespeare regarded as good and necessary for man that he should act (as if it were possible for a man not to act).

> *Die thatkräftigen Männer, Fortinbras, Bolingbroke, Alcibiades, Octavius spielen hier die gegensatzlichen Rollen gegen die verschiedenen thatlosen; nicht ihre Charaktere verdienen ihnen Allen ihr Glück und Gedeihen etwa durch eine grosse Ueberlegenheit ihrer Natur, sondern trotz ihrer geringeren Anlage stellt sich ihre Thatkraft an sich über die Unthätigkeit*

der Anderen hinaus, gleichviel aus wie schöner Quelle diese Passivitat aus wie schlechter jene Thatigkeit fliesse.[6]

That is, active people, like Fortinbras, Bolingbroke, Alcibiades, and Octavius, says Gervinus, are placed in contrast, by Shakespeare, with various characters who do not exhibit energetic activity. And happiness and success, according to Shakespeare, are attained by individuals possessing this active character, but not at all owing to the superiority of their nature; on the contrary, notwithstanding their inferior gifts, the capacity of activity in itself always gives them the advantage over inactivity, quite independently of any consideration whether the inactivity of some flows from excellent impulses and the activity of the others from bad ones. "Activity is good, inactivity is evil. Activity transforms evil into good," says Shakespeare, according to Gervinus. Shakespeare prefers the principle of Alexander (of Macedonia) to that of Diogenes, says Gervinus. In other words, he prefers death and murder through ambition to abstinence and wisdom.

According to Gervinus, Shakespeare believes that humanity need not set up ideals, but that only healthy activity and the golden mean is necessary in everything. Indeed, Shakespeare is so penetrated by this conviction, that, according to Gervinus' assertion, he allows himself to deny even Christian morality, which makes exaggerated demands on human nature. "Shakespeare," we read, "did not approve of the limits of duty exceeding the intentions of nature. He teaches the golden mean between heathen hatred to one's enemies and Christian love towards them" (pp. 561–562).[7] How far Shakespeare was penetrated with this fundamental principle of *reasonable moderation,* says Gervinus, can be seen from the fact that he has the courage to express himself even against the Christian rules which prompt human nature to the excessive exertion of its powers. He did not admit that the limits of duties should exceed the biddings of nature. Therefore he preached a reasonable mean, natural to man, between Christian and heathen

[6] Cf. Gervinus, *Shakespeare Commentaries,* translated by F. E. Bunnètt, 5th ed. (London, Smith, Elder, & Co., 1892), p. 911. Editor.
[7] Cf. English edition of Gervinus, pp. 916–917. Editor.

precepts, of love toward one's enemies on the one hand, and hatred toward them on the other.[8]

"That one may do too much good (exceed the reasonable limits of good) is convincingly proved by Shakespeare's words and examples. Thus excessive generosity ruins Timon, while Antonio's moderate generosity confers honor; normal ambition makes Henry V great, whereas it ruins Percy in whom it has risen too high; excessive virtue leads Angelo to destruction, and if, in those who surround him, excessive severity becomes harmful and cannot prevent crime, on the other hand the divine element in man—charity—if it be excessive, can create crime."

Shakespeare taught, says Gervinus, that one *may be too good.*

He teaches, according to Gervinus, that morality, like politics, is a matter in which, owing to the complexity of circumstances and motives, one cannot establish any principles (p. 563),[9] and in this he agrees with Bacon and Aristotle—there are no positive religious and moral laws which may create principles for correct moral conduct suitable for all cases.

Gervinus most clearly expresses the whole of Shakespeare's moral theory by saying that Shakespeare does not write for those classes for whom definite religious principles and laws are suitable (i.e., for 999 out of 1,000 men) but for the educated.

"There are classes of men whose morality is best guarded by the positive precepts of religion and state law—to such persons, Shakespeare's creations are inaccessible. They are comprehensible and accessible only to the educated, from whom one can expect that they should acquire the healthy tact of life and self-consciousness by means of which, the innate guiding powers of conscience and reason, uniting with the will, lead us to the definite attainment of worthy aims in life. But even for such educated people, Shakespeare's teaching is

[8] Tolstoy is here condensing and paraphrasing a complex passage in G. G. Gervinus' *Shakespeare Commentaries* concerning the principles underlying Shakespeare's moral views. Cf. Gervinus, p. 917. Editor.
[9] Cf. English edition of Gervinus, p. 918. Editor.

not always without danger. The condition on which his teaching is quite harmless is that it should be accepted in all its completeness, in all its parts without any omission. Then it is not only without danger, but is the most clear and faultless and therefore the most worthy of confidence of all moral teaching" (p. 564).[10]

In order thus to accept all, one should understand that according to his teaching it is stupid and harmful for the individual to revolt against or endeavor to overthrow the limits of established religious and state forms. "Shakespeare," says Gervinus, "would abhor an independent and free individual, who, with a powerful spirit, should struggle against all convention in politics and morality, and overstep that union between religion and the State, which has for thousands of years supported society. According to his views, the practical wisdom of men could not have a higher object than the introduction into society of the greatest spontaneity and freedom, but precisely because of this, one should safeguard as sacred and irrefragable the natural laws of society—one should respect the existing order of things, and continually verifying it, inculcate its rational sides, not overlooking nature for the sake of culture, or *vice versa*" (p. 566).[11] Property, the family, the State, are sacred; but aspiration toward the recognition of the equality of men is insanity. Its realization would bring humanity to the greatest calamities. No one struggled more than Shakespeare against the privileges of rank and position, but could this free-thinking man resign himself to the privileges of the wealthy and educated being destroyed in order to give room to the poor and ignorant? How could a man who so eloquently attracts people toward honors permit that the very aspiration toward that which was great be crushed, together with rank and distinction for services, and with the destruction of all degrees "the motives for all high undertakings to be stifled." Even if the attraction of honors and false power treacherously obtained were to cease, could the poet admit of the most dreadful of all violence, that of the ignorant crowd?

[10] Cf. English edition of Gervinus, p. 919. Editor.
[11] Cf. English edition of Gervinus, p. 921. Editor.

He saw that, thanks to this equality now preached, everything may pass into violence, and violence into arbitrary action, and that into unchecked passion which will end the world as the wolf does its prey, and in the end the world will swallow itself up. Even if this does not happen with mankind when it attains equality, even if the love of nations and eternal peace do not prove that impossible "nothing" as Alonso expressed it in *The Tempest,* if, on the contrary, the actual attainment of aspirations toward equality is possible, then the poet would deem that the old age and extinction of the world had approached, and that therefore, for active individuals, it is not worth while to live (pp. 571–572).[12]

Such is Shakespeare's view of life as demonstrated by his greatest exponent and admirer.

Another of the most modern admirers of Shakespeare, Georg Brandes, further adds:

> No one, of course, can conserve his life quite pure from evil, from deceit, and from the injury of others, but evil and deceit are not always vices, and even the evil caused to others, is not necessarily a vice; it is often merely a necessity, a legitimate weapon, a right. And indeed, Shakespeare always held that there are no unconditional prohibitions, nor unconditional duties. For instance, he did not doubt Hamlet's right to kill the King, nor even his right to stab Polonius to death, and yet, he could not restrain himself from an overwhelming feeling of indignation and repulsion when, looking around, he saw everywhere how incessantly the most elementary moral laws were being infringed. Now in his mind there was formed as it were, a closely rivetted ring of thoughts concerning what he had always vaguely felt: such unconditional commandments do not exist; the quality and significance of an act, not to speak of a character, do not depend upon their enactment or infringement, the whole substance lies in the contents with which the separate individual at the moment of his decision and on his own responsibility, fills up the form of these laws.*

In other words, Shakespeare finally clearly saw that the moral of the aim is the only true and possible one; so that,

[12] Cf. English edition of Gervinus, p. 925. Editor.
* Georg Brandes, *William Shakespeare* (1895).

according to Brandes, Shakespeare's fundamental principle, for which he extols him, is that *the end justifies the means.*

Action at all costs, the absence of all ideals, moderation in everything, the conservation of the forms of life once established, and the end justifies the means. If you add to this a Chauvinist English patriotism, expressed in all the historical dramas, a patriotism according to which the English throne is something sacred, Englishmen always vanquish the French, killing thousands and losing only scores, Joan of Arc regarded as a witch, and the belief that Hector and all the Trojans, from whom the English descend, are heroes, while the Greeks are cowards and traitors, and so forth—such is the view of life of the wisest teacher of life according to his greatest admirers. And he who will attentively read Shakespeare's works cannot fail to recognize that the description of this Shakespearean view of life by his admirers is quite correct.

VII

The merit of every poetic work depends on three things:

1. The subject of the work: the deeper the subject, i.e., the more important it is to the life of mankind, the higher is the work.

2. The external beauty achieved by technical methods proper to the particular kind of art. Thus in dramatic art, the technical method will be: a true individuality of language corresponding to the characters, a natural and at the same time touching plot, a correct scenic rendering of the demonstration and development of emotion, and the feeling of measure in all that is represented.

3. Sincerity, i.e., that the author should himself keenly feel what he expresses. Without this condition there can be no work of art, as the essence of art consists in the contemplator of the work of art being infected with the author's feeling. If the author does not actually feel what he expresses, then the recipient cannot become infected with the feeling of the author, he does not experience any feeling, and the production can no longer be classified as a work of art.

The subject of Shakespeare's pieces, as is seen from the demonstrations of his greatest admirers, is that lowest, most vulgar view of life which regards the external elevation of the lords of the world as a genuine distinction, despises the crowd, i.e., the working classes, repudiates not only all religious, but also all humanitarian strivings directed to the betterment of the existing order.

The second condition also, with the exception of the rendering of the scenes in which the movement of feelings is expressed, is quite absent in Shakespeare. He does not grasp the natural character of the positions of his personages, nor the language of the persons represented, nor does he possess the feeling of measure without which no work can be artistic.

The third and most important condition—sincerity, is completely absent in all Shakespeare's works. In all of them one sees intentional artifice, one sees that he is not *in earnest,* but that he is playing with words.

VIII

Shakespeare's works do not satisfy the demands of all art, and besides this, their tendency is of the lowest and most immoral. What then signifies the great fame these works have enjoyed for more than a hundred years?

Many times during my life I have had occasion to argue about Shakespeare with his admirers, not only with people little sensitive to poetry, but with those who keenly felt poetic beauty, such as Turgenev, Fet,[13] and others, and every time I encountered one and the same attitude toward my objection to the praises of Shakespeare. I was not refuted when I pointed out Shakespeare's defects, they only condoled with me for my want of comprehension, and urged upon me the necessity of recognizing the extraordinary supernatural grandeur of Shakespeare, and they did not explain to me in what the beauties of Shakespeare consisted, but were merely vaguely and ex-

[13] Afanasi Afanasievich Fet (1820?–1892), who with Nikolai Alekseevich Nekrasov (1821–1877), is considered one of the best Russian poets of the second half of the nineteenth century. Editor.

aggeratedly enraptured with the whole of Shakespeare, extolling some favorite passages: the unbuttoning of Lear's button, Falstaff's lying, Lady Macbeth's ineffaceable spots, Hamlet's exhortation to his father's ghost, etc., etc.

"Open Shakespeare," I used to say to these admirers, "wherever you like, or wherever it may chance, you will see that you will never find ten consecutive lines which are comprehensible, unartificial, natural to the character that says them, and which produce an artistic impression." (This experiment may be made by anyone.) And either at random, or according to their own choice, Shakespeare's admirers opened pages in Shakespeare's dramas, and without paying any attention to my criticisms as to why the selected ten lines did not satisfy the most elementary demands of aesthetic and common sense, they were enchanted with the very things which to me appeared absurd, incomprehensible, and inartistic. So that in general, when I endeavored to get from Shakespeare's worshipers an explanation of his greatness, I met in them exactly the same attitude which I met, and which is usually to be met, in the defenders of any dogmas accepted not through reason but through faith. It is this attitude of Shakespeare's admirers toward their object—an attitude which may be seen also in all the mistily indefinite essays and conversations about Shakespeare—which gave me the key to the understanding of the cause of Shakespeare's fame. There is but one explanation of this wonderful fame: it is one of those epidemic "suggestions" to which men ever have been and are subject. Such "suggestion" always has existed and does exist in the most varied spheres of life. As glaring instances, considerable in scope and in deceitful influence, one may cite the medieval Crusades, which afflicted not only adults but even children, and other "suggestions," startling in their senselessness, such as faith in witches, in the utility of torture for the discovery of the truth, the search for the elixir of life, the philosophers' stone, or the passion for tulips, valued at several thousand guldens a bulb, which took hold of Holland. Such irrational "suggestions" always have existed and do exist in all spheres of human life—religious, philosophical, political, economical, scientific, artistic, and, in general, literary—and people clearly see their insanity only when they free themselves from them. But so long as they are under their influence, the suggestions appear to them so certain, so true, that to argue about them is regarded as neither necessary nor possible. With the development of the printing press, these epidemics became especially striking.

With the development of the press, it has now come to pass that as soon as any event, owing to casual circumstances, receives an especially prominent significance, the organs of the press immediately announce this significance. As soon as the press has brought forward the significance of the event, the public devotes more and more attention to it. The attention of the public prompts the press to examine the event with greater attention and in greater detail. The interest of the public further increases, and the organs of the press, competing with one another, satisfy the public demand. The public is still more interested; the press attributes yet more significance to the event. So that the importance of the event, continually growing like a lump of snow, receives an appreciation utterly inappropriate to its real significance, and this appreciation, often exaggerated to insanity, is retained so long as the conception of life of the leaders of the press and of the public remains the same. There are innumerable examples of such an inappropriate estimation which in our time, owing to the mutual influence of press and public on one another, is attached to the most insignificant subjects. A striking example of such mutual influence of the public and the press was the excitement which lately caught hold of the whole world in the case of Dreyfus. The suspicion arose that some captain of the French staff was guilty of treason. Whether because this particular captain was a Jew or because of special internal party disagreements in French society, the press attached a somewhat prominent interest to this event, whose like is continually occurring without attracting anyone's attention, and without being able to interest even the French military, still less the whole world. The public turned its attention to this incident, the organs of the press, mutually competing, began to describe, examine, discuss the event; the public was yet more interested; the press answered to the demand of the public, and the lump of snow began to grow and grow, till before our eyes it attained such a bulk, that there was not a family where controversies did not rage about *"l'affaire."* The caricature by Caran d'Ache, representing at first a peaceful family, decided to talk no more about Dreyfus, and then the members of the same family fighting with each other like exasperated furies, quite correctly expressed the attitude of the whole of the reading world to the question about Dreyfus. People of foreign nationalities, who could not be interested in the question whether a French officer was a traitor or not—people, moreover, who could know nothing of the development of the case—all divided themselves for and against Dreyfus, and the moment they met they talked and argued about Dreyfus, some asserting his guilt with assurance, others denying it with equal assurance. Only after the lapse of some years did people begin to awake from the "suggestion" and to understand that they could not possibly know whether Dreyfus was guilty or not, and that each one had thousands of subjects much more near to him and interesting than the case of Dreyfus.

Such infatuations take place in all spheres, but they are especially noticeable in the sphere of literature, as the press naturally occupies itself the more keenly with the affairs of the press, and they are particularly powerful in our time when the press has received such an unnatural development. It continually happens that people suddenly begin to extol some most insignificant works in exaggerated language, and then, if these works do not correspond to the prevailing view of life, they suddenly become utterly indifferent to them, and forget both the works themselves and their former attitude toward them.

So within my recollection, since the forties, there has been in the sphere of art the laudation and glorification of Eugène Sue and Georges Sand, and in the social sphere, Fourier, in the philosophic sphere, Comte, Hegel, in the scientific sphere, Darwin.

Sue is quite forgotten, Georges Sand is being forgotten and replaced by the writings of Zola and the Decadents, Baudelaire, Verlaine, Maeterlinck, and others. Fourier, with his Phalansteries, is quite forgotten, his place being taken by Marx. Hegel, who justified the existing order, and Comte, who denied the necessity of religious activity in mankind, and Darwin with his law of struggle, still hold on, but are beginning to be forgotten, being replaced by the teaching of Nietzsche, which, although utterly extravagant, unconsidered, misty, and vicious in its bearing, yet corresponds better with existing tendencies. Thus sometimes artistic, philosophic, and, in general, literary crazes suddenly arise and are as quickly forgotten. But it also happens that such crazes, having arisen in consequence of special reasons accidentally favoring their establishment, correspond in such a degree to the views of life spread in society, and especially in literary circles, that they are maintained for a long time. As far back as in the time of Rome, it was remarked that often books have their own very strange fates: consisting in failure, notwithstanding their high merits, and in enormous undeserved success, notwithstanding their triviality. The saying arose: "*Pro captu lectoris habent sua fata libelli*"—i.e., that the fate of books depends on the understanding of those who read them. Such was the harmony between Shakespeare's writings and the view of life of those amongst whom his fame arose. And this fame has been and still is maintained owing to Shakespeare's work continuing to correspond to the conception of life of those who support this fame.

IX

Until the end of the eighteenth century, Shakespeare not only failed to gain any special fame in England, but was valued less than his contemporary dramatists: Ben Jonson, Fletcher, Beaumont, and others. His fame originated in Germany, and thence was transferred to England. This happened for the following reason.

Art, especially dramatic art, demanding for its realization great preparations, outlays, and labor, was always religious, i.e., its object was to stimulate in men the clearer conception of the relation of man to God which had at a given time been attained by the leading men of the circle interested in art.

So it was bound to be from its own nature, and so, as a matter of fact, has it always been amongst all nations—Egyptians, Hindus, Chinese, Greeks—commencing in some remote period of human life. And it has always happened that with the coarsening of religious forms, art has more and more diverged from its original object (according to which it could be regarded as an important function—almost an act of worship) and instead of serving religious objects it strove for worldly aims, seeking to satisfy the demands of the crowd or of the powerful, i.e., the aims of recreation and amusement. This deviation of art from its true and high vocation took place everywhere and even in connection with Christianity.

The first manifestations of Christian art were services in churches: in the administration of the sacraments and the ordinary liturgy. When, in course of time, the forms of art as used in worship became insufficient, there appeared the Mysteries, describing those events which were regarded as the most important in the Christian religious view of life. When, in the thirteenth and fourteenth centuries, the center of gravity of Christian teaching was more and more transferred to the worship of Christ as God, and the interpretation and following of his teaching, the form of Mysteries describing external Christian events became insufficient, and new forms were demanded. As the expression of the aspirations which gave rise to these changes there appeared the Moralities, dramatic representations in which the characters were personifications of Christian virtues and their opposite vices.

But allegories, owing to the very fact of their being works of art of a lower order, could not replace the former religious dramas, and yet no new forms of dramatic art had yet been found corresponding to the conception now entertained of Christianity, according to which it was regarded as a teaching of life. Hence dramatic art, bereft of any foundation, came in all Christian countries to swerve further and further from its proper use and object, and instead of serving God, it took to serving the crowd (by crowd, I mean, not merely the common people, but the majority of immoral or unmoral men, indifferent to the higher problems of human life). This deviation was, moreover, encouraged by the circumstance that at this very time the Greek thinkers, poets, and dramatists, hitherto unknown in the Christian world, were discovered and brought back into favor. From all this it followed that, not having yet had time to work out their own form of dramatic art, corresponding to the new conception entertained of Christianity as being a teaching of life, and, at the same time, recognizing the previous form of Mysteries and Moralities as insufficient, the writers of the fifteenth and sixteenth centuries, in their search for a new form, began to imitate the newly discovered Greek models, attracted by their elegance and novelty.

Since those who could principally avail themselves of dramatic representations were the powerful of this world—kings, princes, courtiers, the least religious people, not only utterly indifferent to the questions of religion, but in most cases completely depraved—therefore in satisfying the demands of its audience, the drama of the fifteenth, sixteenth, and seventeenth centuries entirely gave up all religious aim. It came to pass that the drama, which formerly had such a lofty and religious significance, and which can on this condition alone occupy an important place in human life, became, as in the time of Rome, a spectacle, an amusement, a recreation—only with this difference, that in Rome the spectacles existed for the whole people, whereas in the Christian world of the fifteenth, sixteenth, and seventeenth centuries they were principally meant for depraved kings and the higher classes. Such was the case with the Spanish, English, Italian, and French drama.

The dramas of that time, principally composed in all these countries according to ancient Greek models, or taken from poems, legends, or biographies, naturally reflected the characteristics of their respective nationalities: in Italy comedies were chiefly elaborated with humorous positions and persons. In Spain there flourished the worldly drama with complicated plots and ancient historical heroes. The peculiarities of the English drama were the coarse incidents of murders, executions, and battles taking place on the stage, and popular humorous interludes. Neither the Italian nor the Spanish nor the English drama had European fame, but they all enjoyed success in their own countries. General fame, owing to the elegance of its language and the talent of its writers, was possessed only by the French drama, distinguished by its strict adherence to the Greek models and especially to the law of the three unities.

X

So it continued till the end of the eighteenth century, at which time the following happened: in Germany, which had not even got any passable dramatic writers (there was a weak and little-known writer, Hans Sachs), all educated people, together with Frederick the Great, bowed down before the French pseudo-classical drama. Yet at this very time there appeared in Germany a group of educated and talented writers and poets, who feeling the falsity and coldness of the French drama, endeavored to find a new and freer dramatic form. The members of this group, like all the upper classes of the Christian world of that time, were under the charm and influence of the Greek classics, and being utterly indifferent to religious questions, they thought that, if the Greek drama, describing the calamities and sufferings and strife of its heroes, represented the highest dramatic ideal, then such a description of the sufferings and the struggles of heroes would be a sufficient subject in the Christian world too, if only the narrow demands of pseudo-classicalism were rejected. These men, not understanding that, for the Greeks, the strife and sufferings of their heroes had a religious significance, imagined they needed only reject the inconvenient law of the three unities without introducing into the drama any religious element corresponding to their own time—in order that the drama should have sufficient scope in the representation of various moments in the lives of historical personages, and in general of strong human passions. Exactly this kind of drama existed at that time amongst the kindred English people, and becoming acquainted with it, the Germans decided that precisely such should be the drama of the new period.

Hereupon, because of the clever development of scenes which constituted Shakespeare's peculiarity, the Germans chose Shakespeare's dramas in preference to all other English dramas, though these were not in the least inferior, but were even superior to Shakespeare. At the head of the group stood Goethe, who was then the dictator of public opinion in aesthetic questions. He it was who, partly owing to a desire to destroy the fascination of the false French art, partly because he wished to give a greater scope to his own dramatic writing, but chiefly through the agreement of his view of life with Shakespeare's—declared Shakespeare a great poet. When this error was announced by an authority like Goethe, all those aesthetic critics who did not understand art threw themselves on it like crows on carrion, and began to discover in Shakespeare beauties which did not exist, and to extol them. These men—German aesthetic critics, for the most part utterly devoid of aesthetic feeling (without that simple, direct artistic sensibility which, for people with a feeling for art, clearly distinguishes aesthetic impressions from all others), but believing the authority which had recognized Shakespeare as a great poet—began to praise the whole of Shakespeare indiscriminately, especially distinguishing such places as struck them by their effects, or which expressed thoughts corresponding to their views of life, imagining that these effects and these thoughts constitute the essence of what is called art. These men acted as blind men would act who endeavored to find diamonds by touch amongst a heap of stones they were fingering. As the blind man would for a long time strenuously handle the stones and in the end could come to no other conclusion than that all stones are precious and especially so the smoothest, so also these aesthetic critics, without artistic feeling, could not but come to similar results in relation to Shakespeare. To give the greater force to their praise of the whole of Shakespeare they invented aesthetic theories according to which it appeared that no definite religious view of life was necessary for works of art in general, and especially for the drama; that for the purpose of the drama, the representation of human passions and characters was quite sufficient; that not only was an internal religious illumination of what was represented unnecessary, but art should be objective, i.e., should represent events quite independently of any judgment of good and evil. As these theories were founded on Shakespeare's own views of life it naturally turned out that the works of Shakespeare satisfied these theories and therefore were the height of perfection.

These were the people chiefly responsible for Shakespeare's fame. It was principally owing to their writings that the interaction took place between writers and public which expressed itself and is still expressing itself in an insane worship of Shakespeare which has no rational foundation. These aesthetic critics have written profound treatises about Shakespeare. (Eleven thousand volumes have been written about him, and a whole science of Shakespearology composed.) While the public on the one hand were more and more interested, the learned critics on the other gave further and further explanations, adding to the confusion.

So that the first cause of Shakespeare's fame was that the Germans wished to oppose a livelier and freer drama to the cold French drama of which they had grown weary, and which no doubt was tedious enough. The second cause was that the young German writers required a model for writing their own dramas. The third and principal cause was the activity of the learned and zealous aesthetic German critics without aesthetic feeling, who invented the theory of objective art, deliberately rejecting the religious essence of the drama.

"But," I shall be asked, "what do you understand by the words: 'religious essence of the drama'? Is not what you are demanding for the drama religious instruction, didactics, what is called 'tendency' which is incompatible with true art?" I reply that by religious essence of art I understand not the direct inculcation of any religious truths in an artistic guise, and not an allegorical demonstration of these truths, but the expression of a definite view of life corresponding to the highest religious understanding of a given time, which, serving as a motive for composition of the drama, penetrates, unknown to the author, through the whole of his work. So it has always been with true art, and so it is with every true artist in general and especially the dramatist. Hence—as it was when the drama was a serious thing, and as it should be, according to the essence of the matter—he alone can write a drama who has got something to say to men, and that something of the greatest importance for them: about man's relation to God, to the Universe, to the All, the Eternal, the Infinite. But when, thanks to the German theories about objective art, the idea was established that for the drama this was quite unnecessary, then it became obvious how a writer like Shakespeare—who had not got developed in his mind the religious convictions proper to his time, who, in fact, had no convictions at all, but heaped up in his drama all possible events, horrors, fooleries, discussions, and effects—could appear to be a dramatic writer of the greatest genius.

But these are all external reasons. The fundamental inner cause of Shakespeare's fame was and is this—that his dramas were "*pro captu lectoris,*" i.e., they corresponded to the irreligious and immoral frame of mind of the upper classes of his time and ours.

XI

At the beginning of the last century, when Goethe was dictator of philosophic thought and aesthetic laws, a series of casual circumstances made him praise Shakespeare. The aesthetic critics caught up this praise and took to writing their lengthy, misty, learned articles, and the great European public began to be enchanted with Shakespeare. The critics, answering to the popular interest, and endeavoring to compete with one another, wrote new and ever new essays about Shakespeare, the readers and spectators on their side were increasingly confirmed in their admiration, and Shakespeare's fame, like a lump of snow, kept growing and growing, until in our time it has attained that insane worship which obviously has no other foundation but "suggestion."

"Shakespeare finds no rival, not even approximately, either amongst the old or the new writers." "Poetic truth is the brightest flower in the crown of Shakespeare's merits." "Shakespeare is the greatest moralist of all times." "Shakespeare exhibits such many-sidedness and such objectivism that they carry him beyond the limits of time and nationality." "Shakespeare is the greatest genius that has hitherto existed." "For tragedy, comedy, history, idyl, idylistic comedy, aesthetic idyl, for the profoundest presentation, as for any casually thrown off passing piece of verse, he is the only man. He not only wields an unlimited power over our mirth and our tears, over all the workings of passion, humor, thought, and observation, but he possesses also an infinite region full of the fantasy of fiction, of a horrifying and an amusing character. He possesses penetration both in the world of fiction and of reality, and above this reigns one and the same truthfulness to character and to nature, and the same spirit of humanity." "To Shakespeare the epithet of Great comes of itself; and if one adds that independently of his greatness he has further become the reformer of all literature, and moreover has in his works not only expressed the phenomenon of life as it was in his day, but also, by the germs of thought which floated in the air, has prophetically forestalled the direction that the social spirit is going to take in the future (of which we see a striking example in *Hamlet*)—one may without hesitation say that Shakespeare was not only a great poet, but the greatest of all poets who ever existed, and that in the sphere of poetic creation, his only worthy rival was that same life which in his works he expressed to such perfection."

The obvious exaggeration of this estimate proves more conclusively than anything that it is the consequence not of common sense, but of suggestion. If only a phenomenon has become the subject of suggestion, the more trivial, the lower, the emptier it is, the more supernatural and exaggerated is the significance attributed to it. The Pope is not merely saintly, but most saintly, and so forth. So Shakespeare is not merely a good writer, but the greatest genius, the eternal teacher of mankind.

Suggestion is always a deceit, and every deceit is an evil. In truth the suggestion that Shakespeare's works are great works of genius, presenting the height of both aesthetic and ethical perfection, has caused and is causing great injury to men.

This injury is twofold: first, the fall of the drama, and the replacement of this important weapon of progress by an empty and immoral amusement; and secondly, the direct depravation of men by presenting to them false models for imitation.

XII

Human life is perfected solely through the development of the religious consciousness, the only element which permanently unites men. The development of the religious consciousness of men is accomplished through all the sides of man's spiritual activity. One direction of this activity is art. One section of art, perhaps the most influential—is the drama.

Therefore the drama, in order to deserve the importance attributed to it, should serve the development of religious consciousness. Such has the drama always been, and such it formerly was in the Christian world. But upon the appearance of Protestantism in its broadest sense, i.e., the appearance of a new understanding of Christianity as a teaching of life, the dramatic art did not find a form corresponding to the new understanding of Christianity, and the men of the Renaissance were carried away by the imitation of classical art. This was most natural, but the tendency was bound to pass, and art had to discover, as indeed it is now beginning to do, its new form corresponding to the change in the understanding of Christianity.

But the discovery of this new form was arrested by the teaching, arising amongst German writers at the end of the eighteenth and the beginning of the nineteenth centuries—as to so-called objective art, i.e., art indifferent to good or evil, in connection with the exaggerated praise of Shakespeare's dramas, which partly corresponded to the aesthetic teaching of the Germans, and partly served as material for it. If there were not that exaggerated praise of Shakespeare's dramas, recognized as the most perfect model of the drama, the men of the eighteenth and nineteenth centuries would have had to understand that the drama, to have a right to exist and to be a serious thing, must serve, as it always has served and cannot but do—the development of the religious consciousness. And having understood this, they would have searched for a new form of drama corresponding to their religious understanding.

But when it was decided that the height of perfection was Shakespeare's drama, and that we ought to write as he did, not only without any religious, but even without any moral, intention, then all writers of dramas began, in imitation of him, to compose such empty pieces as are those of Goethe, Schiller, Hugo, and, in Russia, of Pushkin, or the chronicles of Ostrovski, Alexis Tolstoy, and an innumerable quantity of other more or less celebrated dramatic productions which fill all the theaters and are prepared wholesale by anyone who happens to have the idea or desire to write a play. It is only thanks to such a low, trivial understanding of the significance of the drama that there appears amongst us that infinite quantity of dramatic works describing men's actions, positions, characters, and frames of mind, not only void of any spiritual substance, but often of any human sense.

Let not the reader think that I exclude from this estimate of contemporary drama the theatrical pieces I have myself incidentally written. I recognize them, as well as all the rest, as not having that religious character which must form the foundation of the drama of the future.

The drama then, the most important branch of art, has in our time become the trivial and immoral amusement of a trivial and immoral crowd. The worst of it is, moreover, that to dramatic art—fallen as low as it is possible to fall—is still attributed an elevated significance no longer appropriate to it. Dramatists, actors, theatrical managers, the press—this last publishing in the most serious tone reports of theaters and operas—and the rest, are all perfectly certain that they are doing something very worthy and important.

XIII

The drama in our time is as a great man fallen, who has reached the last degree of his degradation, and at the same time continues to pride himself on his past of which nothing now remains. The public of our time is like those who mercilessly amuse themselves over this man once so great, and now in the lowest stage of his fall.

Such is one of the mischievous effects of the epidemic suggestion about the greatness of Shakespeare. Another deplorable result of this worship is the presentation to men of a false model for imitation. If people wrote of Shakespeare that for his time he was a good writer, that he had a fairly good turn for verse, was an intelligent actor and good stage manager, even were this appreciation incorrect and somewhat exaggerated—if only it were moderately true, people of the rising generation might remain free from Shakespeare's influence. But when every young man entering into life in our time has presented to him as the model of moral perfection, not the religious and moral teachers of mankind, but first of all Shakespeare, concerning whom it has been decided and is handed down by learned men from generation to generation as an incontestable truth, that he was the greatest poet, the greatest teacher of life, the young man cannot remain free from this pernicious influence. When he is reading or listening to Shakespeare, the question for him is no longer whether Shakespeare be good or bad, but only: in what consists that extraordinary beauty, both aesthetic and ethical, of which he has been assured by learned men whom he respects, and which he himself neither sees nor feels? And constraining himself, and distorting his aesthetic and ethical feeling, he tries to conform to the ruling opinion. He no longer believes in himself but in what is said by the learned people whom he respects. I have experienced all this. Then, reading critical examinations of the dramas and extracts from books with explanatory comments he begins to imagine that he feels something of the nature of an artistic impression. The longer this continues, the more does his aesthetic and ethical feeling become distorted. He ceases to distinguish directly and clearly what is artistic from an artificial imitation of art. But above all, having assimilated the immoral view of life which penetrates all Shakespeare's writings, he loses the capacity of distinguishing good from evil. And the error of extolling an insignificant, inartistic writer —not only not moral, but directly immoral—executes its destructive work.

XIV

This is why I think that the sooner people free themselves from the false glorification of Shakespeare, the better it will be.

Firstly, having freed themselves from this deceit, men will come to understand that the drama which has no religious element as its foundation is not only not an important and good thing, as it is now supposed to be, but the most trivial and despicable of things. Having understood this, they will have to search for and work out a new form of modern drama, a drama which will serve as the development and confirmation of the highest stage of religious consciousness in men.

Secondly, having freed themselves from this hypnotic state, men will understand that the trivial and immoral works of Shakespeare and his imitators, aiming merely at the recreation and amusement of the spectators, cannot possibly represent the teaching of life, and that, while there is no true religious drama, the teaching of life should be sought for in other sources.

18. Bjørnstjerne Bjørnson

1832–1910

Bjørnson became director of the Christiania Theater in January 1865. He had already served as manager of the Bergen theater for the period of two years almost eight years earlier. Before assuming the directorship at Christiania Bjørnson had already published his influential novel Arne *(1858) and his dramas* Between the Battles *(1857) and* Sigurd the Bastard *(1862). It is the novel as well as the trilogy that have earned their author a reputation only slightly below that of Ibsen.*

The first notable performance under Bjørnson's direction at the Christiania was Shakespeare's A Midsummer Night's Dream *(Skjärsommernatsdrömmen) in a translation by Oehlenschläger and using Mendelssohn's music. Bjørnson had been unusually prodigal with the theater's funds for this performance but the critics found it tedious and one reviewer, in* Morgenbladet, *attacked the performance in two scathing articles. Bjørnson rose to the challenge. The present selection is his answer. But it was not merely an apologia. It remains one of the finest examples of Bjørnson the polemicist; a piece of vital, magnificent albeit fanciful prose. As a piece of Shakespeare criticism the article is less profound than interesting. It exhibits once more that dominant tendency in Europe of putting Shakespeare to use in the cause of artistic freedom. In it, Bjørnson speaks out against literalists of the imagination, those critics who insist on elaborate staging with the use of artificial scenery as if the power of the poetry were not enough. But the article is interesting for another reason as well. Although one might suspect the influence of Shakespeare on Bjørnson, it is doubtful that more than a tentative case could be made for it. It is, therefore, fortunate to have the closing section of this article in which he acknowledges his debt to Shakespeare.*

A Defense

Your newspaper has recently published a fine review of this play; [1] but as well as it explained the play's plot, it did not, to my mind, interpret the meaning of the play. And the review in the *Morgenbladet,* which I have waited for until now, explains neither the plot nor the meaning of the play. Clever criticism is the easiest of all forms of criticism; I therefore find it necessary to add a few words so that this wonderful play does not lack a more well-rounded elucidation.

The play is called "a dream," but what does this mean? Certainly someone will answer, it means that fairies play, citizens perform a comedy, sometimes wearing and sometimes not wearing ass heads, lovers pursue one another in a moonlit night—but where is the sense and meaning of these scenes? The dream someone will answer; but what is the sense and meaning of the dream? If it is without sense and meaning, then it is without aesthetic justification.

Dear reader, the sense and meaning are in ourselves. The play takes place all the time—now it happens to you, now it happens to me. A young man who is happily engaged, or an older man who is happily married, dreams at night that this is not at all the case; he has just been engaged to and marries an entirely different person. The memory of his real beloved is present in his mind, but he cannot do anything about it. Though he has a bad conscience, the wedding goes on—until he awakens and thanks God, because it all was only a dream (Lysander). Or a young man is tired of the one with whom he

From *Aftenbladet,* April 28, 1865. Translated by Edward C. Thaden.

[1] Shakespeare's *Midsummer Night's Dream* was given at the Christiania Theater, of which Bjørnson had become director in 1865. Laura Gundersen was Hermia, Louise Bruna was Titania, Lucie Wolf was Puck, and Johannes Brun played the weaver Bottom. The newspaper *Morgenbladet* ran two long articles on April 26 and 27, 1865, about the play and its performance. In both cases the staging of the play was criticized, but Johannes Brun and Laura Gundersen were praised for their performances. Editor.

was shortly before madly in love; he even begins to court another. He even dreams one fine night that he pursues the very woman he has detested with the passion of love, that he solicits her, cries for her, indeed, fights for her (Demetrius). Or a young girl, or a young wife, who loves and is loved, dreams that the loved one flees from her; and when she follows him with tears, entreaties, he beats her, yes lifts his hand against her. She shouts that he should stop, she runs after him but cannot move ahead fast enough, feels the dread of death until she sinks exhaustedly into quiet, untroubled sleep (Hermia). Or she is unfortunate in love but dreams that the one whom she loves, and whose favor she cannot win, comes to her in a large forest and tells her that he does love her, has never loved anyone else, that her eyes are more beautiful than the stars, her hands whiter than the snows of the Tauras Mountains. But this beautiful picture is gradually blurred in a most disturbing manner. Another young man arrives, one about whom she has never thought seriously. He says exactly the same thing that his predecessor did, only more emphatically and blissfully. All ends in antagonism and sorrow, contest and strife, until she cannot stand it any more (Helena).

Here we have the lovers' dream cycle. The poet allows a man to dream that he is unfaithful, or that he is caught by someone whom he does not love. He allows a woman to dream that she is forsaken, or is happy with the one whose heart she was never able to win. Altogether these dreams have one lesson to teach us: guard your thoughts, guard your passions, you who go so confidently alongside of your loved one. These thoughts can produce a flower called "love and idleness" that transforms you before you are aware of it! The dream represents the inversion of reality, but in such a manner that it has the possibility within itself of taking form at any unguarded moment.

This dream of the lovers is paralleled with a parody. A fat, good-natured citizen dreams on the eve of what is anticipated to be his greatest triumph, namely to stand before the duke's throne as the most extraordinary hero, dreams that he cannot get his clothes on, that he cannot wash his head properly because it at bottom is not his own remarkable head but an ass head with long ears, with a snout, with hair that scratches! This certainly goes back to an adventure of my childhood, the man reflects in his dream, and quite rightly so: all of this is an adventure. The mountain opens up, the imprisoned princess steps forth and leads him inside, and he rests his head on her flower-strewn lap, and the beautiful troll comes and scratches his head, and music resounds from the mountain. It is characteristic of Shakespeare that the four lovers do not dream of adventures from their childhood. Because of their superior education they have developed more intensive passions, more forceful personal conduct; they therefore continue in their dreams the ardent thoughts of daytime, except that everything is turned topsy-turvy for them. But the honest weaver who lives corpulently and cheerfully in the praise of his fellow citizens as well in his own conscience, he who has never reflected about anything that has happened to him, but has accepted it as something willed by God—whenever he lays his head on a pillow, he immediately sees both elves and a fairy queen, for him opens up again the magical world of childhood. Only he could wear a strange ass head and feel a curious longing for dry, sweet hay!

Notice, the dream is one thing, and the plot of the play is another. Outwardly this magic is set into motion by the fairies. Theseus and attendants, with whom come the hunting horn, hunting talk, and the festival march, are day and reality, only the animated festival program. But the comedy is placed in opposition to the fine, light thoughts of the dream. It is made up of rational thoughts, the awakened fantasy of accumulated and most troublesome thoughts that result in a display of the fireworks of caprice against the nocturnal background of the dream.

View this play again and again, do not wear Bottom's ass head in the presence of its content. Do not be so blasé and up-to-date modern that you reject the performance because it does not make use of the latest applications of electric light! And with this we have made the transition to a discussion of the play's performance.

II

This play had the good fortune of being staged by Tieck the first time it was performed in Germany. It is his arrangement that is still used in Germany, and from there it was brought to Stockholm, from where it came here [Norway]. An unimportant alteration has been made in Germany and adopted here, namely to discard the division of the scene into two parts that was known from Shakespeare's time. Tieck still used it but it was not necessary for the plot and represented a troublesome reminiscence. Tieck's spirit, however, still is present in the arrangement: it is light and natural; in all respects the dialogue is able to work fully and with its own power. And the dialogue is not obscured by airy schemes or shoved aside by movable scenery. Tieck, who had an excellent understanding of staging machinery, allowed the machines to play their role where all, as in the modern opera, is only machinery; but he allowed spirit to remain spirit.* Mendelssohn-Bartholdy respects the same strict conception; his music has respect for the dialogue of the play. The fairies' speeches are not even melodramas (with the exception of the short formulas for exorcism). He allows the music to follow the play merely as a new fairy who sprinkles several tunes over the scene as a

* *Morgenbladet*'s review calls our attention to England's performance of Shakespeare's fantasy-plays. This must be meant in the sense of parody; because the English give *The Tempest* on a maneuvering ship and all the other plays in a similar fashion. Shakespeare emigrated from England; the English still sit with their machinery out of which Shakespeare's spirit will not rise. It is characteristically the case that Germany's first practical dramaturgist (Herr Generalintendant Dingelstedt) had a plan several years ago to travel to London with Germany's best actors in order to teach the English how to perform Shakespeare. I have seen many of Shakespeare's plays in Germany, among which was *The Winter's Tale* with the music of Flotow. I intend to perform this play next season here. I have also seen one of his major plays at the Odeon in Paris. Both there and in Germany I had to admire the economy with which Shakespeare was given in contrast to all the arrangements with which unimaginative adventure-pieces of recent German origin are helped along. It can well be that someone at one place or another in Germany has allowed the material scenery to strangle Shakespeare; but I have not seen this, and in any case this example should not be imitated.

form of consecration prior to the entry of the spiritual procession, giving it wings upon which it can fly away. Only when the dialogue with all of its dramatis personae have receded into the background does the music hover over the forest as a sort of mist of recollection, in which our fantasy again assembles the picture of what has just taken place. For the fairies' dance, about which one makes so much ado here, he only has several bars of music. Why? Because they are part of the plot, the dialogue, the situation, because the fairies' dance does not require more, the music needs only to suggest. The farmers' dance is also very short. And it can hardly be a consolation for all our foreign travelers—in thought I shall thus inform them—that all of this there in Germany, at least until very recently, is done in conformity with Tieck's arrangement, i.e., with the greatest possible simplicity. With regard to this play, those who want to point with overrefined gentility to materially costly productions abroad are guilty of a comical error. Tieck designed it originally for the restricted stage of the Court Theater at Potsdam. It was not brought to the main Opera when it was moved to Berlin, but to the small royal Schauspielhaus.

I cannot refrain from making the general remark that fantasy which finds satisfaction in the commonplace is stronger and healthier than fantasy which soars upward with desires for unattainable things. To compose one's picture of few and simple hints is the essence of having fantasy, while to allow images to dissolve and blow away means to have nothing. All illusion has some relation to familiar things. When our public, after having been invited to do so over a period of many years, cannot catch the illusion in the *Midsummer Night's Dream* because of this play's inadequate equipment, poor critics are to be blamed. With and without the pen, they have interfered with the public's sense of spontaneity. The motives I shall not investigate. I should take note of such things were the play to be given for a limited Paris audience that had hardly seen the sun among their houses and no trees other than the beautifully trimmed ones in the Bois de Boulogne, an audience that had never truly experienced nature because they have never been alone. But we, who are a hearty people close to nature, who have an infinity of forest impressions behind us, do we need more than a gentle reminder of how it looks? Indeed, this crass attempt to give everything—in the manner of the big operas abroad—can it not only have an unpleasant and disturbing effect on us? I appeal to those Norwegians who have seen performances abroad to tell how miserable they found waterfalls falling down over a back curtain and ships maneuvering on rollers. The new inventions with which technology has supplied the theater still have not been completely mastered and often lead to little more than the corruption of art. One finds himself in a period of transition with all of the ailments that accompany such a period. And we who have gotten hold of the recognized good things of life so recently, should we participate in all the errors on the way to this end?

I shall take care of the complaints about the performance of the play with a few words. The reviewer of the *Morgenbladet* is unhappy that the stage was not high enough; hence his fantasy really must seek to make it a little higher. He is dissatisfied with old Wergmann's forest. He wants a forest in which "it blows and whistles over one's head, in the grass and dew, over the soft moss carpet, where everything is swarming and astir, buzzes, crackles, and chirps, the wild, pungent aroma of the forest"—all of this is almost like coming into the vicinity of a pharmacy. It is possible that one day stagecraft will be so perfected that there will be individual aroma machines for each flower of a stage setting—and that these machines will be maintained in preparation for representations of forests. And when the curtain rises, one bottle will produce the odor of roses, another the perfume of violets, another the smell of tulips. Another apparatus will produce the bird calls of both sparrows and cuckoos. But until then we shall have to try to imagine all of this with our own good will and fantasy. In addition, he complains about the lighting. To this I answer that our apparatus (that cost us over 100 specie-dollars) is the same one that has been used until very recently by the largest theaters. It is truly terrible, in case we are not able to capture illusion with the old one, because we know that the other theaters have got a new apparatus. The main thing is, however, that the staging as a whole, whether it is new or old, has harmonious effect. I appeal to experts to tell us whether ours does this. And one really is trivial to sit and watch the moon while Shakespeare talks through the mouth of Oehlenschläger and Mendelssohn contributes his music.

Another reviewer, whom the *Morgenbladet* itself calls "casual," complains "casually" about the performance and assignment of the roles, but he happens to be guilty—also "casually" —of several serious blunders. He characterizes Helena as an ardent lover that should be played by Mrs. Wolf. I offer Mrs. Wolf running after Demetrius with the most tender names, the patient resignation in the face of his rough treatment and open contempt, and also the monologue in which she charmingly and lyrically paints the childlike caprices of love. He says that Helena's role in no way gives any suggestion of "languishing"; but what does one, then, call sighing with hopeless love and pursuing the object of this love whenever she gets her eyes on him? One indeed calls this languishing. An ardent lover would abandon herself to fury, want to commit suicide or avenge herself. But Helena cannot do this because she stands in the presence of three people, all of whom seem to be making a fool of her. She cannot become angry without immediately falling into mild complaint about her fate or begging them to be nice to her—"she is so weak." And she is so frightened that she flees from a rival whom she has characterized as being less worthy than she herself. When the reviewer himself reads so badly, it is perhaps not so "casual" that he must lecture to us. His second objection and blunder concerns Puck. After having informed us that Puck is a boy, he insists that Puck should be played by a boy: that is to say, that this role should be played without meaning, by an adolescent who would fall all over himself with Puck's first very difficult speech. It is clear enough that Shakespeare's Puck is a boy, but it is equally clear that on the stage boys can only be represented by women in most cases. If someone who has seen Mrs. Wolf play Puck remains in doubt whether or not it was a boy she represented, such a person—despite his philosophical introductory remarks—has such a "casual" conception of the play and its performance that further refutation is superfluous.

III

I cannot conclude without saying something about my personal relationship to the play.

Of all my poetical readings, Shakespeare's *Midsummer Night's Dream* is the piece that has made the most powerful impression on me. It is the richest in fantasy and most innocent work written by Shakespeare. It is fascinating because of its profound play of understanding as well as because of its lofty and humane spirit that speaks and arranges things in their proper order. It was in Eikisdal at the time I was writing *Arne* that I read the play for the first time. The gloom that produced this book then greatly oppressed me. But I made use of this apprenticeship; I felt something inside of myself that could be worked into a play directed against the fantasy and gaiety of the *Midsummer Night's Dream*. I made resolutions. But the conditions under which people of an idealistic orientation live and work in our country are very hard. Our efforts do not accomplish much; we give our blessings and cross ourselves; and the bitterness and passion of daily life take possession of us. I know one thing, however: I now stand much closer to this poem than I did then; I now have more ability to tend herd and guard it against intrusion. When I have not (with my plans and from my nationalistic point of view) on any occasion gotten around to write a play directed against the *Midsummer Night's Dream*, this is because conditions have won out over me, and I was not able to steer against the main course of circumstances.

One naturally wants to show to others a play that has long hovered over him as a lodestar. I understood quite well that a public that comes from *Orpheus* would not immediately follow along with me. But I also thought that the public surely would do this. Hence, as soon as I gained some influence over the actors as director of the theater, I ventured to undertake the experiment. This play is not something that comes to a conclusion. For that purpose it is a too extraordinary fellow worker with regard to what takes place in both the actors and audience. The efforts the actors have made to assure the success of the play seem to me to have been rewarded. The play can be improved (we ourselves shall perform it better next season), some of the performers do not harmonize well with one another, but everything is being brought along in the direction of what is right, and everyone works with such dedication to his task that the last time it ran, as the first time, I had to stay until it was finished. Now one can call this naïveté, poetical simplicity, or stubbornness and haughtiness—whatever it is, this play is something important for me. Because for me this play is a connecting link and appeal to the public. If the public does not want to be led in this direction, then I am not a leader. If one therefore wants to remove me from the theater and separate me from the public, attack me only here; because here I am to be found.

19. Romain Rolland

1866–1944

In 1888 the young Rolland wrote "credo quia verum" across a manuscript in which he had asserted his opposition to the metaphysical absurdities of the post-Hegelian period as well as to the increasing tendency among the "bourgeois" to accept life at a less than heroic level. It is undoubtedly the statement of a young man, but the basic principles, a contradictory mixture of humanist ethics and romantic hero-worship, were ones which he adhered to throughout his life.

Much of Rolland's work, especially the mammoth novel Jean-Christophe *(1903–1912), seems dated. But the eloquent pacifism which emanates from the pages of much of his work has a curious appeal for our time. And it is this pacifism, which sees those moments in Shakespeare when reason and a "great heart" affect a reconciliation of opposing values into a common humanity, that deserves our attention.*

To My Best Friend—Shakespeare

Few friends, few books withstand the ordeal of the days we are going through. The most beloved betray us, we no longer know them. They were the companions of thoughtless hours. The squall blows them away, plants whose roots lie in shallow soil, which a gust of wind uproots. There remain only the souls with deep roots. Many of humble appearance whom one would

From A *Book of Homage to Shakespeare,* edited by Israel Gollancz (Oxford, Humphrey Milford, Oxford University Press, 1916), pp. 411-416. Reprinted by permission of Lady Gollancz and Oxford University Press. Translated by Françoise Rosen.

not notice at all in ordinary life. And a small number of lofty spirits who rise like towers in the midst of the plain and appear greater still above so many ruins. I find again the one who sheltered all the dreams of my life, from the days of my childhood, the old oak, Shakespeare. Not one of his branches is broken, not one of his boughs is blighted; and the storm that passes over the world today makes this great living lyre swell powerfully.

His music does not make us forget the cares of the present. When one listens one is surprised to hear emerging little by little from that murmuring sea the voices of our times, thoughts that seem to be the direct expression of our present judgments on the events which oppress us. On war and peace—on the behavior of politics in the sixteenth and in the twentieth centuries—on the spirit of ambition and cunning of States—on the exploitation of the noblest instincts, heroism, sacrifice, by dissembling interest—on the sacrilegious mingling of the passions of hatred with the words of the Evangelist—on the participation of the Churches and Gods in the killing of people—on the solemn treaties which are only "scraps of paper" —on the character of nations, of armies that are at odds—I have taken pleasure in assembling a series of thoughts of Shakespeare's which, if they were published without his name, would risk awakening the susceptibilities of the censorship of our liberal epoch, more touchy still than that of Queen Elizabeth. So true it is that, in spite of the turmoil of the world, everything is always the same, and that even if man has found new means of ruling and killing, he has not changed (in) his soul.

But the matchless blessing of reading Shakespeare is that in him we taste the rarest virtue and the one we most need at this hour: the gift of universal sympathy, of penetrating humanity, which makes us *live* the souls of others as our own soul. Most assuredly, faith, grandeur, exaltation of life and of all its passions are not at all lacking in our epoch; and it is this which brings it closer to the English or Italian Renaissance—even though, with the difference and to the credit of the latter, one finds in our time none of those personalities boundless (in their capacity) for good or evil, who dominate the crowd; today, greatness is diffused, so to speak, collective rather than individual; and, in the human Ocean, lifted up all in one mass, scarcely a wave rises above the other. But the principal difference is not at all there; it is that this epic spectacle lacks a spectator. No eye encompasses the whole of the storm. Not a heart is wedded to the pangs, the frenzies, the opposing passions of those clashing billows, those shattered barks, those shipwrecks which the whirlpool of the yawning sea closes over. Each one remains walled up in himself and with his own people. That is why one experiences, on reopening a volume of Shakespeare, a solace and deliverance. It seems that in the middle of an oppressive night, in a closed room, the wind forces the window open, and lets in the gentle breezes of the earth.

The great fraternal soul! It is weighted with all the joys and all the sorrows of the universe. Not only does it lend itself with intoxication to youth, to love, to the burning sweetness of springtime passions: Juliet and Miranda, Perdita, Imogen . . . Not only is this soul not like those that are eclipsed in hours of grief, professing the opinion of the old lord Lafeu, that "excessive grief (is) the enemy to the living" (*All's Well That Ends Well,* I, i, 64); but it remains faithfully, affectionately by their sides, to share the burden of their errors, their miseries, their crimes: after having wept over the death of Desdemona, it still has tears for her murderer, more pitiful yet. This soul feels itself closer to the most wretched, and even does not deny itself at all to the most wicked: they are men like us; they have eyes like us, senses, affections, passions like us, they bleed like us, they laugh and weep like us, they die like us (*Merchant of Venice,* III, i). And, says Friar Laurence in *Romeo and Juliet*:

> For nought so vile that on the earth doth live
> But to the earth some special good doth give,
> Nor ought so good but strain'd from that fair use
> Revolts from true birth, stumbling on abuse:

Virtue itself turns vice, being misapplied;
And vice sometimes by action dignified.
(II, iii, 17–22)

The intelligence and the heart of Shakespeare are united in an equal need to penetrate souls. His instinct for justice is complemented by his instinct for love. In the *Merchant of Venice* Shylock and Antonio in turn expound the reasons for the hatred of the Jew for the Christian merchant (I, iii; III, i). Each speaks sincerely and yet each gives quite different reasons. The fact is that both see and make us see the same thing from a different angle. Thus proceeds the creative mind of Shakespeare. Effortlessly, he puts himself in the heart of each character; he clothes his thought, and his form, and his little universe; never does he look upon him from outside. And if none the less with partiality he pours the treasure of his rich sympathy into certain of his heroes, into the children of his fairest or bravest dreams, he is like a good father: in the hour of trial, the less beloved also become as dear to him. The ambitious Wolsey, hypocrite, sleek "fat-cat," has scarcely been disgraced when he takes on an antique grandeur; he sees suddenly the wretchedness of his desires, and in the ruins of his glory was "never so truly happy" (*Henry VIII*, III, ii): his eyes are opened, misfortune has cured him; and this harsh egoist, consoling his weeping friend, leaves him as a testament of his proud life the holiest of sayings: "cherish those hearts that hate thee." The tyrant Leontes, in the crumbling of his happiness, which he himself has ruined by his criminal and raging folly, becomes suddenly sanctified, even to Paulina, who scourges him with the sharpest truths (*The Winter's Tale*, III, ii). Death, which before the bodies of Brutus and Cassius, of Antony, of Coriolanus, makes their irreconcilable enemies bow, transfigures Cleopatra in her last moments and even restores some nobility to the vile Edmund of *King Lear*. It is marvelous to see how, before wretchedness and before death, the poet's great heart is stripped of pride, of rancor, of egoistic passion, to embrace with his immense pity all those who suffer —enemies, rivals, what does it matter?—all brothers in grief.

One of the most touching strokes of this humanity is the action of Romeo, who, coming to die beside dead Juliet, and, provoked by his rival Paris, kills him in spite of himself and lays him in Juliet's tomb, by her side:

> O, give me thy hand,
> One writ with me in sour misfortune's book!
> (V, iii, 81–82)

And when Hamlet torments his criminal mother by cruel words, Shakespeare, unable to check the hero's fit of passion by ascribing to him a pity which Hamlet does not at all feel, inspires this pity in the ghost of the murdered king, who comes, with an accent of moving kindness, to the aid of the overwhelmed woman:

> But, look, amazement on thy mother sits:
> O, step between her and her fighting soul:
> Conceit in weakest bodies strongest works:
> Speak to her, Hamlet.
> (III, iv, 112–115)

This common pity is like a bridge thrown across the moat which separates individuals and classes. It joins the hands of the rich and the poor, the masters and the servants. Although Shakespeare is ranked in politics rather among the aristocrats contemptuous of the mob (no satire is sharper of popular revolutions than Cade's uprising, *Henry VI, Part II,* IV; and Coriolanus is a prototype of Nietzsche's *Übermensch*), his heart has intuitions of delicate tenderness for the lowly; and this delicacy of sensibility he often lends them. Among so many eloquent speeches by the great Roman characters on the Capitol, who is the only one to weep over the body of murdered Caesar? An unknown slave, a servant of Octavius, who comes to bring a message to Antony and who, seeing the slaughtered hero, stops, choking in the midst of his speech: "O! Caesar!" . . . and "gets him apart and weeps" (*Julius Caesar,* III, i). Who dares to take up the defense of Gloucester tortured by Regan and Cornwall? A servant of Cornwall who dares to draw his sword against his master; and other servants receive the old man and bandage his bleeding face. Hamlet is protected against the fearful hatred of the king by the love of the people, whose idol he is—the people which, more clear-sighted than the feeble Henry VI, remains faithful to the loyal Duke Humphreys, even after his disgrace, and which, at the news of his assassination, revolts, breaks down the gates of the palace, and imposes exile on the murderer Suffolk (*Henry VI, Part II,* III, ii). Old Adam makes himself the companion in misery of his young master Orlando; and the young master, in his turn, carries him on his shoulders, seeks food for him, and refuses to eat before him. (*As You Like It,* II, iii, vi, vii). The proconsul Antony, on the eve of the decisive battle, summons his servants and speaks to them like a brother; he would like to serve them in his turn, as well as he has been served by them; and the sweetness of his words wrings tears from them (*Antony and Cleopatra,* IV, ii). Is it necessary to recall ruined Timon, whom his friends betray, with the exception of his servants only, who, scattered by fortune, remain united in Timon ("Yet do our hearts wear Timon's livery . . . for Timon's sake let's yet be fellows," *Timon of Athens,* IV, ii)? But it is in *King Lear* that this divine pity speaks in profoundest accents. The old tyrant, mad with pride and egoism, under the first blows of misfortune, begins to feel the suffering of others. In the tempest that roars over the blasted heath, he takes pity on his shivering fool; and little by little, he discovers universal misery:

> Poor naked wretches, wheresoe'er you are,
> That bide the pelting of this pitiless storm,
> How shall your houseless heads and unfed sides,
> Your loop'd and window'd raggedness, defend you
> From seasons such as these? O, I have ta'en
> Too little care of this! Take physic, pomp;
> Expose thyself to feel what wretches feel,
> That thou mayst shake the superflux to them,
> And show the heavens more just.
>
> (III, iv, 28–36)

This human tenderness which sweeps like a flood over all Shakespeare's work is perhaps what distinguishes it most from the other dramatic works of his time. It is his mark; it is a need for him; he cannot do without it. Even in the subjects which least admit of it, he must make a place for it. In the heart of hard *Coriolanus,* that drama ribbed with iron, that walks in pride and blood, flowers the gentle Virgilia, "my gracious silence" (*Coriolanus,* II, i). And of Portia the stoic, the daughter of Cato, he has made Portia the humane, womanly, weak, feverish, who awaits, consumed by anxiety, the result of the conspiracy (*Julius Caesar,* II, iv). Shakespeare, no more than Montaigne, is not taken in by stoicism; for him, it is an armor that hides the real heart. And what moving sweetness, when the armor is broken and the love bursts out, as in the famous reconciliation scene of Brutus and Cassius, which is the jewel of the play (*Julius Caesar,* IV, iii)! The heart is so swollen with the tenderness that fills it that the tears are ready to flow; but a modesty restrains them and gives to the emotion a supreme beauty. It is only by report that we see the hero of friendship, the enigmatic Antonio, the rich man, happy in the eyes of the world, but gnawed by a mysterious sadness, who seems to live only by his love for his friend, give up the secret of this loving and suffering heart, in the farewell scene where,

> his eye being big with tears,
> Turning his face, he put his hand behind him,
> And with affection wondrous sensible
> He wrung Bassanio's hand.
>
> (*Merchant of Venice,* II, viii, 46–49)

Silence more striking still, when it is that of a child, like little Mamillius—a little, more tragic Dombey—who

> Conceiving the dishonour of his mother,
> He straight declined, droop'd, took it deeply,
> Fasten'd and fix'd the shame on't in himself,
> Threw off his spirit, his appetite, his sleep,
> And downright languish'd.
>
> (*Winter's Tale,* II, iii,13–17)

Even beyond men, this pity is extended to nature. The exiled duke, in *As You Like It,* hearkens to "tongues in trees, books in the running brooks, sermons in stones." And the melancholy Jaques weeps over a dying wounded stag (*As You Like It,* II, i).

Thus, the genius of the poet solders the links of the chain which binds all beings to one another. And nothing quivers in one of them that does not spread through all: for everything is common to us, and it is ourselves that we find on each page of the tragicomedy of the universe.

But, even as we take our part in all joys and all sorrows, while we help each soul to bear its cross, they help us to carry our own.

> When we our betters see bearing our woes,
> We scarcely think our miseries our foes.
> Who alone suffers most i' the mind,
> Leaving free things and happy shows behind:
> But then the mind much sufferance doth o'erskip,
> When grief hath mates, and bearing fellowship.
>
> (*King Lear,* III, vi, 110–115)

Even rancor is blotted out. The spectacle of injustice does not incite the desire to redress it by a like injustice. And the last word, the melody that soars over the last harmonies of this symphony, is that of the luminous Spirit of the Air, which Ariel inspires in Prospero:

> Yet with my nobler reason 'gainst my fury
> Do I take part: the rarer action is
> In virtue than in vengeance.
>
> (*Tempest,* V, i, 26–28)

20. Benedetto Croce

1866–1952

Croce's effect on modern criticism has been immeasurable if not always salutary. His aesthetic theories, while owing much to Kant, diverged from him on several important points. Croce denied Kant's basic a priori categories, time and space, their identity as intuitive forms. And his assertion that the result is the only criterion by which we can measure creative intuition has served to shift the focus of scrutiny from the artist's personality and mind to his work; a doctrine which underlies the "new criticism" of recent decline.

It is tempting to see Croce's aestheticism as the evolutionary offspring of either the Kantian reaction to the British empirical school of the eighteenth century or of the Romantic insistence on a gulf between art and science. But Croce's work resists such easy assimilation. While he disparages, in Ariosto, Shakespeare e Corneille *(1920), the historical criticism in all of its forms because of its imposition of external materials on the work of art, he is equally severe with the a prioristic metaphysics of the Gervinus-Ulrici school. And he does not hesitate in criticizing the "psychologizing" of Georg Brandes.*

All in all, Croce shows little affinity for most of the nineteenth-century methods of criticism: the Romantic imagist-criticism, the rhetorical, the exclamatory, the biographically oriented aestheticism, to mention only a few. Croce insists that, whatever theories are utilized, they must be those emanating from the work of art itself. Each artistic creation has its own laws which cannot be linked with any external laws such as those of sociology, psychology, etc. Shakespeare must be judged by his poetry alone. He "surpasses" the problem of good and evil by making his characters facets of life. But by such assertions as the last two Croce reveals his critical debt to Coleridge. The latter had argued for the doctrine of judging Shakespeare's "organic form" as well as for his poetry.

In speaking of Hamlet *in the first of the following selections Croce describes the young prince's problem as a "tragedy of the will" and goes on to assert that "Life is thought and will" and that Hamlet's crisis is a "perpetual" one "of the human soul." Here, again, Croce's lineage is apparent, this time in Turgenev's famous essay (see above). Nevertheless, while this serves to place Croce's Shakespeare criticism in some kind of perspective, it should not diminish either the justice of many of Croce's disparagements or the extent of his contribution in refining a number of the issues of the criticism of his day.*

FROM Ariosto, Shakespeare and Corneille

Tragedy of the Will

The tragedy of the good and evil will is sometimes followed, sometimes preceded, by another tragedy, that of the will itself. Here the will, instead of holding the passions in control—making its footstool of them—allows itself to be dominated by them in their onrush; or it seeks the good, but remains uncertain, dissatisfied as to the path chosen; or finally, when it fails to find its own way, a way of some sort, and does not know what to think of itself or of the world, it preys upon itself in this empty tension.

A typical form of this first condition of the will is voluptuousness, which overspreads a soul and makes itself mistress there, inebriating, sending to sleep, destroying, and liquefying the will. When we think of that enchanting sweetness and perdition, the image of death arises at the same instant, because it truly is death, if not physical, yet always internal and moral death, death of the spirit, without which man is already a

From Croce's *Ariosto, Shakespeare and Corneille* (London, George Allen & Unwin Ltd., 1920), pp. 241–266. Translated by Douglas Ainslee. Reprinted by permission of George Allen & Unwin Ltd.

corpse in process of decomposition. The tragedy of *Antony and Cleopatra* is composed of the violent sense of pleasure, in its power to bind and to dominate, coupled with a shudder at its abject effects of dissolution and of death.

He moves in a world all kisses and caresses, languors, sounds, perfumes, shimmer of gold and splendid garments, flashing of lights or silence of deep shadows, enjoyment, now ecstatic, now spasmodic and furious. Cleopatra is queen of this world, avid for pleasure, which she herself bestows, diffusing around her its quivering sense, instilling a frantic desire for it into all, offering herself as an example and an incitement, but while conferring it on others, remaining herself a regal and almost a mystical personage. A Roman who has plunged into that world, spoke then of her, astonished at her power, demoniac or divine:

> Age cannot wither nor custom stale
> Her infinite variety.
>
> (II, ii, 240–241)

Cleopatra asks for songs and music, that she may melt into that sea of melody, which heightens pleasure:

> Give me some music; music, moody food
> Of us that trade in love!
>
> (II, v, 1–2)

She knows how to toy with men, keeping their interest alive by her denials:

> . . . if you find him sad,
> Say I am dancing; if in mirth, report
> That I am sudden sick.
>
> (I, iii, 4–6)

Her words express sensual fascination in its most terrible form:

> . . . there is gold, and here
> My bluest veins to kiss; a hand that kings
> Have lipped, and trembled kissing.
>
> (II, v, 28–30)

All around her dance to the same tune and imitate the rhythmic folly of her life. Note the scene of the two waiting women, who are joking about their loves, their future marriages, and the manner of their deaths, with the soothsayer. Listen to the first words of Charmian, so mirthful and caressing in her playful coquetry:

> Lord Alexas, sweet Alexas, most anything Alexas, almost most absolute Alexas, where's the soothsayer that you praised so to the queen? O, that I knew this husband, which, you say, must charge his horns with garlands!
>
> (I, ii, 1–5)

Antony is seized and dragged into this vertiginous course of pungent pleasures, as soon as he appears. In his inebriation the rest of the world, all the active, real world, seems heavy, prosaic, contemptible, and displeasing. The very name of Rome has no longer any power over him.

> Let Rome in Tiber melt, and the wide arch
> Of the ranged empire fall! Here is my space.
> Kingdoms are clay: one dungy earth alike
> Feeds beast as man.
>
> (I, i, 33–36)

As he folds Cleopatra in his arms, he feels that they form a pair who make life more noble, and that in them alone it assumes real significance.

This feeling is not love: we have already called it by its proper name: voluptuousness. Cleopatra loves pleasure and caprice, and the dominion, which both of them afford her; she also loves Antony, because he is, and in so far as he is, part of her pleasures and caprices, and serves her as an instrument of dominion. She busies herself with keeping him bound to her, struggles to retain him when he removes himself from her, but she always has an eye to other things, which are equally necessary for her, even more so than he, and in order to retain them, she would be ready if necessary to give Antony in exchange. Antony too, does not love her; he clearly sees her for what she is, imprecates against her, and enfolds her in his embrace without forgiveness.

> Fall not a tear; . . . give me a kiss:
> Even this repays me.
>
> (III, xi, 69–71)

Love demands union of some sort between two beings for an objective end, with the moral consent of both; but here we are outside morality, and even outside the will. We are caught in the whirlwind and carried along.

Antony it is, who weakens and is conquered. He has lived an active life, which, in the present moment of folly, he holds of no account. He has known war, political strife, the government of states; he has even been brushed with the wing of glory and of victory. He tries several times to grasp his own past and to direct his future. He has not lost his ethical judgment, for he recognizes Cleopatra as she really is, bows reverently before the memory of Fulvia, and treats his new wife Octavia, whom he also will abandon, with respect. For a brief moment, he returns to the world he once knew, takes part in political business, comes to terms with his colleagues and rivals. It would seem that he had disentangled himself from the chain that bound him. But the effort is not lasting, the chain encircles him again; vainly and with ever declining power of resistance, he yields to that destiny, which is on the side of Octavius, the man without loves, so cold and so firm of will. Bad fortune dogs every step of the voluptuary: those that surround him remark a change in his appearance from what he was formerly. They see him betray this change by uttering thoughts that are almost ridiculously feeble, and making inane remarks. They are led to reflect that the mind of man is nothing but a part of his fortune and that eternal things conform to things internal. He himself feels that he is inwardly dissolving, and compares himself to the changing forms of the clouds, dissolved with a breath of wind, like water turning to water. Yet the man, who is thus in process of disaggregation, was once great, and still affords flashes of greatness, bursting forth in feats of warlike prowess, accompanied with lofty speech and generous actions. His generosity confounds Enobarbus, who had deserted him and now takes his own life for very shame. Around him are yet those ready to die for sake of the affection that he inspires. Cleopatra stands lower or higher: she has never known nor has ever desired to know any life but that of caprice and pleasure.

There is logic, will, consistency, in her vertiginous abandonment. She is consistent also in taking her own life, when she sees that she would die in a Roman prison, thus escaping shame and the mockeries of the triumphant foe, and selecting a death of regal voluptuousness. And with her die her faithful handmaids, by a similar death; they have known her as their queen and goddess of pleasure, and now as despising *this vile world* and a life no longer worthy of being lived, because no longer beautiful and brilliant. Charmian, before she slays herself, takes a last farewell of her mistress:

> Downy windows, close;
> And golden Phoebus never be beheld
> Of eyes again so royal! Your crown's awry;
> I'll mend it, and then play.
>
> (V, ii, 319–322)

The tragedy of the will, which is most poetically lofty in *Antony and Cleopatra*, is nevertheless morally a low form, that is to say, it is simple and elementary in its roughness, such as would manifest itself in a soldier like Antony, the bloody, quarrelsome, pleasure-seeking, crapulous Antony.

It shows itself in an atmosphere far more subtle with Hamlet. Hamlet, the hero so refined intellectually, so delicate in taste, so conscious of moral values, comes to the action, not from the Roman forum or from the battlefields of Gaul or Pharsalia, but from the University of Wittenberg. In *Hamlet*, the seductions of the will are altogether overcome; duty is no longer a condition, or a vain effort, but a spontaneous and regular attitude. The obstacle against which it strives is not external to it, it is no inebriation of the senses; it is internal, the will itself in the dialectic of its becoming, in its passage from meditation to purpose and from purpose to action, in its becoming will, true, concrete, factual will.

Hamlet has with reason often been recognized as a companion and precursor of Brutus in *Julius Caesar*, a play which differs from the "historical tragedies," more substantially even than *Antony and Cleopatra*, which is restricted to the practical activity. *Hamlet* attains to a more lofty significance. Here too we find a tragedy of the will in a man whose ethical conscientiousness is not internally troubled, for he lives upon a sublime plane; and here too the obstacle arises from the very bosom of the will. Brutus differs from Hamlet in that he comes to a decision and acts; but his action is accompanied with disgust and repugnance for the impurity with which its accomplishment must be stained. He reproves, condemns, and abhors the political end toward which Caesar is tending, but he does not hate Caesar; he would like to destroy that end, to strike at the soul of Caesar, but not to destroy his body and with it his life. He bows reluctantly to necessity and with the others decides upon his death, but requests that honors should be paid to Caesar dead, and spares Antony contrary to the advice of Cassius, because, as he says, he is a priest bound to sacrifice the necessary victim; but he is not a butcher. Melancholy dogs every step toward the achievement of his end. He differs here from Cassius, who does not experience like scruples and delicacy of feeling, but desires the end, by whatever means. He differs too from Antony, who discovers at once the path to tread and enters it; cautious and resolute, he will triumph over him. He finds everywhere impurity: Cassius, his friend, his brother, behaves in such a way as to make him doubt his right to shed the blood of the mighty Julius, because, instead of that justice, which he has thought to promote and to restore by his act, he now sees only rapine and injustice. But if the spiritual greatness of Brutus shrouds him in sadness, it does not deprive him of the capacity for feeling and understanding human nature. His difference with Cassius comes to an end with his friend's sorrow, that friend who loves and admires him sincerely, and yet cannot be other than he is, hoping that his friend will not condemn too severely his faults and vices, but pass them over in indulgent silence. The reconciliation of the two is sealed when Brutus reveals his wounded heart, as he briefly tells his friend of Portia's death. He enfolds himself in his grief. Brutus is among those who have always meditated upon death and fortified themselves with the thought of it. His suffering is not limited to virtue forced into contamination; for he is haunted by doubt unexpressed. He feels that man is surrounded with mystery, the mystery of Fate, or, as we should say, with the mystery surrounding the future history of the world; he seems to be anxiously asking of himself if the way that he has chosen and followed is the best and wisest way, or whether some evil genius has not introduced itself into his life, in order to drive him to perdition? He hears at night the voice of the evil genius amid the sounds and songs that should give rest and repose to his agitated spirit. He prepares himself to face the coming battle, with the same invincible sadness. It is the day that will bring to an end the work begun on the Ides of March. He takes leave of Cassius, doubtful if he will ever see him again, saying farewell to him forever.

> If we do meet again, why, we shall smile;
> If not, why then, this parting was well made.
> (V, i, 118–120)

Oh, if man could know the event of that day before it befell! But it must suffice to know that day will have an end, and that the end will be known. Mighty powers govern the world, Brutus resigns himself to them: they may have already judged him guilty or be about to do so.

Hamlet has generally been considered the tragedy of Shakespearean tragedies, where the poet has put most of himself, given us his philosophy, and with it the key to the other tragedies. But strictly speaking, Shakespeare has not put himself, that is to say his poetry, into *Hamlet,* either more or less than into any of the others; there is not more philosophy, as judge of reality and of life here than in the others; there is perhaps less, because it is more perplexed and vague than the others, and even the celebrated monologue ("To be or not to be"), though supremely poetical, is irreducible to a philosopheme or to a philosophic problem. Finally, it is not the key or compendium of the other plays, but the expression of a particular state of the soul, which differs from those expressed in the others. Those who read it in the ingenuous spirit in which it was written and conceived find no difficulty about taking it for what it is, namely the expression of disaffection and distaste for life; they experience and assimilate that state of the soul. Life is thought and will, but a will which creates thought and a thought which creates will, and when we feel that certain painful impressions have injured and upset us, it sometimes happens that the will does not obey the stimulus of thought and becomes weak as will; then thought, feeling in its turn that it is not stimulated and upheld by the will, begins to wander and fails to make progress: it tries now this and now that, but grasps nothing firmly; it is thought not sure of itself, it is not true and effective thought. There is, as it were, a suspension of the rapid course of the spirit, a void, a losing of the way, which resembles death, and is in fact a sort of death. This is the state of soul that Shakespeare infused into the ancient legend of Hamlet, Prince of Denmark, on whom he conferred many noble aptitudes and gifts, and the promise or the begining of a fervent life. He then interrupted and suspended Hamlet's beginning of life, and let it wander, as though seeking in vain, not only its proper task, but even the strength necessary to propose it to himself, with that firmness which becomes and is, indeed, itself action. Hamlet is a generous and gentle youth, with a disposition toward meditation and scientific inquiry, a lover of the beautiful, devoted to knightly sports, prone to friendship, not averse to love, with faith in human goodness and in those around him, especially in his father and mother, and in all his relations and friends. He was perhaps too refined and sensitive, too delicate in soul; but his life proceeded, according to its own law, toward certain ends, caressing certain hopes. In the course of this facile and amiable existence, he experienced, first the death of his father, followed soon after by the second marriage of his mother, who seems to have very speedily forgotten her first husband in the allurement of a new love. He feels himself in every way injured by this marriage, and with the disappearance of his esteem for his mother, a horrible suspicion insinuates itself, which is soon confirmed by the apparition of his father's restless ghost, which demands vengeance. And Hamlet will, nay must and will carry it out; he would find a means to do so warily and effectually, if he had not meanwhile begun to die from that shock to his sentiments. That is to say, he began to die without knowing it, to die internally: the pleasures of the world become in his eyes insipid and rancid, the earth and the sky itself lose their colors. Everything that is contrary to the ideal and to the joy of life, injustice, betrayal, lies, hypocrisy, bestial sensuality, greed of power and riches, cowardice, perversity, and with them the nullity of worldly things, death and the fearful unknown, gather themselves together in his spirit, round that horrible thing that he has discovered, the assassination of his father, the adultery of his mother; they tyrannize over his spirit and form a barrier to his further progress, to his living with that former warmth and joyous vigor, as indispensable to thought as it is to action. Hamlet can no longer love, for love is above all love of life; for this reason he breaks off the love-idyl that he had begun with Ophelia, whom he loved and whom in a certain way he still loves infinitely, but as we love one dead, knowing her to be no longer for us. Hamlet can laugh no more: sarcasm and irony take the place of frank laughter on his lips. He fails to co-ordinate his acts, himself becoming the victim of circumstances, though constantly maintaining his attitude of contempt, or breaking out into unexpected resolves, followed by hasty execution.

Sometimes he still rises to the level of moral indignation, as in the colloquy with his mother, but this too is a paroxysm, not a co-ordinated action. Joy is needed, not only for love, but also for vengeance; there must be passion for the activity that is being exercised; but Hamlet is in such a condition that he should give himself the same advice as he gives to the miserable Ophelia—to get her to a nunnery and there practice renunciation and restraint.[1] But he is not conscious of the nature of his malady, and it is precisely for this reason that he is ill; instead of combating it by applying the right remedy, he culti-

[1] There is another meaning for "nunnery" in addition to the one on which Croce bases his statement. Cf. O.E.D., or Eric Partridge, *A Dictionary of Slang and Unconventional English* (New York, 1937), p. 574, or Fletcher in *The Mad Lover* (1617), for "nunnery" as a brothel. In not admitting the double meaning, Croce ignores the frankly sexual nature of the preceding exchange between Hamlet and Ophelia. Editor.

vates, nourishes, and increases it. At the most, what is taking place within him excites his astonishment and moves him to vain self-rebuke and equally vain self-stimulation, as we observe after his dialogue with the players, and after he has heard the passion, fury, and weeping they put into their part, and when he meets the army led by Fortinbras against Poland.

> I do not know
> Why yet I live to say "This thing's to do";
> Sith I have cause and will and strength and means
> To do't. Examples gross as earth exhort me:
> Witness this army of such mass and charge
> Led by a delicate and tender prince;
> Whose spirit with divine ambition puff'd
> Makes mouths at the invisible event,
> Exposing what is mortal and unsure
> To all that fortune, death and danger dare,
> Even for an egg-shell. . . . O, from this time forth,
> My thoughts be bloody, or be nothing worth!
> (III, iv, 43–66)

Finally, he accomplishes the great vengeance, but alas, in how small a way, as though jestingly, as though it were by chance, and he himself dies as though by chance. He had abandoned his life to chance, so his death must be due to chance.

We too have termed the condition of spirit that ruins Hamlet an illness; but the word is better applied to a doctor or a moralist, whereas the tragedy is the work of a poet, who does not describe an illness, but sings a song of desperate and desolate anguish, and so lofty a song is it, to so great a height does it attain, that it would seem as though a newer and more lofty conception of reality and of human action must be born of it. What was perdition for Hamlet is a crisis of the human soul, which assumed so great an extension and complexity after the time of Shakespeare as to give its name to a whole historical period. Yet it has more than historical value, because, light or serious, little or great, it returns to live again perpetually.

Justice and Indulgence

It would be vain to seek among the songs of Shakespeare for the song of reconciliation, or quarrels, composed of inner peace, of tranquillity achieved, but the song of justice echoes everywhere in his works. He knows neither perfect saints, nor perfect sinners, for he feels the struggle at the heart of reality as necessity, not as accident, artifice, or caprice. Even the good, the brave, and the pure have evil, impurity, and weakness in them: "fragility" is the word he utters most often, not only with regard to women; and on the other hand, even the wicked, the guilty, the criminal, have glimpses of goodness, aspirations after redemption, and when everything else is wanting, they have energy of will and thus possess a sort of spiritual greatness. One hears that song as a refrain in several of the tragedies, uttered by foes over the foes whom they have conquered. Antony pronounces this elegy over the fallen Brutus:

> This was the noblest Roman of them all:
> All the conspirators save only he
> Did that they did in envy of great Caesar;
> He only, in a general honest thought
> And common good to all, made one of them.
> His life was gentle, and the elements
> So mix'd in him that nature might stand up
> And say to all the world "This was a man!"
> (*Julius Caesar*, V, v, 68–75)

Octavian, when he hears of the death of Antony, exclaims:

> O Antony!
> . . . we could not stall together; . . . but yet let me lament,
> With tears as sovereign as the blood of hearts,
> That thou, my brother, my competitor
> In top of all design, my mate in empire,
> Friend and companion in the front of war, . . .

Unreconcilable should divide
Where mine his thoughts did kindle, that our stars
Unreconcilable, should divide
Our equalness to this.
(*Antony and Cleopatra,* V, i, 35–49)

It is above all in *Henry VIII* that this feeling for justice widens into a feeling toward oneself and others. We find a particularly good instance of it in the dialogues between Queen Katharine and her great enemy Wolsey. When the queen has mentioned all the grave misdeeds of the dead man in her severe speech, Griffith craves permission to record in his turn all the good there was in him; and with so persuasive an eloquence does he record this good, that the queen, when she has heard him, concludes with a sad smile:

After my death I wish no other herald,
No other speaker of my living actions,
But such an honest chronicler as Griffith.
Whom I most hated living, thou has made me,
With thy religious truth and modesty,
Now in his ashes honour: peace be with him!
(IV, ii, 69–75)

One who feels justice in this way is inclined to be indulgent, and in Shakespeare we find the song of indulgence, in *The Tempest:* a lofty indulgence, for his discernment of good and evil was acute, sense alike for what is noble and for what is base, exquisite. He could never be of those who slip into some form of false indulgence, which lowers the standard of the ideal, in order to approach the real, canceling or rendering uncertain, in greater or lesser measure, the boundaries between virtue and vice. Prospero it is who is indulgent in *The Tempest,* the sage, the wise, the injured, the beneficent Prospero.

The Tempest is an exercise of the imagination, a delicate pattern, woven perhaps as a spectacle for some special occasion, such as a marriage ceremony, for it adopts the procedure of some fanciful, jesting scenario from the popular Italian comedy. Here we find islands unknown, aerial spirits, earthly beings, and monsters; it is full of magic and of prodigies, of shipwrecks, rescues, and incantations; and the smiles of innocent love, the quips of comical creatures variegate pleasantly its surface. We have already noted the traces of Shakespeare's tendency toward the romantic, and those echoes of the comedy of love, of Romeo and Juliet, who are not unfortunate but fortunate, when they are called Ferdinand and Miranda, with their irresistible impulse toward love and joy. But although the work has a bland tone, there are yet to be found in it characters belonging to tragedy, wicked brothers, who usurp the throne, brothers who meditate and attempt fratricide. In Caliban we find the malicious, violent brute, abounding in strength and rich in possibilities. He listens ecstatically to the soft music, with which the isle often resounds, he knows its natural secrets and is ready to place himself at the service of him who shall aid him in his desire for vengeance and shall redeem him from captivity. Henceforth Prospero has all his enemies in his power; he can do with them what he likes. But he is not on the same plane with them, a combatant among combatants: meditation, experience, and science have refined him: he is penetrated with the consciousness of humanity, of its instability, its illusions, its temptations, its miseries. Where others think they see firm foothold, he is aware of change and insecurity; where others find everything clear as day, he feels the presence of mystery, of the unsolved enigma:

> We are such stuff
> As dreams are made on, and our little life
> Is rounded with a sleep.
>
> (IV, i, 156–158)

Will he punish? Finally, even his sprite Ariel, his minister of air, feels compassion for those downcast prisoners, and when asked by Prospero, does not withhold from him that in his place he would be human.

> And mine shall [answers Prospero].
> Hast thou, which are but air, a touch, a feeling
> Of their afflictions, and shall not myself,

> One of their kind, that relish all as sharply,
> Passion as they, be kindlier moved than thou art?
> (V, i, 20–24)

The guilty are pardoned, and finally Caliban, the monstrous Caliban, is pardoned also, promising to behave himself better from that moment onward. Prospero divests himself of his magic wand, which gave him so absolute a power over his like, and while yet in his possession caused him to incur the risk of behaving toward them in a more than human, perhaps an inhuman way.

Shakespeare can and does attain to indulgence toward men; but since in him the contest between good and evil, positive and negative, remains undecided, he is unable to rise to a feeling of cheerful hope and faith nor, on the other hand, to submerge himself in gloomy pessimism. In his characters, the love of life is extraordinarily vigorous and tenacious; all of them are agitated by strong passions; they meditate great designs and pursue them with indomitable vigor; all of them love infinitely and hate infinitely. But all of them, almost without exception, also renounce life and face death with fortitude, serenity, and as though it were a sort of liberation. The motto of all is uttered by Edgar, in *King Lear,* in reply to his old father, Gloucester, who loses courage and wishes to die when he hears of the defeat of the king and of Cordelia. Edgar reminds his father that men must face "their coming here even as their going hence," and that "*ripeness is all.*" They die magnificently, either in battle, or offering their throats to the assassin or the executioner, or they transpierce themselves with their own hands, when nothing is left but death or dishonor. They know how to die; it seems as though they had all "*studied death,*" as says a character in *Macbeth,* when describing one of them.

And nevertheless the ardor of life never becomes lessened or extinguished. Romeo indeed admired the tenacity of life and the fear of death in him who sold him the poison; miserable, hungry, despised, suspected by men and by the law, as he was. In *Measure for Measure,* in the scene where Claudio is in prison and condemned, the usual order is inverted; first we have the prompt persuasion and decision to accept death with serenity, and a few moments later the will to live returns with furious force. The make-believe friar, who assists the condemned man, sets the nullity of life before him in language full of warm and rich imagery: it is troublous and such as "none but fools would keep," a constant heartache for the fear of losing it, a craving after happiness never attained, a falsity of affections, a crepuscular condition, without joy or repose; and Claudio drinks in these words and images, feeling that to live is indeed to die, and wishes for death. But his sister enters, and when she tells him how she has been offered his life as the price of her dishonor, he instantly clutches hold again of life at that glimmer of hope, of hope stained with opprobrium, and dispels with a shudder of horror the image of death:

> Ay, but to die, and go we know not where;
> To lie in cold obstruction and to rot;
> This sensible warm motion to become
> A kneaded clod; . . . 'tis too horrible!
> The weariest and most loathed worldly life
> That age, ache, penury and imprisonment
> Can lay on nature is a paradise
> To what we fear of death.
>
> (III, i, 118–132)

And in the same play the singular personage of Barnardine is placed before us, perfect in a few strokes, Barnardine, the criminal and almost animal, indifferent to life and death, but who yet lives, gets drunk, and then stretches himself out and sleeps soundly; and when he is awakened and called to the place of execution, declares firmly, that he is not disposed to go there that day, so they had better leave him alone and not trouble him; he turns his shoulders on them and goes back to his cell, where they can come and find him, if they have anything to say. Here too the feeling of astonishment at an eagerness for life, which does not exclude the tranquil acceptance of death, is accentuated almost to the point of becoming comic and grotesque.

21. Hugo von Hofmannsthal

1874–1929

Before he was quite twenty Hofmannsthal had written the lyrics which have earned him a place among the greatest German poets. His work of that period is characterized by exquisite rhythms, an aptness of diction, and an ease with his perceptions rare even in older poets.

The lyric phase drew to a close around the turn of the century and Hofmannsthal's gradual estrangement from his spontaneous lyricism found its expression in the remarkable Der Brief des Lord Chandos *(1902). It was at this time that Hofmannsthal became increasingly aware of the disintegration of values and the approaching spiritual anarchy of the times that were to become the themes that would preoccupy much of his mature energy.*

Although Hofmannsthal had a lifelong interest in Shakespeare, he essayed into the expression of that interest only twice in his life. And both times, in Shakespeare's Könige und grosse Herren *(1905), and in* Shakespeare und wir *(a lecture given for the Shakespeare tercentenary, 1916), he performed the function of poet-critic; a function which he took to be one not of analysis but of the rendering of a comprehensive view. In the manner of the great Romantic critics Hofmannsthal urges the consideration of Shakespeare's thoroughly dramatic nature. And finally, the essay is a subtle demonstration that, as T. S. Eliot has said, the criticism of a distinguished poet claims our fullest attention by reason of the magnificence of its perceptions.*

Shakespeare's Kings and Noblemen

I think I know why you called me here to speak before you. It was certainly not the desire to learn something new; you certainly could not expect my handful of observations to add a substantial weight to the load of knowledge about Shakespeare with which your warehouses are overcrowded and your ships overburdened to the point of sinking. None of the obscurities (insofar as there are any left for you) could expect an illumination from me; none of the findings that you have received from preceding generations and will hand on, purified and deepened, to the generations to come, could want confirmation from my lips. But perhaps you feel a trifle oppressed, even overawed, at so much accumulated weath; perhaps you sometimes feel stupefied by the immense flood of tradition in whose tumultuous roar the voice of Herder mingles with that of Sarah Siddons.[1] And an inner voice—was it memory or intuition?—told you that beyond the pure passion of understanding, a less rational, less pure, more heterogeneous instrument is still needed to work the true magic. So you stepped out of the silent study of the scholar into the forest of life, and as the magician reaches for the mandrake you reached for someone alive; you reached for me and set me down in this circle. Accustomed to dissect the marvelous phenomenon into its elements and to dwell with your thoughts in the streaming rays of its divided light, you sometimes desire to call in from outside a living person at whose soul Shakespeare, as an undivided Whole, knocks like Fate demanding to be

From *Selected Prose* by Hugo von Hofmannsthal (New York, Bollingen Series XXXIII, Pantheon Books, 1952), pp. 247–267. Translated by James and Tania Stern. Reprinted by permission of the Bollingen Foundation and Routledge & Kegan Paul Ltd.

[1] Miss Siddons (1755–1831) is considered by many to have been the finest actress England has produced. She was the most popular tragic actress of her time and her performance of Lady Macbeth was especially admired. Her character was impeccable. Editor.

admitted, and for whose eyes this undivided light illuminates the depths and summits of existence. In your memory, which harbors an almost boundless tradition, there stirs an old saying occasionally obscured but never quite forgotten: the true readers of Shakespeare and also those in whom Shakespeare is truly alive are those who carry within them a stage.

"The gift of imaginary performance . . . this very specific creativeness: to produce within oneself action as it is on paper as the most personal experience." For this reason—and the words with which I try to convey it are from one out of your midst—let me believe that you called me here; for this reason, and because, to continue quoting Karl Werder; "Shakespeare's work is action, not mere description. Whoever wants simply to be told stories misunderstands him. Whoever only listens while reading him reads him only half and therefore mishears him. Shakespeare needs to be played, because only then can we hear and see what he does not and cannot say. If he were to say what would be necessary to make uncreative readers understand him without seeing him acted, then he would cease to be Shakespeare."

When I ponder these words and realize that with you they are a tradition—a tradition as unlikely to be lost as anything essential and intelligent ever said by a scholar in your field; and when at the same time I remember a paragraph from Otto Ludwig's [2] essays whose first line runs: "Shakespeare wrote his plays from the core of dramatic art," then it is fully transparent to me what persuaded you to call me here: you presumed I know how to read Shakespeare with imagination. It is with the reader of Shakespeare that you are concerned, with the reader from whom you can assume and demand this "very specific creativeness"; and I feel that if I am not to dissipate your indulgence I must speak to you only of what is a pleasure and a passion, a conscious talent, an imagination, an innate art perhaps, like playing the flute or dancing, a shattering but silent inner orgy—the reading of Shakespeare.

[2] Ludwig (1813–1865) wrote the following tragedies that were well received: *The Hereditary Forester, The Maccabees,* and *Agnes Bernauer.* Some of his novels were also well received by the public. Editor.

I am speaking not of those who read Shakespeare like the Bible or some other true or great book; not of those who lower their faces, tired and wilted by life, over this deep mirror in order to realize that "life has always been like this," and who "cleanse the stuff'd bosom of that perilous stuff"; not of those whose heart is filled with "the ignominy that weighs upon the poor man's shoulder," with "the law's delay, the insolence of office," and all the other terribly real evils of Hamlet's monologue. I am speaking not of those who turn to the wisest of all books, seeking solace when before their outraged eyes the course of the world looks hopelessly out of joint—although it seems to me that it is on them that the marrow of Shakespeare's work continually renews itself. But the readers about whom I wish to speak are those on whom the skin also feeds, retaining forever the brilliant bloom of youth. These are the readers whose passion sees each of Shakespeare's works as a Whole. Those others, driven to Shakespeare by tragic experience, offer their soul—cruelly bent by the pain and harshness of life, like the body of a musical instrument—as the sensitive sounding board for the fall from grandeur, the degradation of the good, self-destruction of the noble, and the ghastly fate of the tender spirit exposed to life. Those of whom I wish to speak are the sounding board, however, not for this alone, but also for a thousand more delicate, more hidden, more sensual, more symbolic things—which, with their intertwining diversity, form the mysterious unit whose passionate servants they are. For them it is not only the great destinies, the sudden turning points of Fate, the tremendous tragedies, that exist. The scene, for instance, where Lear's daughters enter the castle at the approach of rough weather: the heavy door groans to a close behind them and the old man stands there, his white hair exposed to the drenching rain, his heart to the sinister night and the frenzy of his impotent rage. Or the scene in the gloom of the castle yard when Macbeth and his wife, their glances locked in complicity, exchange muttered words. Or that in which Othello steps from the door into the yard, from another door on to the rampart, Iago always one pace behind him, words pouring forth from his mouth like corrosive poison, a devouring, inextinguishable fire-poison eating through the bone into the marrow, Othello listening all the time and protesting, his tongue twisting in his mouth like that of an animal about to be slaughtered, his rolling bloodshot eyes as helpless as a tortured steer's; and Iago, his fangs always in the other's entrails, dragging him, the dog the steer, through rooms and corridors, doors and courts, letting go only in the final death struggle . . . Although nothing created by human beings can be compared with these scenes, it is not for them alone that the readers about whom I wish to speak lose themselves in a world built by a genius. For them there are innumerable encounters during which the soul does not have to hide fearfully in the dark and cry out to itself: *Guarda e passa!*

These dramas are not exclusively filled with events whose aspect is of the same order of things as the maelstrom, the surging sinister sea, the landslide, or the human face frozen in death. Not everything in them emanates the dread loneliness that hovers round the monstrous fates as it does round the summits of icy mountains. At times in one of these dramas the human destinies, the dark and shining, yes, even the torments and degradation and bitterness of the death hour, are so well woven into a Whole that their being side by side, their merging and disappearing into one another, creates something like a deeply moving, solemn, and woeful music. In *Henry VIII* Wolsey's fall and his calm acceptance of it, the clear sound of his great, resigned words, and again the dying of Queen Katharine, this fading away of a gentle, suffering voice, the festive music surrounding the King and the Queen, all merge inextricably into a melodious Whole, which, in its heroic elements and the recurrent theme, is reminiscent of a Beethoven sonata. In the romantic plays, in *The Tempest,* in *Cymbeline, Measure for Measure, As You Like It,* and in *The Winter's Tale,* the Whole is interwoven by this music. Or rather everything surrenders to this music, everything which is placed side by side, everything breathing at the other, mingling love and hatred in their breath, everything which glides past the other, that delights or terrifies, all that is sublime and all that is ridiculous—yes, all that is there and not there, insofar as in each work of art those things which do not appear in them also play a part by spreading their shadows round the Whole. Only the combination of all this can produce the unutterably sweet music of the Whole. And it is precisely of the reader who can hear this music that I wish to speak to you—because he is the person who reads Shakespeare with all his heart, with all his soul, with all his strength. And of him in whom this passion dwells let me speak to you as of a figure, as Milton in his verse speaks of L'Allegro and Il Penseroso, or as La Bruyère [3] speaks of the Distracted and the Ambitious. I feel that such plays as *Cymbeline, The Tempest,* and the others possess the power to produce again and again in the imagination of the creative reader an inner stage on which their magic can live and their music be heard as a Whole.

In the same way the figures of Lear and Shylock, of Macbeth and Juliet, overpower the body of the great actor in order to live and die in it—for there is no doubt that Shakespeare's reader and Shakespeare's actor are closely related. The difference is that round the actor a single figure wraps itself like a skin, whereas in the reader all figures want to live simultaneously. The former is beckoned aside by a phantom: "Give me all your blood to drink," while the latter is surrounded by a host of phantoms. I do believe that with this mysterious awakening of a "specific creativeness" on a day unlike other days, under a wind and weather unlike other wind and weather, the figure will demand to be played by the actor (who is powerless to refuse) and the drama demand of the reader: "Today you read me, and I live in you." I don't believe that the reader who "carries within him a stage" could have read *Romeo and Juliet* on the day he was destined to read *The Tempest.* Perhaps he reached out for *Romeo and Juliet;* he leafed through it, but the play left him cold. It didn't tempt him. The lines of verse whereon his eye fell

[3] Hofmannsthal is probably referring to *Les Caractères de Théophraste, traduits du grec, avec les Caractères ou les Moeurs de ce siècle* (1688). Editor.

today seemed to him indifferent, not like eyes, not like the calyx of a flower through which one can peer into its depths. The stage directions for the acts and scenes did not seem like little hidden doors in a mysterious wall, not like narrow clearings which open and lead into the dusky heart of the forest. So he laid the volume down and was about to go off without Shakespeare when his eye fell on this title: *The Tempest*. And in a flash he knew: "I can, after all, create life. Today I am able to revive within myself Prospero and Miranda, Ariel and Caliban, more effectively than water can revive wilted flowers. Today or never I am the island on which all this has happened. Today or never I carry within me the cave before whose entrance Caliban suns himself, the thicket of high fantastic trees round whose crowns Ariel glides like a miraculous bird: within me also is the air of this island, a southern evening breeze of gold and blue wherein Miranda's beauty swims like a wonder of the sea in its element. Today or never am I all these things at once: I am Prospero's magnificence and Ferdinand's youth, Ariel's elflike devotion and Caliban's hate; I am Antonio the evil, Gonzalo the honest, Stephano the drunken villain. And why, pray, should I not be all these beings? In me there are so many. In me so many meet one another." True, in each of us there live more beings than we care to admit to ourselves. Somewhere lying dormant within us are the shadows and fears of boyhood's twilight hours forming a cave for Caliban. There is so much space within us. And over many things drifting about in us we have no more power than a shipowner over his vessels tossing about at sea.

So the reader walks off with *The Tempest* in his pocket. The meadow is too near to the highway, the forest already too dark. For a while he strolls to and fro unable to decide, until he settles down on a tree trunk between gossamer threads and mossy branches, and projects his magic theater. It requires a supreme effort of imagination; he has to efface himself, become completely empty, become the scene of action, that island, become completely a stage. Then Prospero emerges from the cave, a shadow of tiredness on his noble face, and Miranda's flowerlike hands reach for the clasp to loosen the dark magic cloak from his shoulders. And now he, the reader, is nothing but an instrument: now the book plays on him.

You will tell me that my reader's name is Charles Lamb or Theophile Gautier, that he is a poet in whom the poems of others come once again to life. But that should make no difference. What matters is Shakespeare's music, and that again and again there must be someone to whom it is granted to hear the whole music of these poems. But it must be as a Whole. Take *Measure for Measure,* a play full of harshness, with somber passages, with strange, tart blending of the high and the low; more difficult in language, its motives moving us less quickly than the others—a play that begins to live only after we have heard its whole music. It resembled the faces of certain rare women whose beauty is known only to him who has been happy with them. How frightful is this action in itself, this story of the disloyal judge, disloyal to his profession, disloyal to the wretched convicted, disloyal to the good sister—how harsh and sinister, how heart-constricting, how outrageous, repulsive, and revolting all this is! How harsh and sinister, how painful is Claudio's fate, his fear of death, his clinging to the straw that can save him! And all this only because of a senseless law, because of something no better than a trivial coincidence, a "blank in the lottery"! And grafted on to this misfortune which so outrages us, more misfortune. What a wonderful composition it is! what lights thrown on darkness! what life these lights give the shadows! In the mouth of the one who has to die and is afraid of dying, what a voice, what eloquence, what language, wiser than himself, more profound than his shallow virtue—how death squeezes out of him the best sap! And in the mouth of the girl who is helpless, who is betrayed, what strength, what a sword of God suddenly in her hand! And the others! See how their lives intertwine, how their very presence changes the air: the presence of the old murderer Barnadine, who has been condemned to death for seven years, next to the boy Claudio, who was condemned twenty-four hours ago. Friar Thomas and Friar Peter in the quiet monastery with its peace and seclusion, next to the prison, next to the palace wherein the evil Angelo lurks like a poisonous spider in the masonry. Then all of a sudden we are out of town and there sits Mariana before the "moated grange" and a boy's voice singing that sweet song "Take, O take those lips away" . . . And between this world and that, combining everything like a chorus, the disguised Duke, who now sees at close range those whom he has formerly seen only from above, from afar, he whose presence calms our heart as during a nightmare does the deep knowledge "It is only a dream!" and from whose lips fall those incomparable words about life and death. Between these figures, so that life and light shall play everywhere over living flesh, the shadows emphasizing life, there is still this company of commoner, lower beings, even the least among them not completely denuded of some goodness or wit, some grace or courtesy, not quite incapable of showing good will, of saying something kind or uttering an apt analogy. And between all these human beings, what an atmosphere, what a co-existence on this earth, what little yet immeasurably deep and tender gestures toward one another, what looks of pity or mockery exchanged between them! What a Whole, not of calculation, not of reason, not even of emotion, a Whole not so much from the point of view of colors alone or from that of morality, not from the contrast between heaviness and lightness, sadness and gaiety—but from a combination of all this, what a Whole "before God"! What music!

In the performance of *Twelfth Night* by Beerbohm-Tree [4] and his troupe, the play ends—and it is said that this was not the director's brilliant idea, but an old English tradition—with each gentleman offering a hand to his lady, and thus, in couples, the Duke and Viola, Olivia and Sebastian, and behind them their retinue dance across and off the stage. Hand in hand they dance, those who had inflamed and tortured one another, sought and deceived and enchanted one

[4] Sir Herbert Beerbohm-Tree (1853–1917), half brother of Sir Max Beerbohm. He managed the Haymarket Theatre from 1887–1896, and later became the manager-proprietor of Her Majesty's Theatre. Editor.

another. Thus these figures become figures of a dance, pursuing and not finding, chasing the Wrong and fleeing the Right. This is now the final figure, and for an instant something wafts past it like a shadow, a fleeting memory of the Dance of Death which also makes everything equal, as everything here is equal and together, hands in hands, is creating a double chain, a "figure" wherein the single destiny has as much value as a single spot of color on an ornament, as a single theme in a symphony. Even if this idea were re-created out of an old tradition, it was nevertheless once, the first time, a stroke of genius on the part of one director who invented this perfect symbol of binding together the human bodies (in whose gestures he has expressed for five acts the experiences of each single character), of binding them together at the last moment by a rhythm and expressing in them the wholeness of the Whole. You will say that this director was also a poet. But every creative stage director is a poet. Again and again throughout history Fate chooses one man from among those who "carry within them a stage" and who, in luxurious solitude, play Shakespeare for themselves—chooses the man, gives him a real stage.

And thus, among the hundreds of stages on which Shakespeare is played for show—where he is played, I mean, for tradition's sake, because he constitutes part of the repertory or because his plays contain fine roles—there shines out one stage where he is performed out of sheer passion. Just as Macbeth and Shylock, Othello and Juliet, continue to overpower the body and soul of an actor of genius, so the music of the dramas continues to overpower the soul of a creative director and his whole stage, and lives anew. For everything alive lives only from the living, and the flame only from that which wants to burn.

On announcing that I was going to talk to you about Shakespeare's kings and noblemen, it was agreed that I would not speak of anything but the Whole in Shakespeare's work. It's as though I had said I wished to talk about the solemn and sublime sounds in Beethoven's symphonies, or of light and color in Rubens. When I say "kings and noblemen" your memory is inundated with a flood of figures and gestures incomparable to any vision unless it be that which was granted to the old men on the walls of Troy when before their eyes the dust clouds parted, and the sun was seen gleaming on the armor and faces of the countless heroes so akin to the gods. More figures, images, feelings surge up in you than you can grasp. You are reminded at once of Lear, who is a king, every inch a king; of Hamlet, who is a prince, a prince to his fingertips; of Richard II, that elder "brother" of Hamlet who talks so much about his royal blood, round whose shoulders hangs the royal cloak as agonizing to wear as that garment immersed in the blood of Nessus and which, when finally torn off, spells certain death. And the face of Henry VI, pale as though his head had been cut off and stuck on a pike, rests for an instant in you, and the face of gentle Duncan, too. In a flash you see the royal, commanding gestures of Antony and feel a breath of the spirit-kingdom on Prospero's island, of the fairy-realm of those idyllic kings in long red cloaks and scepters in their hands—Leontes of Sicily, Polixenes of Bohemia, Cymbeline, and Theseus. But this flood of visions continues to rise, and you look into an imbroglio of noble gestures until your head begins to swim. The gestures of command and contempt, of haughty defiance and magnanimity, glitter before your eyes like a thousand flashes of lightning. The words "kings and noblemen" have the power to make continuously fresh floods rise from the well of a memory steeped in Shakespeare. Swamped by a vision and figures almost impossible to grasp, you will search within yourselves for a word that can compress in one idea this whole imaginary world of spirits. You sense that these words conjure up not only three-quarters of all figures created by Shakespeare, but also what happens between these figures as well as what happens between them and those of less importance who stand beside them; you sense that these words apply not only to these figures but also to the empty space around them and to what fills this empty space—what the Italians call *l'ambiente*. You slowly realize that in this world of Shakespeare there really exists a line leading from one point to another, some true relation between the scene in which Kent, the unrecognized, offers his services to Lear because he had something in his countenance which "he would fain call master," and the sylvan idyl of King Cymbeline's sons who grow up in a cave, unfettered, like beautiful young animals although of royal blood; between the sullen feuds of the English barons in the dramas of the kings and the benevolent master's tone in which noble Brutus speaks to Lucius, his page; between the tone of proud Othello, yes, between Cleopatra, a queen, and Falstaff, who is—after all—a nobleman. You feel, as I do, this imponderable, this intangible element, this nothing which is nevertheless everything, and from my lips you take the words wherewith I wish to name it—the atmosphere of Shakespeare's work. This word could not be more vague, yet it belongs to those of which we may have to make a very definite, very productive use.

At no other time of the year, however, would I have dared to speak of something so vague and in it to seek something so great than now, that spring has come.

> Now with the drops of this most balmy time
> My love looks fresh

and now greater than ever is the courage to see all beautiful things afresh, to dismiss all those clearly defined subjects which are usually discussed—characters, actions, ideas—and to follow this fleeting, barely palpable truth which pervades all of Shakespeare's work.

The moment itself has so much atmosphere. I mean this very moment in the life of Nature, this moment of the not yet fully awakened, not yet luxuriating, still yearning spring in which the death anniversary of a human being unites us here, a human being who has become almost a myth to us and of whom we can scarce believe that he ever was a presence among mortal men. It does not appear to me as something essentially different whether we sense the atmosphere of spring, the atmosphere of a Shakespearean drama, or that of a picture by Rembrandt. Here as there I feel a gigantic ensemble. (Let me take this sober word from the technique of painting rather than any other. There are many at my disposal: I could speak of the music of the Whole, of a harmony, of a spiritualization, but all these words strike me as somewhat wilted, slightly soiled by the touch of human hands.) An ensemble wherein the difference between great and small has been canceled insofar as one lives for the sake of the other, the great for the small, the dark for the light, where one seeks the other, emphasizes and restrains the other, colors and discolors, and where finally for the soul there exists nothing but the Whole—the indivisible, intangible, imponderable Whole. To dissect the atmosphere of spring was always the passion of the lyric poet. But its essence is nevertheless the ensemble. Everywhere the world is burgeoning. The far and the near whisper to one another; the tepid breeze gliding over the still-naked earth breathes an air of oppressive sultriness. Light, like water, is melting everywhere, but no moment is more pregnant with the abundance of spring than that of noon, when darkness falls and heavy, sinister clouds brood over the earth-brown hills and the clamor of delirious bird voices rises from the bare branches into the gloom. And as in a phantasmagoria, everything has changed. The naked landscape, hitherto so sad and deserted, is full of voluptuousness. The darkness doesn't oppress, it exalts. The near is as mysterious as the far. And the voice of a single bird contributes no less to the Whole than the dark forest which lends to the wind the scent of moist earth and budding green.

I could continue to offer you this notion of atmosphere were I not sure that you have understood me immediately and completely, and were I not afraid to tire you. The death of a human being has its atmosphere, like the spring. The faces of those in whose arms a man has died speak a language that defies words. And in their presence inanimate objects join in this language. A chair that has always stood elsewhere, an open cupboard that has never remained open for long, and a thousand trivial signs appearing at such a moment like traces of ghosts' hands: this is the world which ends at the windowpanes. But the outside world, too, in a mysterious way, shows this fateful, deeply knowing face: the street lamps are burning as on any other day; the passing of the unsuspecting strangers, turning a corner, passing the house, turning another corner—all this condenses itself into something that drags along like an ominous chain. These are the moments when the long-forgotten friends return: the emergence of those whose behavior has become queer, who are embittered or utterly estranged, and out of whom now break forth words and looks never heard or seen at any other time. The sudden astonishment: how did we part? how did all this happen? The quick realization: how futile everything is! How alike we all are, how similar to one another! This, too, is atmosphere. Here, too, something indefinable connects the near with the far, the great with the small, one moving the other into its proper light, intensifying and subduing, coloring and discoloring one by the other, annihilating all borderlines between the seemingly important and seemingly unimportant, the common and the exceptional—and creates the ensemble out of the whole existing material, considering no elements to be incompatible.

The atmosphere in Shakespeare's work is nobility: the king is merely the greatest nobleman among great noblemen, and each of them has in him something of a king—nobility in the sense of the cinquecento—that is, infinitely freer, infinitely more human, more colorful than anything which we are accustomed to associate with this notion. It is not only the characters and their feelings born out of Shakespeare's soul which are imbued with this nobility, but precisely and above all the atmosphere, the air of life, *ce grand air* pervading everything. All these characters (the duller few who do not belong to them exist only to create contrast) are steeped in the element of nobility as the figures in the paintings of Titian and Giorgione are stepped in the golden, luminous element of color. It's in this element that such groups as Romeo, Mercutio, Benvolio, Tybalt, as well as Antonio the noble merchant and his friends, move. The banished Duke in the Ardennes and all those who belong to him, above all Brutus and his household, are surrounded by this aura. This light, this air, is around them in such abundance and with such intensity that it cannot be ignored. A noble consciousness—nay, deeper than that—an existence of almost conscious nobility, a noble breathing, and closely connected with it a remarkable tender and strong feeling for the other person, a mutual almost impersonal affection, a tenderness, reverence for the human. Have I not recalled to you with these words—too weak to express what is ineffably alive—what all these different young people have in common: the melancholic Jaques with the lighthearted Bassanio, the passionate Romeo with the shrewd, shy Mercutio? The element in which these beings are bred is delicately suspended between arrogance and courtesy. It is the youthful attitude of defiance which is nevertheless shocked at the thought of having offended—a readiness to open up and form attachments, yet at the same time remaining detached and complete. Their equilibrium is one of the most beautiful things I know. Like graceful, well-built ships they lie rocking to and fro above their own shadows on the flood of life. Round them there is something exultant, something expansive overflowing into the air, an abundance of life, a glorification of life itself, something definitely welcoming life, something that evokes the Pythian and Nemean odes of Pindar, those radiant salutations of victors. Not only is Prince Henry ultimately their brother, but so, to a certain degree, is Falstaff. They are youths, but Brutus is a man. They are without any other destiny but the destiny of love; they seem to be placed in this picture only as a glorification of life, like glowing reds and resplendent yellows in a painting. Brutus, however, has a lofty destiny of his own. He is modeled of the same clay as they, but he is a more mature person. It is not the manner in which his soul interprets life, but his attitude in life, this nobility without harshness, full of generosity, of goodness and gentleness, this tone whose harmony could shine forth only from a soul in whose depths the profoundest self-respect is rooted. Apart from his destiny which fulfills itself in him—"the genius and the mortal instruments are then in council"—and drives him to the great deed of his life which is then followed by everything else, even by death, as water follows water when a dam is opened; apart from his inner destiny this tragedy (whose hero is Brutus) is illuminated almost exclusively by the light of this noble being in whose ray all other characters mold themselves by coming closer to him. What occurs between Brutus and Cassius is nothing but the reaction of Cassius (who is less noble and knows himself to be less noble) to the atmosphere around Brutus. In Cassius there is a vain, mute, inner wooing of Brutus, a wooing with every torment of jealousy which Cassius does not admit to himself, which Brutus, too, perhaps, if aware of, does not admit, doesn't want to know, certainly doesn't want to analyze. And in Brutus an amazing forbearance for Cassius; up to the moment of his single outburst he places himself tactfully on the same level; and even then it is his nerves, not his will, which give way. (An hour ago he has received the news of Portia's death, yet refrains from mentioning it.) And then, on parting, once again: "noble, noble Cassius." Imagine him being capable of saying this, the noble one to the less noble! Of feeling driven to say it twice! This is the attitude of Brutus toward Cassius. And Portia! She has but this one unforgettable scene. Enveloped in the atmosphere of Brutus, her noble face is molded from the light emanating from him. Or does this light emanate from elsewhere? Are both Brutus and Portia molded out of this light and its shadows? Who, before a Rembrandt, can say whether the atmosphere is there for the sake of the figures or the figures for the sake of the atmosphere? But certain places exist simply to catch the whole light, which is the soul of the atmosphere. I have in mind the scenes with the boy Lucius and the other servants. The considerate tone of his voice when he apologizes to Lucius for shortening his sleep to which his youth has so much claim. And this: "Look, Lucius, here's the book I sought for so; I put it in the pocket of my gown. . . . Bear with me, good boy." And then, as Lucius falls asleep while tuning his lute, Brutus steps forward to remove the lute on which his arm has sunk in slumber: "If thou dost nod, thou break'st thy instrument." I don't know what can bring tears to a reader's eye if not such a detail. This is the man who was Caesar's murderer. He is the general in his tent. He is the last Roman; tomorrow at Philippi he will die. And here he is, bending down, and from under the sleeping boy removing a lute so that it shall not be broken. And at the moment of making this small gesture, this plain, homely, almost feminine little gesture—more natural to a woman, a housewife, a mother —at this moment, so near his death (Caesar's ghost is already standing there in the dark), I see his face: it's a face he has never had before, a second face as though taking form from within—a face in which male and female features mingle, as in the death masks of Beethoven and Napoleon. It is here that we are moved to tears, rather than at Lear's curses, rather than when Macbeth, strangled in his own iron torments as in a hundredweight of armor, turns his eye on us and constricts our heart. From such minor details our admiration for Shakespeare is intensified to the pitch of worship. Indeed, in a work of art there is no difference between great and small. Here, when Brutus, Caesar's murderer, picks up the lute so that it shall not be broken, here as nowhere else do we face the tornado of existence that sucks us down. These are the flashes of lightning wherein a heart reveals itself completely. We are reminded of Ottilie in the *Elective Affinities,*[5] who could never forget the anecdote about how Charles I of England, already dethroned and surrounded by enemies, drops the knob of his stick. He looks round and, dumfounded to see that no one picks it up, stoops himself for the first time in his life. This incident so engraves itself on her heart that from then on she stoops whenever anyone, even a man, drops something. Again, we think of the howl suddenly uttered by Natasha during the hare hunt in *War and Peace,* that wild, triumphant howl of a hound from the throat of an elegant young lady. These are the flashes of lightning I have in mind. And in Shakespeare they are legion. They are the cataclysms of his atmosphere.

I know nothing that so grips the heart as the tone of Lear's voice when he speaks to Edgar. To his daughters he talks like a furious prophet or a patriarch drunk with pain. To his fool he speaks harshly. But to Edgar, that naked madman whom he has found in a cave, he speaks in a tone (wherein,

[5] Goethe's novel, *Wahlverwandtschaften* (1809). Editor.

to be sure, there is something of madness) whose keynote is an extraordinary politeness of the heart, an indescribable courtesy, which makes us realize how this king could sometimes make his people happy when in a gracious mood. It is that same politeness whose glow hovers over gentle Duncan when he comes in and suggests that the air round Macbeth's castle ought to be good since swifts nest there. The same light, too, shines over that brief scene between Richard II and the groom (shortly before his death); and the same but stronger, more exotic, more resplendent light in each scene between Antony and Cleopatra, between Antony and his friends, Cleopatra and her attendants. What reverence for themselves and the grandeur of their existence! What "Olympian air," what magnificent style, when the affairs of the world have to wait in the anteroom while they embrace: "The nobleness of life is to do thus . . ." The same light again, as if penetrating dense storm clouds with furious flashes of lightning, falls on the hundred figures of the proud peers of England whose self-esteem (one of them calls it "our stately presence") shrouds them in wide folds grander, wilder, more real than any ermine-trimmed cloak. But I could continue endlessly saying, "It is here! It is there!" for I see it everywhere. I could spend another hour describing how I see in this aura the figures of all these regal, noble women, from Cleopatra to Imogen. I see it everywhere so much, in fact, that I am deeply perplexed when perceiving a figure like Macbeth with almost nothing of this atmosphere around him. This suggests to me that Shakespeare meant to endow him with a peculiar frightfulness, meant to let him be shrouded by an icy air of death. It seems as if the ghastly breath of Hecate had eaten away from the world around Macbeth everything alive, everything that ordinarily unites mankind, leaving nothing of that which surrounds Hamlet as a breath of life. Take the scene with the actors, where Hamlet's whole being expands in a princely, gracious self-indulgence and joy, even delighting others with his self-indulgence. Or the scenes with Polonius, Rosencrantz, and Guildenstern as a conscious use of his princely eminence, an ironic and grievous demonstration of his superiority—implying that even this prerogative is worth nothing, even this privilege is of no avail save as an instrument of self-torture.

Gentlemen! The ideas I have been expounding here seem to me to bind together the whole of Shakespeare's work. They are a mystery and the word "atmosphere" describes them in as unsatisfactory and almost as superficial a manner as the word "chiaroscuro" describes a similar mystery in the work of Rembrandt. Were I thinking of the figures alone—and it is the isolated figures, as though standing in a vacuum, that are usually made the subject of observation—then I would have tried to talk of the Shakespearean "attitude." For the important point is to see or to sense the common ground whereon, in life, all these figures stand. Dante's figures are placed in a gigantic architectonic system and the place on which each stands is its place according to mystical designs. Shakespeare's figures, on the other hand, are determined not by the stars but by themselves; they carry within themselves hell, purgatory, and heaven, and instead of their place in life they have their attitude. I, however, see these figures not each by itself but each in relation to all the others, and between them not a vacuum but a space mystically alive. I don't see them next to one another separately, like the figures of saints on a painting by an early primitive, but standing out from a common element like the men, animals, and angels in the paintings of Rembrandt.

The drama (I don't mean only Shakespeare's drama) is just as much a picture of the absolute solitude of the individual as a picture of the co-existence of mankind. In the dramas cast out of the volcano of Kleist's [6] fiery soul, this atmosphere, this co-existence of characters, is perhaps the most beautiful part of the whole. His creatures, you will remember, are continually lusting after one another; suddenly, when addressing one another, they change from the distant you to the naked thou, caress one another with amorous

[6] Heinrich von Kleist (1777–1811), the renowned German dramatist and poet. Editor.

glances, seize one another with violence, the one yearning to merge into the other but promptly turning cold, flying asunder in estrangement, then to go all over again in ardent search of one another. All this fills Kleist's space with passionate life and movement and creates something living out of the void.

To sum up: Whatever occurs between these figures seems to me filled with a life flowing from the same mysterious sources as the figures themselves. This mirroring of one another, this humiliating and exalting, restraining and fortifying of one another—all this, for me, is as much the work of a hand of a gigantic genius as the figures themselves. And it is because I cannot, in Shakespeare's work any more than in Rembrandt's, draw or admit a dividing line between the figures themselves and that part of the picture without them that I have seized upon the word "atmosphere." The lack of time and the urgency of immediate understanding between us has prevented me from employing a word even more appropriate and more mysterious—the word "myth."

Had I been able with greater intensity than today to evoke in your minds the power of Rembrandt and with comparable intensity the power of Homer, then these three primeval forces —Shakespeare's atmosphere, Rembrandt's chiaroscuro, Homer's myth—would for a moment have merged into one. Grasping this glowing key, we would have descended to the mothers, and there, where "neither Space, still less Time" exists, have visualized the deepest creating and longing of distant spirits in mystical union with the deepest creating and longing of our own epoch—to generate atmosphere for its existence, to let its figures move in the lightness and darkness of life, to imbue its breath with myth.

22. José Ortega y Gasset

1883–1955

Spanish interest in Shakespeare, unlike that in France and Germany, has been sparse and unsystematic. Spain, preoccupied with its own literary tradition (see introduction), has never needed Shakespeare as a weapon against classicism. A number of major writers such as Jacinto Benavente (1866–1954) have rendered Shakespeare into Spanish. Others, such as Pío Baroja (1872–1956), Gustavo Bécquer (1836–1870), and Pedro de Alarcón (1833–1891), have left brief notices of their appreciation of the English poet. But Shakespeare has never been the subject of a mania or of a controversy in Spain as elsewhere in Europe, and not until recently have Spanish thinkers moved beyond their domestic concerns to deal with the contemporary of their own Cervantes.

Among the handful of present-day Spanish thinkers who have shown an interest in Shakespeare, Ortega occupies a special place. With the appearance of his La rebelión de las masas *(1930), Ortega became the foremost Spanish philosopher of his time and one of the profoundest of modern humanists. The book promulgated a humanism based on an ideal of culture and "true" democracy. The critique embodied in the work was in the mainstream of Ortega's thought; a mainstream clearly distinguishable from the first. Few modern thinkers have been as consistent as Ortega.*

But one characteristic of Ortega's work, a characteristic which he shares with the chief humanists of the day, is the inability to refrain from preaching. Ortega, from the beginning, has sought to develop a position in which a new conception of reason could be reconciled with the advances in the social and historical sciences. His commitment to humanistic ideals as well as to scientific method made such philosophies as the vitalism of Bergson or the irrationalism of Spengler impossible. Until recently there has not been a great deal of interest in Ortega, possibly because of the didactic nature of much of his work, but since 1955 there have been a number of fine studies devoted to his thought.

The following essay, Shylock, *was written in 1910 during the first period of Ortega's work. During this "objectivist" phase, which lasted from 1904 until the outbreak of World War I, Ortega's work is characterized by his method of using the particular case to illustrate the universal. As in much of his other work, Ortega wanders far afield here, but the total impression is one of coherence.*

Shylock

Some nights ago I saw *The Merchant of Venice* in Lara. Novelli, with his face like that of an enormous chimpanzee, played the Jew splendidly in Titian-like hues and lineaments. The rest of the actors committed a collective crime which I will not allow to pass without protest.

No one will accuse me of maintaining an individualistic vision of history: to explain human evolution according to Carlyle's concept in terms of the pure and exclusive results of some great men's acts has always appeared to me a poetic commonplace which can only interest us in our twenties; the very age at which the hope to become a great man is forever lost. Soon we begin to think that, without the need of becoming great men, life proposes some lofty duties to us, some superior activities which render it worth living, and from this point we are led into a more or less collectivist conception of history.

From *Obras Completas* de José Ortega y Gasset, Tomo Uno (1902–1916), Segunda Edicion (Madrid, Revista de Occidente, 1950) pp. 522–526. Reprinted by permission of the Revista de Occidente. Translated by the editor.

However, the second part of Carlyle's formula—*Heroen-worship*—the cult of geniuses, seems necessary to me, and it deserves to be fought for. In my opinion there is no pedagogy without a study of the classics, as there is no instruction on virtues without saints. All men have brought, or were able to bring, their own share to the great edifice of culture; but there are great men who have brought the plan, the main idea of the construction. The meaning of our life, less powerful and more modest, is to work inside the thought of these men as a honeybee works inside the hive.

Such men are examples, as much a sample and a model as the plan of the temple is for the apprentice craftsman who works on the ornaments of a voussoir at the rear of a cloister. In this way we control our work: the classics are an invitation to historical humanity, and, like foremen, they direct us to posts in the common task. We should work as if we were not men of genius, and this thought, wherever else it may fit, fits the Spanish people even more, inclined as they are to do no less than to discover the Mediterranean Sea every day.

It is thus necessary to open our hearts again to the cult of the classics, taking care to be more intimate with this cult, more rebellious and without any of the official pomposity of ancient rhetoric.

I was shaken in my respect toward such a classic as Shakespeare the other night when I became aware of the frivolous atmosphere that descended from the stage down into the audience.

These Italian companies generally formed by a sole actor backed by nonentities should have provoked a greater reaction from the public. Is the good actor present only in those who succeed in moving their facial expression in a certain manner? The whole of contemporary art aims precisely at the creation of a total atmosphere: in painting and in novels it has become the main subject, and individual traits of the characters have become sheer matter which helps the artist to build a world of centralized relationships, capable of living a life independent from the actuality of such matters. Only the art of the comedians refuses to transform itself in such a way. Thus Novelli, in spite of being a great artist, cannot help creating a dislocated, trivial, and nightmarish Shylock; a *reductio ad absurdum* of the great Shakespearean suggestion. This amounts to a lack of respect for the soul of the great poet, whose creative art is classical precisely because he neither tells us anecdotes nor takes picturesque profiles out of the tapestry of life. Shakespeare is what he is for us nowadays because each of his works is a small universe, a microcosmos, enclosing, in a condensed form, the complete substance of the real world, the macrocosmos, a world of less intensity, for in itself more extensive, where, in order to coalesce two energetic emotions, we have to go from one to the other by a stupid way of ten and twenty years.

The works of Shakespeare, like the pictures of Rubens, have unalterable orbits. Shakespeare organizes with great care the distribution of aesthetic values in every one of his works, thus achieving perfect balance. He composes elements like Rubens. If in *The Merchant of Venice* the figure of Shylock, the regulating weight, appears however more accentuated by the insignificance of the actors who play the other roles, the work fails, losing absolute balance, and falls into pieces over the head of the aloof spectator with all the weight of its age-old materials. If Antonio, Portia, Bassanio, and Jessica do not enter the realm of our perception, the moneylender will remain, to us, reduced to an old and shaggy dog that, from his kennel, barks at passers-by.

And, for the love of Shakespeare, Shylock means far more than that!

II

The miserable howls of the Venetian Jew direct our attention to one of the worst evils of history: anti-Semitism.

Such a passion is not a fleeting one; Shylock is not an anecdote extracted from a frivolous Italian "centon."[1] The poor wandering Jew who trudges, his head bent, over the

[1] A poem of 100 lines, each of whose lines is borrowed from other works and arranged so as primarily to demonstrate cleverness. Editor.

roads of history, under the weight of infinite misfortunes is as legendary as the millennium. He is, however, alive. I have seen him in the *Brühl* of Leipzig, in front of his miserable shop, where the most expensive furs are displayed. I have seen him, stoop-shouldered, dressed in a worn outer coat, his nose bent over an enormous red beard. I have seen him more erect and with a more tranquil bearing walking by the *Zeil* of Frankfurt. And one day, in a third-class car on my way from Wittenberg to Berlin, I recognized him sitting in front of me. He was a small ball of old flesh under a round little head with its pointed nose and the eyes of a sparrow; and all that set in perpetual restlessness. "I cannot stay silent, I confess," he said to me, "are you a German?" Spanish! "I have read Lope de Vega. I am Jewish and I have a small shop of clocks and watches in Berlin." The car had been filled with Germans, commissioners, students, soldiers. The moment they heard the word "Jewish" they started with jokes and insults against the short traveler. I felt ashamed, I confess; I was afraid those stolid burghers would attribute a Jewish origin to my Spanish paleness and black beard. I was ashamed and did not defend him, and the other night, seeing *The Merchant of Venice*, the small Jewish seller of watches appeared in my memory, and looked into me with his eyes of a malignant bird, and I felt a pain in my heart.

How this great race has suffered! The other races have let fall on the Jews, drop by drop, all the might of their hatred. Jews have been ill-treated, scorned, and exploited a thousand times. They have lost all their rights, they have been driven into seclusion, like cattle into their compartments, inside the ghettos and Jewish communities branded with the sign of the red wheels. When a medieval Christian wanted to praise God in a very special way, he would kill Jews. One should read the very curious laws of Ferdinand I concerning the "chuetas" [2] or, under another name, the rabble, in which so many privileges were forbidden them including, among other things, the title of *Don*.

Poor immortal race! From remote centuries European na-

[2] The converted Jews of Mallorca. Editor.

tions, the Arabs, and later the Turks, have exerted upon Jewish flesh their utmost capacities to torture. In the pallid and swarthy flesh they have tested the sharpness of their knives. What has it gotten them? Pain, that divine teacher, which has made the Jewish soul more sensitive, has given this people an arduous energy more suited to the sublimest of tasks. We have killed Jews, and their blood, to the extent that it became more rare, became also more exquisite, more spiritual, and converted itself into pure psychic energy, becoming the least of vehicles and the greatest of the intellectual powers. Through Jewish veins only spirit flows, only philosophy, revolution, lyricism, and double-entry bookkeeping.

Wherever there are Jews there are always two things: melancholy and filth. But principally there is melancholy! They have, in the attics of their soul, collected bitterness enough to inundate the planet; they are teachers of melancholia. Their scholars, like their poets, cry lamentations, and the sun comes, without gaiety, to their Paris benches. As Heine once said:

> The great and the small weep,
> and even the frozen governors,
> the women and flowers weep,
> and the stars are suffering.
>
> And all the tears spill
> south in speechless league,
> flowing until they fill
> the Jordan deep.[3]

I would never stop talking about Jews, nor do I believe that there is a more delicate topic for a poet's sensitivity than the millennial pain of a people who once chose God as the vessel to contain them. Poor magnificent Yahwe, God of

[3] The above is a version of the poem sent by Heine, in a letter of October 25, 1824 (together with "To Edom!") to Moses Moser. Heine had wished to write the four stanzas as an inscription in, and a prologue to, "The Rabbi of Bacherach" (which he had sent Moser earlier). Ortega quotes the last two stanzas of an excellent Spanish translation whose author I have been unable to identify. The translation is from the German and was rendered by me. Editor.

restlessness and melancholy; Thou who once hadst the fire in one hand, and the manna in the other, and set Thyself afire in the bramble bush by the wayside! Still do the Russian police set illiterate laborers, not yet purified by the caustic words of the prophets, on the people of Thy choice. The horror of it! Only recently did Alexander III expel all the Jews, and the Jewish women, in order to be allowed to remain, had to use the yellow tickets of prostitution. That was yesterday: today . . . Kishinev, Bialystok,[4] blood, streams of blood; the blood of Reuben, the blood of Naphtali!

On the occasion of the anti-Semitic riots of 1892, Julius Huret reported in *Figaro* from Russia the text of a conversation he had with a Jew from Lodz; a man whose son had just been murdered and of whom the following question had been asked: "Is it not said that there are too many Jews in Lodz?" "Yes," he answered—"many. But where do you want them to go? They have been driven off everywhere. When they were expelled from St. Petersburg, a Jew I once knew went to see Gresser, the chief of police, and told him: 'You can put up with dogs in Petersburg . . . I have eight children to support, I earn my living with great difficulty. Please, let me stay, and I will walk on all fours like the dogs!' 'No,' Gresser answered, 'you are a Jew. You are less than a dog. Make a Christian of yourself.' "

Poor Yahwe! According to Nietzsche, you have become the God of the slums!

Mr. Novelli, Mr. Novelli, why transform Shylock into a picturesque figure? In the Venetian Jew Shakespeare conjures up a millennial pain: with poetic license, unflinchingly, he portrays the cruel image of hate among the races, and of enmity among their Gods.

And now, dear reader, study the third volume of the *History of the Novel in Spain* [5] which has just been published. In it there is a splendid study of *The Celestina,* in which

[4] Sites of particularly bloody pogroms. Editor.

[5] Ortega is here referring to a monumental work whose actual title was *Origenes de la Novela* (Madrid, Bailly-Bailliero i hijos), by Menéndez y Pelayo, 4 vols., published between 1905 and 1915. Editor.

Menéndez y Pelayo [6] tells how its author, a Jew, was involved in an Inquisitional trial, instituted by his father-in-law, old Alvaro de Montalbán, for eating unleavened bread, entering the Holy Tabernacle, and for certain expressions by which, in this world, he was criticizing the next. The principal witness—the parish priest of San Gines.

[6] Marcelino Menéndez y Pelayo (1856–1912). A major critic and literary historian of his time. Editor.

23. Salvador de Madariaga

1886–

Salvador de Madariaga has been a journalist, literary critic, historian, Spanish ambassador to the United States, League of Nations delegate, professor, and novelist. He is recognized throughout the world together with Miguel de Unamuno (1864–1936) and Ortega as a major bearer of twentieth-century Spain's contribution to European intellectual activity.

De Madariaga has written frequently on English literature. His Shelley and Calderón *(1920) demonstrated a profound grasp of the character of English Romanticism and of its unique relation to the spirit of Spanish* renascimiento *literature. In* On Hamlet, *de Madariaga rehearses many of the Romantic attitudes to Shakespeare and echoes, as well, some Crocean positions. But the book is interesting not merely as the first extended study of a single Shakespearean play by a Spaniard but also because of its introduction. It is in the introduction, reprinted here, that de Madariaga asserts that "the era of Shakespeare is the era of Spain." The introduction further develops this theme of the sixteenth and seventeenth centuries as "the Spanish era" and continues on to a brief review of the chief tendencies in Hamlet criticism. He concludes the introduction with a sound critique of the Stoll-Schücking type of historical criticism.*

FROM On Hamlet

Introduction

To be a constant reader of *Hamlet,* and to hold it as one of the few great masterpieces of the European spirit, is no claim to write on it; to have attempted a translation of it into Spanish verse may, however, be considered by the more generous sort fit credentials for admission into and even for a modest share in the permanent debate on the great tragedy and its meaning. For a translator must retrace every mental step of the author, without skipping a single shade of meaning; and so may come into closer familiarity with the intentions of the mastermind than even the national critic—granted, of course, his own power to do so. Let this consideration be remembered before I am condemned for venturing to rush in where so many angels and ministers of literary grace have dared tread before me. The list is now long in which names as great as Coleridge and Bradley shine with a light so dazzling. *"On a honte d'écrire des vers quand on en lit de pareils"* [1] —said Voltaire in self-disgust, reading a page of Racine. It is with feelings akin to this shame that I venture on my present task.

The more so as *Hamlet* is the masterpiece of an English genius, a genius that is foreign, in this case, to his would-be interpreter. One who has only too often had occasion to observe how the keenest and even the most creative minds, foreign to Spain, are apt to fall into the bog of incomprehension when trying to interpret Calderón or Cervantes, cannot be unaware of the fact that a similar fate may well be in store for him in an attempt to present his own *Hamlet* to the people in whose midst it was born. There are, however, some ways in

From *On Hamlet* (London, Hollis & Carter, 1948), pp. ix-xii. Reprinted by permission of Don Salvador de Madariaga.

[1] One is ashamed to write poetry when one has read such as this. Editor.

which a Spaniard may claim to be less foreign to Shakespeare than most other men, leaving of course aside his own kith and kin. It is not in vain that Shakespeare shone in the European firmament when the sun never set on the Spanish domains. The era of Shakespeare is the era of Spain. Now nations reach the apex of their power when the genius of the time is in harmony with their own genius; when in other words the age acts as a sounding board for their own peculiar note. The sixteenth and seventeenth centuries were the Spanish era because then the subject of the world's debate was man on a background of absolute values—God, evil, death, love, free arbiter, and predestination; all pre-eminently Spanish themes. The eighteenth century was French because by then the world's debate had shifted from the spirit to the mind, from inspiration and revelation to inquiry, from synthesis to analysis, and from religion to politics. The nineteenth century was English because by then politics had grown so thin that one could see the economic bones through the ideological skin, and the once religious or theological ethics had become secularized into social morality. And we are now entering a new era in which social mechanics or behaviorism threatens to oust social morality, an era therefore which will be the century of the U.S. or the U.S.S.R., as the case may be.

If this be true, Spaniards should be particularly apt to appreciate the spirit of the sixteenth century; for in that century what came to the surface in any one nation was that which in that nation was most in harmony with Spain. Shakespeare in particular looks upon the world with the serene eyes of an artist, indifferent to all teaching, impartial between good and evil, i.e., with that mood of the man of passion I have analyzed elsewhere, as typical of the man of Spain. I have there shown that the natural attitude of the "pathic" man, of whom the Spaniard is the prototype, is that of the spectator (the Englishman, a man of action being the protagonist; the Frenchman, a man of thought, the critic). Now, in his deepest sense, Shakespeare is *a spectator of genius.* An explanation of his works and characters which overlooks this fact, and therefore attributes to him a purpose, a bias, a tendency, should be suspected as likely to lead to error. Shakespeare just looks, sees, and re-creates what is there.

The purely fortuitous fact that such is the specific natural attitude of the Spaniard is therefore my second excuse for venturing to write on *Hamlet.* In the course of my translations I had often to consult the many and admirable essays written by English and American critics on the play and its characters; and, to be sure, met more than once with this central thought of all Shakespearean criticism set down as clearly as could be wished, i.e., that Shakespeare is unbiased, all-embracing, "above the strife." But it soon became evident to me that the principle, once stated and proclaimed, was apt to be forgotten when it might have been invaluable to explain a character or to analyze a situation. It is, of course, utterly impossible even to attempt a criticism of *Hamlet*'s critics; for our present purpose, however, it is necessary to point out that, after having been made to indulge in an orgy of character interpretation, which naively identified Shakespeare's characters with human beings, we are now led too far in the opposite direction, and bidden to be content with a Shakespeare who *depicted* characters without bothering as to their motivations. The greatest poet, the keenest observer of human nature is thus declared to have taken no interest in the motives which made his characters act as they did. This conclusion, convenient though it be for the critics whom Shakespeare's subtlety—and occasional lapses into carelessness—baffles, must be brushed aside as irrelevant. The principle that shall rule over all our inquiries is that Shakespeare knew what he was doing—even if, at times, he fell below his own, or our, standards of craftsmanship.

Here is the *Gioconda.* Of course, it would be childish to describe her as an actual woman; and those critics who tell us all about Hamlet's youth or how Ophelia may have learned those unseemly songs from her wicked nurse, do fall into that mistake. But are we to follow the "historical" critics whose theory amounts to solemnly warning us that the *Gioconda* is just a piece of cloth covered with oil and pigment so as to *depict* a woman? No more but so?—as Ophelia would ask. Was then Leonardo so indifferent to the inner Mona Lisa that he paid no attention to co-ordinating eyes and lips, cheeks and forehead, into a spiritual and psychological perspective? Of course, we know that out of words and lines, images and situations, Shakespeare was but cleverly contriving an illusion. But the force, the depth, and the creative quality behind this illusion come from the fact that it is conceived from the intuition of a coherent psyche living behind its seemingly incoherent gestures and motions—that, in Shakespeare's own words, though "infinite in faculty, in form and moving," it is "express and admirable in action." *

* It is significant that such a prominent exponent of the historical school as Dr. Stoll discusses little else but Hamlet's *character* which otherwise he apparently denies. "But what of our hero?"—he asks at the end of an utterly unconvincing refusal to see any procrastination in Hamlet—"In ridding his (whom? what *person*?) of his fault have we also robbed him of his charm? If not weak and erring, he is still unfortunate enough, unhappy enough to be tragic." Stoll-H, p. 68. See also "By his tone and bearing, likewise, and a conduct that is (if we be not cavilling) irreproachable, and a reputation that is stainless, is Hamlet to be judged."—Stoll-A, p. 104. (The above references are to *Hamlet: An Historical and Comparative Study,* University of Minnesota Studies in Language and Literature, Minneapolis, 1919; and to *Art and Artifice in Shakespeare,* Cambridge, England, 1938. Editor.

24. Giuseppe Ungaretti

1888–

Italian writers have been among the most active of the twentieth century. Two world wars have not managed to diminish their energies. Italy's literary scene, since the end of the last century, has been in a constant state of upheaval. Manifesto has followed manifesto. Futurists have been stacked side by side with crepuscolario *contemporaries and those who have practiced other "isms." But through it all the most noticeable strain has been that of the poet's striving after a* poesia pura; *a poetry, which as its epithet implies, is rooted in the tradition of Petrarch and, more recently, of Mallarmé and Valéry. It is a poetry of tension, obscurity, and what its generally most esteemed practitioner, Ungaretti, has termed a "pristine intellectual distinction."*

What criticism has emanated from this movement is of a piece with its aesthetic practice. It eschews much of nineteenth-century "rhetorical" criticism, the modern historico-realists, and is in general close to the main Crocean position. Indeed, if looked at carefully, its aesthetic seems to be a rehearsal of Croce's central doctrine of "lyrical intuition."

Ungaretti is generally considered Italy's major poet after the First World War. His work has been marked by a consistent search for clarity and "pure" diction of a kind neither effete nor intellectually impoverished. His criticism is sparse and little known. It has not been gathered systematically. Between the wars Ungaretti was co-editor with Henri Michaux and Jean Paulhan, two French poets, of the enormously influential journal Mesure.

The origins and motives of the following essay, Appunti sull'arte poetica di Shakespeare, *are both evident in its autobiographical passages. But the essay is more than the recount-*

ing of an autodidactical experience. It offers a significant doctrine of translation. But of even greater value are its embodiment of the aesthetics held in common by many of this century's Italian poets as well as its assertion that Shakespeare's art is the result of a fusion of classicism and Romanticism.

Notes on Shakespeare's Art of Poetry

Had not its printing been delayed by a forcible removal of paper, together with the many other obstacles which marked those terrible weeks, this translation would have appeared eight months ago, as announced. I had been planning the work since 1931, which is to say, from a time when I had begun to strive for a profound self-renewal. In my attempt to solve problems of both a technical and a purely inspirational nature, or at least to certify the validity of this kind of endeavor, I was driven to analyze in depth certain very specific aspects of a number of writers of widely differing disposition and origin. This is a thing which is possible only when one engages in translation. The immediate result was the volume of *Translations*, published by "Novissima," which appeared in 1936. The volume contained poems by St. John Perse, Essenin (in my interpretation of his work I owe much to the aid of Maria Miloslavsky and Franz Hellens), Gongora, Blake, and Paulhan. How was it possible for a translator to find equivalents which can capture the wondrous effects of certain modes of expression particularly notable for their sheer simplicity? How could I do justice to other expressions which were striving to reveal a new and unfettered message of a unique and inimitable nature, by falling back upon traditional forms and time-worn themes? My own ideal was to achieve a poetry in which inwardness of spirit, neither betrayed nor falsified by sentimentality, would be wedded to great sophistication in diction.

From *Poesia*, Quaderno primo, February 1945 (Roma, Quaderni internazionali). Reprinted by permission of Giuseppe Ungaretti. Translated by Alfred Triolo.

Now the ancient themes are timeless, and indeed they are the property of popular poetry itself. From Petrarch's time on, however, they had come to mean that poetry has its initial impulse in the memory, whence it tends to move out along a path of autobiographical revelation. Without any loss of variety and concreteness poetry progresses toward a depuration of ideas, which themselves point to a certain continuity of culture and unity of feeling through the centuries. During the fifty years just passed, Petrarchism had been revitalized by Mallarmé, and with the rehabilitation of Donne and Scève it had recaptured its pristine intellectual distinction. I therefore realized that the mere translation of a handful of Gongora's sonnets could not give me a grasp of the vast import of Petrarchism. During this very period I had begun to turn my thoughts to an interpretation of Shakespeare's lyrics. I was doubly drawn to him because I knew of no other genius, save perhaps Michelangelo, in whom Romanticism and classicism had so spontaneously fused in the creation of models of superb diction.

I did not then suspect that this work would turn out to be so arduous, at least for a considerable period of time; and during my sojourn in Brazil I tortured the page for months on end without a whit of progress. I had cast it all aside, when one evening a year or so ago in Rome, in pursuit of some sort of relief from the troubles afflicting me, I quite mechanically began to tamper with changes in a line here and there. Quite suddenly the realization dawned on me that, while it is certainly not presumptuous to persist in the attempt to transpose a poetic content from one language to another with some degree of precision, it is entirely absurd to restrain languages so dissimilar as English and Italian from pursuing the logic of their own genius in the matter of sound. I now began to understand the nature of a difficulty into which no insight was possible while I limited myself to the translation of Gongora's Spanish into Italian, for the very good reason that Spanish words are practically equal to ours in number of syllables. If we keep in mind that, in an identical group of words, the quantity of Italian syllables is greater than that of English by a ratio of about sixteen to ten or twelve, the difficulty resolves itself. The reader will judge as to whether the result of such meticulous attentions, in metrics as well as elsewhere, is convincing.

Now with respect to word meaning the task entailed lesser difficulties, but when put to the test in this area taste and ingenuity run the serious risk of falling into a variety of snares. How, I asked myself, is one to take precautions against them? What means can be found to sidestep them? Is there any sure guide to be followed for the attainment of literal perfection? The answer is, of course, that there is none. Let me cite one example. When Shakespeare's text (Sonnet CXL) says "tongue-tied" to represent the idea of an inner emotional agitation which occasions such anxiety that one is rendered powerless to speak, however he may try to master himself, was I to choose a bland, chaste turn of phrase, as some translators have done, or should I be content to say bluntly as the poet has it, *"lingua legata"*? If I wished to get the effect conveyed by the entire sonnet, the effect, that is, of a moral torment which is almost physical torture, wherein the expression "tongue-tied" takes on the obsessive force of a dominant image, there was no room at all for hesitation. These are trifles, and yet they lead to all sorts of trouble if one fails to detect them on his own. They are indeed of such importance that I would feel very proud if I might one day manage to identify all of them in an edition arrayed with footnotes. In the present edition I must limit myself to the affirmation that, after having consulted the commentaries of illustrious predecessors and the extant translations, I sought in my own choices to hold fast to the way which best maintained a direct channel of communion with the poet.

I was very much concerned to formulate, chiefly for my own benefit, an interpretation of Shakespeare which should not mislead. There were various aberrancies which had to be eschewed, ranging from blunders in word choice, in particular, to lack of discretion in the choice of a manner, in general. Examples of the latter are the excessively rhetorical manner of the Romantics, the petty long-windedness of twentieth-century commentators, and the general obscurity of so many others.

My postulates and the very type of choice I made were, moreover, an index of the tone to which my translation proposed to adhere. Careful examination of the text convinced me that it was a tone which derived its particular accent and even the articulation of its syntactical structure from Petrarch at his most vigorous:

> I know how Love hurls his darts and flees,
> And how first he feints and then he strikes,
> How he will rob by force and filch by stealth,
> And how inconstantly his wheel revolves,
> How fitful is the hope he gives, how sure the woe,
> How faithless all his promises;
> I perceive how his fire steals into the marrow,
> And how the covert wound festers in the veins
> Whence open flames and death burst forth.*

This is the tone which Dante seems to foreshadow in the following pair of lines from his sonnet to Cino da Pistoia:

> And I know how he bridles and how he spurs,
> And how beneath his ride we laugh and cry.

Now it must be said that one's success in the discrimination of the tone of a poem does not automatically encompass the solution of the problem of the relationship of this tone to thematic exposition. In the poem taken as a model, however, the leading theme, the ravages of time, and the minor ones which emerge from it, are so closely wedded to the tone that I was quite naturally led to pose this question: Could it be, as I had hoped when I first conceived the work, that a definitive illumination was to be achieved by simply allowing myself to be guided by what these themes suggested? Happily such was indeed the case.

Petrarch's love stubbornly dwells upon repairing the ravages of time moment by moment, and it is virtually insensible to time's flight. And yet this love gradually endows time with the spatiality of an infinite historical depth, thus giving rise to a

* F. Petrarch, *Triumph of Love,* Ch. III, lines 175–183. Ungaretti uses one version of a difficult manuscript tradition. Translator.

form which is both an earthly beauty and a beauty residing in the realm of unchanging ideas; this is what Laura symbolizes. The process goes on by means of a series of slow gradations in light intensity up to the point at which advancing age discloses that what awaits the poet is a gaping tomb. Now blinding and terrifying the light finally reveals that love, beauty, and fame, in a word, Laura, are supernatural. It was, of course, possible for Petrarch to impoverish his thematics through the dialectics which characterize his *Triumphs,* but his fundamental melancholy will remain something ineffable, and his confessions which are always an internal dialogue will ever remain highly personal.

In contrast, Shakespeare at all times feels that growing old is a progressively more crushing burden, and he refuses to seek a compensatory redemption in memory. Why? Because the memory only relentlessly records the increasing weight of the burden and the weakening of our life force. For him then the theme of immortality will derive, in the flesh, from our progeny (Sonnets II and IV) and, spiritually, from the concrete beauty of the mind's work (Sonnets XV and XIX). Within such limits memory surely cannot offer the ineradicable vision of a progressive extension but only a series of brilliant images. As a result we are struck, for example, by the figure of the advancing years which besiege a face and furrow it in Sonnet II, or by the resigned satisfaction of a graying father as he rediscovers his youth in the fresh beauty of his son, or again, by the Apocalyptic panorama of Sonnet XIX.

It is no wonder, therefore, in the light of these Shakespearean propensities, that a current event should beautifully conspire to render an expressive truth more vivid, so that in Sonnet VI, for instance, the practice of usury (whether or not to continue the ban on it was a lively subject of discussion at the time) could suggest the violent coupling of the financial interest rate and the morally remunerative rate of family growth. And there is more. Anyone who delights in impetuous expression may well gaze in envy at the artistic effects which the clever use of a local phenomenon can bring off in one sonnet. I refer to Sonnet LXVIII in which the union of the theme of aging with that of naturalness—done in a somewhat ill-humored fashion—gives us an originality approached only in the fine arts by a Rembrandt or a Goya, or more recently, by our own great Scipione.

Needless to say I could continue on in this vein until the day after tomorrow. But I cannot resist another example. Whereas Petrarch makes the theme of absence memorable of and for itself

> And the light has remained impressed in my mind,

proof could be heaped upon proof to support the contention that in Shakespeare, at least at first glance, it is not the theme of absence itself that remains with us but rather a particular circumstance: a seemingly endless journey astride a stumbling nag (Sonnet L), or the blood brought forth from a horse by a spur gash, or (in Sonnet LI) a headlong ride reminiscent of the Arabian Nights. On the other hand the theme of absence may go so far as to waste the soul away to its very depths by dint of weeping, as we see in Sonnet XXX, a gem of sadness and tenderness, anguish and limitless renunciation.

For me the way of circumspection in translation was to avoid straying from my source and, by repeated rereading, to restrain myself from slighting the cry of anguish in favor of the images; for the important thing is the cry, which the images merely localize and date. What I allude to is that cry of the love passion which is no less imperious in Shakespeare than in Petrarch. In the latter it is an almost muffled outburst, uttered without witnesses, while in Shakespeare it is, so to speak, filled out by the voices of bystanders; it is, in short, a shout. By what manner of miracle, we may ask, is the explosive compound which amasses such disparate elements as the picturesque and the madrigalesque, the enchanting and the horrible, the moralistic and the despicable, transubstantiated, in the rereading, into a most wondrous sign of harmony by virtue of one cry of desolation?

By following the path I have described one comes to know that despite irremediable regrets and inextinguishable desire, advancing age possesses the power to prescribe youth as its medicine and mean—an impossible mean, alas—and further that it has sufficient strength to preserve the essence of youth within and despite the turbulence of soul, flesh, and mind, and to give it the name of youthful worth and virile beauty, or virtue pure and simple (Sonnet LXII). Thus also Eve, the dark beauty, working within the frailty of his being, will overpower a man and corrupt in him the fair hope of repossessing youth (Sonnet CXXXIII).

In the midst of this sea of poetry the ship of discourse was about to reach port. By this time I no longer had to concern myself about such questions as whether a poet like Shakespeare was able to disengage himself from the two inclinations contending within him, and join them himself, so that the three characters might follow the action as spectators look on at the unfolding of a drama. Of what importance is it to know whether the Young Lord existed in reality, or whether there had really been a Dark Lady, since the very color is more than anything else a moral attribute; what does it matter how many unconfessed and unconfessable things the words may contain and the extent to which they are due to causes of which the poet himself was unaware; of what consequence is all of this as against the fact that herein each one of us can mirror himself in accordance with his own individual experience and that all of us can detect the reflection of our mysterious humanity?

There will never be a poetry which fails to bear deep within itself an inviolable secret, from which it draws its breath of life.

25. Jean-Louis Barrault

1910–

Barrault is considered by many people to be France's outstanding régisseur. *He has made an equal impact as an actor, teacher, director, and, when the spirit moved him, as critic. His criticism has been published in two influential works,* Reflexions sur le théâtre *(1949) and* Nouvelle reflexions sur le théâtre *(1959).*

As a critic, Barrault seems intent on reconciling a broad humanism with the sanest French "aestheticism." Although always rational, Barrault sees the value, as well, of a criticism which emanates from the internal coherence of the work itself; an organic coherence which can transcend the measured limits of classical drama. In preferring Shakespeare to Molière, Barrault invokes the former's modernity and scope. But it is a modernity, as Barrault observes, which is visible, paradoxically, as a result of the English poet's detailed and faithful observation of "an age of transition" similar to our own. The value of criticism like Barrault's lies in its implicit conviction that the critic must bring the work of literature down to ourselves.

The following essay is the text of a lecture given during the Edinburgh Festival in September 1948 before the performance of Hamlet *in French.*

Shakespeare and the French

From the second half of the eighteenth century onward, Shakespeare has been regularly played in France. Voltaire is supposed to have been one of the first French writers interested in Shakespeare; we shall see later the various stages he went through. The most recent lovers of Shakespeare were Antoine, who produced practically every play, including *Titus Andronicus,* Gemier who is supposed to have been an extraordinary Shylock, Charles Dullin who produced *Richard III, Julius Caesar,* and *King Lear,* and Gaston Baty who produced *Macbeth, The Taming of the Shrew,* and *Twelfth Night.* The latter play was also produced by Copeau. Then came the Pitoëffs who produced *Hamlet* and *Romeo and Juliet.* Last but not least the Comédie Française gave *Coriolanus* in 1937, and in 1945 *Antony and Cleopatra,* which I directed. Finally, Jean Vilar produced *Richard II,* and quite a few new companies have followed this lead and produced *A Midsummer Night's Dream, Much Ado,* etc. And of course here I have only been concerned with Shakespeare played in French translations. All these examples show that in France Shakespeare is given practically as often as Racine and Molière, and is therefore a necessity to us. Yet Shakespeare's entry on the French stage begins with a crime. In order to cross the Channel he has to be shorn of his poetic garb. The poetic atmosphere of his art which rises toward suprareality and ideal forms is cruelly dispelled by the cold light of our severely rationalized language. Shakespeare, whose thought belongs more to poetry than to pure reason, has his wings severely clipped by the logic which destroys rhythm and music, and seeks to pierce the most shaded and mysterious recesses of his poetry. This is altogether a very great handicap which seriously hampers even those who love Shakespeare. When he is shorn of his poetic appearance, there are people who only see in him the representative of a barbarous age, dealing in ghosts, female pimps, murderers, and plotters. Such has been for many centuries the opinion of many French purists, and such would normally be the opinion of most French people who are so form conscious; and yet the descendants of Malherbe, La

From *The Theatre of Jean-Louis Barrault* (London, Barrie Books Ltd., and New York, Hill and Wang, Inc., 1961), pp. 89–100. Translated by Joseph Chiari. Reprinted by permission of Hill and Wang, Inc., and Barrie and Rockliff.

Fontaine, Boileau, Voltaire, and Chénier love Shakespeare even if he has been rendered somehow ungainly and lame by translation.

The three books which I always keep by my bedside, and which I should wish to take with me if I had to leave hurriedly without any warning as so many had to do during the dark years of the occupation, are the Bible which contains our sources, Racine with his artistic beauty, and Shakespeare which contains life. Today I should like to add a fourth: Molière for his studies of men. Shakespeare is always ready at any moment to offer us an injection of life; he is by far the best "blood donor"; he revives us whenever we need it and that we do often enough. France's spiritual life could be represented by a passionate yet brotherly conversation between three people. What a remarkable trio that would be! Let us imagine the passionate Pascal clashing against the logical genius of Descartes, with Montaigne as a smiling referee, or let us imagine La Fontaine caught between Ronsard and Malherbe, or coming to our times, let us imagine Gide encouraging Valéry to bait Claudel! These examples show that we have in France three different attitudes which are in constant conflict. The three attitudes summarize French thought. For the foreigner it is the Cartesian attitude which best represents France, generally described as Descartes' country. This statement is often followed by well-known tags such as: *"Enfin Malherbe vint; ce qui se conçoit bien s'enonce clairement,"* * etc., or this sentence which has dominated French art: "Art separates what Nature confuses."

One of the most striking features of French life is the luminous clarity of the French genius which can lift to their highest pitch logic and common sense. If logic and common sense are the hallmarks of the French character, taste, control, and subtle discrimination are the hallmark of French art. How can one account for these traits? Are they due to France's geographical position and to her temperate climate and her varied landscape? Indeed in France everything is varied and temper-

*At last Malherbe came; what is clearly thought out can be clearly expressed. Translator.

ate, and wherever we look, whether northward or southward, whether we look at forests, mountains, or rivers, we never have the opportunity of seeing anything which horrifies through excess in one direction or another. Everything is varied, and temperate; the result is that wherever he goes, the French artist moves about with a rubber or a file in his hand to polish and repolish ceaselessly. France is the land of thrift. "Thrift, thrift, thrift, Horatio." All this makes France one of the very few countries where a genius like Racine could be born; Racine the acme of taste, control, and discrimination, whose vocabulary does not exceed 1,500 words and whose alexandrines could not be improved. Valéry once tried to do so, and after three days gave it up. Racine deleted from his masterpieces only what ordinary minds could have left in and he draws from his audiences the tears which fall from Orpheus' lyre and which are prompted more by admiration than by pity. But one must not forget that the love of control and measure above all things, together with a tyrannical passion for taste, can become a weakness through which art could become anemic and die. Constant rubbing and filing can end in rubbing out the edges, in thinning out the material, and in conferring upon it the worn-out, thin look of an old coin. The fear of ridicule and excess of refinement and polish can lead to dryness and lack of life. That is the moment when we can only be saved by calling upon Shakespeare with his exuberant life, his fecundity, and his genius.

France, exhausted by "le Grand Siècle," was in need of rejuvenation; her blood had become too blue. The trees of the French garden had been overpruned and they had lost their sap. Shakespeare's appearance on the French stage was eagerly welcomed by those who, later, made possible the Romantic revolution. They took to Shakespeare as if he were the long-awaited wholemeal bread. Voltaire, who had introduced Shakespeare, was swept by a great enthusiasm, which later he tried to temper with criticism. Having praised before the fecundity, the sublime power of Shakespeare's genius, he proceeded to reproach him with lack of tact and ignorance of the rules; and he ended by describing Shakespeare's tragedies as works which contained splendid and majestic scenes but were in fact nothing but monstrous farces. There certainly was gold in them, but according to him it was still too mixed up with the dross, and his final conclusion was that one had to keep a firm check on such a source of mediocrity, triviality, and long and tedious improbabilities. So the classical corset was again tightened up on a chest which for a while had breathed freely and which now was made to pay for the folly of having deified "the drunken savage." Taste was again in conflict with genius and life, and the pattern of Voltaire's behavior was repeated by many of the following generations who, like him, oscillated between enthusiasm and coldness. The truth is that the Frenchman is less a gardener than a horticulturist. When he realizes that his beautifully planned garden has too many graveled paths, he is overwhelmed with nostalgia for an English lawn; so he plants a lawn; but as soon as it has grown, he covers it with geometrically laid out flower beds "in the French style." This is part of the agelong debate between good taste on one side and genius on the other; and the Frenchman constantly knocks his head against both.

Taste and genius exist in every age, but it is only at certain given moments in the life of nations that they harmonize; then the lyre only produces the sound which it ought to produce. These moments are as rare as the meeting of stars and they have only a very brief duration. They form our golden ages, the ages of our masterpieces; in such ages we have: *Andromache, Hamlet, Britannicus, Macbeth, Bajazet, Antony and Cleopatra, Phaedra, The Tempest,* and Racine and Shakespeare rise above the problems of genre into a world which is their own. There, Shakespeare's restraint is as elegant as Racine's, whose cruelty has nothing to envy in Shakespeare's. It might very well happen that if there were an international competition, Racine would be given the prize for taste and Shakespeare for abundance; but that simply means that the world is conventional and loves labels, and nothing can alter that. Yet it remains true that when we are tired of looking for rare things, Shakespeare is the supreme refuge to bring us back to life, to revive our hearts and to return us to the human world. You might ask, "Why Shakespeare and nobody else? Is he the only one to possess such virtues? Is there not in the French patrimony a writer who blends taste and genius perfectly and who, like Shakespeare, has ferocity and strength and is fully immersed in life? What about Molière, why do you prefer Shakespeare to him?" My reply would be: I do not prefer Shakespeare, but the point is that Molière is ourselves, quotations from his plays are part of our minds since our earliest age; we have grown up with him, yet I must admit that at this moment I feed more on Shakespeare than on Molière. The probable reason is that Shakespeare has more in common with us and thus his situations and themes are closer to ours than those of Molière. Such a remark does not take anything away from Molière who in genius and taste is equal to the greatest.

Shakespeare is topical to our time, he lived as we do now, in an age of transition, an age of revolutions and calamities in which the old faith had been lost, and the new one had not yet appeared. His world was, like ours, in the throes of doubt. Molière on the contrary lived in an age of prosperity and brilliance, in an orderly society dominated by monarchic authority. Wealth, prosperity, order, authority, all these notions are very remote from us; Molière stands for equilibrium and at this moment we do not know what equilibrium is. If therefore I am prepared to take with me Shakespeare, leaving behind Molière (although I should very much like to take both), it is because at this moment, and I mean at this moment, and not in fifty years' time when things will be different, Shakespeare is more modern than Molière. He is closer to us, and the conditions in which he lived are also closer to ours. In order to make this point clear it is hardly worth while recalling the long imprisonment of Mary Stuart and her end on the block, the great Elizabeth dining to the sound of bugles and drums, Murray's vices in Scotland, Rizzio's and Darnley's murders, Dunbar's flight, or Morton put to the torture. It is hardly worth mentioning the Low Countries and their suffering, or Spain where Philip II, dying, said to his doctor: "Why do you fear to draw a few drops of blood from a man who has spilt so much?" It is hardly worth while mentioning Wallenstein in Germany, the Cenci in Italy, St. Bartholomew's Day in France, Charles IX, Henry III, the barricades, the death of the two Guises at Blois, the death of Henry IV, etc. All these things testify to the troubled state of the age in which Shakespeare was living. The genius of the age fed his genius, and more than anyone else he immortalized the turmoil of his time. The Middle Ages were fading away, and with them the faith which united the Western world; the religious reformation begun under Henry VIII was still in progress, and the political revolution which reached its climax with Charles I was about to begin; the modern age was about to be born, and Shakespeare was, as we are now, struggling in a vale where murders and catastrophes were parts of life, and where all human values were again questioned. At the age of twenty-six in *Henry VI* he makes a father who has killed his son say:

> O, pity, God, this miserable age!
> What stratagems, how fell, how butcherly,
> Erroneous, mutinous and unnatural
> This deadly quarrel daily doth beget!
> (3 *Henry VI*, II, v, 88–91)

To us, who still have present in our minds the memory of Buchenwald and Auschwitz, the retreat of Dunkirk or the horrors endured by Coventry and Hiroshima, these cries of despair easily find an echo in our souls. We must confess that we feel rather remote from the antiquated common sense of Chrysale and the arguments of les Femmes Savantes. Shakespeare's age is, like ours, an age most aptly described by Hamlet's phrase, "The time is out of joint."

What does Shakespeare do in such a situation, what example does he offer us; does he forsake his age for the shelter of an ivory tower? No, he replaces the poet in his true function which is to be the summary and brief chronicle of his time, by borrowing subjects from life to give to his age its style. Had he emerged like us from the Second World War, and had he lived, as we do, through the anxieties caused by the behavior of the two world powers which are holding peace in their hands, I doubt if he would alter in any way Enobarbus' words when he says about Antony and Caesar who are now face to face:

> Then world, thou hast a pair of chaps, no more;
> And throw between them all the food thou hast,
> They'll grind the one the other . . .
> (*Antony and Cleopatra,* III, v, 14–16)

"What we must imitate from this great man," said Stendhal, "is his way of studying the world in which we live and the art of offering our contemporaries the kind of tragedy which they need (but which they dare not ask for, terrified by their habits and their mania about taste). What matters is not so much to write plays which resemble Shakespeare's as to study the world in which we live in just the same way as Shakespeare studied his; for we too have conflicting paths and conspiracies, and we too have men who today laugh and joke in drawing rooms and will be in prison a week later, or men who laugh and joke with those who, a few days later, will choose the jury which will sentence them to death." The age of Stendhal was like ours, in tune with that of Shakespeare. Therefore Shakespeare with his social message which corresponds to our time can be considered as something like the patron of the artist who is committed, and, the more one thinks about this point, the more truth one finds in it; yet we must of course be very careful about this kind of assertion. True, Shakespeare walks about the streets of the cities of his time, but it is in order to bear witness and not to take sides, and that is of supreme importance, for, if we do not bear this point firmly in mind, we might discover that our age, which is thoroughly infected with politics, has managed to ascribe to Shakespeare a definite political party and ideology. We have only to think of the protracted anguish which followed the production of *Coriolanus* at the Comédie Française in 1937 at the time of the Popular Front. Shakespeare was very nearly transformed into an apologist of fascism. Shakespeare is an artist and as such he has no politics. When, for instance, in *Henry VI,* Part II, he deals with Jack Cade as the representative of the masses in rebellion against the privileged classes, he remains above the masses and above the privileged classes; he does not take sides. If he concedes a point to the privileged classes by making Jack Cade foolishly say: "But then are we in order when we are most in disorder" (2 *Henry VI,* IV, ii, 199), he follows that by paying homage to the eternal greatness of oppressed people, through the words which he puts in the mouth of Jack Cade dying in the garden of the wise Iden: "For I, that never feared any, am vanquished by famine, not by valour" (IV, x, 80–81). Shakespeare teaches us that politics bring out futile hatreds, and Stendhal used to say that: "Any political admixture in the work of art was like a pistol shot in the middle of a concert."

With the exception of a few examples of jingoism which could irk a rather sensitive Frenchman, Shakespeare's art is always above politics. He always manages to avoid propaganda, even in his most "official" plays. He never preaches morality or politics; he is only concerned with justice, and that is why he is a great dramatist whose wisdom is enriching. For him a dramatic subject is first and foremost a problem of mechanics involving conflicting human forces; the dramatist must control the conflict and find a solution. A dramatic theme is a kind of complicated clockwork mechanism which has more or less broken down under the impact of the passions which are part of it, and which has to be repaired and made workable in the course of the play. The balance wheel of the mechanism is out of order and must be adjusted or put right. The complicated clockwork, its balance wheel and its problems represent life in the broad context of the universe. The equilibrium of life is as unstable as the mechanism of a clock, and life, like man, endeavors to stand up, in spite of the law of gravitation. The conflicting forces, the passions, the balance wheel out of order, are the images of men who oppose one another, who fight and plead for their rights, who use all kinds of means, in bad faith as well as in good faith, simply because their hearts are swamped by their passions, and their heads are cracked like old walls by the fury which sweeps them away. To find the solution to this problem of mechanics, to repair the clock by adjusting the wheel, means in terms of drama to settle all accounts, to cleanse man from his passions, and to restore health and life which in the end will be all the better for what preceded. It is in fact to perform the act of true justice. That is the real task of the dramatist, and it is the basic social function of the theater.

The theater is only useful to society if it cleanses men, adjusts and restores them, and it can only reach that aim by being, above all, the art of justice. It is in the name of justice that we witness the entry in the lists of young Henry Richmond, the future Henry VII, who to the trumpets' sound, and like St. George, comes to defeat the monstrous Richard III. By his deed he brings justice to the most beautiful piece of historical pageantry which exists in the theater, something which is comparable to our best tapestries, and which is a splendid slice of English history from Richard II to Richard III painted by Shakespeare. The blood of Richard III finally washes away the plot of Bolingbroke. The same aura of justice surrounds Fortinbras when he arrives on the stage at the end of *Hamlet*, bringing to a world of death and suicide a breath of new life and a positive solution to what looked like an insoluble problem; it is the fulfillment of Hamlet's prophecy before his death: "I do prophesy the election lights on Fortinbras."

Richmond, Fortinbras, are the characters who enable Shakespeare to develop for us Richard II, Henry VI, and Hamlet, and at the same time to preserve justice; they are the axles of the scales and we could not do without them; they anticipate the angels of judgment day. A tragedy can only end, not by the death of a hero but by the complete solution of the problems dealt with; a play is a complex of parts and not one single part; a tragedy can only end with the appearance of the one who administers justice, and not simply through the death of a victim. The fanfare which meant the close of great tragedies is reminiscent of the trumpets of judgment day. To deal with the real, to give a style to an age, to go down in the street as a witness and not as a militant propagandist, to restore morality to its proper place, all in the name of justice, such are some of the aims of Shakespeare which one might also describe as his social message. But he does more than that, he brings on a new hero; he adds to the gallery of tragic heroes a new one, one who is specifically his creation, and who does not belong to antiquity or to the Middle Ages; it is the Renaissance hero, the hero who, tired by the mediocrity of life, tortured by madness, is assailed by the highest form of doubt and is so exactingly scrupulous as to put all in question. He is chaste, pure, admirable, fascinating; his name is Richard II, Henry VI, or Hamlet. He is the hero who fails to save Macbeth and so lets him go to his death; he is the one who gets hold of Antony, he is the voluptuous victim of the Sonnets, and if he is not Shakespeare himself, he is the most typical hero of a period of renaissance, whether it is Shakespearean Renaissance or any other renaissance. Shakespeare communicates to us the experiences of this hero, and with him we see that paradise has once again been lost and with it faith. Everything is again put into question; men have to endure the test of doubt and live through the drama of belief, and the Shakespearean hero preserves through all his trials a chaste nature, a scrupulous intelligence, and a noble heart. Whenever confronted with action he doubts its necessity, for in ages of conflict a morality of action is an encouragement of mediocrity, cupidity, and injustice; everything is dirty and vulgar, all flesh is threatened by worms whether it is alive or dead, therefore every gesture is a crime against human love and true friendship: and one cannot go on acting without soiling one's very soul. That is the problem:

> How so ever thou pursuest this act
> Taint not thy mind,
> Taint not thy mind!

The moment the consequences of an action are in doubt, the moment one asks oneself whether the action one is about to perform is not only useful but just, everything collapses. As soon as a man becomes lucid, as soon as he ceases to act according to his faith, without the slightest reflection, even if it is only "for an eggshell," or even if there is "no cause why the man dies," everything grows blurred. Night and day, morning and evening, sun and moon, joy and hatred cease to exist as such; a kind of twilight hour, in which Nature herself seems to be at a loss, wondering whether "to be or not to be," descends upon our earthly world and heralds the coming night. It is an ambiguous world very much like the one we are living in now, and the Shakespearean hero generally finds himself caught between light and darkness, between the real and the unreal, between being and not being, in a most ambiguous and dangerous, albeit superior position, which if one becomes conscious of it, makes action impossible.

> Thus conscience does make cowards of us all. . . .
> And enterprises . . . lose the name of action.
> (*Hamlet*, III, i, 83–88)

This incapacity to act feeds the *taedium vitae,* the bitter intoxication of despair, and the longing for suicide and death, through the bare bodkin which could bring about quietus:

> How weary, stale, flat and unprofitable
> Seem to me all the uses of the world.
> Fie on't! O fie!
> (I, ii, 133–135)

> I do not set my life at a pin's fee
> (I, iv, 65)

> Since no man has ought of what he leaves,
> What is't to leave betimes?

But despair is only a transient phase, which leaves the hero's soul uncontaminated, and by submitting to his fate in time, he wins a transcendental victory. The hero has lived too long with his eyes fixed on the window which opens upon the infinite to miss his moment of illumination and to fail to see from under his closed eyelids the glimmering lights of infinity beckoning him to their bourns. Having rejected suicide, he accepts death as a kind of solution to the problems which beset him, and he can prophesy the advent of action in a world which will bathe in a new faith. The trial by doubt is ended; the hero has been on the verge of the void, and now he knows that his sacrifice, accepted in the perfect lucidity of his mind which has trodden every corner of the maze of doubt, will bring forth a new world and a new faith.

Such is, as far as I can see, my understanding of the fascinating and complete Shakespearean hero, whom I like to call the hero of superior doubt, which for me is best represented in its purest and most chaste state by Hamlet. But we shall never repeat often enough that everything in Shakespeare is certainly complex; great poet that he was, Shakespeare could not fail to touch upon all the aspects of the problems which beset man and which as soon as they are observed become as varied in their aspect as Hamlet's cloud; they can look like a camel, like a weasel, like a whale. The Shakespearean hero is the great human contribution to modern civilization; he is his spiritual message to us all. Besides his social and spiritual message, is there a kind message which in spite of the loss of his splendid language, the great and universal William sends to us Frenchmen, or rather to us men? I think there is, and it is a message on the plane of art. Shakespeare gives his art the apparent confusion and complexity of Nature. He composes musically, and most of his great works are composed like symphonies; one of the most musical of his compositions is *Antony and Cleopatra* which I used to love passionately. My love of this play brings to mind the extraordinary skill with which Shakespeare plays with words. He squeezes the last ounce of life out of them, he turns them inside out in the most brilliant puns, of which he is the supreme master; all sorts of puns, earthy, coarse, or refined, they all spring from the very roots of the words. This leads to a final remark about poetry and about Shakespearean realism.

Shakespeare's poetry generally begins to soar when after having started from reality it rises above it. Let us take the example of *King Lear,* which is the play which moves us the most. Whenever I hear the words: "My God, make me not be mad. . . ." I burst into tears. I saw Laurence Olivier play the part of King Lear, and he was unforgettable. The way he played the part was for me a revelation. When he came on the stage, crowned with flowers, I noted that Olivier had followed realism as far as daubing his feet with blood, which for us spectators looked like real blood. Looking at them, I suddenly realized that the blood on the feet made it possible for Olivier to forget about trying to show that his feet were bruised and sore and on the contrary to concentrate all his energy in rendering the sublime and serene poetry of Lear. Realism, pushed to its extreme limit, frees poetry. In France King Lear would have had no blood on his feet, and the actor playing this part would have been compelled to show that this part of his anatomy was troubling him; this would have been a kind of stylization which would have detracted from his concentration on rendering the turmoil of his mind and soul and therefore from the poetry. Shakespeare offers us the best examples of poetic realism: he is one of the three or four universal geniuses. He soars above nations and it is quite natural that whenever we wish to draw him to us we should look for what is universal in him. We are instinctively inclined to denationalize him and to leave behind his national garb; the English follow the opposite process, and it is right and natural that it should be so. For England he is universal, no doubt, but he is British born, and Rosencrantz and Guildenstern are students who belong more to Oxford than to Wittenberg. We all like to pull Shakespeare to ourselves; we take a leaf from Bottom's aesthetics, Bottom who in *A Midsummer Night's Dream* nimbly manages to produce "Pyramus and Thisbe" by representing a wall with one hand, and a moon by using a lantern and a faggot. We take away from Shakespeare his props and crenelated walls, and we try to draw him toward the abstract, producing him with curtains and costumes which do not belong to any definite period. The English people try with all their might to hold him back in the midst of their chivalry and to prevent him from crossing the water; we on the other hand try to draw him to us. Can we be blamed for that? I think not, for Shakespeare is for us a vital need.

Selected Bibliography

GENERAL

Herford, C. H., "A Sketch of the History of Shakespeare's Influence on the Continent." *Bulletin of the John Rylands Library,* Vol. 9 (1925), pp. 20–62.

Robertson, J. G., "Shakespeare on the Continent." *Cambridge History of English Literature,* Vol. 5 (1910), pp. 283–308. With bibliography.

Thimm, Franz, *Shakespeareana from 1564 to 1864.* An account of the Shakespeare literature of England, Germany, France, and other European countries during three centuries, with bibliographical introductions. London, 1865. vi, 92 pp.; 2nd ed., 1872, viii, 120 pp.

FRANCE

Haines, C. M., *Shakespeare in France.* Criticism: Voltaire to Victor Hugo. London, 1925. viii, 170 pp.

Jusserand, J. J., *Shakespeare in France Under the Ancien Régime.* London, 1899. xxviii, 496 pp.

Lounsbury, T. R., *Shakespeare and Voltaire.* London, 1902. 476 pp.

SPAIN

Fitzgerald, T. A., "Shakespeare in Spain and Spanish America." *Modern Language Journal,* Vol. 35 (December 1951), pp. 589–594.

Par, Alfonso, *Shakespeare en la Literatura Española.* Madrid and Barcelona, 1935. Vol. 1, 359 pp.; Vol. 2, 320 pp.

Ruppert y Ujaravi, R., *Shakespeare en España.* Traducciones, imitaciones e influencia de las obras de Shakespeare en la literatura española. Madrid, 1920. 107 pp.

ITALY

Bellezza, P., *Shakespeare e Manzoni*. Milano, 1927. 191 pp.

Collison-Morley, L., *Shakespeare in Italy*. Stratford-upon-Avon, 1916. 180 pp.

Fucilla, J. G., "Shakespeare in Italian Criticism." *Philological Quarterly,* Vol. 20 (1941), pp. 559–572.

GERMANY

Böhtlingk, A. R. A., *Goethe und Shakespeare*. Leipzig, 1909. xii, 320 pp.

Joachimi-Dege, Marie, *Deutsche Shakespeare-Probleme im 18 Jahrhundert und im Zeitalter der Romantik*. Leipzig, 1907. 296 pp.

Pascal, R., *Shakespeare in Germany*. Cambridge, England, 1937. 199 pp.

Price, L. M., *English-German Literary Influences*. Bibliography and survey. Berkeley, Calif., 1920. 616 pp.

SCANDINAVIAN COUNTRIES

Bolin, Wilhelm, "Zur Shakespeare-Literatur Schwedens." Shakespeare Jahrbuch (Shakespeare Yearbook Series) Jahrgang 50 (1880), pp. 73–128.

Molin, Nils, "Modern Shakespeareforskning." *Göteborgsstudien i Litteraturhistoria Tillägnade Sverker Ek* (Göteborg, 1954), pp. 10–25.

RUSSIA

Friedrichs, Ernst, "Shakespeare in Russland." *English Studies,* Vol. 50 (1916), pp. 106–136.

Gibian, George, *Tolstoy and Shakespeare*. 's-Gravenhage, 1957. 47 pp.

Lirondelle, Andre, *Shakespeare en Russie* (1748–1840). Paris, 1912. 248 pp.

OTHER EUROPEAN COUNTRIES

Haraszti, Z., *Shakespeare in Hungary*. Boston, Trustees of the Public Library, 1929. 36 pp.

Klajn, Hugo, "Shakespeare in Yugoslavia." *Shakespeare Quarterly*, Vol. 5 (1954), pp. 41 ff.

Pennink, R. *Nederland en Shakespeare*. 's-Gravenhage, 1936. 304 pp.

Popovic, V., *Shakespeare in Serbia*. London, 1928. vi, 128 pp.

Wagner, Wilhelm, "Shakespeare in Griechenland." Shakespeare Jahrbuch (Shakespeare Yearbook Series) Jahrgang 12 (1877), pp. 33–56.

Zyczynski, H., "Mickiewica i Shakespear." *Pamietnik Literacki* (Lwow, 1921), pp. 94–109.

Index to Plays Mentioned

NOTE: Only Shakespeare's works mentioned in the text have been indexed. All plays are indexed in alphabetical order under the titles by which they are most commonly known. All characters are indexed under the plays in which they appear in alphabetical order and under the names by which they are most frequently mentioned. Characters alluded to but unnamed are represented by italicized numbers.

About the Author

OSWALD LEWINTER, born in Vienna, Austria, in 1931, was educated in the New York City public schools. After several years in the Merchant Marine he completed his education at the University of California in Berkeley. He has held positions with the United Nations, with a major textbook publisher, and as a resident art critic in a leading gallery in the Northwest. He has published poetry and criticism in such periodicals as *The Paris Review, Contact, Hudson Review, The Literary Review, The Noble Savage,* and *The Walt Whitman Review.* At present Mr. LeWinter teaches English and Humanities at The Pennsylvania State University.